Let the Mocking Bird Sing Herbal Praise

(from the Old Barn)
Volume I

By
Sandy Bradley, V.M.D.

TEACH Services, Inc.
Brushton, New York

Copyright © 1995, 1996 Sandy Bradley, V.M.D.

ISBN 1-57258-123-7
Library of Congress Catalog Card No. 96-61231

Published by

TEACH Services, Inc.
RR 1, Box 182
Brushton, New York 12916

A SPECIAL PAGE of DEDICATION

TO MY FRIEND
AND
SISTER IN
CHRIST YESHUA

CHERYL CHAPMAN

WHO PROVIDED THE MEANS, THE CARE AND
THE HOPE TO MAKE
<u>LET THE MOCKING BIRD SING HERBAL PRAISE</u>
<u>(from the Old Barn)</u>

A REALITY.

Table of Contents

Dedication

These pages of dedication are of extreme importance to me because without the following individuals <u>Let The Mocking bird Sing Herbal Praise (from the Old Barn)</u> would not have come into existence.

To *Yeshua* (Jesus) Christ, my God and my Fortress, without whom none of this would be possible. Let me briefly explain who *Yeshua* is.

"Yeshua" is the actual Hebrew birth name of Jesus when He was born and walked this earth. It is equivalent to the Greek transliterated name "Jesus" (our English translation).

Yeshua and Jesus also mean "Joshua" — all meaning help of Yehovah (Jehovah) or saviour Yehovah's salvation relating to God, the Son.

"Yahweh" is the Hebrew name for God, the Father taken from the tetragrammaton — YHWH. The Hebrew language does not have "J"s, therefore where you see "J" it is really "Y."

I choose, by revelation of my Father, to call my Saviour by the name He was given when He walked this earth — *Yeshua*. Although it is my choice to do so, I do not in any way mean to insinuate that one should not call Him "Jesus" (that is the Greek name for Him).

If I had a friend from France named "Pierre", I would <u>honor him best</u> by calling him "Pierre" (his birth name), not "Peter" the English translation. Therefore, I honor my Saviour and God best by calling Him by His birth name *"Yeshua"* who is God *Yahweh* incarnate.

I realize that many religious groups <u>do not</u> believe that *Yeshua* God (Jesus Christ) is actually God, but only a teacher or one of the masters of the universe. I want it made clear that when I say "God" I mean God the Father (Yahweh), God the Son (Yeshua) and God the Holy Spirit. It is not my intent to offend anyone of contrary persuasion. My purpose is simply to affirm my own belief and how it has sustained me through the darkest of times.

To my parents who bore me — who taught me values of truth, integrity and justice, who also instilled in me a love for my Creator, my sisters and brothers around the world, and all His beautiful creations near and far.

To my grandmother who, because of her Native American heritage, was able to provide advice that saved the life of my first patient who I treated with herbs and dietary management - my own beloved little Toy Poodle, "Peet."

To "Cody," that mighty giant of a Shepherd whose strength, courage and gentleness was unmatched. Whose death will not have been in vain. Whose condition was initially curable through natural remedies, but lack of funds and proper facilities became the fatal flaw in the plan. What I learned from Cody has since formed a thread of knowledge throughout my work as a physician.

To "Cindi," a very special Dalmation whose pain and agony from kidney failure was alleviated and was reversing through herbs and diet, but again circumstances rendered proper facilities unavailable. Her peaceful death at home is attributed to the assistance of herbal comfort.

To Bob Anderson and Elizabeth Kirk, a husband and wife team who gave me the opportunity to expand my gifts of leadership and to give a better life to "Sweet Pea," a very special second "Cody."

To all those beautiful supportive people at Tri-County Animal Shelter of Hughesville, Maryland, especially Kathy Delosier and Sally Gardella.

To the caring staff at Inner Harbor Animal Hospital for extending their time and efforts to help me with Sweet Pea.

To every one of my clients who have become extended family and were there in my times of desperation - Thank you from the bottom of my heart.

To Sam Linton, who extended credit for hay that my animals be fed while I completed this book.

To Frank Robinson, who also extended credit for grain and hay that my animals be fed.

To Bill Coxe and Bill Peterson, my friends who saw to the needs of all my animals while I was flat on my back.

To my graphics and illustrative team, Virginia and Chris Butcher, for doing their best with high volume and little economics.

To Maria Jesteadt, my typist, who sacrificed time and sleep to help make this book possible.

To Randy Bryant, my printer, who stepped out on faith and invested time and money.

To my friend Clarissa Bowie, who helped to make this book an improved piece of work.

To Roger Coleson whose generous contributions of honey needed for treatments helped to save many patients.

And last, but not least, Connie and Don Livengood, whose faith and products help provide this book.

A special thanks:

A special thanks to my fellow herbalists who gave me such a warm welcome both Christian and non-Christian alike at the Fifth Annual Symposium of the American Herbalist Guild of 1994, as well as the West Virginia Herbalist Association.

There is much information to be gotten from the books of many members of the Guild.

Thank you Father for
what has been accomplished
on less than a "shoe-string" budget
and more on the power of prayer and faith.

Foreward

"He causeth the grass to grow for the cattle, and herb for the service of man: that he may bring forth food out of the earth." Psalms 104:14 KJV

Jesus's ministry consisted of physical, mental and spiritual restoration. The majority of His ministry was devoted to healing the sick and feeding the poor. He offered His gift of eternal life to all people, rich and poor, free and bond. He came to break down every wall that divides humanity. He came to show that His gift of mercy and love is as free as the air that we breathe. Christ's life and death established a faith in which there is no social standing, a belief by which all races, both poor and rich, are linked in a common brotherhood and are equal before God. He passed no human by as being unworthy of His notice, but healed all who came to Him in faith. His heart was filled with love and sympathy for all creation.

Everywhere people are sick and perishing for lack of knowledge of the truths that have been with us since the beginning of time. It is not the Creator's purpose that humanity shall be weighed down with disease and pain. When we transgress God's laws of health, pain, sickness, and death are the result. When sickness comes, it is essential that we assist nature's efforts to rebuild the body and restore our bodies to its natural state.

In our present system of medical education, we have thrown out the priceless treasures that are hidden in the scriptures, and we have glorified science. This is simply man's attempt to worship and glorify creation instead of the Creator. Because of this rejection of truth, medical knowledge has not benefited from the remarkable healing properties that have been provided for us in nature. But we are living in the times of great medical and spiritual enlightenment. We are beginning to unite the wisdom of the scriptures and medical science together for the benefit of mankind.

In this volume, the author, a woman with a vast amount of experience in the field of wholistic veterinarian medicine, and one particularly favored with rare insight and knowledge, has brought within reach of every person, lay, and professional, a great amount of information on the use of herbs for the restoration of health. She provides animal health care through the use of drug-free remedies using vitamins, herbs, and food supplements whenever possible. Her practice is a unique blend of the latest scientific research and the word of God.

I highly recommend this book to you. It is written in clear, simple, beautiful language, instructive to the learner, hopeful to the desperate, cheering to the sick, and restful to the weary. Use it as a learning tool and a source of practical information. She shares not only her knowledge in regards to animal health care, but her personal medical experiences. It is our hope to encourage the reader to take an active part in the maintenance of your health and the health of your pets.

Susan Zaharie-Johnson, B.S.,
and Herbal Consultant

I would like <u>every</u> reader to not only enjoy and understand this book's contents but also to use it as a reference book.

I have purposely included selected medical terms to familiarize the reader with language health care professionals may use without explanation. Instead of providing a glossary, I chose to write out the meanings next to the terms.

To the reader who is not a health professional I <u>encourage</u> the use of a medical dictionary, a book of medical conditions, or just an unabridged dictionary, <u>if it is possible</u>.

I hope this book helps stimulate a desire for the reader to seek other sources to either confirm or reject what your are reading.

If you already have a mastery of medical jargon, I recommend or encourage you to study the technical data, the chronology of events, and proposed conclusions.

To write simplistically about complex matters for a broad audience is not easy, at least for me. I seek your patience and understanding.

Stop! Look! Read before You Go On!
What I Want <u>You</u>, the Reader, To Know

<u>What This Book Intends to Do</u>

I intended for this book <u>to be more complete</u> in the following ways:
* the information I so desire to share with you;
* the stories related to each case;
* documents I am still waiting to receive;
* testimonies (many were not available in time for print;
* my comments and approaches that I feel will help you.

Despite the book's appearance of not being ready, I have decided to go ahead with publishing it for the following reasons:
* The health care system is in serious condition and in desperate need of repair before damage becomes so great that even the best solutions are too late.
* People and their pets are suffering needlessly. I believe the information I have to share <u>now</u> can help save lives.
* The attention needed by my patients overrides the additional time needed to complete the book as intended, therefore I wish to share the information that <u>is</u> prepared.

I have decided to solve this problem by printing two volumes at different times. In this volume, Volume I, I did not have time to write extensive explanations; therefore, I am urging and encouraging readers to seek creditable materials to read on the subject of herbs and organic eating.

This volume includes the following: documents and testimonies that show a pattern of herbs and diet combating disease; a few selected stories about my own pets and clients; a few selected stories that have merit and important information, even in their infancy; a few selected herbal combinations used in my practice that work for me, that may help the reader; a selected list of readings to help educate the reader about how to improve their health at whatever level they might be; and information that may enlighten the reader about herbs and their general uses.

This book focuses on giving the reader principles, not specifics, because the Food and Drug Administration (FDA) does not permit certain types of formuals as it is translated as issuing a prescription. Further, this book provides encouragement to the grass roots of America to demand change for the health care we deserve.

I plan for volume II to contain, where applicable, more documents and testimonies, stories in their completion; actual formulas for general care and treatment, and suggested meals.

What This Book Does Not Intend to Do

This book is not extravagant in its efforts to prove by conventional scientific standards that the findings are true and credible. Why? I have been a practicing veterinarian for more than sixteen years. I have devoted eleven of those years observing and using naturopathic medicines in both humans and animals. There is no literature, to my knowledge, available to the masses that shows any of the following: the conversion of a highly <u>malignant</u> cancerous tumor to a <u>benign</u> lump (that was confirmed by a scientific diagnostic tool, such as histopathology) accomplished by the use of simple vegetables, fruits and herbs; or the conversion of a diabetic patient presented in a coma-like (ketoacidosis) state, with a glucose level of 324 lowered to 63, without adverse clinical signs — the diabetic condition being controlled and maintained by mere diet and herbs; or the reversal of a totally crippled patient painfully suffering from a condition originating from birth (supported clinically and radiographically) to an able-bodied being, living well into expected years. This book will not allow anyone, based on the above facts, <u>to discount</u> the empirical value of the observations included.

With regard to my own personal health and encounters with various physicians, I do not intend to blame or incriminate, for the purpose of lawsuit, any one person, specific health care institution, or health care professional. However, I will not fail to accept the responsibility of pointing out to the reader that there is undoubtedly a general tendency for gross error, lack of concern, and unwillingness to present the patient with <u>already existing knowledge</u> of the keys to better health cited in books, such as <u>Back to Eden</u> by Jethro Kloss, the Paul Bragg nutritional health series, and books by many other early pioneers as well as contemporary authors in the field of alternative medicine. The American Herbalist Guild has many authors who have and are sharing a tremendous wealth of knowledge in their books.

What I Desire To Do For My Loyal Clients

Because my clients are of all races, cultures, ages, socio-economic, and educational levels, I have attempted to write this book so that all may enjoy and benefit from its contents. Many of my clients who are senior citizens must use magnifying glasses or have someone else to read to them. It is my desire to accommodate the people who have supported my practice these fourteen years that I have been in the Washington metropolitan area. For this reason I ask that those who are blessed with the ability to read and understand more readily than others to be patient. Information is provided for those who wish to examine the more complex and detailed medical evidence. Whenever possible information will be bite-sized and easily digestible. To some it may seem over-simplified. The <u>messages</u> of this book <u>are aimed</u> at <u>being thought provoking</u> and <u>motivating</u>.

Some pages may contain statements and information that are repeated in various forms. Many of us learn by repetition (memory is enhanced by repetition). A point is often driven home by repetition.

I cannot determine for another person what helps him or her solve his or her problems in life, but I can say with all assurance and assertiveness that the One who <u>some claim never existed</u>, <u>never died</u>, <u>never rose from the dead</u>, *Yeshua* Christ, is my source of wisdom, knowledge, and accountability together with my God-given gifts that were created to help mankind.

I invite you, the reader, to **look beyond the differences of our spiritual orientations** and **join in a common cause** in restoring the power of choice for better health back to the people.

I have no doubt some will question my sincerity and commitment to Truth and proceed to misuse and misinterpret the contents of this book, <u>discounting the real purpose for which it was written</u>. Unfortunately, this is the nature of controversy. The reality of hope is that the Truth shall be revealed and the power of choice for better health is restored.

A Page to Remember — Please

This book is not intended to be typical or conventional in its format, contents, or style.

Not all aspects of this book is for every reader.

For those health professionals who need to see detailed information confirming diagnosis and the course of the injury it is there.

For those who question the financial effects of my injuries and the gross improprieties of our existing welfare system — the basic evidence is there.

For those who doubt the legal entanglements stemming from the retained attorney — samples of evidence is there.

The evidence of specific events submitted in part or whole is intended to provide the reader with support for my story.

For those of you who are not interested in the details of any of these supportive documents, I urge you to skip over them bearing in mind that their purpose is to provide interested readers the chronological (where applicable) documentation they need to consider my saga real and noteworthy for discussion.

Issues not able to be addressed in volume I will be done so in either volume II or my autobiography.

If I had to choose a single concept to leave with you above all others it would be this: that none of us are perfect in word nor deed — but if each one of us takes the responsibility to do the right thing according to our best and sincere understanding of the Spiritual laws of this universe, then God's grace is ever with us.

I introduce my presentation with these words, Yeshua said, "But I say unto you, **love your enemies**," therefore my friends, love is more than a feeling — it is the right thing to do. Yeshua's quote: Matthew 5:44 KJV

Preface
The Reality of Conventional Medicine

There is one question that is paramount and inevitably posed by allopathic or conventional practitioners and that is, "Are these alternative methods of medical treatment a cure or quackery?" Before I attempt to answer this question, let us look at some of our most serious medical problems and what conventional medicine has offered to date. I'll let the reader decide which approach is closest to a cure and/or better quality of life.

Heart disease is among the top <u>five</u> killers in our country. By-pass, double, triple, and even quadruple heart surgery is very commonplace today. But what about the longevity and the quality of life of those individuals who undergo these surgeries and other chemical-based modalities of treatment? What kind of exercise tolerance can most individuals endure? How permanent are the repairs and is the damaged tissue involved really restored and stronger or merely a bandage buying time? What should be the important emphasis of diet and its effects on our bodies? Are we being told the truth about the dietary contents of our foods?

Though heart disease is just one of the foremost conditions leading to death and debilitation, what about others such as diabetes mellitus, or breast and prostate cancer, or malignancies of all sorts in adults and children, debilitating conditions of any or all of our organ systems — kidney, lung, skin, bone, muscle, etc.

Malfunctioning carbohydrate metabolism is on the rise in this country, whether it be diabetes or hypoglycemia. I have had personal experience with both conditions — my mother, who is currently a diabetic, and myself, confirmed a hypoglycemic while in veterinary school in 1977.

The questions then become, "How serious is the condition being examined? Is the diagnosis confirmed by accepted scientific methodology? Is the mode of treatment and results reproducible by other qualified medical personnel?"

In the jungles of South America, Africa, Australia, our own Native American cultures and many other civilizations of what modern societies term "developing" and often "primitive," with the exception of the first question, the answers are largely irrelevant. In many of these cultures, the qualified personnel may be the medicine man or woman who has been trained in knowledge passed on to them from generations before.

Introduction

There I sat — Saturday, November 6, 1993, 4:00 pm — in a pick-up, slide-on camper not more than twelve-feet long and three-feet wide, its base resting on two-by-fours surrounded by cold muddy ground. The camper sits inside a corral that a friend and I had built in May 1992 in the middle of a large field just behind the west side of a huge tobacco barn. The farm itself is more than 600 acres, and I rent twelve acres to house two horses, four dogs, three cats, one goat, four chickens, and myself.

I sat with my warm three-quarter down coat zipped to the top and head covered with my "Champions Start Here" cap given to me by Rick Grant. Rick is the owner and trainer of Grant Canine Training Institute and the Greater Maryland Rotweiller Club whose facilities are next door to me.

"Sweet Pea," the latest medical miracle in my life, lay a foot and a half away all curled up on one of my not-so-old woolen fleeced jackets. The air below must have been fairly cold because my legs were chilly. "Chloe" (my ten-year-old apricot Toy Poodle and side-kick) lay above on my cabin-like bed sound asleep.

I was surrounded by the necessities of life, all within one arm's reach or two steps forward. A jar at my feet for liquid elimination, a quarter roll of toilet paper to my left in a small open cupboard, a pot of lamb stew on my little four-burner aqua-blue propane stove (meat is no longer part of my diet). On one side of the stove was my battery-operated combination siren, florescent nightlight, headlight flasher and AM/FM radio. On the same stove, my ever-ready solution of lemon lotion for skin lesions, insect repellent, and general first aid. My two bowls for eating were on the counter: one for salads and one for main entrees. Also on the counter, in a cup, were syringes (without the needles) I used to give Chloe and Sweet Pea their daily oral tonics. Sweet Pea's wipe-on herbal lotion for skin restoration and the Clorox for cleaning were all on the left side of the camper, with one gallon of drinking water below.

Above my cabin-like bed sat my trusted battery-operated alarm clock whose alarm now sounded like a muffled baby duck with laryngitis. It had fallen into a bowl of water not too long before.

My eyes were getting very heavy. The heat from the little propane furnace had started to kick in. While my upper body had gotten warmer, my feet and lower legs were still a bit chilled. My head and torso began to fall to my right, where I have a mixture of clean and soiled clothes piled up next to the window on my little diner-like, cafeteria-style bench chair. This bench had three sides with a small table in the middle.

Unfortunately, sundown drew near. Soon, I would not be able to see very well. The propane tank was about empty. I had to make a decision to either allow it to empty and fight the elements of pitch black darkness and freezing cold using only a flashlight — a flashlight with batteries more dead than alive — or change to the full tank now, while I still had some light, thus eliminating the opportunity to use up the very last bit of propane. The small propane tanks of twenty pounds usually gave only two to three days of heating. This was the weekend and I would not be getting paid until Monday unless I had a house call. I had only three dollars in my pocket for gas money to and from the animal shelter on Monday.

I had just lit a candle. The week before I purchased twenty-one of them at a dollar store (three for $1.00). I've always admired Abraham Lincoln, but I never thought our lives would be so similar. No running water, no electricity, no central heating, no plumbing, just living by the elements provided by mother nature.

Sunset was but a few moments away, yet the furnace seemed to continue heating. I knew, however, it would not continue much longer; the tank's weight was very light just hours ago. I decided to change rather than wait. Midnight did not seem a very appealing time to do this necessary task.

The sun set, and at 5:52 pm while sitting in the outhouse built by me with Yeshua's help, the voice-mail beeper clipped to my belt brought an uncanny reality to mind. Today's world with its highly advanced technology and mind boggling achievements had permitted and cultivated a legal system that had forced a trained professional with fifteen years of clinical experience to live in circumstances comparable to those of the young Abraham Lincoln.

My candle began to fail. Thank God I had twenty more. Light was restored. There was a song taught to us in grade school that went something like "but if everyone lit just one little candle, what a bright world this would be." How precious light is when you are surrounded by "unwanted" darkness.

Let The Mocking Bird Sing Herbal Praise (from the Old Barn) was conceived as I sat and pondered over some difficult questions. Two of those questions were, "Why am I here?" and "Why would I *choose* to be here after having had a $67,000 investment in education and an unlimited choice of professional positions throughout this country and abroad?"

I continued to think and ask myself why would I choose to live in the middle of a farm field in an old tobacco barn with my animals having little or no heat for fifteen months? A brief explanation is summed up in *one* word - "commitment"!! (The details of this answer are discussed in my autobiography.)

Commitment to God Almighty of this universe and commitment to myself to do the best that I can do with the God-given talents that I have. That these talents be used and shared for the betterment of animal kind and ultimately mankind.

While speaking one morning with Connie Livengood, the president and founder of Live-N-Good International, whose herbal and aloe products I use and endorse, we prayed together over the phone that this book would be a blessing to *all people*, and especially those who believe in God's miracles.

I shared with her that I had miraculously been given an opportunity to purchase an eleven-acre piece of property for approximately $190,000. An inspired couple was willing to give me a chance in spite of my badly damaged credit, resulting from the traumatic physical injuries I had sustained over the last few years, beginning with a botched surgery performed on my hand.

And now, eight months later, another dream has perished - the dream of a clinic in my home has evaporated because of circumstances beyond my control. The water on this piece of land had become so contaminated that it was not fit for animal or human consumption.

What Is This Book Really All About?

Economic exploitation and manipulation of the masses by the "powers that be," i.e. the U.S. Department of Agriculture (USDA), the Food and Drug Administration (FDA), Congress, the pharmaceutical and insurance industries, the American Medical Association (AMA), and the American Veterinarian Medical Association (AVMA). Without sugar-coating and without dancing around the bush, this book is about <u>righteous indignation</u> — about speaking out — about making a change — about anger toward the powers that create a network that controls our health, that sentences men, women, and children to their deaths or ill health every hour of the day.

These last few days and weeks (before going to press) have allowed me to see and hear about medically related events increasing in scope and number almost daily. These events are so appalling that I can no longer be silent nor be content in not trying to make a difference.

I am tired of watching people and animals die needlessly. I am tired of seeing them and their loved ones watch as their conditions worsen and being told there is no other way except failing conventional methods. I am tired of watching patients being sent home with no hope when there is hope — **if not for total recovery then certainly hope to improve the quality of life they have remaining**.

Books are being taken off the shelves that contain life-saving herbal formulas because the FDA deems it unlawfully writing of prescriptions — <u>the type of books which helped to save my life</u>.

It is expected that some will attempt to discredit me and the evidence I present. Some will pass me off as feeble-minded, half-baked, ill-trained, lacking true understanding of medical science.

I find it difficult to believe that anyone of a true searching heart will ignore my experiences, my background or my findings.

Over the last eight years I have been admitted to or seen in nine different hospitals and treated by more than fifteen different allopathic physicians, four chiropractors, and one occupational therapist. I believe that I am more than qualified to make at least plausible assessments of our health care system in more ways than general observations.

Doc Bradley - Am I Really Cured?

Do I Have a Personal Testimony?

I believe this chapter to be one of the most important in this book. On August 26, 1994, I attended the Fifth Annual Symposium of the American Herbalist Guild. There my deepest commitments to herbal healing and diet management were solidified. Herbalists from around the country converged to share their personal knowledge and experiences of the medicinal plant world. I was the only veterinarian who attended. My attendance was by invitation as a teacher and speaker.

It did not take me long to realize from the lectures the confirmation in my mind of the parallels that exist between man and beast, especially mammals. The presentation of success stories paralleling identical diseases common to man and animals was not surprising; diseases such as cancers of all types, diabetes, blood disorders, muscle and bone disorders, skin abnormalities and many others.

As a doctor of medicine and a surgeon by profession, I do realize that there may be certain conditions and defects that cannot be changed without surgical intervention, such as the separation of Siamese twins and the correction of a hair lip or cleft palate. If there are herbal and dietary remedies for these types of conditions, it is beyond my knowledge and that of most alternative medicine practitioners I have met or know about.

This chapter is important because it demonstrates the ability of phytotherapy and phytomedicine — or therapy and medicine using plants for treatment — to reverse severely debilitating conditions of humans, using myself as the primary example.

Notation: It is important to note that my hand did not progress to the favorable outcome expected but that the original injury triggered further damage by the presence of more painful neuromas. SAMPLE documents of each condition are found at the end of this chapter in chronological order. Please note the dates to understand the sequence of events. COMPUTERIZED TESTS REVEAL MY RIGHT HAND HAS BEEN COMPLETELY RESTORED to function. Photos in the middle section of the book demonstrate the condition of my hand and leg injuries before herbal treatments and dietary management and after these changes.

Brief Background — What Happened To Doc Bradley?

Doc Bradley began as a student desiring one thing: to become a competent and caring veterinarian. In 1971, there was no other Afro-American female attending a white veterinary school in the entire United States of America, creating a set of unbelievable circumstances discussed in my autobiography. I had also received a scholarship to the University of Pennsylvania and I was accepted at Tuskegee Institute as well, the only source of our black veterinarians at that time. This information is only mentioned to support the fact that it was an act of God that I overcame the trials and tribulations associated with that particular experience of higher learning. Post graduation proved to be yet another set of unforgettable experiences. I moved from Pennsylvania to Washington, D.C. in 1980. Finally I aquired my own clinic, after three years of working for others -- a dream shared by most graduates -- to have their own veterinary hospital. For many it often takes several years to fulfill this dream.

After only five years into my commitment I showed definite signs of accomplishing my goal to serve: more than a 3,500 client base, two to three new cases daily, equipment almost paid for, established reputation in the community, surgical contracts for spay and neuter programs with the local animal welfare league, established first emergency clinic for D.C., expanded in scope to cover metropolitan area, would begin showing a profit within another year, considerations for a satellite hospital or relocation, had grateful clients (viewed as extended family), a definitely sound beginning of a rewarding career.

I sought the services of an orthopedic surgeon for a minor lesion on my ring finger, the surgeon proved <u>incompetent</u> and <u>dishonest</u> by a jury of his peers - costing me permanent (determined at that time) damage to my hand. A nerve was cut and partially removed creating a 2.5cm deficit or gap, assessed by Johns Hopkins University Hospital. I then reluctantly sought the services of a <u>respected attorney</u> for a medical malpractice charge. The attorney proved quite competent but there were numerous occasions where total honesty was lacking which prompted questions of moral intentions. This resulted in a long emotional and financially altered journey that I might not otherwise have had.

A second surgery was required due to the onset of contractions of the hand (leading to the progression of a bird claw appearance) with tremendous and constant pain. An excellent surgeon, Dr. Russell Moore (Johns Hopkins University), removed two large neuromas (nerve tumors) created by the first surgeon and performed a nerve graft or nerve transplant. Initially the condition <u>improved</u>, however, the degree of <u>permanent</u> damage from the first surgery overrode the second, leading to greater pain as the nerves attempted to heal. Discovering the dishonesty of both the first doctor and the attorney led to a stressful sequence of events creating a domino effect which resulted in the loss of my home and business. The injury to my hand reduced my ability to function adequately as a professional, as well as my personal capacity in handling animals, consequently serious bodily injuries occurred as a consequence of my malfunctioning hand. I developed a condition called Tinel Syndrome which is characterized by shock like sensations that rendered my hand almost useless without protective bandaging or padding. Sensitivities to cold temperatures and extreme numbness added to the total dysfunction of my hand.

An auto accident (four months after the nerve was cut) occurred and I was rear-ended by a driver who had fallen asleep at the wheel. CAT and bone scans were required and the results showed a bulging vertebral disc of the lower back (L5 - S1) and arthritic changes. Cervical spine spasms were also diagnosed and treated. The first horse accident worsened my back injury and the bulging disc progressed to a herniated disc with complications. Several large areas of hematomas or blood clots led to severe back spasms, muscle damage, a concussion, colonic impaction and intestinal blockage. I was in and out of the hospital four times — literally dying slowly, I had no insurance and had no ability to buy any. The second horse accident my horse slipped on damp ground and my leg was quickly pinned underneath her side. My body faced one direction while my leg faced the opposite direction. This led to several spiral fractures which included the tibia, the fibula and the ankle bone. The inside bone of my ankle was crushed and became literally invisible. I required a full leg cast for four months and a half leg cast for two months. The first two settings were not good alignments. My leg was set and healed in a terrible twisted position. This led to a deformity in appearance and gait; yet the x-ray reports state excellent alignment (see x-ray documents). In truth, the bones were in good apposition (near each other) but not in good alignment — otherwise, how do you explain a leg so horribly rotated and distorted? I was unable to walk without my foot turning over and my knee rotating totally inward. The use of a cane and crutches became necessary beyond seven months. I experienced severe pain, constantly. One of the bones of my small toe nearly protruded through my skin at the bottom of my foot.

By June 16, 1993 the doctors declared there was no hope without cutting my leg and twisting it back to its normal position, then stabilizing it with pins and screws. There was no guarantee of full restoration, a definite risk of infection, requiring a minimum of six months in the hospital with I.V. antibiotics if osteomyelitis (bone infection) developed and perhaps amputation (see hospital records). The doctor commented, "a lot of people have deformities; you can accept it and live with it or you will come back when the pain is too great." Three attempts were made to align my leg and were obviously unsuccessful. It was difficult to entertain any thought of trusting anyone severing my leg in order to turn it around, drive pins and screws into it and face the possibility of serious bone infection or amputation. This was not a pleasant thought, nor a viable choice, especially being offered by the same source where the misalignment originally occurred. Because of the history characterizing the success rate of my own patients with musculo-skeletal conditions I <u>insisted</u> on using the same herbal formulas I used on them — specifically remembering "Killer" (see story). I used the "H" formula, Rheum-aid, and B F & C (bone, flesh and cartilage) (see hospital records), daily; also 8 oz. glasses of water with a tablespoon each of organically grown apple cider vinegar and unfiltered honey with a pinch of organically grown cayenne. I made my own liniment using wintergreen alcohol, olive oil, fresh squeezed lemon, peroxide, and Yager's liniment. I applied it every few hours along with two capsules of each formula mentioned above and a super garlic capsule (16,860 mg) every two to three hours for two days, then every six to eight hours for one month. Within the first twenty-four hours of treatment the PAIN STOPPED. By July 17, 1993, the bones in my leg and ankle had remodelled, turned around ninety-eight percent of its normal position. I was NO LONGER WALKING WITH A LIMP.

Before February 5, 1986 (the day the first surgeon severed the nerve in my hand), I had never missed one day of attendance in my clinic since January 1981 for any illness or medical condition.

As an undergraduate at Pennsylvania State University where I started as a biology and physical education major in 1965, I had a long history of athletic activities. I enjoyed the following sports until the ensuing injuries:

1. track and field / cross country - -50 yard dash was a favorite
2. tennis - amateur and semi-professional (1969-71) achieved USLTA ranking (mid-Atlantic states)
3. basketball
4. archery
5. bowling
6. volleyball
7. badminton
8. fencing
9. softball
10. horseback riding
11. field hockey
12. roller skating
13. Judo
14. Karate (received first belt)
15. swimming
16. billiards
17. gymnastics

This list of sports is not for the purpose of boasting, but to illustrate the emotional devastation I felt when I could no longer participate due to my injuries. I no longer participate in Judo or Karate not because of any physical limitations but by personal choice discussed in my autobiography.

How Herbs and a Changed Diet Saved My Life
and Continues to Strengthen It

Before herbal treatments:

* It seemed I had no hope, no life as I knew it, as reflected to me by the allopaths.
* Conventional medicine had no more answers without tremendous risks.

My Leg - From June 1992 to May 1993:

1. I could not walk without pain.
2. I could not physically run at all.
3. I could not enjoy the pleasure of romping with any of my five playful dogs across the fields — without pain.
4. I could not walk along a country road, leading my beloved horses with a rope, without pain.
5. I could not walk without my foot being turned over, having a grossly exaggerated limp, without pain.
6. I could never again play tennis or basketball or run track, according to the physicians, without surgery. "You are trying to walk normally, but you can't. Many people have deformities, and they must learn to live with it," the words kept ringing. "When the pain gets severe enough, you will come back to see us," they said.
7. **I could not imagine having my leg cut off below the knee**, turned around, a metal pin shoved into the middle of it with two screws driven in to anchor it at the top and bottom — **without more pain.**

My Hand - From February 5, 1986 to May 1993:

1. I experienced excruciating pain and more pain between the first and second surgeries.
2. I could not touch anything without protective padding.
3. I could not shake your hand without pain.
4. I could not hold a glass of water or a pencil without electric shocks radiating throughout my hand and often up my entire arm.
5. I could not tolerate extreme temperatures, cold or hot — especially cold — without pain.

<u>My Back - From June 12, 1986 to January 1992</u>:

1. I could not bend over — without pain.
2. I could not carry more than five pounds — especially uphill — without pain.
3. I could not sit or stand for even short periods — without pain.
4. I could not drive — without pain.
5. Back spasms travelled up the spine leading to unending debilitating migraines.
6. I had <u>non-stop</u> severe to excruciating pain from <u>1986 to 1992</u>.

I do not need to offer statistics to support my position. **I am a statistic** — one reality out of many!

Statistics mean nothing when misused. Scientific studies mean nothing when subject to manipulation in order to <u>fit</u> the goal it is attempting to prove, for example:
* fudging the figures
* changing the variables
* making conclusions to <u>fit</u> the proposed problem; preying on the fact that most of the population does not understand how to determine good studies from bad ones.

I am not offering scientific studies, but <u>raw evidence</u> using:
* <u>myself</u> - before and after herbal intervention and diet change;
* <u>my patients</u> - before and after herbal intervention and diet change;
* <u>testimonies</u> - eyewitness accounts - before and after herbal intervention and diet change.

Some of this evidence is acquired by using accepted methods of scientific measurements. It is no question that in conventional medicine the following procedures are considered valuable diagnostic aids:

* x-rays or radiographs
* blood tests
*. histopathology reports (biopsies, etc.)
* photographs depicting the disease

In summary, I performed my duties the best I could between the pain,despite the pain. <u>The need of my patients to reduce their pain often quieted my own</u>. My animal friends made unbelievable recoveries before my eyes — offering me hope that otherwise I would never have had — gave me life. In turn, the wisdom gained from their experiences and mine allows me to offer a better hope for you and your pets than with what conventional medicine has offered me and mine.

I make one request of you as the reader — my fellow human being. Help me to help you so you, too, can be free. Stand up for your <u>inalienable</u> right to make choices about your own bodies that is within the reasonable scope that God allows for us.

The point of this book is to fight the enemy - the father of lies - for your sake and for mine. "<u>And you shall know the truth, and the truth shall make you free</u>." <u>John 8:32 NKJ</u>

By The Power of Forgiveness

Some Conclusive Thoughts on How These Events Have Affected Me

By the power of forgiveness is the beginning title of my autobiography. The <u>choice</u> of <u>forgiveness</u> does not mean that <u>accountability</u> is not <u>expected</u>. My attending physician and my attorney were legally and morally wrong and should be accountable for their actions by law. Though it appears they have slipped through the cracks of justice accountability is a <u>spiritual</u> law that is <u>always</u> enforced. I forgive this attorney (whose actions caused more emotional pain than the physician) and only hope that this <u>gifted</u> person will choose to be used for the good of the people he serves and that he will benefit from the lessons of the past. My prayer is that someday my attorney and physician will admit their wrongdoings and <u>attempt</u> to make amends for the pain and suffering they have caused to those who trusted them.

An extended account of this scenario will be discussed in my autobiography. There are <u>two</u> testimonies which include statements of support for me long before the birth of this book. Those references have been blotted out as are many others to protect the rights of all parties concerned.

Medical Documents
Relative to Right Hand Injury
(in Chronological Order)
Includes Computerized Documentation
of Total Recovery of Right Hand and
Lifting Abilities
(Showing Restoration of My Back).
Right Hand Strength
Now Exceeds That of The Left.

February 11, 1986

Clinton, MD 20735

RE: Dr. Sandy Bradley

Dear ▮▮▮:

Thanks for referring Dr. Sandy Bradley to me for evaluation today. Dr. Bradley is a 38-year-old, right-hand dominant veterinarian who underwent removal of a mass from the right ring finger approximately on week ago. Following that, the patient stated that she had numbness of the ring finger. During the operation, a flexor tendon mass was resected.

At this point, the patient is about one week post-op. She has diminished range of motion and some tenderness of the hand in general; however, there is minimal if any swelling. The wound is benign, and there is no inflammation around the sutures. The patient has a transverse incision at the level of the MP flexor crease of the ring finger. She was tested for sensibility and has intact two-point discrimination on the ulnar border of the ring finger; however, the radial border shows that she has somewhat diminished two-point discrimination.

At this time, I think that it is important that she maximize range of motion in her digits and we have given her instructions on how to perform physical therapy for her hand. She will begin soaks and apply skin cream to the hand. She is going to have her sutures removed by you in about one week, and I would like to see her back in several week's time. I think that in a couple of weeks she should be able to return to her normal veterinary activities. If it seems as though she is not getting any functional return in the radial digital nerve, she may have to have a nerve graft in the future; however, this could be done as an elective procedure. It is possible that she has a neuropraxia or stretch of the digital nerve at this point, and this may return spontaneously.

In all, I do not think that she will be severely limited from her operating duties, and at least for the time being, our efforts will be aimed at getting her back to her job since this is a critical time for her.

Sincerely,

▮. Russel▮▮▮▮, M.D.
Associate Professor of
Orthopaedic Surgery

HOSPITAL OF MARYLAND, INC.
Baltimore, Maryland 21239

DEPARTMENT OF PATHOLOGY

ACCESSION NO.:	86-S-1109
PATIENT NAME:	BRADLEY, Sandy
HISTORY NO.:	16-040-4416
LOCATION:	Outpatient
AGE:	39
RACE:	Black
SEX:	Female
PROCEDURE DATE:	3/19/86

PHYSICIAN :

Dr. Russell

TYPE OF PROCEDURE: Exploration and possible nerve graft to right 4th finger.

CLINICAL IMPRESSION: Digital nerve injury of right 4th finger.

The specimen is labeled "proximal neuroma of right 4th finger". The specimen is received in Formalin and consists of two pieces of tissue. The larger piece of tissue measures 1.5 x 1 x .5 cm. and consists of dense white, firm, fibrous, soft tissue. This piece is sectioned and entirely submitted. The smaller piece is yellow in color and has a consistency of adipose tissue and measures .7 x .4 x .2 cm. The piece is submitted in tact.

MICROSCOPIC DIAGNOSIS:

    RIGHT 4TH FINGER; SUBCUTANEOUS TISSUE WITH SCARRING AND CHANGES COMPATIBLE WITH NEUROMA.

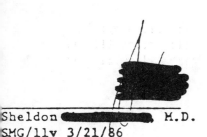

Sheldon   , M.D.
SMG/llv 3/21/86

SCHOOL OF MEDICINE
DEPARTMENT OF ORTHOPAEDIC SURGERY

 M.D.
Associate Professor

October 23, 1986

RE: Dr. Sandy Bradley

To Whom it May Concern:

Dr. Bradley at this time is recovering from reconstructive surgery on her hand, and at this time, although her range of motion has returned nicely, she has problems with heavy manual activity that is required in her work as a veterinarian.

For this reason, she is unable to use her right hand in forceful types of activities that are required in her everyday handling of animals, that include such minor procedures as injections.

I feel that Dr. Bradley is temporarily unable to perform her everyday activities. Currently, she is undergoing physical therapy to ameliorate her symptoms. If any further information is needed, feel free to contact my office.

Sincerely,

M.D.
Associate Professor of
Orthopaedic Surgery

cc: Dr. Sandy Bradley
Washington, D.C. 20018

GREATER CHESAPEAKE ᴴAND SPECIALISTS, P.A.

, M.D.
, M.D.
, M.D.
, M.D.
, M.D.
, M.D.

August 4, 1987

Washington, D.C.

Re: Sandy Bradley, V.M.D.

Dr. Sandy Bradley was seen in follow-up on July 31, 1987, following nerve grafting for the radial digital nerve to the right 4th finger. She has minimal if any swelling today and has a good range of motion to the finger. However, she does have pain along the area of the scar and also states that she has impaired feeling or sensation in the fingertip. She states that she is unable to do her activities as a result of the discomfort.

Two-point testing was performed and she has approximately 5 mm two-point discrimination on the ulnar aspect of the tip of the ring finger; however, she has greater than 10 mm of two-point discrimination on the radial aspect. She does have protective sensation and I would have to state at this point that she may have some neuromatous type pain in her hand; however, I don't feel that she has any reason for re-exploration of the wound at this point and feel that she should be treated with external means such as padding or splinting as is necessary.

I feel, as a result of the injury and discomfort Dr. Bradley is having, she has a fifty percent (50%) impairment for the ring finger of the right hand. Also, I think that her hand is disabled at least another ten percent (10%) because of the weakness and overall pain problem that she has, and this would calculate out to be a total of fifteen percent (15%) hand impairment. I think that the only corrective measures that should be taken at this time are protective in nature, and I do not feel that repeat surgery would be beneficial at this time and, in fact, I think that this could set off a worse pain

Re: Sandy Bradley, V.M.D.
August 4, 1987

problem. It is understood that she might never have a normal
hand and that she may always have some difficulties in performing
her duties as a veterinarian, especially on larger animals.

Sincerely,

M.D.

**Hand Surgery
Rehabilitation Center, Ltd.**
██████ Medical Center

███████ Virginia ██████

██████

Hand Surgery:
████████ M.D.
Medical Director

October 22, 1987

████████████████
████████████
2███████████████
Washington, D.C. ████████

RE: Dr. Sandy Bradley

Dear Mr. ████████:

In followup to your request, Dr. Bradley was <u>interviewed on 23
August 1987</u>, following a chart review of records on 14 August 1987. It
<u>would be my</u> feeling that this lady probably had a volar flexor sheath
cyst or ganglion over the right ring finger which was removed and/or
decompressed at a surgical procedure on or about 31 January 1986 by Dr.
████████, apparently without benefit of an operating tourniquet in
a blood obscured field in which a piece of the radial digital nerve was
removed, demonstrated by pathological examination at the time of the
initial surgery and confirmed in followup surgical procedure by Dr.
Moore on or about 19 March 1986. At that procedure, nerve grafting from
the medial antebrachial cutaneous nerve to the radial digital nerve of
the ring finger was performed. Subsequently, the patient has had
problems with pain in the hand particularly upon trying to grasp with
apparent neuroma formation at the proximal graft anastomosis. This
precludes her being able to grasp animals securely in her line of work
as a veterinarian as well as interfering with other activities. She
apparently has almost constant electrical shock phenomenon in the hand
in this area at the base of the ring finger whenever she tries to grasp
things.

It would be my opinion that operating on a hand without the
benefit of an operating tourniquet is substandard medical care and that
the removal of the piece of digital nerve at the time of the initial
surgery would also obviously be substandard and that this has

resulted directly in the patient's present problems of electric
paresthesias in the right palm and right ring finger and is the direct
cause of her hand disuse.

    If you should have comments or questions, please feel free to
write or call.

                              Sincerely yours,

                                      ███████████████, M.D.

███████
Dictated/not read

BRADLEY, Sandy, D.V.M.

OFFICE FOLLOWUP VISIT

2-14-89

Dr. Bradley has had ongoing pain involving the right hand, primarily the palmar surface and also the right fourth finger and the metacarpal phalangeal region.

EXAMINATION: She is alert and fully oriented. She is profoundly tender on palpation at the base of the right fourth and fifth fingers just at the metacarpal phalangeal joint. There is also a palpable lump at the base between the right fourth and fifth fingers. There is a wedge-shaped area which resembles a "V" between the right third and fifth finger with an area of discoloration also noted at the base of the fourth finger. The latter region is profoundly tender on palpation at this time. There is a puffiness that is noted distally at the base also of the right fourth proximal phalanax. Other modalities are essentially unchanged.

IMPRESSION: Status post neuroma resection at the base of
                the fourth finger.
                Myofascial-type syndrome.
                Causal-type syndrome.
                Possible recurrent neuroma involving the
                digital nerve.

DISCUSSION: Overall, subjectively this patient has gotten somewhat worse since the time she was last evaluated as far as her symptom complex is concerned. Conservative modalities should be continued. I shall re-evaluate her in three months or before if necessary.

M.D.

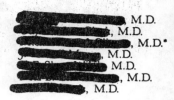 HAND SPECIALISTS, P.A.

███████████, M.D.
███████████, M.D.
███████████, M.D.*
███████████, M.D.
███████████, M.D.
███████████, M.D.

September 10, 1991

████████████
Director
████ Rehab. Center
████████████

Ft. Washington, MD. ████

Re: Sandy Bradley

Dear █████████

Sandy still has pain in the ulnar aspect of her ring finger and she states that she has a neuroma that changes in size slightly. She also states that she has numbness in her long finger at this time along the ulnar border.

I do not feel that physical therapy or desensitization would help her at this point; however, she is going to pursue this just in case it is of benefit to her.

Sincerely yours,

, M.D.

JRM/pcf

7/21/92

████████████

Landover, MD 20785

Sandy Bradley
Route 23
Middle House #2
Tenafick, MD 20612

* reconstructive plastic surgery

 **INDEPENDENCE TRAINING**
FT. WASHINGTON, MD. 20744 TEL. NO.

June 25, 1994

Sandy Bradley, V.M.D.
P.O. Box 4001
Upper Marlboro, MD 20775

Dear Dr. Bradley:

I was indeed pleasantly impressed with the progress you have made in your right hand when I saw you on 6/20/94. I recall our last meeting around October, 1991. At that time your right hand was severely contracted in the carpal as well as the metacarpal joints and there was indication of atrophy in the thenar and intrinsic musculature. Above all, I remember the bird's claw like appearance of the hand and your report of pain and other sensory changes in the hand as well as in the arm itself. I was saddened by the fact that since I saw you initially around June of 1986, your hand got worse. Therefore, seeing your hand in it's full functional capacity was truly impressive. I am glad that I have a computerized functional capacity evaluation equipment in our clinic (The Baltimore Therapeutic Equipment-BTE). Your performance on the BTE certainly demonstrates your current capacity to tolerate external challenges (in the right hand as well as in the lower extremities).

Thank you for giving me the opportunity to see you in your present state of recovery. Best wishes for success with your research and practice in the use of herbal medicine.

Sincerely,

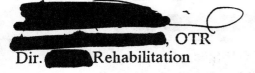, OTR
Dir.   Rehabilitation

```
BTE QUEST          Maximum Strength Comparison        Static/Isometric
--------------------------------------------------------------------
Patient ID: 160404416        Name: SANDY BRADLEY
Attachment: 162&  GRIP STRENGTH              Height: 38
```

LEFT	RIGHT
1 : 287 inch-lbs.	1 : 340 inch-lbs.
2 : 293 inch-lbs.	2 : 354 inch-lbs.
3 : 270 inch-lbs.	3 : 292 inch-lbs.
Average : 283 inch-lbs.	Average : 329 inch-lbs.
Coeff. Of Variation : (3.4%)	Coeff. Of Variation : 8.1%

CV ±10% is considered within normal limits.

Left Is 14.0% Less Than Right

```
    June 21, 1994 At 16:21 From ▮▮▮▮▮▮▮▮▮▮▮▮ TRAINING CENTER
```

6 inch pounds = 1 pound

Demonstrates right (injured) hand
now exceeds strength of left (normal) hand

BTE QUEST   Six Second Strength Trials   Static/Isometric

Patient ID: 160404416   Name: SANDY BRADLEY

Attachment: 162&   GRIP STRENGTH   Height: 38   Side: LEFT

Peak Force: 272, 280, 255   Average: 269   Average (6 Seconds): 245, 256, 235

Average (3 To 5 Seconds): 259, 263, 236   Coeff. Var. (3 To 5 Seconds): 4.7%

June 21, 1994 At 16:36 From ████████████████ TRAINING CENTER

Demonstrates as time went on my right hand did not become fatigued and continued to be strong with a peak force of 280 within 3-5 seconds

Patient ID: 160404416   Name: SANDY BRADLEY
Attachment: 191L LIFTING ABILITY   Height: 9   Side: BOTH

```
  91

  77                                          Total Time
                                              135 Seconds
  63
I       52 inches                             Range Dist
N                                             43 inches
C  49 ---------------------------------------
H                                             Rep. Count
E  35                                              14
S
  21                                          Maximum Lead
                                                 52 lbs.
   7 ---------------------------------------
        9 inches
Weight    52
Time     6   9
Power    30
```

June 21, 1994 At 17:14 From ██████████████████████ TRAINING CENTER

Minimum knee bend.
S/P Rt. tibia & ankle FX & medial rotation of
Rt. knee.

This graft
proves that fractures of right tibia and ankle including the
medial (inward) rotation of knee (by being healed) no longer
impair ability to lift and stand while in a positional stance for lifting; also
therefore the herniated disc problem is not a functional threat.

**Documents to Verify Pathology
Ensued by Auto Accident of
June 12, 1986
(in Chronological Order)**

December 5, 1986

████████████
Suite 300
████████████
College Park, MD ████

Re: Dr. Sandy Bradley
D/A: (June 12, 1986)

Dear Ms. ████

Dr. Bradley reported to my office on June 19, 1986, complaining of pain in the neck and mid-back areas and weakness and aching in the right arm following a rear-end auto accidnet in which she was involved on June 12, 1986.

Physical, orthopedic, and neurological examinations and review of cervical X-rays were performed.

DIAGNOSES: 1. Acute hyperflexion/hyperextension injury of the cervical spine with paravertebral myospasm.
2. Acute sprain/strain of the thoracic spine with paravertebral spasm and subluxation complex T9/T10.

PRONOSIS: Guarded for full recovery to pre-injury status.

TREATMENT: The patient was treated with Fluorimethane Spray and Stretch for myospasm. She did not return for further treatment.

Sincerely,

████████████

████████   D.C.

████

Hospital
DEPARTMENT OF RADIOLOGY
Lanham, Maryland 20706 •(301)
, M.D., Chairman

X-RAY   NUCLEAR MEDICINE   ULTRASOUND   COMPUTERIZED TOMOGRAPHY
IMAGING REPORT

PATIENT'S NAME BRADLEY, SANDRA	AGE 40	REFERRED BY	HOSPITAL/E.R. NO. 6750103	ORIGIN OP	DATE OF EXAM 3-20-87	X-RAY NO. 37183

NAME IS ISOTOPE 99m Tc MDP	COMPOUND 99m Tc MDP	DATE OF ASSAY	ASSAYED (uCi,mCi)/ml	PAT.RECD. (uCi,mCi)	GIVEN I.V.	19.0 mCi P.O. LOCAL I.T.	DATE GIVEN 3-20-87

BONE SCAN:
Multiple scintiphotos including the skull, cervical spine, thoracic spine.
lumbar spine, pelvis and both hips, both upper and lower extremities, including
both hands and feet show no increased activity throughout the visualized bony
structure.

CONCLUSION: Normal bone scan.

CERVICAL SPINE
Routine views with lateral views with flexion and extension show no limitation
in the flexion and extension views.

Multiple views of the cervical spine show no evidence of fracture, subluxation
or bone destruction. The intervertebral disc spaces and neural foramina are
normal. The odontoid process is intact.

CONCLUSION: Normal cervical spine.

THORACIC SPINE:
There is no evidence of fracture or bone destruction. The intervertebral
disc spaces are normal. The pedicles are intact.

IMPRESSION: Normal thoracic spine.

LUMBOSACRAL SPINE AND PELVIS
The SI joints and hips are normal.

The intervertebral spaces are normal. There is no spur of the lumbar vertebrae.
There is no spondylysis or spondylolisthesis. There are degenerative osteoarthritic
changes in the facet joints at L3-4, L4-5 and L5-S1.

IMPRESSION: Mild degenerative osteoarthritic changes in the facet joints.

, M.D.
Radiologist

3-22-87

PATIENT: BRADLEY,SANDY   MRUN: 14-81-70 AGE: 40Y
ORDER #: 77585   ADMIT DR: ███████████████
ADMIT DATE: 03/26/87   DISP 03/26/87 FROM OP
SERVICE: 03/26/87   ACCOUNT #: 167053
DICTATED BY: ███████████████ D
REPORT STATUS: COMPLETE

L SPINE WO   (CC:3107805)
CT SCAN OF THE LUMBAR SPINE: The examination was performed from L3
thru S1 to exclude a disc herniation.

L3-4:   No significant bony or soft tissue abnormalities are seen.

L4-5:   No significant bony or soft tissue abnormalities are seen.

L5-S1:   There is mild disc bulging lateralizing very slightly to the
right side on cuts #13 and 14.   A focal disc herniation is not seen.
No significant bony abnormalities are present.

IMPRESSION:
MILD DEGENERATIVE DISC DISEASE AT L5-S1.

RN/snb
03/27/87
9:33 AM

                              ███████████████████ MD

Documents Relative to
Further Back Injury
Caused by Horse Toppling Over on Me
Includes:
1) Hospital Records
2) Doctor's Bills
3) Letters of Verification

Referred to as Horse Accident #1

MEMORIAL HOSPI

LA PLATA, MD. 20646
(301)

	5 BC/BS PROV. NO.	6 FEDERAL TAX NO. 52-0445374	7 MEDICARE NO. 210035	8 MEDICAID NO. 00033	3 PATIENT CONTROL NUMBER 277938 /165

10 PATIENT'S LAST NAME / FIRST NAME / INITIAL / **11 PATIENT'S ADDRESS** / CITY / STATE

BRADLEY, SANDY — STAR RT 2 BOX 2167 — LAPLATA, MD

12 BIRTH DATE	13 SEX	14 MS	15 DATE	16 HR.	17 TYPE	18 SRC	19 A.H.	20 D.H.	21 STAT	22 FROM	THROUGH	23 COV.D.	24 N-C.D.	25 C-LD.	26 L.R.D.	27
02/13/47	F	S	08/14/89	15	4	7		12	01	08/14/89	08/18/89	4				

28 OCCURRENCE CD / DATE	29 OCCURRENCE CD / DATE	30 OCCURRENCE CD / DATE	31 OCCURRENCE CD / DATE	32 OCCURRENCE CD / DATE	33 OCCURRENCE SPAN FROM / THROUGH
11 07/02/89					277938 /165

BRADLEY, SANDY
STAR RT 2 BOX 2167
LAPLATA, MD 20646
(301) 753-9091

CONDITION CODES 35 36 37 38 39	BLOOD RECORD (PINTS) 40 FURN 41 REPL 42 NOT RP. 43 DED.	44 SP. PROG.	45

46 VALUE CD / AMT	47 VALUE CD / AMT	48 VALUE CD / AMT	49 VALUE CD / AMT
01 278.35			

50 DESCRIPTION		51 R. CODE	52 S. UNITS	53 TOTAL CHARGES	54	55	56
ROOM-BOARD/SEMI	278.35	120	4	1113.40			
ADMIT CHARGE		221	1	88.38			
PHARMACY		250	8	2.63			
IV SOLUTIONS		258	19	87.80			
STERILE SUPPLY		272	5	77.64			
CLINICAL LABORATORY		300	5	160.26			
DX X-RAY		320	5	309.87			
CAT SCAN		352	1	189.24			
TOTAL CHARGES		001		2029.27			

Handwritten notes:

Dr. AlFano
① 1st to Diagnose (Dx) — Recommended
   Herniated DISC — ORTHO MD
   X-RAY 7/6/89 TOO SERIOUS

57 P
② Hospitalized by PG + PMH
   X-RAYED — missed diagnosis

A
B
C

③ HERNIATED DISC — not
   Dx until April 1990 by
   CONVENTIONAL DOCTORS via CT
   SCAN Dr. SIDHU — see Letter

65 IN

60 DEDUCTIBLE	61 CO-INSURANCE	62 EST. RESPONSIBILITY	63 PRIOR PAYMENTS	64 EST. AMOUNT DUE

DUE FROM PATIENT ▶ 2029.27   2029.2

67 CERT.-SSN-HIC.-ID. NO.	69 GROUP NAME	70 INSURANCE GROUP NO.

71 EID	72 ESC	73 EMPLOYER NAME	74 EMPLOYEE ID.	75 EMPLOYER LOCATION

UB-82 HCFA-1450   PATIENT COPY

 CHIROPRACTIC OFFICE

La Plata, Maryland 20646

November 2, 1994

Re: Patient: Sandy Bradley

To Whom It May Concern:

Doctor Bradley was seen in my office from <u>July 6, 1989</u>
through the beginning of August 1989.

She reported that on the previous Sunday a horse had fallen
on her. She could not rise and reported being in a semi-
conscious state for three hours. Her pain was constant and
there were bruises noticeable on her lower back area.
She also reported lower back pain with sciatic radiation down
the left leg, numbness and tingling. She stated that she was
losing strength in her big toe on that side as well.

After several treatments, I received a phone call from a
friend who was with her on that particular day and was told
that she was in extreme pain and of course, there was still
swelling. It was my advice at that time, that she be
transported to the hospital and more invasive procedures be
employed.

The last time I saw Dr. Bradley was the beginning of August
and at that time, I had again advised her to seek medical
attention and told her that I would be available for any
problems as they occurred in the future. As I then believed
and still believe now that her main problem was an herniated
disc in her lower back which at times can be painful and
incapacitating.

Sincerely,

_____, D.C.

  **HOSPITAL**

La Plata, Maryland 20646

(301)

DATE: October 24, 1990

PATIENT: Sandy Bradley

Dear

It has been requested from this hospital that the following medical information be obtained:

☐ Verification of Birth: Please be advised that _____

was born at Physicians Memorial Hospital on _____ and discharged on

_____. The patient's parent is_____ (Mother's name).

☑ Verification of <u>Inpatient</u> and/or <u>Outpatient</u> Treatment:

To Whom it May Concern:

This is to verify that ___Sandy Bradley_____

was treated in our hospital on July 7, 1989, July 12, 1989, July 24, 1989, August 14, 1989

~~and released~~ to August 18, 1989, March 23, 1990 to March 24, 1990 and July 23, 199

If additional information is needed, please contact the Medical Records Department at **645-0184**.

Medical Records Department
_____Hospital

MR-005   dick wildes PRINTING. co., inc.

, M.D.

LA PLATA, MARYLAND 20646
(301) █████████
██████████ D.C.

ACCT# NEEDED TO PROCESS PMT.

PATIENT   08102

SANDY   BRADLEY
ST RT 2, BOX 2167
LAPLATA   MD 20646
165215   753 9091

DATE	DESCRIPTION	PROC CODE	CHARGE
07/07/89	X-RAY LUMBAR SPINE MULT.VIEWS	72110	26.00
07/07/89	X-RAY THORACIC SPINE	72070	19.00

DR ID# 506-56-3775

DIAGNOSIS:
  INJURY,TRUNK,BACK
  INJURY,TRUNK,BACK

FACILITY-████████████ HOSP.
LA PLATA,MD 20646

CHARGES	CREDITS	BALANCE DUE
45.00		45.00

TO CLAIM INSURANCE BENEFITS:
    1. COMPLETE THE PERSONAL INFORMATION ON YOUR FORM.
    2. ATTACH A COPY OF THIS RECEIPT & MAIL TO YOUR INSURANCE COMPANY

5/9/91

District of Columbia ██

To Whom it May Concern:

This statement is my recolection of events concerning Dr. Sandy Bradley's accident in July 1989. Dr. Bradley contacted me one afternoon (cannot recall exact date) stating that she had a horse accident one week prior. She stated that she was having difficulty and wanted me to take her to the local emergency room (████████████████████ Hospital). My father and myself escorted Dr. Bradley to the emergency room. Dr.Bradley was having trouble walking on her left leg.

Approximately one week after the visit to the emergency room, Dr. Bradley called me to say she still wasn't feeling well. while on the phone with Sandy, she dropped the phone to vomit. I ran across to her home where I found her in the bathroom vomiting into the toliet. I then escorted her to her bed and she stated that she felt lightheaded and very weak. Approximatley 5 mins after Dr.Bradley got into the bed, she started to lose conscienceness. I proceeded to call her Dr. (Dr. ████████). Dr.████████ instructed me to call an ambulance to pick up Dr. Bradley. When I got back into the room with Dr.Bradley, she was unconscience. I ran and called 911 and when I returned to her room she was starting to ragain conscienceness.

Upon the ambulance's arrival, they immediately began to conduct a full patient assesment. This assesment included a head to toe survey on the patient. The ambulance crew decided to MediVac the patient to a trama center due to the fact she was having possible neurological problems.

After Dr. Bradley was MediVaced to ████████████████ Hospital, I called a friend of her's and made her aware of the situation. I then called Mr. and Mrs. ████████ (more friends of Dr. Bradley) and asked that they please call her parents.

During Dr. Bradley's stay at the hospital my family and I took care of Dr.Bradley's animals. We took care of her two white German Shepards as well as her two horses. After Dr. Bradley was released from the hospital, she was forced to give the two shepards to a shelter because she was in no physical condition to take care of them.

Approximately one month later Dr. Bradley called me once again and stated she was having similar problems as before. I took her to her family physician (████████████) and the dr. instructed her to go to ████ and be admitted for treatment. I then took Dr. Bradley over to ████████████████ Hospital where she stayed for 3 days. After being released from ████, Dr. Bradley was obviously still in distress from her injuries and to this day she states she is still having back problems and headaches.

Sincerely,

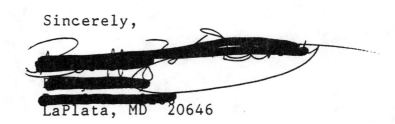

LaPlata, MD 20646

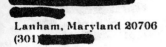
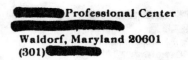
, M.D., P.A.

NEUROLOGICAL SURGERY

, M.D., FRCS(C)   By Appointment Only

February 26, 1990

TO WHOM IT MAY CONCERN:

Ms. Sandy Bradley was seen in the office on February 20, 1990 for the treatment of back pain. Ms. Bradley will be admitted as soon as arrangements can be made for a myelogram and CT scan of the back at ▇▇▇▇ Memoiral Hospital.

Thank you.

Sincerly,

M.D.

kmh

Lanham, Maryland 20706
(301)

Waldorf, Maryland
·(301)

, M.D., P.A.
NEUROLOGICAL SURGERY

April 27, 1990

Sandy Bradley:

The patient was seen in the office on April 27, 1990.

The patient has been complaining of pain in the lower back with
intermittent pain radiating down into the left leg and some
soreness in the right leg. Her neck has not bothered her too
much recently but does get stiff from time to time.

On examination the patient has tenderness at L4-5--S1 level and
left sacroiliac region. Straight leg raising is 90 degrees
bilaterally.

Neurological examination is unchanged from before.

The patient's myelogram and CT scan findings have been discussed
with her. These have indicated some right lateral disc
herniation at L5-S1. The patient is advised that her symptoms
are more on the left side and the disc seems to be more abnormal
on the right side. She is advised continued conservative
management and if her pain gets worse then further treatment
might have to be considered. She is advised to take it easy and
avoid strenuous activity. She is advised to do Williams
exercises. She is to return in four to six weeks time for
further evaluation.

, M.D.

(1) Hematoma
   in left back
   directly from horse injury

(2) initially disc-bulging
   from auto accident
   now herniated
   from horse accident

1

Documents Relative to
Contorted and Fractured Leg
(Referred to as Horse Accident #2
in Chronological Order)
Includes:
1) Eyewitness Testimony
2) Hospital Records - Chart & X-ray Reports
3) Applications Submitted via Hospital
for Medical Assistance
4) Disability Determination Records via Hospital

On June 19, 1992, I was present when Dr. Sandy Bradly broke her leg in a riding accident. Her leg was twisted at an angle. During the next 6 months, I saw her frequently in a full or near full length cast. She complained of the pain and the angle at which the leg was mending thru June of 1993. At this time, she told me she was going to begin treating herself with "herbs." When I next saw her a month later, she was walking better and she said her leg was straightening out. I have since observed her walking with a much improved gait and motion.

DEPARTMENT OF RADIOLO

 # HOSPITAL CENTER

CHEVERLY, MARYLAND 20785

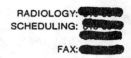

RADIOLOGY:
SCHEDULING:
FAX:

ATIENT'S NAME	AGE	REFERRED BY	HOSP./E.R. NO.	ORIGIN	DATE OF EXAM	X-RAY NO.
BRADLEY, SANDY	02-13-47	STAFF/ORTHO CLN	10346101	ORTHO CLN	07-01-92	328923

PATIENT ACCOUNT #: 203671722 **REPORT**
PROCEDURE CODES: 7305-9, 7306-7

INDICATION: Fracture.

RIGHT LEG: A spiral fracture of the distal tibia is noted and a spiral fracture of the proximal fibula is noted. Relatively good alignment is maintained on two projections. The fracture line appears to extend into the ankle joint.

LEFT ANKLE THROUGH PLASTER: A hairline fracture extends through the tibia into the ankle joint. Excellent alignment is maintained.

Should say
Right ankle

_____ M.D.
Radiologist

D:07-01-92
T:07-02-92

State of Maryland
DEPARTMENT OF HUMAN RESOURCES
EVALUATION OF IMPAIRMENT & DISABILITY
. . . .

████ HOSPITAL Department of Social Services Address: _____

Part I: *(To be completed by Client)*

Name: _____ _____ _____
                                            Date of Birth   Last Grade of School Completed

Address: _____ Telephone No. _____

1. What is your usual occupation? _____

2. How long have you been unemployed? _____ Why? _____

3. What illness keeps you from working? How? _____

4. Have you received treatment (doctor's office, clinic, hospital)? If so, Where? _____ When? _____

TO THE PHYSICIAN/HEALTH PRACTITIONER: Please complete the following statements. I authorize you to release any information regarding my medical condition required by the State to determine my eligibility for benefits.

Applicant's Signature ___*Nancy Bradley, W.M.D*___ Date ___7/1/92___ ✳

Part II: *(To be completed by Examining/Treating Physician/Health Practitioner)* see reverse side for instructions

1. How long have you known patient? ___*1 wk*___ Date of current examination ___7/1/92___

2. Physical data: Height _____ Weight _____ Blood Pressure _____ Pulse _____

3. a. Please record a complete list of current disorders as diagnosed by you with estimated date of onset: _____
   ___*Fx Rt Tibia*___
   _____ ICD Code: _____

   b. Is the patient's condition worse since the last examination? ☐ Yes, ☒ No. If Yes, how? _____
   _____

   c. Describe current/future treatment: ___*Casting*___

   d. Any additional comments: ___*Pt is on crutches*___

4. PROGNOSIS: From your diagnosis of the patient's condition, please check the current level of his/her work capacity:
   ☒ No Work Capacity **or** ☐ Full Work Capacity, **or** limited to ☐ Sedentary Work, ☐ Light Work, ☐ Moderate Work
       • for ☐ 12 months or more, **or** ☒ less than 12 months.
   Is the patient's condition ☐ Permanent or ☒ Temporary. Can the condition be corrected with treatment? ___*yes*___
   ___*will be healed in 2 months*___

   Record any significant laboratory data: _____
5. a. Patient is unable to work from (Month/Year) ___*6/19/92*___ through (Month/Year) ___*8/19/92*___
      - OR -   *took long.*
   b. Patient is unable to participate in Project Independence classes/training through (Month/Year) _____

Please Continue to the Reverse Side and Sign in Part IV

First 2 sessions to reduce fracture not successful *Dec 28, 1992*
Cast off

State of Maryland
DEPARTMENT OF HUMAN RESOURCES
EVALUATION OF IMPAIRMENT & DISABILITY

Category _____

Case No. _____

Worker ████████████

Telephone ████████████

PG HC.   Department of Social Services   Address: _____

Part I: *(To be completed by Client)*

Name: Sandy Bradley   2-13-47   V.M.D.
                        Date of Birth   Veterinarian Medical Degree
                                         Last Grade of School Completed

Address: General Delivery Upper Marlboro, Md.   Telephone No. (301) 249-4879

1. What is your usual occupation? Veterinarian – Clinical Practitioner

2. How long have you been unemployed? 1 yr.   Why? June 19 - horse fell on leg

3. What illness keeps you from working? How? the above - severe external rotation - pain & swelling inability to walk, bend leg properly

4. Have you received treatment (doctor's office, clinic, hospital)? If so, Where? PEH   When? June - Dec 92

TO THE PHYSICIAN/HEALTH PRACTITIONER: Please complete the following statements. I authorize you to release any information regarding my medical condition required by the State to determine my eligibility for benefits.

Applicant's Signature Sandy Bradley V.M.D.   Date (6-16-93)

Part II: *(To be completed by Examining/Treating Physician/Health Practitioner)* see reverse side for instructions

1. How long have you known patient? 7/1/92   Date of current examination 6/16/93

2. Physical data: Height _____ Weight 120   Blood Pressure _____ Pulse _____

3. a. Please record a complete list of current disorders as diagnosed by you with estimated date of onset: _____

SPIRAL FRACTURE RIGHT TIBIA

_____ ICD Code: _____

b. Is the patient's condition worse since the last examination? ☒ Yes, ☐ No. If Yes, how? _____

MORE ROTATION, SYMPTOMS FROM KNEE/ANKLE

c. Describe current/future treatment: OSTEOTOMY & INTERNAL OR EXTERNAL FIXATION

d. Any additional comments: _____

4. PROGNOSIS: From your diagnosis of the patient's condition, please check the current level of his/her work capacity:
☒ No Work Capacity **or** ☐ Full Work Capacity, **or** limited to ☐ Sedentary Work, ☐ Light Work, ☐ Moderate Work
   • for ☒ 12 months or more, **or** ☐ less than 12 months.
Is the patient's condition ☐ Permanent or ☐ Temporary. Can the condition be corrected with treatment? _____

Record any significant laboratory data: _____

5. a. Patient is unable to work from (Month/Year) 6 /93 through (Month/Year) 7/1/94
      - OR -
   b. Patient is unable to participate in Project Independence classes/training through (Month/Year) _____

Please Continue to the Reverse Side and Sign in Part IV

Part III: SPECIAL MEDICAL NEEDS *(To be Completed by the Examining/Treating Physician)*
see below for instructions

1. Pregnancy Confirmed? ☐ Yes, ☐ No. EDC: _____ Date of Examination: _____
2. Receiving Prenatal Care? ☐ Yes, ☐ No.
3. Telephone required in the home because: _____
4. Supervised care is needed at the following level: *(See definitions below)*
   ☐ Domiciliary Care, ☐ Protective Payee, ☐ Care in Own Home, ☐ Other (specify) _____

Part IV: REQUIRED SIGNATURE

_____
Print/Type Name of Physician/Health Practitioner

_____
Signature of Physician/Health Practitioner

Prince George's Hospital Center
Medical Out Patient Clinic
_____
Board of Medical Examiner's I.D. No./Certification/License No.

6/16/93
_____
Date

Cheverly, MD, 20785
_____
Address of Physician/Practitioner

(301)
_____
Telephone Number

Part II INSTRUCTIONS: (To be completed by Examining/Treating Practitioner
if the patient has been seen or treated in the past 90 days)
This form will be used to determine eligibility for assistance that is based upon the mental or physical impairment of the applicant.
It will also be used to determine exemption from work/training programs and capacity to care for children in the family.

Please complete and return this form to the local department of social services as soon as possible. Thank you.

1. Please record the date you first began to treat this patient and the date of your most recent examination.

2. Please record data obtained in the most recent examination of the patient.

3. a. Please give specific complaints, observed symptoms, etc. which contribute to the diagnosis and illustrate the exact nature and extent of impairment. For example, if seizure disorder is diagnosed, please record the severity, frequency and date of last seizure. Please add the ICD code.
   b. This information will help us determine when we should refer the patient to the Social Security Administration to reapply for federal disability benefits.
   c. Information required to determine eligibility.
   d. Please record any additional information you feel would help us make a decision on the patient's eligibility.

4. Please state if patient is unable to work given his condition or if he retains some limited capacity to work.
   Is patient totally unable to work or is it advisable for patient to seek other kinds of employment?
   Please record whether EEG, EKG, psychiatric therapy, psychological evaluation or other kinds of follow-up treatments are needed. Give dates when the results of any current testing will be available.

5. a. Please refrain from the use of "indefinite". Program payments may be limited based on the months you specify the patient will be impaired.
   b. This information is needed to determine if an Aid to Families with Dependent Children recipient should be exempt, due to an impairment, from the requirement to participate in job-related/education-related activities.

Part III INSTRUCTIONS:

This information is needed to determine eligibility for Public Assistance Programs for Pregnant Women,
the medical need for a telephone or the need for supervised care for the disabled or elderly individual.

Domiciliary Care: A protective institutional/home-type environment needed because of advanced age and/or physical/mental impairment.

Protective Payee: A responsible person to act as the payee for benefits.

Care in Own Home: Nursing/personal/housekeeping service to an individual in the home.

MARYLAND MEDICAL ASSISTANCE PROGRAM
VOCATIONAL, EDUCATIONAL AND SOCIAL DATA — ABD

_____ H. C. D.S.S.   390610   46   F
DEPARTMENT OF SOCIAL SERVICES   CASE NUMBER   AGE   SEX

Name: __Bradley, Sandy__   __S__   __160-40-4416__
   LAST   FIRST   M.I.   MARITAL STATUS   SOCIAL SECURITY NUMBER

I. EMPLOYMENT HISTORY

A. Usual Occupation: _Veterinarian_

   1. When did the applicant or recipient last work at the usual occupation? _June 1992_

   2. When and where did the applicant or recipient last work? _Self-employed in_ _P.G. & Calvert Co._

B. List other types of work performed by the applicant or recipient.

PLACE OF EMPLOYMENT	DATES (FROM/TO)	TYPE OF WORK OF ACTIVITY PERFORMED	REASON FOR STOPPING

C. What is the applicant's or recipient's opinion of his/her ability to work?

   1. At present: _unable_

   2. For the future: _unable._

II. EDUCATION AND TRAINING

A. Is the applicant's or recipient's ability to read and/or write limited in any manner? ☐ Yes ☒ No If yes, describe: _____

B. Complete the following regarding the applicant or recipient:

   1. Highest grade (through 12) completed? _12_ List main course(s) taken, e.g., Industrial Arts (speciality), Commercial (speciality). _____

   2. College or University? ☒ Yes ☐ No If yes, major or speciality: _V. M. D._
     Degree received? ☒ Yes ☐ No If yes, type: _V. M. D_ ; If no, number of semester hours completed _____ . How many hours did the applicant or recipient complete in his/her major or speciality? _____

   3. Military (active or reserve)? ☐ Yes ☒ No If yes, years active _____ reserve _____ . Job speciality? Primary: _____ Secondary: _____

   4. Vocational training, for example, Business School(s), Correspondence Course(s), Technical Institute(s)? List place and/or training received and experience: _N/A._

III. SOCIAL DATA

A. What is the applicant's or recipient's living arrangement? Living: ☐ Alone ☐ With others
☐ Nursing Home ☐ Chronic or other hospital ☐ Institution ☐ Private Home ☐ Own Home or Apartment
☒ Other: _in a truck-camper & a barn, no running water._

B. Does the applicant or recipient provide for self? ☒ Yes ☐ No If no, describe care received: _____
as best she can

6/16/93
PAGE 1

C. Does the applicant or recipient need personal services? ☐ Yes ☒ No   If yes, describe services required:

_____
_____

*D. Briefly describe the applicant's or recipient's current daily activities: At present she is doing none as little as she can; it is hard for her to get around — she can not drive drive properly.

_____

IV. PHYSICAL DATA

A. Briefly, describe the applicant's or recipient's physical appearance: She is thin and in need of bathing.

B. Complete the following evaluation of physical mobility regarding the applicant or recipient:

ACTIVITY	DEGREE OF DIFFICULTY		COMMENTS
Walking	☐ None ☐ Minimal	☐ Moderate ☒ Extreme	
Standing	☐ None ☐ Minimal	☐ Moderate ☒ Extreme	
Lifting	☐ None ☐ Minimal	☐ Moderate ☒ Extreme	
Bending	☐ None ☐ Minimal	☐ Moderate ☒ Extreme	
Climbing	☐ None ☐ Minimal	☐ Moderate ☒ Extreme	
Other: _____	☐ None ☐ Minimal	☐ Moderate ☒ Extreme	

Use of device needed? ☐ Yes ☐ No   If yes, explain: _____
_____

V. REHABILITATION AND DISABILITY COMPENSATION REFERRAL(S)

A. Has the applicant or recipient been referred to a vocational rehabilitation program? ☐ Yes ☒ No   If yes, name and address of referring agency: _____
_____ ; and

name and address of rehabilitation agency: _____
_____

B. Has the applicant or recipient applied for any disability related compensation, e.g., Social Security, SSI, VA, Workmen's Compensation? ☐ Yes ☒ No   If yes, complete the following:

TYPE	DATE APPLIED	DECISION (i.e., Eligible, Ineligible or Pending)

C. If the applicant or recipient was determined ineligible for Social Security and/or Supplemental Security Income (SS/SSI), state the reason(s) why: _____
_____
_____

VI. BRIEFLY DESCRIBE OTHER PERTINENT FACTS

Dr Bradley, in her line of work makes housecalls, she must be able to get around and be mobile to properly care for the animals. At this point her mobility, even just standing for long periods, is difficult.

_____

Eligibility Technician: ▓▓▓▓▓▓▓▓▓   Date: 6-16-93   pkg

Supervisor: _____ ▓▓▓▓▓▓   Date: 6-16-93

DIMENSIONS HEALTH CORPORATION

☐ ~~Prince George's~~ Hospital Center
☐ ~~Central Laurel Bethesda~~ Hospital
☐ ~~Greater~~ Health Center

☐ OB GYN CENTER

☐ MED SURG CLINIC

NAME: Bradley Sandy   NO. _____

| DATE | Medicine_____ | Surgery_____ | Gyn._____ | E.N.T._____ | Ped._____ | Ortho._____ | Other_____ |

3-16-93

Here because of knee + ankle
symptoms from skeletal reduction.
Long discussion c Dr. G. _____
regarding operative and non-operative
options, including osteotomy, internal +
external rotation, options, risk,
including infection, non-union, and
(amputation)

Patient is a DWM, wants to
use holistic healer.

Hi - Rheumison; RFC are
holistic and she wants to
try.

Will try herbal remedies
for 3 months & decide.

Given Kolliabate & Glucosamine
___ for F/U

Left c nursing Sout - _____, R.L.

Breast Cancer and Me
Perhaps You Don't Have to Die

This chapter is not a promise to life when death is meant to be. It is a window of hope through the knowledge of prevention using diet and herbal treatments. Every woman - every female must be concerned.

On August 2, 1994, **I viewed a special show born out of Oprah Winfrey's concern** for all women of all races who are dying of, diseased with, and vulnerable to this devastating killing condition of breast cancer.

On that show, Oprah asked what can women do to prevent and be more informed to help protect themselves. The answer given was that the mode of treatment, prevention, and diagnosis has not <u>drastically</u> changed over the last twenty years. In part because breast cancer does not affect men with the frequency that it does women. Breast cancer research is not focused for a cure with the zeal that prostate cancer is (which now has a blood test to help determine diagnosis). The problem for the general public remains the same. They are not given the whole truth, both as to the actual <u>cause</u> of the cancer involving the breast or prostate or the treatment; nor any cancer for that matter. I am not alone on this position. There are many books and speakers who know the truth and are making it known.

The greater issues on which to focus for all concerned, I believe, are the following:

1. What are the right questions to ask?
2. Do we as a society have the answers for prevention and treatment?
3. If the answers were truly available twenty years ago, why were they not revealed to us, at least for discussion and education?
4. Why aren't naturopathic approaches publicized or accepted by the conventional medical community?

The answer, I believe, is a complex one that can be summed up in one word; "**control**." In any given population, if the powers that be <u>control</u> the very foods you eat and how you get them, those powers invariably determine the course or pattern of that population's ills. They also determine the medical abnormalities that develop with and without environmental variables or changes. We as individuals have lost the ability to have the power of choice over our own bodies - beginning with what we eat to how we treat our bodies in times of illness.

Let me use myself as an example. I will be the first to admit that I am not eating as well as I know I <u>should</u>, so if I have the knowledge to do better, then why don't I? The most obvious answer is a simple, but sad reality: Like many of you, I cannot afford the prices of most organic or near organic foods.

But a second answer goes far beyond finances. Being a woman, breast cancer has to be one of my concerns. Why? Part of my own personal reason, again like many of you, is my lack of control in the quality of foods available to me. Women and men are being ill-informed and misled about lifesaving information regarding the quality of the foods they eat and how the quality either can lead to or prevent not only these conditions but also many others. What makes a veterinarian qualified to speak on issues concerning human medicine? I realize, from everyday contacts, that the background of veterinarians is not common knowledge to many people. Therefore, I will take a moment to briefly explain using my own personal experience.

During the time I matriculated at the University of Pennsylvania, Penn was known as the only veterinary school (in the United States) whose history originated from its medical school, hence our degrees read V.M.D. (veterinary medical doctor) and not D.V.M. (doctor of veterinary medicine). It was not established as a vet school separate unto itself as are most veterinary schools in the United States. With that beginning, the first two years of a four-year veterinary program was primarily devoted to understanding the dynamics of human physiology, biochemistry, pharmacology, microbiology, pathology, biostatistics, epidemeology and other related sciences integrated with the comparative studies of many different animal species. All veterinarians are trained to have a basic working knowledge of nutrition as well as the development and usage of various drugs and pharmaceuticals used in both animal and man, at least in this country.

Further, during the seventies, aspirants to veterinary school were told the more science background you had, the better your chances of admissions to veterinary school. My particular background, before veterinary school, includes cytology, histology, physiology, inorganic and organic chemistry, physics, elements of botany and zoology - all human oriented with the exception of zoology. Comparative medicine in the fullest scope was not focused on until the junior and senior years of veterinary training. Being human, being a veterinarian, you are naturally curious about the pathology of your own body; therefore, you see parallels in the animals you treat and study. There is a natural motivation to seek and to search for the real information the general public is not privileged to have nor understand. Based upon my educational background, I believe that most properly trained veterinarians are qualified to offer worthy opinions concerning issues of human medicine.

It has been my experience that many doctors and knowledgeable health care professionals do not subscribe to most of the medicinal drugs put out there for the average citizen to use. The sole reason I am writing this book is to provide the professional and lay person alike valuable information that they may not have —knowledge enabling you to learn how to protect yourself and to equip you to fight for the only life you have. I feel strongly that it needs to be

70

known that the information that I and others offer to share with you today is not well received by some because the power of wealth and prosperity has become terribly unbalanced. Uncontrollable crime and drugs have become worldwide epidemics in societies today, particularly the U.S. The simple ways of life are no longer profitable. Cover-ups and outright corruptible tactics by many leading institutions are being revealed daily. Why?

Information to cure and prevent has been available since man's existence, but passed off as ludicrous, fictitious, medieval, wives' tales, folklore and unscientific. Books that have been around for years yet scorned as folklore and unscientific hold the key to the much needed cures and prophylactic approaches. One such book is Back to Eden (written more than fifty-five years ago). Yes, that very same one that many of you have stuffed away somewhere in a closet or the kitchen shelf.

In their rudimentary, unscholarly (to some), and simplistic approach, books like Back to Eden have the real answers for prevention, cure and treatment for not only cancer, but many other diseases. Upon close inspection, these books offer realistic advice and sound reason to a better understanding of the aging process. The Bragg health science series is also an excellent source of basic information to get basic results (see bibliography).

Breast cancer is no different than any other cancer of the food-related diseases. We do become what we eat and drink, it is such a basic concept. **Plain natural foods equal good health.**

Every physician knows that all cancers or tumors, which medically are called "neoplasms," are ultimately caused by the invasion of viruses. I will attempt to explain a basic concept to help you understand how your body works with viruses involving tumors. These viruses generally fall into two categories, DNA (deoxyribonucleic acid) and RNA (ribonucleic acid) viruses. They attack your very genetic coding, the information in your genes. What makes them able to do that? These viruses have actually come into each normal cell that has fallen sick and weak. When the wall of the sick cell breaks down, it no longer has a protective shield and the virus then merely walks in and injects its own DNA or RNA genetic code into your now collapsed and defenseless cell. Then it replicates itself into each cell nearby that it can take over. If your immune system recognizes the virus as not being "self" or a natural part of your body, it will immediately stop it. The immune system will proceed to encapsulate or separate the cells that have been destroyed by the viruses.

How does this tumor or lump become malignant or "cancerous?" All tumors are cancerous. They are either benign or malignant. The cells in that lump have done their damage in that region where it sits and now has become strong enough to invade cells in your entire bloodstream. They are no longer encapsulated and restrained. Your cells have lost the battle with that virus which has set up house. In other words, the intruder has taken over your home and now has become part of the community, masquerading. The community of

71

cells, having been won over, now provides a channel for the invader to travel beyond the community. It now targets the county, then the state, the nation, and finally the world via the transient system of the bloodstream. The virus, then having the ability to travel all over the world (your body) in a matter of minutes, plants its seeds of destruction until there are no soldiers of your immune system left.

Once the cells of your major strongholds (heart, liver, lung, kidneys, intestine, pancreas) are weakened, your body no longer has pockets of fortresses. Your body has become totally defenseless and now awaits the complete take over by the enemy, which feeds itself more and more on the denatured foods that opened the window for the virus in the first place.

If your immune system is strong enough, at the very beginning, when the lump is benign or before it actually becomes a lump, it can be extruded (or kicked) out of the body on its head - never to be seen again - unless similar conditions prevail allowing again another invasion and take over. Now, your body is not only vulnerable to other viruses but to every germ or threatening condition to destroy your health. You have now acquired a state of immune deficiency. You are vulnerable to all kinds of attacks.

We talk about AIDS (acquired immune deficiency syndrome) as that horrid disease that takes life via body fluids, i.e. sexual contact, transfusions, drug use, and the like. What of the AIDS inflicted and perpetrated by powers outside of yourself? We as consumers have no control from the time that an animal is born or the seed is planted to the time it reaches us for consumption. What happens in between is where most of the toxicity occurs. Therefore, what you are eating is not nutritious. It is not feeding your immune system to strengthen it, but injecting poison, whittling away at the fighting soldiers of the primary system designed to protect you.

Because there are just not enough USDA inspectors, some processing plants (meat and fish) admit they police themselves. The threat of intimidation in the world of meat inspection toward the inspectors themselves has been validated by real life encounters of professors who shared their stories with the classes in veterinary school.

Let me provide some personal experiences related to breast pathology that have shown me that allopathic physicians do not provide the answers to a healthy life.

My first experience began in my junior year of veterinary school. I had episodic periods of profound tenderness in my breasts and an increasing pattern of lumpy texture in parts of my breasts, and one in particular. The student health physician recommended a mammogram. I was only thirty at the time in 1977. Heavy scheduling demanded either an immediate appointment or a six week wait. What bad timing! Finals were on the same day. What a decision to make! Given the troubles I already had with the school (explained in my autobiography), the importance of these finals meant the difference between

72

graduating and not graduating. The importance of the mammogram could mean life or death. Six weeks later could be too late if the lumps were malignant. My request to take exams later was denied.

To say the least, worry and concern was a preoccupation as I did not yet have a personal relationship with Yeshua. I was instructed to see a surgeon immediately after the mammogram. He appeared to be quite upset believing that it was not necessary for me to have had the exposure based on my age. I was confused and angry. It seemed that the right hand did not know what the left hand was doing and my career was caught in the middle. The final diagnosis was that I had cystic and fibrotic breasts, a very common affliction of women across the country, that were to be monitored for change. I don't remember doing anything differently until 1983 after having an improved diet for almost two years. The cystic/fibrotic state had all but disappeared, but I did not really draw the connection or have a conscious awareness until I was confronted with the problem again in 1989. Surprisingly, much of the observation on myself in this matter was in retrospect. However, I distinctly remember a revival of the problem in 1989 because my trial was just over and I had moved into my recently purchased handyman's special in La Plata, Maryland. It was at that time I rekindled my passion for a particularly well-known brand of ice cream I grew up on. I began to notice within hours after eating the ice cream an increased activity of the lumps. They appeared to increase in number and size with an overall tenderness increasing as well. This time I had thirteen years of clinical experience, having seen the effects of hormones in man and beast. I suspected the ice cream, knowing that estrogens are used heavily in the dairy and beef cattle industry to increase milk production and as a growth stimulant.

Just a few months earlier I, unknowingly fed my male Doberman imported chickens raised on estrogen compounds. This led to a dramatic enlargement of his breasts within three short days of feeding. As I flashed back in time, I remembered how amazed I was that his breasts had become even larger than my female Doberman's breasts who had a litter some time ago. The startling thing was that after immediately withdrawing those chickens from his diet, his breasts receded to normal within just three days. I continued to be surprised that it took three days to develop obvious enlargement and another three to return to normal size.

With this memory in mind, I immediately began to correlate this estrogen-containing compound I so freely consumed with the activity in my breasts and terminated my now week-long consumption right away. Inside of a week, the newly found lumps and increased cystic activity disappeared, returning to the character of palpation before I began eating the ice cream. This was enough to confirm in my mind that there was a real cause for concern. A local butcher told me that at the last seminar he attended in Pennsylvania, only three farmers did not yield to hormonal supplementation in their cattle's feed.

Several months later I had an overwhelming urge for more of my

73

favorite ice cream. Giving in to the rationalization that perhaps it was not the hormones in the ice cream but something else that precipitated those changes in my breasts, I ate some for several days. It did not take long before the scenario repeated itself. Only this time the signs appeared sooner. This led me to conclude that I had created an increased sensitivity to substances in the ice cream.

When I first committed to a total vegetarian diet back in 1983, I no longer had a problem with cystic/fibrotic breasts nor any tenderness. By July 1990, I was forced to compromise my eating habits by having to receive and use food stamps I accepted foods given to me by charities and neighbors, grateful to receive anything edible. It proved to be a great insult on my body and it has taken years to recover.

There are many women as well as men with problems of the reproductive organs because of hormones included in their diet through meats and dairy products. By God's grace there are natural hormones — natural steroids — designed to work with your body and not against it. Substances that try to fool your body but never become part of your body by their very synthetic nature become enemies of your body. By adding them to your diet, you are planting seeds of destruction. I personally have used natural plants time and time again in cases of pathology of the uterus, breasts and prostate glands with a good measure of success clinically.

My Current Pets

Each has a miraculous tale to tell; most of these stories will be told in Volume II.

Zach and Meshi are featured on the front cover of this book:

Zach - Destined to be euthanized just twenty-four hours before I reached him. Only a year old, his time had run out at the shelter. Already they had kept him a week longer. Zach later revealed hypothyroidism with almost complete loss of hair. Herb combinations and diet change restored him to the <u>picture you see</u> without conventional thyroid medications.

Meshi - My beloved trail horse and barrel racer (when she wants to). She and I are partners and must agree on the activities in which she wishes to participate. She became deathly ill shortly after her purchase as she was boarded away from home. Herbal combinations and no commercial feeds restored her soundness and keeps her that way.

Chloe - My five-pound Toy Poodle who thinks she's a Rotweiller in disguise.

Zachariah - My Doberman Pincer who sprints speeds faster than a bullet. He makes running a way of life and not just a way to get around. (The very same one on the cover.)

Sarah - My Great Dane who teaches deer how to jump.

Sweet Pea - "There's something in that water" - a survivor of survivors.

Iron Fortress - The big fellow with the bad feet and legs, but not anymore.

Cayenne, Sr. - My two-year-old cat who says, "Red pepper was a heck of a wake up call!"

Cayenne, Jr. - Cayenne Sr.'s one-year-old son. "It couldn't be done" proof of Cayenne Sr.'s recovery.

Meshi - My buckskin dun Quarter horse / Arab. Instead of being full of stuff in her lungs (bilateral pneumonia), she's just "full of it." (The very same one on the cover.)

"Peet" - The Little Ball of Fur who Started it All

The phone rang as it always does. "Abe Lincoln Animal Clinic, may I help you?" answered my secretary and technician. "It's the Animal Rescue League, Doc." Mrs. Bell wanted to know if I would look at a Toy Poodle already eleven years old that had been declared hopeless by the veterinarian in the building next door. Diagnosis: Evidence of bilateral congestive heart failure with severe pulmonary edema and arthritis involving front and back legs. The good news was they had a home for her if she could be stabilized. An older patron who desperately wanted her was more than willing to pay for any expenses to get her well, if possible. The League's expression to me was, "We know it looks bad, but we want to check with Dr. Bradley first and wait for her recommendations." It was a comfort to know that their confidence in me had grown to that level. My greatest concern was then and still is that I do my best and offer the ultimate care I can give to all who sincerely seek my services for their pets.

Without hesitation I instructed Mrs. Bell to send her over as I've done many times before. However, this little dog was one of the worse cases I had seen in congestive heart failure with the degree of pulmonary edema (fluid in the lungs) that she had. She was very cyanotic. Indicated best by her bluish purple tongue.

Peet was immediately digitalized (given a loading or concentrated dose followed by a maintenance dose), given lasix (the diuretic of choice), and put on an entire week of oxygen therapy and neubulization before she was stabilized. It became obvious that Peet would not be a good candidate for the average person to adopt. Her personality and will to live won my heart and Peet became mine to keep.

She unexpectedly rewarded me by appearing in the exam room one day having jumped off her recliner, where she was usually restricted, wagging her tail and barking at the patient on the table. Needless to say my joy was unspeakable.

Since Peet was my very first case using a wholistic approach, I was not yet experienced in how important **real** diet management or the ingestion of herbs played in her recovery and in preventing the recurrence of her condition. Therefore, Peet remained on conventional therapies for another twelve months fairly stabilized until one day, unbeknownst to me, Peet was dying from "heart attack and stroke" in the private bathroom of the clinic. I believe I felt the Spirit of Yeshua urge me to go and check on Peet immediately after the last patient left. I began to run, my heart rate accelerating. Upon reaching the doorway of the bathroom, there I found Peet. Peet was not moving. Her breathing was so shallow she appeared dead. Serous (clear) fluid was coming out of her nose. Her pulse was almost nonexistent. She was extremely comatose, twisted in position, and slipping into death. I became very personally involved at this point.

Here I had been spending so much time treating someone else's pet while mine lie in the bathroom dying. This, to me, was a very selfish, fleeting thought - but nonetheless I thought it. I asked God to forgive me and prayed for His guidance and asserted that I <u>willed</u> to listen to His instruction, that if it were in His plan for Peet to make it to <u>please show me what to do</u>. The message plainly came through to call my grandmother, a woman of Cherokee extraction.

"Grandma," I said frantically over the phone (for she was in Philadelphia, Pennsylvania and I in Washington, D.C.). "I have done everything known to man that I have been taught to do, the digoxin, lasix, and all that other stuff is just not working anymore. Peet is dying!" She immediately responded without so much as a hesitation. She told me to use three different herbs and natural substances (explained in volume II) to be rubbed on her chest and nostrils and put into her mouth. I could not believe my eyes and ears. Within minutes she was cognizant of her surroundings and me, responding to my words, and moving her limbs. Restoration of her vital signs was complete and strong. As an oath to God and to all who read these words let the truth be recorded that Peet was up and about walking where she wanted to walk and taking care of bodily functions within <u>one-half hour</u>!!!

Coming back to my sense of control, <u>my immediate response was</u> - they have been lying to me! I have become indebted to a system for the sum of $67,000 for an undergraduate and professional education - only to be fed lies.

These very agents of healing I was told to use by my (then) seventy-seven-year-old grandmother — who is, by the way, over ninety — were to be looked upon as idiotic, wasteful, unscientific, wivestales, and folklore. Let me tell you from that day forward I have thanked and will continue to thank Almighty God for those <u>unscientific wivestales</u> and <u>folklore</u> — **the real medicine of this world.** That day I began my search in learning about the healing plants that have been here for centuries long before the United States of America even existed.

I am dealing with those lies I have been trained to believe in today. I believe it to be part of my purpose to, at least, try to open <u>your</u> eyes to the truth as mine were opened. It just takes a listening ear and a willing heart to test the validity of God's "untampered-with herbs," plants of the universe.

I invite you to walk the road of TRUTH.

The Herbs Don't Care

The herbs do not care whether the disease has two names or twenty names, three syllables or ten syllables, they just go in and begin the process of healing. A partial or total <u>cure</u> depends on several factors similar to those of some aspects of conventional medicine, since a great deal of allopathic medicine has its roots in phyto or plant medicine.

Some of these <u>factors</u> are the following:

1. Getting to the patient <u>in time</u> to assess the problem.

2. Choosing <u>the most effective herb</u> or <u>combination</u> of herbs for <u>the</u> particular problem or <u>set</u> of problems specific to that patient.

    a. Often the specific <u>cause</u> of the disease is irrelevant, but knowing which system(s) (respiratory, neurological, etc.) or organ(s) such as liver, kidney and so on is most affected is important for the proper choice of herbal treatments and dietary reform.

    b. Like conventional medicine, the patient recovers from illness without ever knowing the direct cause; therefore <u>it is unacceptable</u> for the "powers that be" <u>to expect</u> herbalists to show justification of their use of a particular herb because the direct cause in unknown. **The herbs know the way**. Building and nourishing the immune system, which in my opinion is not just those designated cells labeled by man, but <u>each and every cell</u> in your body created for a particular function. If that one cell is incapable of functioning, then you have a breakdown in your immune system, period. Therefore, AIDS (acquired immune deficiency syndrome) can be applied to <u>any</u> disease process, just in varying degrees. **All of your body comprises the essence of immunity**. We compartmentalize our bodies like we do conventional medicine — cardiology, endocrinology, dermatology, and the list goes on and on, increasing more every day. The systems of our bodies do not function separately; therefore, we should not treat them separately, but as one highly integrated system with a common function, to sustain life.

3. Combining herbal foods with <u>other</u> foods that are, at least, complimentary (friendly to) if not completely compatible (totally nourishing) with your human body. <u>Anything</u> less will not only be rejected, but gain entrance and sit somewhere in your body awaiting the opportunity to begin the process of putrefaction and death to some, many, or all of your viable cells. The molecular structure of the causative agent is irrelevant. The process of AIDS has then begun.

4. Subjecting your body to the same routine, environment, and exposure will, at the very least, minimize anything you do herbally (externally or internally). For example, I may use a very effective herb to heal my lower back of its herniated disc problem. But if I am compelled to haul 110 gallons of water daily to sustain my animals, then it becomes a situation similar to constantly pulling the scab off a healing wound.

5. Having the best quality of herbs and other foods to be assimilated into your body. **The quality of the product is only as good as the quality of its ingredients.** Herbs or foods raised in toxic environments will carry those toxins with them into your bodies.

6. Being aware that the water we drink and the air we breathe must be devoid of impurities or to expect breakdowns in immunity. There can never be an absolute 100 percent total cure, indefinitely, as long as these variables (water and environment) transmit toxins to the living organism - man, beasts and plants. **Man has created his own iron-lung trap** and the use of any herb or any food anywhere **can only** serve to **help** control, maintain, and combat the daily onslaught of agents designed to kill. But for the grace of God go we!

7. Stopping your herbs too soon. Like conventional medicine, to halt consumption or the external applications of your treatments (even after the desired results seem achieved) will either open the door for a reversal of the condition or the level of progress will stop there. But if you maintain a fair intake of nourishing foods, the affected area may stop at the level of healing achieved and not regress when the appropriate treatment continues. **This I have discovered countless times in my patients as well as the injuries with my own back and hand.** When I do see definite regression of the condition is when there is consumption of toxin-laden foods, usually acquired from supermarkets.

8. In complex cases, working toward a cure usually requires the help of an experienced herbalist. Just as successful brain surgeries require the confidence in the track record of an experienced brain surgeon. The wide range of knowledge must be passed on, tried and proven to the individual guiding the patient. Notice I have said guide because the patient, when possible, is involved in decision making of his or her body.

9. Exercise is important and beneficial. But **extensive exercise is not imperative for optimal health.** The appropriate exercise acquired in outdoor occupations such as farming is plenty for proper circulation and muscle toning of all body parts. Urban living creates a need for artificial and often harmful means to maintain body functions.

10. **Mental, spiritual and physical factors must all work together to bring about maximum cure for whatever time.**

**Cases
with a Story
Completed
for
Volume I**

"Killer" and Me

"Killer" was my very first miracle case of a crippling musculo-skeletal disease. At six months of age, this German Shepherd was brought to my emergency clinic completely unable to walk using his hind legs. He dragged himself along using only his front legs. He was the classic picture of the genetic disorder of hip displasia, most prevalent in certain large breed dogs and particularly the American-bred German Shepherds. He had been seen by at least one other conventional practitioner who, by conventional standards, gave Killer's owners, the Tysons, the information we are taught in veterinary school — that is, the only hope of correcting this disorder is to cut the pectineus muscle or saw off the femoral head (top part of the thigh bone) to reduce the pain caused by that bone rubbing against the acetabelum of the coxo-femeral joint (the ball and socket joint of the hip). There is also a ball and socket joint of the shoulder, called the scapulo-humeral joint. Removing a portion of such a critical part of the anatomy would not guarantee a better gait and not necessarily reduce pain. Prosthetic hip joints were in their early stages for veterinary medicine. Besides, the Tysons were hardworking people who did not have a thousand or more dollars that most orthopedic surgeons required to handle Killer's case. I informed the Tysons of their options. It was either put Killer out of his misery now, try the less expensive surgery, or try using herbs, making Killer my first patient using an herbal treatment for such a problem. They agreed to treatment with herbs. Within twenty-four hours, the Tysons called to say Killer was walking up the stairs unassisted.

Even today, in my personal opinion, prosthetic joints could never replace the beauty of the patient's own body-restored!

Killer also had a fractured cervical vertebrae above C6 (broken bone in his neck) and recovered well after three days of hospitalization and cage rest with herbs and diet change.

Killer walks well today. He may exhibit occasionally a little problem getting up and down for several reasons. His diet still consists of supermarket dog food because of convenience and finances. Herbal supplementation to neutralize or offset the toxins of commercial feeding is often irregular unless Tracy, the daughter, and the author of Killer's testimony, is there to feed him. **Urban pets often do not get the exercise and fresh air that will promote and maintain good health in addition to the exposure of natural wild medicinal plants.**

Over the years, Killer has had a variety of ailments. My treatments for

Killer have been strictly internal and external herbal applications with the exceptions of the required vaccinations and occasional use of Penicillin (oral and injectable) and vitamin B complex. All of Killer's musculo-skeletal disorders were treated with **the same herbal formulas I used on myself** to restore the twisted and deformed leg, knee and ankle I acquired through my horse accident in June 1992!!!

As a matter of fact, I owe my ability to walk without deformity to God first, and then to the use of herbal treatments, such use being inspired by Killer's miraculous recovery. **We both are walking free because of God's** (*Yeshua's*) **pharmacy of medicinal herbs.**

July 12, 1994

Re: Killer Tyson

I met Dr. Bradley in Sept. of 81.

Killer my German Shephard was having a leg problem. My father and I took him to an animal hospital on Connecticut Ave. ████████ We were told there was nothing they could do for him because most Shephards have this problem and if it got too bad he would have to be put to sleep forever. He was in so much pain we would have to pick him up and carry him out to ŧelieve himself. We were told it was nothing we could do but give him aspirin for pain.

We didn't stop believing that there was someone to help somewhere. We took him to the ████████ Animal Rescue League about his legs that's when they told us about Dr. Bradley. She explained to us that there was nothing she could do, but she would try something on her own because there was really no medicine for his condition. The miracle drugs were herbs and vitamins and it really worked. She was a God sent woman. Killer's legs are healthy and strong today and when I see him limp I know what to do thanks to Dr. Bradley. She's been his keeper and I can call her anytime and she's right there for him and me.

Killer has had a broken neck and Dr. Bradley mended him again. He had a broken leg. We took him to another hospital because Dr. Bradley was out of town. The hospital took x-rays and never wrapped or put a splint on Killer's leg just gave him aspirins. Two days later we got in touch with Dr. Bradley she came to our house and put a splint on his leg about a week later he was good to go. Thanks and we love you.

Good Luck

submitted by ████████

My Cat Lives Because of Cayenne Pepper.
Yes, Red Pepper.

I'll never forget that day. I remember it was around the 4th of July of 1992, and I was propped in a wheelchair, leg raised wearing a full-length cast. It was one of those days when I was asking not, "Why me, Lord?" but, "Why not me?" There was a sudden knock at the door. It was the postman. "You're a veterinarian, aren't you?" I cautiously responded, "Yes". "I found this little kitten on the side of the street. I think it's been hit by a car, and you'll probably have to put it out of its misery. Can you do that?" I nodded in the affirmative and said, "Sure. Where is it?" He stepped outside for a moment and brought in one of the most pitiful sights I had seen in my then fourteen years of practice. He looked to be not more than six weeks of age. His frail little body twisted with forelegs pointed east and back legs pointed west. His neck was in severe contortion. His eyes had rolled totally upward and back. There was fecal or waste material all over his rear end. There was urine on his belly. He was totally limp and lifeless. His tongue was blue. The heart rate was extremely rapid and there was hardly a pulse. He was not aware of his surroundings at all; in essence he was unconscious, unresponsive, simulating a coma-like state of shock.

The postman left. I gently placed the cat onto the floor on a bed of towels I grabbed that were near by. I did not have a light to check his pupillary response (pupils opening and closing in response to light), but he appeared to have some palpebral response. This is when you touch the corners of the eyelids and they move. It was faint, but there. I quickly struggled to wheel myself to my crutches and hobbled to the kitchen to get my trusted bottle of liquid cayenne extract. I thought if anything was to help restore life to this little guy, it would be this. "Dog gone it! Where is that cayenne?" I became a little frantic. I was renting a room, and the landlady was not at home. Doctor's orders were not to go up and down stairs. I remembered that it was upstairs in my bedroom. I had been staying downstairs because the bathroom was downstairs. "Oh no, God help me to find it in time," I whispered. I had not really mastered getting up the stairs with any kind of grace or timing, so I turned myself around, sat on the lowest step and raised myself step-by-step backwards. Finally I had reached the top. It had only been a couple of weeks since my horse accident and the first cast was plaster of Paris and extremely heavy.

When I finally got the door open, I crawled on the floor of the bedroom because it was just too complicated to stand up and move; besides, I forgot and left the crutches at the bottom of the stairs. I dragged myself onto the bed to peer into adjacent boxes, my bewildered cat "Danielle" looking on. I kept saying, "Father, if you want me to help him, please show me where the cayenne is." Within minutes I found the cayenne in an unpacked box in the closet. Clutching the bottle tightly in my left hand and with my glove-covered right hand, I carefully but hurriedly turned around backwards holding onto the steps and bannister with my right leg sticking out and my left leg bent, using a sort of sliding motion to get down. When I reached the bottom step I had to turn around with my rump on the step before I could use the crutches. I kept telling myself, "Hurry, hurry". Patients in shock do not have much time.

Once I reached him I had to lay the crutches down, stick one leg out, bend the other and crawl over to the spot where he lay. "Please God, let him still be breathing." He was, but fading quickly. I reached over, turned his head, tilted it where his nose was pointed upward, opened his tiny jaws, and squirted about one fourth of a small dropperful of the cayenne right onto his tongue. To my amazement, his head shook frantically, his front legs stretched out, his eyes opened with the pupils focusing forward as they should be, and within ten minutes, he had total control of eye movements and was very cognizant of his surroundings, responding to sound and touch.

I conducted a cursory neurological exam and discovered that his patellar reflexes were completely absent (no jerk response occurred when the knee caps were tapped). I squeezed each toe of both hind legs with a pair of hemostats (scissor-like clamps) but he felt absolutely nothing, not even with the strongest pressure. He showed no indication that he could move his legs at all. When he began to look around, I could see a noticeable head tremor that he still has to this day - two years later. Though I had no means to x-ray his body, my clinical experience combined with his clinical signs told me that there was probably cerebellar brain damage as well as a good possibility that the spinal cord was at least partially severed or crushed, or that a hematoma was causing a mechanical obstruction over the cord leaving him totally paralyzed from the waist down.

There was no doubt of there being some damage to the spinal cord.

He had a fever of 104. I decided to inject penicillin and vitamin B complex (I.M.) into the muscle. Penicillin, vitamin B complex and vitamin C injections may be the only preparations of conventional medicine I will consider using in any given situation unless I just have no other choice and depending on what I have on hand. While he was resting, I hobbled back to the kitchen and retrieved my old standby tonic (changes with availability of herbs), which I usually keep ready for use for my other pets as a supplement to their diets as part of their prevention and maintenance program. By the time I returned, he was trying to crawl out of the little fortress of towels and large pillows I had built around him.

I had just bought time-released multi-vitamins and B complex tablets to supplement my herbal regime. That evening, Cayenne and I started to take them together. The next day Cayenne was dragging himself all around, up and over his little fortress. He would no longer be contained. He still could not move his back legs, but he had amazing strength in his forelegs. It was funny to watch his tiny little head twitch while he pursued his course with so much determination. For several days I had to express his bladder and squeeze his intestinal tract to help him eliminate. Within one week after doses of tonic every few hours, Cayenne shockingly was not only able to move his back legs, but he could curl up like a normal kitten and go to sleep. This was just unheard of, at least in my hearing. Like most active kittens, he became very mischievous and began climbing up on everything, including the sofabed I was sleeping on. Weeks went by — people and friends were amazed at his progress. I would sit him on my lap while I sat in the wheelchair and give him all of his medication, then put him down and let him follow me. He was soon able to eliminate on his own. This was a big concern for me because if the nerves from his lumbosacral plexus (located in the lower spine) were not restored, he would not be able to go on his own, and a possible reason to someday euthanize him.

Another bad habit that Cayenne developed was a voracious appetite. You might ask, "Well, what's so wrong with that? You want him to be healthy, don't you?" My response to that question is, "Yes, but leave some for the rest of the family." There were two other cats and my Toy Poodle, Chloe, who resided in the house. After Cayenne began to walk, he would attack a bowl of food as a lion on a gazelle. I realize certain supplementation can make one hungry, but Cayenne was the first to clean his bowl and the last to clean out everyone else's.

As time went on the injury to his back showed evidence of being both permanent and severely handicapping. Spinal injury was shown because of how he walked very wide-legged in the back, with his sides swinging out, like a duck waddling . His front legs and head movements were indicative of damage to the cerebellum, the part of the brain that controls balance and accurate placement of limbs for walking. Cayenne still has a slight head tremor, and he hyper extends each foreleg (called a hypermetric gait). Cayenne grew to run better than he walks. When he ate, his head would start to bob and weave so erratically that he was hitting himself in the face each time he got his head close to the bottom of the bowl.

When Cayenne was almost a year old, we had moved to the barn. He chased birds, caught mice, and did everything else cats do except he looked a little funny doing it. I was not concerned about Cayenne; after all, his back had been broken. I just knew he would not be able to express his natural calling to procreate given his physical disabilities. What Cayenne showed me was that he either had no pain, or if he had pain, it was not enough to suppress that natural urge. Therefore, the herbal and dietary changes were sufficiently effective to make him a functional being despite the appearance of his disabilities. Today

Cayenne has a beautiful young son that is his spitting image. It is obvious, I hope, that my lack of concern was expressed by not neutering Cayenne. **Cayenne and I both have overcome our dysfunctions from injuries and conditions seemingly permanent.**

I chose the herb cayenne because it has several excellent features. One of its most incredible qualities is its ability to help control internal and external hemorrhage. It will increase oxygenation to all tissues, including the brain, and it will restore the original elasticity and pliability to arteries and veins. It also rejuvenates calcified joints. Any or most cardiac arrhythmias are corrected if cayenne is used early enough and carefully monitored for necessary changes of dose or intervals of treatment. Cayenne also serves as a catalyst therefore enhances the effects of other herbs taken at the same time. I have used it as a respiratory stimulant on newborns who were thought to have taken their last breaths, when a drop or two on the back of their tongue quickly revived them among the living within minutes. I have seen the best results with cayenne extract or tincture (in a vegetable glycerin which improves penetration of tissues) reaching the bloodstream within two minutes. Tinctures made with apple cider vinegar are even better because of the natural replacement of the essential natural potassium for the strength and integrity of each cell. I have seen some startling results with cayenne in most any form, but this case is without question the most dramatic recovery of such severity. I cannot prove to you these claims by scientific findings, but what I can prove is the clinical evidence shown by medical improvements.

Only with the help of Yeshua God and His herbs have Cayenne and I become healthy and functional beings. We may not yet be devoid of **residual scars** that **identify those injuries**, but our performance shows that **we are more than overcomers.**

> "But in all these things we overwhelmingly conquer
> through Him who loved us."
>
> Romans 8:27 NAS (New American Standard)

Throughout the ages claims of cures using herbal treatments and proper restorative diets have been totally ignored by modern medicine. To cure diabetes is not to give insulin from another living being but to heal and restore your own pancreas. Buying and using insulin makes one dependent on the arrogance of man. To cure breast and prostate cancer is not the injection of human altered drugs called chemotherapy or radiation implants, but using the plants known to heal and restore those organs.

Christa Star — One Horse That Owns Part of My Heart

Christa Star was a very, very special horse. She saved my life on three separate occasions. The story of Christa should not go untold. For this reason the details of her life with me are preserved in my autobiography. Her story goes beyond the scope of this book, which deals primarily with the herbal approach to medicine. In light of this objective I will attempt to share with you the important highlights of her case that helped to mold my wholistic approach of practicing medicine on the equine species.

I first met Christa (who was called Tom then until I renamed her years later) as a "hack" horse I rented for regular trail rides in early 1982. I had only been in practice for a year on my own. The practice was located in Northeast, Washington, D.C. I was truly blessed to own and manage the Abe Lincoln Animal Clinic and Emergency Center, the only emergency clinic in the city at the time. Horseback riding was my heartfelt choice of relaxation.

Though Tom was fifteen in 1982, she was one of the most gorgeous red-toned chestnuts I had ever seen. She was strong, well proportioned, and extremely healthy looking. She had the strength of an ox, the quickness of a deer, and the gentleness of a lamb. She was also very alert and well poised. Everyone asked for Tom because she worked so hard to please her rider.

It is now 1987. I had been away, working hard at the clinic, prior to my hand injury in February 1986. When I returned to the farm I asked to see Tom. She wasn't available right away. A few days later she was brought back to the hack stable so that I could see her. I intended to buy the beautiful horse I left behind, if I could. When I saw her, the sight almost took my breath away. She had endured too many unkind, "wanna be cowboys," too many beatings, too many long hours, too little food, and not enough shelter. Her spirit had been broken. Her body was badly abused.

I stood there gazing with my mouth open and my eyeballs stretched. My heart gasped in the silence of my chest. My beautiful Tom, no longer beautiful. She stood there with her head hanging down, eyes drooped. Her coat no longer a bright sorrel chestnut trimmed with flaxen mane and tail, but a dingy gray without shine, without life. Her lower lip hung down and quivered. As I approached her, I called her name. She did not respond at all. Her ears didn't twitch. Her tail did not swish with that old familiar "welcome home" body language. She just stared at the ground.

The owner said I could choose another horse, that I was not bound to purchase Tom. If I wanted to take her out, I could. She could hardly walk up a hill. She would heave and choke, gasping for breath. Her chest had the classic barrel-like appearance from the labored breathing that the condition called "heaves" brings about. The ankles of her front legs had become terribly knobby and severely arthritic from the constant pounding while running on hard surfaces. Her back legs at the knee joints were stiff and were locking in position — what we call upward fixation of the patellar (or knee cap). Tom and I walked a little ways. I promised her she would never see an unkind rider again, that I would take her off this cursed hack line.

I returned to the stable to negotiate, believing that I would truly be relieving the owner of an expense of vet bills. Surely, he could not want much for Tom. Instead, he demanded $1,000 or more because of the money she brought in on the weekends. I cannot explain the anger that wrenched my soul that day. To even think of it brings a terrible lump in my throat and tears to my eyes. Tom had become a part of me and that part of me had been badly abused, used, and tormented and someone whose values had obviously become so distorted owned a part of me.

I had just begun preparing for a medical malpractice case. My hand was seriously injured and had undergone a nerve transplantation. Just fourteen months ago I had to give up my clinic because of the surgeries. I had no money to speak of, certainly not that kind of money anyway. But I promised Tom I would not leave her to the mercy of evil again. So, I made the owner a proposition based on a successful outcome of my trial if he would lower the price. He agreed to lease her to me for $100 a month, without a stall (because he had none available) until I could pay him $750. That was the best he was willing to offer and he would supply her hay. Up to this point, Tom and the other hack horses where fed loaves of bread (an arrangement the owner had with a local supermarket) along with communal hay shared as a group. He promised me that Tom would be taken off the hack line and not used for any rides weekends or otherwise.

Of course I discovered that she was ridden on occasion when I was not there. "Everyone asks for Tom." I would find Tom standing with girth marks around her belly, sweating, and looking worn. Were I to call the Humane Society, what then would I do? I had no money to stable Tom. She would most likely have been taken away from me, too. I just didn't know, and I did not want to take the chance. I was new to the Washington area, but I had been here long enough to see how wayward politics operated.

I am providing this background information to give the reader a sense of how special Tom/Christa Star was to me. Like the native American (of many tribes) who views himself as one with his champion steed, I too share this feeling - this belief - this gift. There has never been a spirit like Christa's that has touched my heart so profoundly as hers. I never thought I could miss any creature as much as I missed her. She was a gift sent to me by the Almighty of this universe to help me learn how to live and how to die.

Because of the objectives of <u>this</u> book, I must reflect on issues of medical relevance. Initially, when I first saw Christa again in 1987, I gave her a cursory exam. Her pulse was weak and extremely slow. Her gums were pale and circulation poor, demonstrated by what we call capillary refill. Her heart rate was slow and had irregular beats. Her breathing was obviously labored, and it was not until a few days later that I noticed how jaundiced her eyes were. A long-time employee shared with me that Tom was seen by a vet not long ago and proclaimed to have liver problems. When I confronted the owner, he responded that it was a while ago and that Tom seemed to have gotten over it, yet he had not re-called the vet for verification. Again, I bit my tongue and was determined to scrape or borrow enough money to purchase Tom. He accepted, as I recall, the $100 that I had quickly borrowed. Christa was my Mother's Day present.

The very week I treated Tom, now renamed Christa Star, her improvement was amazing. Within just hours of a little cayenne and honey mixture, infused directly into her mouth, her lip stopped quivering, her eyes brightened and she became alert. She tossed her head up and down and pranced around exuding life again. Her pulse, heart rate, and respiration approached normal the first day of treatment. Of course, the condition of heaves itself took a couple of weeks to overcome. In addition to her cayenne-honey mixture, I chose to administer a tea containing such herbs as red clover, burdock, parsley, willow bark, and sarsaparilla. The jaundice was completely gone inside of two weeks. Her left front leg, which had been so wobbly and weak, was now firmly planted on the ground. Her back legs dragged less. In only three months, the knobby (periosteal) thickening of her ankles (carpal joints) were reduced to obscurity. It was the sliding knee cap of her left leg that occasionally prevailed until the day she died, not because it couldn't be cured, but because I lacked the funds to do what I knew was necessary to continue treatment.

Christa also had a heavy worm burden of Ascarids, better known as roundworms, a common intestinal parasite. Although tube worming was becoming obsolete, I chose to use it to ensure being ridden of them quickly, using a safe worming agent, garlic water. Tube worming is merely a technique when a pliable plastic tube is inserted through the horse's nostril to the stomach. It was the method of getting it in that was a little dangerous. The danger of tube worming a horse is the possibility of inserting the tube into the trachea leading to the lungs instead of going into the esophagus which leads to the stomach, and thus pouring fluid into the lungs causing aspirate pneumonia and possibly death. Christa made me look like an experienced veteran even though it was only my second tube worming since graduation. She regained her weight within days since improved absorption of nutrients was achieved.

Christa's diet initially was quite simple, but very expensive for me since my income was extremely meager at the time. Most days I barely had gas money, but I had to get to the barn no matter how I did it.

As in the days of old, I resorted to feeding her the best I could buy of plain oats (initially rolled as in oatmeal) and corn (grits) supplemented with wheat bran that I bought at a health food store in Mt. Rainier, Maryland, where I shop for myself. I mixed and poured over her food blackstrap molasses (because of its high calcium, protein, and iron), clover honey (unfiltered and unheated), and cayenne pepper. All were organically grown. I also poured over her food one-half cup of garlic/onion water as a prophylactic dewormer and immune system builder. She never had problems cleaning her plate.

Her recovery was unbelievable to all. Before she reached her peak of recovery, Christa was on the trails again with the rough riders of Runaway Farm. She was one of the smoothest horses I've ever ridden bareback. She still jumped higher over logs and other obstacles on the trails than most horses her junior. And she still fiercely competed for the lead. But Christa had two episodes that almost killed her before the seizures started.

The first episode really tested my self-control and faith as a Christian. I just had not realized how protective I had become over Christa. I remember the day as if it were yesterday. Thank God it was a fairly warm day, not hot. I was feeling so forlorn. I was forced to leave Christa in a pasture with two horses I knew were extremely aggressive, and there was nothing I could do about it. Things just were not going well with the progress of my hand. I was plagued with constant pain. I had bad times with my lawyer, and my favorite and closest friend on four legs was just miserable. She had no clean, comfortable stall to rest. Her knees were bothering her because I had been out of her herb supplements for that problem for several days now, and I had never been able to procure all that she needed for total and complete recovery, just enough to restore good function.

She could barely walk, and I had to leave. I coaxed her over to a corner of the pasture closer to the road away from the other horses so that I could leave her hay for the evening. I was only up the road a few seconds when I felt the need to return and make sure she was okay. It was a decision I'll never regret. In horror I saw my friend trying to hobble for shelter to the entrance of the barn, but she was being pinned against the wall of the barn by the two renegades. The larger black gelding was reared on his hind legs biting her neck trying to force her down. The second horse, a mare, was biting at her chest and flanks. She was crying out. No one seemed to see it. Horrible pictures raced through my mind. If they got her to fall they would stump and crush her to death.

I don't know what came over me, but I forgot all about my hand. It was always in a protective padded splint. I jumped out of my van, leaving the door flung wide open. I climbed and jumped over the wooden fence, running full speed toward both horses. They were in a frenzy to kill the weak one. I can't remember exactly how I did it, but I picked up a two by four lying on the ground near by and rushed the gelding, and he was no small horse. He could easily have reared and killed me, but I challenged him to get off Christa and come to me instead. The mare stopped when she heard me shout, "Get off her you no good son of a gun." The owners of these horses were nice people, but I couldn't think of them now. Their horses were out of control and I was going to do whatever it took to keep them from killing mine. The gelding was persistent, stopping only for a moment, then proceded to bite Christa again. My rage was now totally out of control. I ran toward him shouting with the board raised. He then turned toward me and began to trot. I met him with a "Come on buddy, help me, Lord" and I whacked him across the side of his head and face with as much force as I could muster. It stunned him. It put fear in him while I stood my ground for another. He turned and ran away with his female companion following.

I dropped the board and ran to my friend. She was literally so frightened that she just shook and shook with beads of sweat all over her body. Her breathing was fast and heavy. Her eyes looked as if they would pop out. She stood stiff and could not move. When she could look at me and hear my voice, her eyes began to recede back into their sockets, but she could not stop shaking. I tried to calm her. I did not want to leave her. I needed a lead rope. I just needed help. We were on a 250-acre farm and nobody seemed to be around. I started screaming, "Somebody help, I need help." Soon two of the guys I rode with scurried around the side of the barn. They were shocked. They had never seen a horse in Christa's condition and, frankly, neither had I. My specialty was and is small — not large — animal medicine and surgery. One of the fellows offered to put Christa in his horse's stall until she was well again. She literally could not move on her own. All of her muscles had tightened up. Both knee caps were locked or semi-locked in position. We had to put a rope-like tie beneath her rump and semi-circled her legs with one person on either side with someone up front to lead her. It took us almost an hour to move her fifty feet. I was so grateful to those fellows, and I can't even remember which friends they were. At least it is only their names I cannot remember.

I just kept thinking, if they had gotten her to the ground I would have had to witness a horrible, horrible scene. And yes, I thank God again that I did not. It took her several days to regain her confidence. A lot of herbal liniment was necessary to relax her muscles. I made and used a combination of wintergreen alcohol, garlic powder, cayenne pepper, Yager's liniment, olive oil, and fresh-squeezed lemon along with the oral combinations. I did not wrap her legs.

Even after that terrible experience, a twenty-mile hike was not a problem. But a two-day event, without a proper rub down and care (being away from home) proved almost a disaster. We got lost from the group. It must have been nearly thirty miles of travel that second day. It was just too much for her, and it became evident one day.

It was a clear, brisk day and I was riding her around in the pasture where she and the other boarders were kept. She just didn't seem to be herself that day. Since the two-day trail ride, she appeared to be a little slower and less alert. We were heading back toward the stable to unsaddle. We had only been out for a half hour when suddenly I felt her stumble from underneath me and her knees started to buckle. As she fell over to her left side, I instinctively jumped off rushing toward her head to assess her conscious state and vital signs. Her heart rate was extremely fast, pulse thready, eyes rolling, muscles twitching. She was grunting and moaning. She was turning blue. I became petrified. I cried out, "Oh, Lord don't let my horse die." She was experiencing a syndrome similar to a stroke. "Yeshua, what should I do" What should I do?" I had to regain my composure and think. I believe it was the Holy Spirit of God that led me to use the right combinations of natural ingredients to save my horse. John 6:45 says, "And they shall all be taught by God." While John 7:39 says, "The Holy Spirit was not yet given," referring to Christ not having gone to the cross yet. I believe God's word; therefore, I know that it is the Holy Spirit of Yeshua who guided and taught me what to do.

I then made a paste of cayenne pepper, honey, sarsaparilla, and hawthorn berries and placed it on the back of her tongue as far as I could and encouraged her to swallow. I did not want to chance liquids at this time because she might aspirate. I also took a large swab of Vicks Vapor Rub (one of my favorite respiratory stimulants) and spread it along the inside walls of the entire nasal cavity of both nostrils. She began to take deep breaths and swallow the balls of paste. Again, within minutes her breathing improved. Her eyes stopped rolling, her color came back and her vital signs changed for the better. She slowly picked her head up, and I rushed around to the back of her neck to help her get sternal (on her stomach). It was hard because she was heavy and my hand was in a splint, but she soon helped me and was lying on her stomach like a dog.

I now took the opportunity to run back to the stall and get her garlic / onion /cayenne combination I always kept for feeding. I then used a 60cc syringe and slowly infused it along the side of her mouth. She was swallowing quite easily now. Within ten minutes from start to finish, she was up on her feet and able to walk to her stall which she had had now for approximately five to eight months, just before we left the farm. Again I applied my favorite liniment to her whole body and placed a borrowed blanket over her. I stayed until the wee hours, and when I felt she was out of danger, I went home.

The very next day she looked as if nothing had happened, but I never rode her like a "wanna be cowgirl" again. There were several times before this episode that I had to treat my horse in the middle of the fields. Sometimes I treated her in pitch darkness to soothe her joints and aching limbs. She did not have a stall, spring, summer, fall, and winter from May 1987 until early 1989. Christa was never the same after that trip.

We had now moved from the farm, and Christa was all mine. Three years had passed, and I had paid nearly $2,500 for Christa in past due lease payments, since I could not afford to pay the remaining $650 until I received monies from my trial awards to purchase her in August 1989.

Christa was so much happier now that she was in her new home. She could see me and I could see her from the large, bay picture window of my kitchen. I had gotten another horse to keep her company in her aging years. From the window, I would see him kick Christa in the head with his hind feet when she stood behind him. They were on five acres of land, so there was no good reason for his behavior. By the time I got outside to reprimand him, he would take off. My poor Christa. It took no effort to rid her of him, but I'm afraid the damage was already done. Christa was now twenty-three years old. I had still not received monies due me from the trial. Her left eye had become slightly more noticeable in size than her right. I am investigating the validity of iridology for reasons I will not mention in this book. I will say that the area of Christa's left eye, which coincides with liver function, had a persistent waxing and waning of a lesion when she became jaundiced. While she was on sufficient amounts of her herbs, all signs abated. But the intervals of not having them available grew longer and longer.

One day she began to have full-blown seizures called clonic, tonic seizures. Christa would just give this terrible grunt and fall over with her head and all four legs moving fiercely. Another terrifying thing to watch. Thanks to a book by Dr. D.C. Jarvis, a physician from Vermont who wrote <u>Folk Medicine</u>, in which he talked about how apple cider vinegar and honey replaced potassium in the cells of the body. All damaged, sick, or worn cells will lose their potassium. I would rush to make up a glass — one tablespoon honey and one tablespoon of vinegar, but on my own I added cayenne pepper. It was amazing. I timed her response. From the moment she went down from the seizure until the time she was up and eating grass was less than three minutes. These seizures became more frequent, but she would get up each time.

The pressure behind the eyeball, which seemed to be the cause of the eyeball protruding, became quite evident. So much so that there was a great fluctuation in size when she ate regular horse feed, which often contained animal sterol. This was feed that would be given to me, not any I had bought. When I recognized the effects, I removed it totally from her diet and the eye protrusion was not visible until one day when she just began to walk in circles. The day I had dreaded. The day I knew was to come. One day her head was of normal size and the next it was twice as big on one side as on the other. It was evident that Christa had a brain tumor or some space occupying lesion. Based on her history, clinical signs, and the lesion seen in her iris, I suspected that a metastatic tumor from the liver had spread to the brain. A metastatic lesion of the brain would be a definite possibility for the cause of the seizures with a history of liver problems. The details of her death are reserved for Volume II and my autobiography, but this I will share. Though I did not have sufficient quantity nor type of herbs to reverse her condition, those that I did have, mullein, chamomile, passion flower and hops, **kept her from an agonizing death.**

95

With all my heart, I believe, that the horse is special and close to the heart of the God I serve because His word says the following:

> "The chariot with the black horses is going forth into the north country, and the white ones are going forth after them . . ."
> "Behold these that go toward the north country have quieted My Spirit (of wrath) and have caused it to rest in the north country."
> Zechariah 6:5 & 8 King James (amplified version)

I pay tribute to one of God's (Yaweh's) anointed creatures who has touched my life.

Cash — The Cat Who Almost Owned Up to His Name

All my patients are special. All of my pets are special, but this little kitty is special in a special way. I was uniquely introduced to Cash during the brief period that I managed the Inner Harbor Animal Clinic in Baltimore, Maryland. The ironic thing about this story is that I was committed to overseeing that the execution of conventional medicine be properly carried out according to standards.

The owners accepted my commitment to naturopathic medicine, and acknowledged my assertion that I could, and would (to the best of my abilities) follow the established policies of the previous veterinarian for the time I would have the position.

My primary responsibility was to reorganize and restructure a situation that went awry, while serving as the head veterinarian, as well. Had I not been in this position, I would not have been able to help Cash.

Cash was a two-year-old neutered male with a history of possible cardiomyopathy (diseased heart) that may or may not have been associated with toxic ingestion. A battery of tests was ordered and performed by one of the part-time veterinarians hired at the clinic. An electrocardiogram (EKG) and blood tests were obtained. Clinical signs of lethargy, depression, anorexia, arrhythmia, and alterations of vital signs were compatible with problems of the heart. According to the conventional approach, the veterinarian correctly urged a rescheduling for x-rays, since the equipment was in repair the day of his exam. The couple was convinced that their hard-earned money was not being used for Cash's best interest, especially since there was no promise that he would improve. They were informed that Cash may have to be on medication the rest of his life. That evening, I called them.

My feelings were correct. They felt they were being taken for a ride because of the high costs already encountered and no promise that Cash would feel better without being maintained by artificial means — on medications for his lifetime. They were not intending to return for the prepaid x-rays, scheduled in a few days. The couple did agree to come in and let me examine Cash and place him on a naturopathic program, including a total diet change, and use of herbal supplementations. Cash's response was remarkable.

Read the testimony on Cash.

Princess Tela

Princess Tela who is really the Mighty Queen of "Tiny Terror." In 1985, Tela came to my office as a small fur-ball, submissive, cuddly, and cute. She was first presented with various degrees of upper and lower respiratory clinical signs. Her cooperation was appreciated and predictable.

Her mother, Mrs. Hughes, was always so concerned about her "little Tela." As a puppy, Tela's treatments for her conditions, though herbal in nature, were symptomatic according to her clinical signs and history. "She sneezes and coughs as if she's going to vomit" as Mrs. Hughes continued to worriedly describe Tela's major complaint. "She has also vomited twice in the car."

Tela was recently acquired from a local rescue league and the very common condition of kennel cough was high on the list of differentials. Often, regardless of the quality of the shelters and kennels (and this one was well kept) the kennel cough viruses may occasionally persist to pathogenic levels particularly in unvaccinated animals. Upon palpation and pressure on the cricoid cartilage of her trachea, she demonstrated the diagnostic duck-like honking cough. I chose to use a combination approach of conventional and wholistic treatments.

I initiated her treatment with an injection of procaine penicillin G with an iron and vitamin B complex followed by one-half teaspoon of fresh-squeezed lemon. Not a very sophisticated approach by some. Often this condition is self-limiting and requires little or no treatment at all, but can be disheartening for the client to hear. The worse scenario is a progression to a nasty ocular and nasal discharge caused by a concomitant secondary bacterial infection. This stage, gone untreated, may lead to the demise of the patient, which in most situations is not the case since the advent of the multi-valent vaccines which now include fractions for most of the incriminating viruses. Tela successfully reached adulthood uneventfully.

Adulthood for Tela and me seemed to be a dog of a different color. During her entire puppyhood, Tela allowed me to treat her almost gleefully. Suddenly she must have seen me as the local burglar; but then again, she was like many other patients who are just grand in the office, but transform into little hellions on their own turf. She so surprised her mother. "Tela! Why are you acting so ugly? Dr. Bradley is trying to help you," as the three of us (Mrs. Hughes, her physically fit son, and myself) struggled to hold down this twenty-pound biting, jumping jellybean - and just for her heart worm test! Sometimes it took seven to ten minutes just to get the muzzle on, only to discover that she had cleverly removed it if you took your eyes off her or turned your back to prepare your syringe. Tela would growl and snap terribly, but for the most part, once the muzzle was secured, taking her blood and giving her shots was, as some would say, "a piece of cake".

"I am so glad you called, Dr. Bradley. I was getting nervous that I couldn't reach you. I don't know why Tela is acting so ugly," she repeated. As I repacked my bag, finished recording Tela's record and stood to walk out the door, Mrs. Hughes unwittingly remembered and asserted, "Her nails, Dr. Bradley, can you do Tela's nails?" In all honesty my heart skipped a beat. I thought of my injured back, my aching hand and looked over at Tela with the muzzle now hanging around her neck and not her jaws. I gathered a smile of all I could muster, looked at Mrs. Hughes and said, "Sure - let's go to it" and proceded with round two with the "Queen of Terror".

On October 14, 1987, the incident that Mrs. Hughes refers to in her testimony began as a call from her that day. She had been trying to reach me again and was forced to seek another vet in Lanham, MD. She was told that only a vet qualified in orthopedics could help her. Two German Shepherds had attacked Tela. Bitten into her right thorax, the left caudal tibia fractured and chip fractures of the same knee accompanied by associated torn ligaments, Tela's body had been quite traumatized and required hospitalization. She had now been stabilized and released. Cautioned and warned that Princess Tela would never walk properly again without surgery, Mrs. Hughes attempted to find me. I do not remember how we made contact, but it may very well have been that I called her, ironically, at the same time she needed me. A happening that seems to occur frequently with my clients.

Upon examining the quite swollen leg and reviewing her x-rays, I had to concur with the attending physician; from a conventional approach, he was correct. I had arranged to meet Mrs. Hughes right in her upstairs office at the day care center that she owned and managed. I got the usual Tela greeting but tempered by her injury. My right hand at the time was hampered by the nerve that had been severed and partially removed. A padded glove, similar to those worn by weight lifters, allowed me to treat Tela. A veteran colleague of mine in Newark, Delaware, who attended special orthopedic seminars, shared with me a principle that is the basis for my entire approach to any orthopedic problem. This principle states that if you can obtain and maintain just minimal juxtaposition of the bone fragments, a bridge and callus formation will result with proper external fixation. This just means that if the broken ends or parts are close together and stay that way, it will heal. This is unlike most conventional approaches which insist that only internal (surgical implants) fixation is the answer to the same problem.

A "malunion" refers to an improperly healed fracture and a "sequestrum" refers to a piece or pieces of bone broken away from the main bone, still lodged in the tissue. I have discovered that the problems of malunion and sequestration which are a concern of conventional medicine, have not occurred in the cases I have treated, such as Tela's, where there was definite evidence of chipped bone fractures. The herbs seem to remodel and restore degenerative or injured bone as well as heal detached ligaments and tendons.

Therefore, I proceeded to construct and apply an external splint that I termed a modified Robert Jones (a type of splint used with a lot of padding). Tela had to be sedated to obtain proper setting and alignment while I placed on the splint. Every splint I use, unlike many of the conventional splints, is contoured exactly to the curves and measurements of each patient. Within twenty minutes, Tela was up and about and able to stand on all fours. Specific herbs for the musculo-skeletal system were administered and given to go home. At the end of four weeks, Tela was standing and walking on both hind legs.

See photos.
See testimonies:
Muscle and Bone Disorders

10/14/87—fx Tibia
Was told leg would never mend
without surgery.

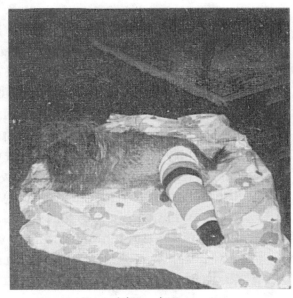

1 hour later
Applied custom designed splint
and herbs orally.

Four weeks later.

Iron Fortress — The Big Guy with the Bad Feet (and Legs)

I acquired Iron from the Equine Rescue League in ███████████████ I chose Iron (then called Forty) because he did have a medical problem, but just looking at him I knew, with God's help, he could be cured. I had treated worse cases than Iron. Also healthy animals have much less of a problem being adopted. It is my feeling that I am in a position to help where the average person adopting would have to spend hundreds or thousands of dollars for veterinary care and may still end up euthanizing the pet of their choice.

Iron's diagnosis, as shown by the following document, was arthritis of the right rear fetlock (ankle joint) demonstrated by enlargement of the joint with right and left front and rear lameness. His condition was severe enough that he could not be ridden or exercised without painkillers and at best not more than a few times a week. Iron had been on daily doses of butazolindin (a drug known to depress the bone marrow that causes bleeding disorders, and may be fatal to animals with cardiac problems, and invariably affects the kidneys) and had difficulty even coming out of his stall with obvious stiffness.

His background included a line of jumpers and racetrack achievers. Iron is a tall, standing seventeen-two hands, dark bay, Thoroughbred - gentle, attentive, and so responsive that he rides with a hackamore (a bridle without a bit).

I knew about Iron's arthritic problems, but I later discovered with the help of my farrier, ████████████████ that Iron had chronic and persistent problems with abscesses of both front and back feet. He was extremely sensitive in the front and virtually became a cripple without shoes.

Before he left the farm in Virginia, to come to my barn, I instructed the owners of the League how to apply the liniment and oral herb combinations. The liniment was applied to <u>all four</u> legs from top to bottom as well as the entire foot. It contained cayenne pepper, wintergreen alcohol, olive oil, lemons, B F & C (bone, flesh and cartilage capsules - opened), Rheum-aid, and camphor. The oral included dried cut sarsaparilla, willow bark, cayenne, wintergreen, marsh-mallow, black walnut hulls, cider vinegar, and honey. Within twenty-four hours, the owners, voluntarily, offered information that Iron Fortress was running to the gate of the pasture he had been in for grazing. Something he'd never done since he was brought there. There was, they said, a noticeable difference in attitude, alertness, and definitely his gait. He was picking his legs up higher and only needed one dose of bute. They were afraid of complete withdrawal of the painkiller since they had little or no experience in the use of herbs with animals. Forty showed so much improvement that the owners decided to use similar combinations on another horse who was to be put down if she could not walk soon. The results were so dramatic that the mare was able to be used for lessons.

Forty was delivered to the old barn where I was staying. His story is quite simple. From the day he arrived I never had to give him any analgesic or painkilling drugs. Within three days of intensive herbal rub downs, oral herbal combinations every few hours, and diet change, Iron Fortress trotted three miles without so much as slowing down along side of my barrel racing mare, Meshi.

I cannot emphasize enough that herbal treatment is similar to conventional (in my experience) in that once medication is started (particularly for tough, severely debilitating problems), a certain level of the herbs must be obtained and maintained in the bloodstream until total recovery is complete or healing will stop where it is. Progress may cease or even reverse under certain negative conditions. Iron has recovered from worm infestations and a case of rain rot - all herbally.

A large horse like Iron requires at least four medium or two large onions and one-half bulb of garlic per gallon of water with a minimum of one tablespoon of cayenne pepper added. Initially, give 30cc infusion daily and one cup of the solution poured over food. It is best to use organic or near organic grains such as corn, oats, barley, or any combination above. I, personally, have never had a problem of heat build up in the feet or laminitis (Founder's Disease) from feeding corn - especially if supplemental herbs are used daily to enhance absorption and digestibility. This high concentration of garlic and onions can be used three to five days and then be reduced to maintenance and prophylactic levels by just adding one-half to one cup of solution per feeding. The extra trouble of making your solutions is well worth the worse problem of expensive veterinary bills, recurrent worms problems, and the risk of liver and kidney damage using conventional wormers. Not only are you ridding your horse or pony of worms, but you are enhancing the immune system and preventing the susceptibility of all sorts of diseases.

Rain rot is generally reversed by first thoroughly cleansing the area with a good soap such as olive and aloe or olive and honey (Kiss My Face - an excellent brand). Make sure all areas of pus underneath the hair is exposed and cleaned. Apply a combination similar to the liniment used for the legs (wintergreen alcohol, peroxide, cayenne pepper, olive oil, and sea salt) - Yager's Liniment, if available or Bigel oil or camphor can be used as an additional ingredient. This should be applied liberally and rubbed in at least twice a day until almost healed then once daily. For very severe or tough cases, one tablespoon of Clorox per gallon of water can be used as a rinse after the soap wash.

VETERINARY ASSOCIATES

D.V.M.
Equine and Farm Animal Practice

Purcellville, VA
(703)

Owner:	FCRL			Telephone: Home:	
				Work:	
Address:			S.S. #	Barn:	

Animal	Species/Breed	Professional Services	Date: 7-20-93	Amount
Whisper	BAYTBF	EXAM: GRADE I lame (RF) - no head bob just ↑ wt. on (LF); off + on low grade lameness in (RF) probably 2° to (club foot) condition - Rec. shoe w/ pad and rolled toe		18.00
IRON FORTRESS	BAYTBG	EXAM: GRADE III LAME (RR) and (LR) w/ bilateral shortened stride but worse on (RR); very strong ⊕ flexion test or the (RR) ankle - ankle enlargement noted. DX: (ARTHRITIS) OF THE (RR) fetlock Rec. use 2g Bute once or twice daily prior to riding as needed		25.00

		Dispensed Medications/Supplies		
		Rx: Anthelcide Paste × 24 @ 6.00		144.00

		½	Farm Call/Mileage	10.00
		15%	Total	197.00
			Amount Paid	-29.55
			Amount Due	167.45

Receipt No. 5418

Method of Payment

**Cases with a Story
to Be Completed in
Volume II**

They put Cody to sleep today. As I held back the tears I can visualize that gentle giant of a Shepherd called "Cody." His trusting eyes I will never see again until Yeshua returns.

The pain his owners must be experiencing now. I know his mother made the decision she only knew how to make - not to see or believe that her beloved "Cody was suffering any longer. Oh no, this is it," she said. "He must be suffering. His feet are still bleeding". I'll never forget that look on her face when she looked into my eyes as she spoke those words.

Little ████, the twelve-year-old daughter, looked bewildered and hurt. Elwood, the father, stood shaking his head quietly saying that Cody didn't look better.

In vain I tried to show and explain that though Cody had areas of intermediate stages of healing and that the bleeding under the scabs was part of the healing process, all Mrs. "B" could see was the scene she <u>experienced</u> before I started the case - blood, blood on his feet, blood between this back legs, scabs under his chin and around the front part of his neck. They couldn't realize that the reasons for the blood they saw was totally different from the reasons before I took the case. The reason I say <u>couldn't</u> is that they had been so indoctrinated to the concept that they as owners were instruments of torture and suffering for this pet they supposedly love by allowing him to go on with enlarged bleeding feet and oozing scabs.

"Sweat Pea"
and Two Eyewitness Accounts

Friday, September 24, 1993, I had only been working at the shelter two days. This day proved to be an eye-opener, a tragic experience and a revealing ray of hope all at once.

I walked back to the treatment room. How ironic to be termed the "treatment room." The girls, Kathy and Sally, were mildly joking as the wardens routinely brought in the strays and unwanted call-ins, as well as the cruelty cases and just unwanted creatures, whether they be dogs, cats, rabbits, or ferrets. I could not fight a feeling of helplessness. A feeling of somehow being responsible for allowing this situation to come about. This shelter alone was obliged to euthanize more than 10,000 animals the last year. Most of them healthy and many pedigrees. What took place in the next few moments changed the way I see pets in this country and my role as a veterinarian and a pet owner.

This scene I will never forget. Initially, I smiled and joked with the staff as the cute kittens and puppies, as well as the young and middle-aged adults, paraded through the back doors to the treatment room. Some in cages, some on leashes, some in the arms of the wardens.

As each warden from their respective counties began to initiate in placing their animals on the table, my observations suddenly began to challenge my emotions to the logic of what I was about to witness. I was not prepared for the following events.

The first, I believe, was a gorgeous black Labrador retriever who was gently placed on the stainless steel table. Sally and Kathy soothingly spoke to him as the blue solution was drawn. "He was brought in as unwanted and there was no room. Hey big boy, it'll be all right." The warden helped to hold off the vein while one of the girls skillfully injected the solution of death. I watched his body slowly slump on the cold table. I watched him being packed up and placed into a large metal barrel in the cooler.

I have seen this before. I am a veterinarian. After all, I've worked with shelters in the past. I've had to put several animals to sleep, and I've seen them being placed in those barrels before.

Cat after cat, dog after dog, kitten after kitten, puppy after puppy, all getting the "blue juice." I could not fight the tears back any longer. I had to leave the room, leaving my co-workers to continue their hateful duties. The tears came actually my first day, Wednesday, September 22, 1993. The shelter's supervisor, Bob Anderson, had told the staff, "If I was able to cut the ice, then the treatment room would determine it." He, personally, never allows his staff veterinarians at his hospital to perform the euthanasias in numbers. To be trained to save life and to watch a seemingly senseless execution of dozens and dozens of healthy animals, to have their breath just snuffed out in minutes, is a multiple perforation to the soul, an axe hacking away at one's living spirit. Kathy and Sally this day were euthanizing.

There's something about death in masses. Mass murders of beast and man incite a magnitude of grief that boggles the mind beyond comprehension. As a veterinarian, I've never had to euthanize more than one patient at a time. On occasion, with severe viral epidemics, we as veterinarians have either watched patients not respond to therapy and die in numbers or had to euthanize them relieving them of their suffering, but were never forced to **routinely** end the life of a perfectly healthy animal.

These animal health technicians and wardens were chosen for the job because they care about the well-being and treatment of animals. I was trained and took an oath to preserve life, yet here we stand observing and participating in this travesty of unnecessary premeditated murder.

Their joking and laughter had now become a defense tactic to hold their tears into the caverns of denial in order to do their jobs.

Soon to follow was a long oblong trap-like metal cage containing, at least, five or six kittens approximately four months old. They were barn cats, I was told. The owner had several of them and did not want to be bothered with them anymore. There were a total of about twenty or thirty who needed to be gathered up. They were the cutest, most precious little creatures of all color patterns.

Again, the animals were placed on the table. This time a needle and syringe containing a tranquilizer was inserted into their abdomen as the cage was positioned over the table allowing the technicians access by the square holes of the cage. Each one slowly slumped and became lifeless. Each was carefully taken out of the cage and gently placed on the cold stainless steel table.

Step two is the injection of the solution of death, the blue solution, placed very carefully into the animal's pumping heart until the heart is no longer pumping. Because many of the animals are feral, the type of cages used are necessary for accessibility and restraint before the super-concentration of phenobarbital can be administered.

Right after that, another cage load of puppies came in through the infamous double doors. Again, I watched the same procedure. My question then became, "Why are these young ones being put to sleep (PTS)?" The answer, oddly enough, was not surprising, but still astounding and shocking to the psyche. "We have no room. None of the (associate) humane societies have space either." I learned that strays have a mandatory five-day reclaim period and turn-in's must be PTS if there simply is no physical space. "We try to keep as many of the kittens and puppies that we possibly can or turn them over to either the local humane societies if they have room or any of the local foster groups. Some of our purebreds, such as Danes and Dobes, are often taken by the rescue leagues if they are adoptable." If they had been wild for a period of time or displayed any type of aggressive behavior, a decision could be made to PTS rather than chance a bite problem with a prospective owner, particularly one with children.

It was now nearly four o'clock. Again, cage after cage, dog after dog, cat after cat took their turn on the table of death. But the ray of hope and the glimmer of gleam triumphed when that fortunate kitten or puppy, dog or cat would be placed on that same table and be given its vaccinations and kept for possible adoption when there was room at the inn. Not all were to be immediately euthanized. These moments of joy are what keeps many of these caretakers literally sane and able to do the hideous job they are expected to do. Most of the puppies and kittens, if possible, were held if there was room or sent to the various Animal Welfare groups such as the Lucky Ones or foster homes from the St. Mary's County Animal Welfare League or one of the humane societies. There are other individual groups for various breeds, such as the Doberman, Great Dane or Labrador Rescue Leagues.

This day the supervisor, Bob, was in the treatment room watching the wardens bring the animals in. Suddenly, in comes this small Shepherd-like puppy, not even a year old, with hardly any hair. It's skin was severely scabbed from the tip of its nose to the end of its tail. Pus and blood oozed from multiple areas all over its entire body, particularly the elbows, head and neck and along the dorsum or top of the spine. Her feet were swollen and legs were somewhat twisted outward and her back was slightly hunched in the middle from a not so obvious source of pain. Her eyes were crusted and full of mucoid discharge.

My immediate thought was that the dog had a severe case of demodex mange with secondary bacterial infection. I thought, "Oh another case similar to Cody's. Maybe I could help this one by the knowledge I gained from Cody." I quickly turned to Bob and asked, "Can I work with this one? How long can we keep a stray? Give me three days to show improvement." The allotted time for strays by law is five days.

Bob, knowing my zeal to show how herbal treatment and diet work and also knowing the necessity of documentation, looked at me, hesitantly at first, then quickly responded, "Go ahead. We'll keep her at least five days. She's yours."

I quickly went over to Sweet Pea — who then had no name — and began to talk to her and give her a cursory exam. No one really wanted to touch her. She had the classic, end-stage (advanced) moist eczema with secondary bacterial infection odor, which is very characteristic and unmistakable to anyone who enters the room. As I examined her, I could literally see her heart pounding through the chest wall. I allowed several of the employees to witness this, in particular, warden Drew Wrinkler, then a new animal control officer. He was astonished to be able to feel and see her heart pound so vividly through the chest wall. Her breathing was somewhat labored, very audible, and she expressed subtle moaning, but only when lying down. Sweet Pea's feet were swollen and the toes spread far apart. She dripped blood on the floor everywhere she walked from the oozing open sores. The saga of Sweet Pea and her miraculous recovery will be completed in Volume II.

See testimonies of <u>two</u> eyewitnesses on the following pages.

Reference: "Sweet Pea"

Animal Welfare League

Baltimore, MD

June, 18, 1994

To Whom I May Concern:

I am not a veterinarian. But, I have worked for over fifteen years in the rescuing of dogs and cats. During those years I have worked with a few good veterinarians and have learned much from them.

When I first saw "Sweet Pea" at the shelter I was all in favor of immediately putting her down. She had over 50% of her body covered from what looked like Sarcoptic Mange and Secondary Infection. There was thick wrinkled areas with crusty patches on her head, body, tail head, and feet. Her spine was bent with hips not in align with the rest of the body. In non-medical terms "She was a mess".

Dr. Bradley took "Sweet Pea" out of the shelter and started a regimen of natural medication. Over the next several months Doc. Bradley brought to my attention other ailments with the root cause being a depressed immune system.

At this time "Sweet Pea" is much improved with all the crusty patches gone, no obvious secondary infection, and her spine/hip alignment is close to normal. She does have some thick wrinkled areas but the hair is growing back.

Respectfully submitted,

, V.P.

lag

Having been a euthanasia technician for nearly three years at a county run animal shelter, I can honestly say that I have seen some of the saddest sights come through the doors of the euthanasia room. Living in a mostly rural, small - town type community. I have grown to learn that putting food on the table take's priority over putting food in the mouth of the family dog chained to the dog box in the back yard. And certainly if you can't afford to take your child to the doctor a trip to the veterinarian is absolutely unheard of. Therefore, I soon developed a belief that the kindest thing that could be done for many of the animals that came in to the shelter was to end their suffering as quickly and painlessly as possible knowing that a compassionate touch of the hand and the soothing sound of a voice may be the most affection that animal received in its entire life.

The dog that would one day be known as Doc Bradlys "Sweet Pea" was no different. When this poor, pitiful animal came through those doors, what I saw standing before me was just another one of the thousands I have seen in the past and one of the thousands I knew were still to come in the future. I honestly marveled at how an animal that looked so sad with her head down and her back arched up as though she were in great discomfort could have the heart to get up and walk with total strangers. If you have ever seen someone in their bare feet try to walk down a gravel road you will be able to picture the slow, deliberate, seemingly up - on - the - toes way that this dog walked. Her feet and legs were swollen and encrusted with dry, cracking skin and her muzzle, up to and around her eyes, was one large swollen skin crust. I would have to say that there probably was not a square inch on her body that did not show some form of hair loss or skin eruption. Admittedly, what I saw before me was one of the more severe skin conditions that I have witnessed in the years that I have worked at the shelter.

Although I believe that at times it is better to end an animals suffering, I must admit that Sweet Pea has been lucky to become the "exception to the rule." Over the months that she has been under Doc Bradlys care she has developed a very special personality not often seen in dogs that have had such hard beginnings. Sweet Pea absolutely loves interacting with people and not only people she knows but total strangers are greeted with great interest. In fact, she has such a wonderful disposition that I truly believe that she hasn't a clue that she is not just like you or I. As far as her skin condition, I would have to say that her progress is nothing short of miraculous. I never would have believed that her healing process could have progressed so far. When I last saw her, she was growing a beautiful coat of hair. Only her neck still showed the signs of the ordeal she had been through as the hair had not yet grown back. She holds her head high now and actually prances around from person to person as if to say "look at me aren't I beautiful." With out a doubt Sweet Pea has been lucky to become the "exception . . . " because only Doc Bradly could see her potential. She saw in Sweet Pea something that no one could even begin to fathom. And that vision is truly paying off.

1. Remember every herb is a plant, but not every plant is an herb.

2. What do garlic, onions, and eggs have in common? Natural sulfur compounds, natural antibiotics.

3. From what herb does the penicillin mold come? Hyssop; King David said, "Cleanse me with hyssop, and I will be clean; wash me, and I will be whiter than snow."

4. What really makes a drug a drug? Allopaths and naturopaths will not, in most cases, agree on its definition. As a naturopath, I view a drug as any substance placed on or taken into the body that cannot be recognized as "self" by the body and therefore, is automatically foreign and will either be immediately extruded by the body's defense mechanisms or fool the body and seed itself in one or more places creating diseases of all sorts. Anything other than a foodstuff that is not totally assimilated by the body - external or internal - is a drug. Remember, not all foods are nourishing for the human body (i.e., poisonous mushrooms can mean death to us but life and nourishment to other creatures).

> "And God said, Behold, I have given you every <u>herb</u> bearing seed, which is upon the face of all the earth, and every tree, in the which is the fruit of a tree yielding seed, to you it shall be for meat.
>
> "<u>And to every beast</u> of the earth, and to every fowl of the air, and to every thing that creepeth upon the earth, wherein there is life, I have given every green <u>herb</u> for meat: and it was so."
>
> Genesis 1:29 & 30 King James Version

5. It has been my experience, clinically, that herbal medicine crosses <u>all</u> species' lines, just as the above Biblical passage indicates.

6. There are many modalities under the umbrella of holistic medicine. I do not subscribe to all of them, but I believe that given sound evidence that the approach is effective and no more dangerous than that of chemo- and

radiation therapy and any other high-risk therapies, that the information should be readily available <u>equal to that of conventional approaches</u> and the choice be up to the patient!

7. Eating herbs is as natural to your body as eating an apple.

8. How may diseases of our children are diet related? For example refined sugar can cause hyperexcitability, tooth decay, diabetes; causes of chronic ear infections - I have seen definite reversals often with mere diet change (people and pets).

9. Can food that is good for you taste good to you? You bet it can! All kinds of harmful chemicals (artificial flavorings, colorings and preservatives) are added to our already inferior foods to make them look and taste attractive (see document on common additives in pet and people foods).

    Good tasting ice cream, milk and cheese (cow or goat) can still be enjoyed without the estrogens and the antibiotics (in the feeds of these animals).

    Have you ever asked yourself the question, "If the organic stores can keep and maintain foods long enough to sell, why can't the supermarkets do it?"

    Fruits and vegetables not loaded with residues from herbicides, pesticides, and radiation will not only taste better, but heal your body rather than destroy it.

    Your grains, legumes, home-baked breads, casseroles, desserts, and fruit drinks will taste just like great, great grandma use to "make 'em" with the real cane sugar straight from the fields while they still had all the minerals and vitamins locked inside, not totally devoid of them like the stripped white, refined sugar on your tables that's causing senseless deaths around the globe - particularly in this country! White flour follows close behind. Investigate. Find out for yourselves. Demand a change for better health with better taste!

10. Some of the largest and strongest creatures on earth have no meat in their diets, such as the horse and elephant, and they require the same proteins as we for survival. Meat is not only the primary source of proteins for many people, but a very poor choice for any human. Fowl and fish are among the most digestible sources of flesh protein, for humans.

Nutritional Nuggets - More Food for Thought
for Man and Animals of All Sorts

1. <u>Sugar</u> (refined white) - all nutritive value of vitamins and minerals are removed. <u>It will kill you</u> - I urge you to <u>read</u> up on sugars. Excellent sources of nutritional sugars are honey, black strap molasses, maple syrup, sucanat (the granulated juice of cane sugar), turbinado, barley malt, and brown rice syrup (<u>both good for diabetics</u> and those dieting).

2. <u>White flour and white rice</u> - no nutritional value - like white refined sugar
    a. will kill you - read - do not be ignorant of what you consume
    b. unless label says 100% whole wheat you are usually getting white flour not wheat, since they are used interchangeably

3. <u>Juices</u> - get yourself a good quality <u>juicer</u> - If you desire faster healing and a better quality of maintaining your body - fruits usually cleanse the body while vegetables are usually protein builders - requires almost no break-down of the body and goes immediately into the bloodstream - results are astonishing if educated to their uses - wash and cleanse thoroughly if not organically grown

4. <u>Herb teas</u> - high in vitamins and minerals - can mix and match creating all kinds of beverages not only of nutritional support but therapeutic value regardless of FDA claims.

5. <u>Vitamins and minerals</u> - Never, never take in isolation - always take in a food or herb that is high in the desired vitamin or mineral necessary to overcome the condition or a dangerous imbalance is ultimately created setting you up for more disease.

6. Most of us choose what we wish to eat. I'm just fighting for an **informed** choice.

Alternative Pharmacy

The Origin of Drug Development Concerning Medicinal Plants from Past to Present

Presented by Mary C. Marquis, R.P.H.

October 22, 1994

The origins of pharmacy began during the Norman Conquest when the mercers, who operated the mercery, controlled the trade of drugs and spices. Eventually, these businesses evolved into peppers and spicers. The peppers and spicers became known as grocers, whose responsibility was to garble drugs and spices and to inspect the apothecaries. It was during the 1600's that the apothecaries began to assume control of the industry, establishing a charter of their own in order to prevent them from being a subordinate guild to that of the grocers. In the words of King James, "Grocers are but merchants. The business of an apothecary is a mystery."

In colonial America, the physician and pharmacist continued to combine two sciences. Usually, the more prosperous physicians would also prepare and sell medicaments to their patients, perhaps in response to competition from the independent professional druggist, who was beginning to advertise and gain prominence. Most physicians were also apothecaries.

Most of the medicaments sold were from formulations based on the theories of heroic medicine, which included bleeding, blistering, and purging the patient.

But as patients began to see problems with this type of treatment, the family caregivers began to seek alternative remedies. Tradition held that the woman was the primary caretaker within the family, often serving as physician and druggist when, especially in remote areas, no doctor or apothecary was available. Women would exchange different medical remedies, leading to a resurgence of the time-tested cures made from roots and herbs. Of course, the profit-minded merchants selling painted jars filled with various white powders tended to override the use of home-remedy plant medicaments.

Today's pharmacist is the result of a circuitous route whereby the pharmacist is a specialist in the use, preparation, and application of various medications, whether oral or intravenous.

As a backdrop for this role, the pharmaceutical industry is charged with the development and marketing of drugs. In 1993, Fortune magazine identified the pharmaceutical industry as one of the most profitable in this nation. Its immense profitability is the result of a strong dynamic: marketing muscle, patent protection, and a unique relationship with its customers.

Today, pharmacists dispense most drugs, using unit dose systems in which manufactured dosage forms are delivered to the patient. A unit dose system employs unit dose containers in which a single use container is intended for administration by other than the parenteral route as a single dose direct from the container.

Many drugs, approximately twenty-five percent, used in the pharmaceutical trade are derived from plant origins. Given pharmacists' traditional use of medicinal plants, and with the growth in knowledge in the chemical arena, it is not surprising that pharmacists began isolating the main chemical constituents of plants such as the cardiac glycosides, digitalis and digitoxin, and the opiates such as morphine. This created a pharmaceutical revolution in which alkaloids and glycosides generated an expansive list of new drugs. Some of these include morphine, codeine, quinine, cocaine, colchicine, ephedrine, atropine, physostigmine, reserpine, and many others.

Hence, the pharmaceutical industry grew out of the pharmacy and changed the use of drugs from the plant-based materia medica into standardized, quantifiable drug. Pharmaceutical companies — then and now — have very heavy overheads. As many prominent scientific researchers have demonstrated, it can take years of patient teamwork, as well as extensive phases of clinical research trials, before a promising therapeutic substance results. In addition, the companies must satisfy the stringent requirements of the Federal Food Drug and Cosmetic Act of 1938.

The financial investment necessary for procuring a new drug is monumental: Approximately $250 million. And, as any astute businessperson will tell you, the market for the new drug must be readily available.

For the most part, manufacturers did not automatically assume that plants could continue to provide badly needed drugs, so they focussed most intensely on developing chemical compounds. Of course, an even more compelling concern was the financial one. How can you patent a whole plant? Without the ability to patent, a company could not profitably market a product. In many cases, the active constituent was impossible to synthesize. All of these concerns put an end to most pharmaceutical research on medicinal plants.

Quantification of the plant's ability made it extremely difficult to standardize into an acceptable dosage form such as a pill or capsule, creating another obstacle to medicinal plant research and development. Hence, scientific researchers began to look askance at the use of plants, turning instead to synthetic compounds in the creation of drug products.

This is a real shame. Especially when our European contemporaries are so forward-thinking with regard to using herbs as drugs. In Germany, for example, the Federal Ministry of Health provides monographs for the medicinal uses of herbs.

In the last twenty years, the resurgence of self-care in this country, people have begun to question the superiority and wisdom of traditional

118

allopathic or Western medicine methodology. Amazingly enough, pharmaceutical companies themselves have joined this movement to some extent, and are actually starting to examine the shaman's practices with medicinal plants. For instance, the National Institutes of Health, along with Bristol-Myers/Squibb, Virginia Polytechnic Institute and State University, and the Missouri Botanical Garden have teamed up in the Amozonian country of Surinam to study medicinal plants. Bristol-Myers/Squibb has agreed to pay royalties to the indigenous people there and to share patent rights with them for any drugs derived from plants gathered there. As the use of medicinal plants is re-examined, quantification has begun. Another company, Shaman Pharmaceuticals, is exploring the medicinal uses of plants and has begun to extract plant constituents for possible assimilation into drug products.

To me, this practice of examining the plants that native people have used as medicine for centuries makes a lot of sense. In a laboratory where one in thousands of chemically created synthetic compounds will result in a useful drug, why not bet on a surer thing? As stated by Gordon Cragg, chief of the NCI's Natural Products Branch in the May 10, 1994, issue of the Washington Post, "Nature is still in many cases the most economical source for medicines."

At last, maybe the tide has turned and we will finally see the recognition that medicinal plants — herbs — deserve.

Bibliography

Blanton, Wyndham D. Medicine in Virginia in the Eighteenth Century, Richmond, VA: The William Byrd Press, 1930

Virginia Pharmaceutical Association, A Century of Virginia Pharmacy, Richmond, VA: VPMA, 1981

Bavitt, Todd L. Medicine and Slavery: The Diseases and Health Care of Blacks in Antebellum Virginia, Urbana, IL: University of Illinois Press, 1978

Cowen, David L. and Helfand, William H., Pharmacy An Illustrated History, New York, New York: Harry N. Abrams, Inc., 1990

Griggs, Barbara, Green Pharmacy, Rochester, VT: The Healing Arts Press, 1991

Foster, Steven Ph.D. and Duke, James A. Ph.D., Peterson's Field Guides: Eastern/Central Medicinal Plants, Boston, MA: Houghton Mifflin Company, 1990

Feldmann, Edward G. Ph.D., <u>Handbook of Nonprescription Drugs, 9th Ed.,</u>
Washington, D.C.: The American Pharmaceutical Association, 1990

Weiss, Rick, "Plants That Heal," Health, The Washington Post, 16 May 1994, p. 14

"Bitter Medicine For the Drug Companies": U.S. News and World Report, 24 October 1994, p. 72

Astounding Medical Recoveries by Herbs and Diet;
Yes I am boldly making therapeutic (healing) claims
contrary to what the powers that be dictate
- because they concern me-

These are medical facts!

The FDA dictates that herbal or vitamin usage cannot be claimed for anything more than nutritional support — never for therapeutic or medicinal value.

The shoe has always been on the other foot. The FDA, pharmaceutical companies, and allopaths (in general) have always demanded that users of natural medicine prove their claims — prove that their approaches really work.

I now challenge the establishment to prove to the American people that herbs and proper dietary changes DO NOT WORK!

I remind these "powers that be" and the reader that I am a trained physician (a Veterinary Medical Doctor) from one of the most esteemed institutions of progressive learning in this entire world, ranked among the top five when I attended.

Am I being boastful? No, just truthful, channeling constructive indignation! The University of Pennsylvania School of Veterinary Medicine taught me that folk medicine was ineffective, unproven quackery that should be regarded as nonscientific and rebuked as medieval and backward thinking. After eight years of less than good experiences with hospitals and ill-prepared physicians, it is not the naturopaths that are the backward thinkers.

I am angry! Angry that I was charged $67,000 for an education that robbed me of the real and most effective ways of practicing medicine. At the very least, folk medicine should have been taught along side of conventional approaches instead of being relegated to primitive, ignorant thinking when in essence it is the very opposite.

At no time is there ever a mention of phytotherapy (plant medicine) with the emphasis of unadulterated diets and foods devoid of harmful chemicals that we can truly avoid by using organic farming techniques and the proper use of natural food preservation.

Diet is placed far down the list as a causative factor of disease. The drugs they create are evaluated for their so-called "active ingredient." The integral parts of the plant are created to help you. There is no such thing as an active ingredient in nature, but the use of either part or all of the plant. Everything that makes that plant what it is is important, synergistically, to help heal your body. Herbs are not drugs, unless you make them so by extracting out their chemical composition, putting them in test tubes, and then introducing them into your body. They would no longer be the natural substances they were created to be, but now foreign substances capable of inducing cancer and all other types of destructive conditions. Herbs are not drugs but foodstuffs that are totally absorbed and assimilated by your body, and used by it as nourishment automatically strengthening every one of your cells. The essence of your health takes place on the cellular level, the place where you and I cannot see with the naked eye, but we can feel by the strength and endurance of our bodies.

Every "true" herb has multifunctional properties — that is, it will not only help and strengthen the organ you desire to heal, but it will go to other troubled areas as well as to healthy cells, enhancing their maintenance levels. Conventional medicine, on the other hand, invades the body, uses its chemical muscles to intimidate the virus, bacteria, toxin, or whatever the offending agent, but it never really leaves the body because it does several things. First, it will never really nourish your cells because it is foreign, it is not food, and will never be accepted; therefore, it is never properly used by the cells it's trying to protect.

Second, it becomes part of the problem because either the kidneys or the liver will have to use great amounts of energy and immune responses to rid the body of the residue invariably left behind by this chemical. This residue sits as a nidus or seed, dormant until the opportunity arises when the body becomes further weakened from more of the same or other incriminates such as chronic ingestion of toxic foods until the threshold is reached in which there no longer is an immune response. Then disease sets in.

The third thing a drug does is leave your cells weaker and more susceptible when it does try to exit the body because while in your body it has done absolutely nothing to really nourish your healthy soldiers, let alone your sick ones. A drug provides only temporary and euphoric relief: A false sense of well-being or improvement. Our bodies have the capability to regenerate to a tremendous capacity fed the proper nourishment that leads to self healing. Eighty-five percent of the liver can be destroyed, yet proper nourishment through herbs and diet will regenerate that liver to excellent function. This applies to kidneys or virtually any organ of your body treated in time with the right combinations, environmental controls, and moderate exercise.

Herbal Medicine -
What I Have Found Clinically to Work

I vary the combinations, dosages, and duration of times herbs are taken, depending on the severity of the problem, the animal's response, ability of the owner to assess signs and administer recommendations, and my availability to see the patient as needed. Distance is often a factor between success and failure.

When Do Herbs Not Work?

1. As in conventional medicine, when the condition is not treated in time.

2. When there is an improper assessment of the system involved. Often the specific organ involved must be identified.

3. When the selection of the proper herb or combination of herbs for the condition is not accurate. One of the reasons that this approach to medicine is a lost art is that the wisdom is usually passed on from generation to generation to a specifically trained few in a given culture. There is still a knowledge of the general use of herbs among the masses, similar to that practiced by our forefathers and ancestors in our own country not too long ago.

4. When there is little attention paid to a proper diet, meaning one that is devoid of or at least reduced in toxins (artificial flavors, colorings, preservatives and herbicide or pesticide treated food). A proper diet is especially important in a recovering patient afflicted by a terminal illness.

5. When the herb being used is not the herb you expected - in other words, mistaken identity.

6. No herb or food will reverse a process if one continues to subject oneself to the same damaging conditions, be it either a physical condition, as with an injured back, or an organic condition, as with a cirrhotic liver brought on from alcohol consumption.

All herbs have the inherent quality of possessing their own group of vitamins and minerals. Therefore, usually, if one should take an herb that is not for purposes intended for a specific course of treatment, one would still receive the benefits that herb has to offer.

How Do I Select the Herbs That I Use?

On this planet there are probably thousands upon thousands of different herbs, many indigenous to only certain geographical locations. Like the traditional pattern of choice even used by most conventional doctors, I tend to stay with those herbs I know the actions of best. I personally try not to use any herbs with known abilities to cause toxic effects, such as the foxglove plant from which comes the drug digitalis, used in treating heart conditions. I prefer instead to use a much more innocuous herb such as dandelion or cayenne, which can be used with a much wider margin of safety. It must be emphasized here that <u>any</u> substance consumed in excess can be toxic; for example, water toxicity occurs in cattle (or any species beyond the limits of its natural consumption).

Don't Let the Establishment Fool You!
Conventional Medicine Aims at cultivating a
Dependence on It and Not Really a Cure for You

Conventional medicine often aims at cultivating a dependence on it and not really a cure for you. Why do I make such a rash statement being a V.M.D. (Veterinary Medical Doctor) myself? When I became so ill and after seeing my pets and patients becoming so ill or afflicted by disease or parasitic invasion — only to be met with the response, "There's nothing else we can do except give you these" — my despair became overwhelming, then it turned to outrage after I made discoveries that boggled my mind.

The health care system today promotes death just as Dr. Robert Mendelson declared years ago when he called hospitals "temples of doom." They don't have to be. Yes, there is good that comes out of hospitals and the offices of many well-intended physicians, but not enough to heal a nation and keep it healthy. Why? Because the keys — the truth — to real health is concealed, not discussed and never presented, except in despicable terms and labels the patient to be ignorant and backward to believe "such nonsense."

Let's take a simple illustration of real medicine versus counterfeit medicine. Let's look at the problem of diabetes (especially in this country). The pancreas is the source of the disease in that it is not functioning by either secreting enough insulin or the insulin is not getting into the cells that depend on it. The treatment does not focus on healing the pancreas and all the other organs with which it shares a responsibility. Instead, treatment is a daily injection or oral consumption of a form of insulin, not of your own body, that does absolutely nothing to restore the function of the organ. This makes you and your body dependent emotionally, financially, and physically on the powers that be who supply this drug, a drug that leaves your pancreas to fall into a more depraved state. Every organ or tissue then weakens more and more and pressure builds in various parts of the body. The foreign insulin sets up seeds of destruction. We as a society, continue to eat refined sugar, white flour products, white rice, and carcinogenic sugar substitutes like Nutrasweet and Saccharin and wonder why we have high blood pressure, glaucoma, and loss of limbs from compromised circulation.

Healing begins on the cellular level. We must treat our bodies as one big cell with many smaller cells inside. **That cell must receive the proper nourishment in order to function according to its design or it will die.** To provide anything less is fruitless. It would be like putting a fish in the desert sand instead of a tank of water. Why accept the nitrates, the MSG, the BHT, BHA, colorings, preservatives, and other toxins we readily consume every day for years? Don't believe the lie that a little bit won't hurt you — a pebble in a brook causes many far reaching ripples downstream. All diseases approached by modern medicine are treated in a similar manner with the focus <u>not on</u> <u>healing the tissue</u> but the focus bent on producing a response in your body that is just as artificial as the drugs introduced into it.

There are herbal combinations all over this world — right here in the U.S. that can restore a diseased heart, a failing pancreas, a shattered limb, a foul cancer, and an epileptic seizure. With God's help, I have been able to reverse and see the changes before my eyes of my own body as well as my patients.

Sadly, many of us believe that everything that is released through the media (radio, television, newspapers, magazines, etc.) is true as long as the statements are accompanied with the words "scientists say" or "the latest studies show." I implore you — as a doctor of scientific background — do not believe everything passed on as truth solely because claims are associated with these phrases.

Scientists vary in their approaches and beliefs just as you and I do. Not all studies are presented with results that are not affected by biased and prejudiced theories.

We are constantly told that the average citizen would have to consume tons of a specific carcinogen or harmful chemical agent used to preserve or color our foods before we are lethally or noticeably affected. Have you ever thought about the accumulative affect of the total number of toxins incorporated in every kind of food you eat or liquids you drink and the frequency with which you consume them over a period of time?

How long would it take you to die or be adversely affected if you continuously ate a peanut butter and jelly sandwich sprinkled with arsenic? Not only your sandwich but your water, your sodas, teas, coffee — everything you consumed had just a touch of arsenic? Let's suppose your favorite foods are not only sprinkled with arsenic but a little cyanide. Perhaps one or two occasions may not matter, but even the smallest amounts from the cradle to adulthood will eventually kill you.

Think about it! Not only do we have just <u>one</u>, <u>two</u>, or even <u>ten</u> harmful chemicals in our food supply, but dozens and dozens of them from fertilization of the lettuce in the field to the carrots in your T.V. dinner and baby foods.

And we wonder why there is so much cancer — so many medical disorders. Please examine closely the document on <u>Common Additives in People and Pet Foods</u>.

I have had personal experience in knowing and feeling the difference in medical recoveries supported by adulterated (toxic-based) foods versus those that are not. Had I not experienced the difference, I would not have a testimony.

Arsenic is used as a growth additive to stimulate the maturity of a baby chick to an adult chicken in far fewer days than it actually requires.

Health cannot be **restored** or **disease prevented** if the foods are irradiated or pumped full of harmful chemicals consumed on a **daily** basis.

For those of you who **do not care** and like things just the way they are

— please be my guest — but for those of us who do care what goes into our bodies and wish to be in the best health that we can and want to provide the same for our children we demand the right to do so. It's time for truth to come out of the closet where it's been a prisoner too long!

What We Eat and How We Treat Our Bodies Should Be a Matter of Choice — An Inalienable Right

There will be those who are extremists as with any issue noteworthy of controversy.

There will be those who will insist on the use of herbs in ways that most reasonable and honest people will be totally against - just as in a similar analogy, where persons who <u>claim</u> to be Christians do horrific things in the <u>name of Christianity</u> and God when in truth, God never approved of such behavior.

<u>There is room for both naturopathic and reasonable approaches to conventional medicine.</u>

The primary care physician and herbalist can work hand in hand — particularly with patients who need treatment at home after complicated conditions or end-stage diseases are treated at the hospitals. **Herbal hospices can be cost effective as well as restoring human dignity and the quality of life.** As I have chosen to use conventional diagnostic aides, such as blood tests, x-rays, and histopathology (biopsies), so can modern day practitioners — working together as a team — come up with the best treatment for the patient by making all information available as to the known successes and failures of both worlds and allowing the patient to choose. <u>There should be no other way to practice medicine.</u> To do anything less would be a monopoly of mind, body and soul - stealing the very essence of life's function <u>the ability to choose</u>!

<u>The caution is this</u> - The choice of one human being cannot and should not destroy the existence or well being of another, for we are then breaking a <u>spiritual law</u> that does have severe and eternal consequences whether we choose to believe this or not.

<u>The following statements are for the purposes of thought — to accept or reject as a possible truth</u>:

One can <u>sincerely</u> believe something <u>all his or her life</u>, but be sincerely wrong - because one believes a thing does not make it so; for example:

*   One can believe <u>with all his or her heart</u> that the sun will not rise the next morning, but regardless of your belief <u>the sun will rise</u>;
*   One can believe that just because a <u>fleet</u> of airplanes all look alike that all are going to the same place, only to find that flight 7 is going to <u>Israel</u> (where you want to go) but you get flight 3 going to <u>Egypt</u>. You will not get to Israel no matter how hard you believe it to be so, but instead you will be in Egypt, a place totally different from what you expected.

Your Children - Their Food is Important Too

<u>Your children do not have to</u>:

1.   Have tubes implanted in their ears for chronic ear infections

2.   Be put on deadly chemicals and drugs for hyperactivity, which is caused by the foods in their diets

3.   Be sent home to die from curable cancers

4.   Be put on drugs for seizures that are most likely cased by diet

And what about the poisons you eat being passed on to your unborn child or your young nursing child? Don't believe the lie that it makes no difference - smoking and alcohol kill - <u>so do drugs in foods</u>.

You and your children do not have to suffer from the various ailments that you do.

Just as there are charlatans and quacks in the area of modern medicine or <u>any occupation</u> there are and will be an increase of quacks in alternative medicine. Be careful and first examine <u>the success rate</u> of the practitioner, the <u>length of time</u> in practice, and the <u>testimonies</u> of those who have actually been helped by that practitioner. Support him or her according to your own spiritual orientation, if you have one.

When Do Harmless Herbs Become Dangerous?

1. When man has tampered with and manipulated the medicinal essence of a plant to where it has been destroyed for its intended uses. Specifically in the so-called process of extracting the active ingredient as discussed earlier. The rest of the plant is discarded - this now <u>altered portion</u> (a new substance) is introduced into our bodies no longer natural, but a toxin is the <u>real reason</u> for severe and fatal reactions to penicillin and aspirin.

2. Did you know that penicillin is derived from the mold on the leaves of the herb hyssop? The "powers that be" instead of using this great medicinal plant, not only extracts portions of it, but <u>adds</u> all kinds of toxic preservatives such as FORMALDEHYDE (an embalming fluid) and then blames the resulting reactions of the patient being allergic to the penicillin when in fact for most cases it is the toxic <u>additives</u> causing these reactions. This is what I firmly believe happened with Joe and Fran Berry's dog "Biddie" (see testimony).

3. Biddie was doing extremely well <u>until</u> the introduction of prescribed amoxicillin from the pharmacists. "Sweet Pea" (now my dog) who had the severe skin lesions and generalized organ-system breakdown with lymphadenopathy (all lymph nodes of the body enlarged) also responded extremely negative - reversing in clinical signs, which had formerly progressed well. If the body has little leverage to fight back even the penicillin and its derivatives (with its additives) seem to worsen the conditions. Look on the bottles of any injectable penicillin and you will see formaldehyde listed as a preservative along with other preservatives.

4. Instead of the "powers that be" making available the willow bark — the medicinal plant which contains the ingredient "salicin" in aspirin — the process of so-called "extraction of the main ingredient" is used and we are given man-made poison resulting in all kinds of side effects, such as internal hemorrhage by thinning of the blood. It is not the plant itself but the creation of another substance by <u>man's intervention</u>.

5. Encouragement should be directed into the safer and cheaper alternative medicines and dietary or nutritional approaches to our devastating and chronic diseases.

6. Herbs do not care what <u>we</u> call a disease. They just heal all of the body.

7. "And their fruit shall be for food and their <u>leaf</u> for healing." Ezekiel 7:12

8. <u>My ideas and realizations are not new</u>. People throughout history, from the beginning of time have known that herbs heal and good <u>unadulterated</u> foods <u>restore and maintain</u> our bodies' functions for which they have been designed.

9. Regardless of our spiritual orientations, something motivates each human being to rise everyday and seek to maintain the essence of his or her body and if this essence is lacking in food and water we will surely die. It does not matter if you are an atheist, Christian, Buddhist, etc. - refraining from foods <u>indefinitely</u> brings physical death to our "earth suits" as I call them.

10. I choose to believe the Biblical scriptures when God says:
    "I have given you every herb bearing seed...to you it shall be for meat..
    And to every beast of the earth...I have given every green herb for
    meat;"   Genesis 1:29 & 30

11. Herbs such as garlic, cayenne, and horseradish will also nourish your vegetable garden or any plant and enhance their growth and endurance. I see it every day.

What I Think about Doctors

I am a doctor. I am a servant to the people who seek my services.

Doctors are no greater or no less than any other human being. We all are precious in the sight of God.

We sit in a seat of great honor to offer the gift of healing in the face of suffering and disease. Fellow human beings place their most precious possession in our hands - their bodies. In the case of a veterinarian, the life of the pet is placed in our hands. We must treat life as a sacred gift and not ours to abuse and use but to restore in every way **possible by the most natural means.** Too often it is we doctors who act out the notion that the patient is here to serve us; forgetting that the true mandate of the Hippocratic oath is one of service aiming for perfection in diagnosis, treatment, and restoring the patient to physical, mental, emotional, and spiritual wholeness — working together with the patient as a team with the goal of preserving a quality of life for that patient.

The insurance companies, the FDA, the pharmaceutical companies, and the administration of aberrant hospital policies too often undermine and prevent the purposeful goals cited above in those health care professionals who wish to accept their mandate to heal, not steal from the people they serve.

What Do I Think of Chiropractors

Like any profession, there are the competent and the incompetent.

One of those competent saved my life in 1989 (see testimonies of Dr. Frank Alfono and Buffy Denny). He was the first to correctly diagnose my herniated disc by x-ray in July 1989. It took the conventional process a whole year to diagnose my condition by the use of a myologram, which translated into extra money, extra pain, extra emotional stress. Thank God for Dr. Shidhu who confirmed Dr. Alfono's original diagnosis.

After her examination, Dr. Denise Conner (of College Park, Maryland) gave me excellent advice immediately after the auto accident and referred me to the office of Dr. Mitchell, explaining they were better equipped to handle my injuries.

Dr. Mitchell of Silver Spring, Maryland then treated me for disc and acute muscle strain problems. I was very impressed with her clinical exam, assessment, diagnosis and treatment (see documents).

To my surprise I was forced to change from her excellent chiropractic care to a conventional orthopedic surgeon. The same attorney who had questionable ethical tactics insisted on this change not because I was receiving inferior care (which was hardly the case) but because in his words he "wouldn't know what to ask a chiropractor in the courtroom."

I have had one unpleasant experience with a chiropractor — not because of excessive charge but a lack of professionalism in approach and in executing his skills. In my opinion, as a doctor of conscience, I could not refer him to anyone with assurance their problems would be met with their best and total interests in mind or that he would have the capability to do so. Perhaps I am wrong. I hope so.

Good chiropractors can be invaluable in conjunction with a competent herbalist and/or primary care physician.

Make Your Doctors and Hospitals Accountable

1. Get your doctor to explain your condition to your understanding.

2. Demand an explanation of why they are choosing or have chosen a certain drug to use in your case.

3. Ask for a discussion of side effects and how the doctor expects them to affect you — if at all.

4. **Never allow surgery to be scheduled without your absolute understanding and consent.**

5. We as patients should never accept this trend of "just fifteen minutes with the patients and move on" attitude. Good, caring doctors and nurses do not like this movement any more than we do. I am a doctor, but I have been on the patient end of things more times than I cared to, and it has opened my eyes to the great travesty in which this country is involved. **Too many people are shuffled, misused, and abused by the system of a few who control the dollars and cents.**

6. As doctors we are servants - gifted to bring healing to the soul that seeks us out - granted there are suit happy derelicts who have no just claims, but our system must change back to the era of the Marcus Welby's, the Ben Casey's, the Hippocrates of yesteryear, at least in commitment of heart. When medicine becomes motivated by the dollar, that soul will pay the consequences, whether we believe it or not, we do have to answer to a higher authority!

What Do Herbs Do When Death Is Inevitable?

1. <u>Relieve pain</u> naturally, without side effects of drowsiness, incapacitation, and dementia. They will relieve your pain or help to relieve it.

2. Within twenty-four hours of the dreaded diagnosis to amputate and rearrange my leg as the only way to relieve my pain and distortion, <u>three</u> herb formulas <u>removed</u> all pain I had suffered from for more than a year. These formulas — H formula, Rheum-aid and B F &C are mentioned in other chapters.

3. <u>The pain disappeared or was reduced</u> from my herniated disc, my back spasms, my shingles, my hand, my nerve-exposed tooth, my nail punctured foot — all were relieved of agonizing pain.

4. <u>Organic</u> (not distilled, which is robbed of its vitamins and minerals) apple cider vinegar; raw, unfiltered honey; and organic cayenne all worked synergistically to naturally replace the potassium loss from damaged and aging cells, restoring the rejuvenating energy needed for healing.

5. Just these few selected foods and herbs offer so much more in terms of their healing properties. Time does not allow in Volume I to expand. **I urge readers to do their own research and try for themselves.**

6. <u>Anecdote</u> - Keep in mind that some of the very same drugs used for anesthesia in animals are also used for anesthesia in people; therefore, if these herbs will relieve pain or discomfort in animals (particularly mammals) then they will for people. **The issue of euthanasia and suffering in people must be addressed in light of this fact. People should have the right of discussion and choice.**

What Can We Do to Help the Organic Farmer?

How Can We Get Better Foods on Our Supermarket Shelves Instead of Way Out Places with Way Out Prices?

1. Go to your local supermarkets and ask to speak to the produce manager. Tell them you would like to see more organic products or you will be forced to shop elsewhere, such as stores like Fresh Fields, where you are able to get chemical free produce.

2. Challenge the farm credit system to be accountable to their own mandates.
   a. a government-sponsored agency set up by Congress to give loans to those who need them; an establishment that we as consumers need to know more about
   b. they've been deliberately discriminating against qualified organic farmers with good credit (some turned down six to eight times within the last ten years) therefore, farmers must pay everything out of pocket
   c. major difference between conventional and organic farmers is that natural fungicides are not as effective as synthetic (or chemical) fungicides by comparison therefore, there is a greater risk of crop loss - organic farmers provide more jobs for laborers because they are needed to manually remove weeds - USDA and FDA therefore determine residue levels to assure safe food supply by conducting studies to determine long term and accumulative effects.

3. Buy directly in groups or via wholesale/retail distributors.

4. Contact your congressman and express your desires for better chemical free foods to be available in local supermarkets.

5. Keep accurate records of all legitimate medical recoveries diagnosed as irreversible but were reversed or improved by natural means of diet or diet plus other modes of alternative medicine.

6. Support all your trustworthy organic merchants and growers.

There Are Good People out There Who Want to Listen

I know that there are good people of conscience belonging to these "powers that be" - Congress, USDA, FDA, pharmaceutical companies, insurance companies, AMA, AVMA, and the other industries which help to control all aspects of our health care system.

They just need to be educated to the truth - like myself. What person would deny the best for all concerned once exposed to the truth?

Unless, of course, greed, self grandisement, individual gain, power and control be the motivating factors smothering the <u>desire</u> to cooperate and compromise - to make things work for the good of all.

This book is appealing to those of conscience. To those in high places of policy change as well as to those on the grass roots level. Working together in truth always brings about better changes. Not everyone can get everything they ask for, but thirteen colonies came together to bring about this United States of America - not perfect, but better than most.

Can You Make a Difference?
Can You and I? You Bet We Can!
Stand up for Your Health! Stand up!

Why am I so adamant in exposing the hidden agenda of the establishment? The answers to cancer cures and other medical conditions have been denied to the public. Just think carefully about what you are about to read.

1. I almost died - Had I accepted the conventional response of "there's nothing more we can do" or "your job is quite stressful, perhaps that's why your back still hurts" — a ridiculous answer for a patient with a history of a 1,200 to 1,500-pound animal falling on her only one and a half months before with hematomas of the back and blocked bowels.

2. I almost remained a cripple. Misalignment led to horrible rotational distortion, PERMANENT PAIN, distortion of my limb, and NO better answer than amputation and reconstruction with pins and screws.

3. I almost became virtually a one-handed individual. With time, my hand may have totally contracted to a bird claw position, with constant, shocking pain.

This was the legacy that modern medicine had to offer me. Keeping from me the valuable information that saved my life, the work and writings of Jethro Kloss in his book Back to Eden, the classic guide to herbal medicine, natural foods, and home remedies in the authentic Kloss Family Heirloom Edition. As of August 16, 1994, I have the explicit written permission of Jethro Kloss' family granddaughter, Doris Kloss Gardiner, to reproduce any information from his writings I deem necessary to include in my book (see document at the end of this chapter).

I hereby state, without flinching, that as a practitioner of the healing arts I AM ANGRY to have been deceived and duped into thinking that the methods of modern medicine are the only effective ways to treat life-threatening diseases such as cancer, diabetes, and many others as well as many chronic and acute disorders of every system of the body. As a matter of fact, Jethro Kloss, more than 55 years ago tried to offer the world, through the National Cancer Research Institute, his definitive cures through the very simple things of life. But greed, power, and arrogance of the powers that be then, just as they do now, ignored him and rejected this man's desire to help reduce the suffering of Americans, which I will go so far to say is not only caused by the powers that be, but are perpetuated by them. The love of and the compulsion for power and control of the masses is their motivation.

It was the work of Jethro Kloss that saved my life and the lives of many of my patients. His book was used almost exclusively to lead me in a modified approach to successfully convert a fulminating bone cancer called fibrosarcoma to a benign lump called a fibroma on the leg of a dog named "Deja" (see documents). Dogs and cats are mammals just as we are and are prone to get the same diseases we do: cancers of all types, diabetes, blood disorders, skin disorders, epilepsy, leukemia, AIDS, etc. Therefore, if herbs and diet can help reverse their conditions, it certainly can help reverse ours. It did for me and I choose to <u>share</u> the information.

I owe my recoveries to people like Jethro Kloss and Paul Bragg (see bibliography) and I refuse to allow the work of these men of God to be further hidden from the American people and the world if citizens s<u>o choose</u> to know what <u>they said</u> and what they <u>did</u> to help end the suffering they saw around them.

Following is a copy of Jethro Kloss' heart-felt letter to the National Cancer Research Institute and statements of their response to Mr. Kloss.

Help me to help you and your loved ones. Let's make the powers that be accountable for the unnecessary deaths that have gone on for the last fifty-five years or more. The insurance companies must include <u>creditable avenues</u> of alternative medicine - <u>if we choose to</u> include them as part of our health care system.

(The following excerpt from p. 459 of <u>BACK TO EDEN</u> is reprinted with permission from BACK TO EDEN BOOKS, Copyright (c) 1992, by the Jethro Kloss Family.)

"Many years ago, before I attempted to treat cancer and had taken it for granted that there was no cure, I made up my mind I would find out the cause of cancer; so I looked up the records to find out in which countries of the earth cancer was most prevalent. When I learned this, I looked to find out what food the peoples of these countries ate. I found that in the civilized nations of earth where a large amount of meat and rich and luxurious foods were consumed, cancer was more prevalent. In the uncivilized nations where they ate plain, natural foods, cancer was very rare. In some instances where cancer was rare, when the people there learned of the diet used by civilized peoples and used it, cancer increased.

People used to think meat was the great cause of cancer, but in my research I found that people who did not eat meat at all had cancer, and I also found that people who did not eat meat at all, with whom I was well acquainted with their habits of diet, had cancer. They were eating denatured foods and bad combinations of foods of such a nature that these caused much waste matter to accumulate in the system, which caused the different organs to become diseased, and cancer many times resulted.

After learning this, I felt quite sure that I was on the right road to find out the cause of cancer, and since then I have known it. Denatured foods have been robbed of their minerals and vitamins, which are the life-giving properties, the very parts which God put in the different foods to keep the blood pure and to sustain the nervous system.

BACK TO EDEN BOOKS®

P.O. Box 1439 • Loma Linda, California 92354 • Phone (714) 796-9615
FAX (714) 796-9746

August 16, 1994

We are happy to give you permission to use material from
BACK TO EDEN. We only request that you give credit, such as:

"Reprinted with permission from BACK TO EDEN BOOKS, Copyright (c)
1992, by the Jethro Kloss Family."

Good success to you in marketing your new book.

With kindest regards,

Doris Kloss Gardiner

DOCTORS OF THE NATIONAL CANCER RESEARCH INSTITUTE
WASHINGTON, D.C.

Dear Gentlemen:

Knowing that you are vitally interested in the work to which our government has called you and in which it has shown a deep interest by the large appropriation it has allowed, and realizing that the people generally are looking and watching for the National Cancer Research Institute to accomplish great things for the benefit of the many, many rapidly increasing sufferers from cancer, I am constrained to write you and tell you that I absolutely have a cancer cure that will cure any cancer which has not gone too far.

I know the cause, prevention, and cure of cancer, also of heart diseases, pneumonia, asthma, infantile paralysis, gonorrhea, syphilis, and tuberculosis. I use no poisonous drugs. What I use would harm no one, no matter what his trouble, but would benefit him. I have spent a great deal of money, much labor, and deep research in finding out these things.

I am getting along in years and do not myself want any practice. I wish to give what I have discovered to practitioners who have a license to practice. This is what I would like to do for the benefit of the Cancer Research Institute that the people of the world may have the benefit of what I have found to be a real cure.

Will you permit one or more of your research doctors who know of a cancer patient who has not been treated by radium or X-ray to let me treat this patient under their special observation by the methods which I have found successful? Thus they will see everything done for this patient and will know that a cure really can be effected by the means which I use. You may provide the patient and the patient may be kept anywhere where there are necessary facilities for treatment.

Not a few prominent citizens of this city who know of my work are urging that I write you thus. They feel sure that you will be pleased to give me this opportunity, for we all know that the government has appointed you to make every effort to find a remedy for cancer. I feel condemned that I have not done more to make public my findings. I must make them public and I would like to do it through you.

If the above terms do not meet with your approval, please advise me.

Most respectfully yours,

JETHRO KLOSS

The Cancer Research Institute doctor who answered my letter said they were not in a position to accept my offer, but they suggested that I go to some hospital which takes cancer patients or to some regular practitioner.

They asked me to write out my treatment. To do this means a great deal. Other physicians have asked me again and again to put my findings on paper, not only on cancer but on other diseases as well. One army surgeon asked if I were going to take all this knowledge with me into the grave. Because I am willing to help any physician or group of physicians in helping humanity, I am now presenting the treatments which I have found to be highly successful.

No animal experimentation is required. Nothing poisonous is used. What I use would benefit anyone.

I have been asked many times by physicians and others how I knew that certain cases were cancer. My reply was that I knew only what their physician said it was, and what the laboratory test showed.

In advanced cases of cancer and in other serious cases, it is necessary to have a nurse who is very thorough and persevering in her work and who understands the value of the treatment, diet, water, massage, herbs, sunshine, fresh air, exercise, and rest.

It is very hard to write out all my findings and practical experiences, but I trust I have said enough and made it plain enough so that somebody will be benefited by them.

What Do My Pets Eat? Does Fasting Help?

If finances permitted, like many of you, I want my pets to have the very best that I can afford. Any medical and nutritional knowledge helps me to provide them with optimal health as domesticated animals, when I can.

Given a choice, I would not feed my animals processed feed at all - so-called "natural" or otherwise. Be mindful, the same cattle fed estrogens and antibiotics consumed by your pets are causing similar problems in yourselves — breast, prostate and uterine diseases. I have had dogs all of my life - from cradle to present. Ever since I was mature enough to care for a pet I have been blessed to be taught just how precious Yeshua's creatures are to Him. For those who are of the Christian persuasion, let me remind or inform you that God made a covenant not only with man but with the animal kingdom as well, that He would not totally destroy life by a flood again by displaying the seal of this covenant with a bow (rainbow) in the sky.

"I will [earnestly] remember my covenant or solemn pledge, which is between Me and you and every living creature of all flesh, and the waters shall no more become a flood to destroy and make all flesh corrupt."

"And God said, Noah, this rainbow is the token or sign of the covenant or solemn pledge, which I have established between Me and all flesh upon the earth.

Genesis 9:15 & 17 King James Amplified

One day a week, do not give your pet any solid foods. Instead offer just honey, lemon, and water. This is very cleansing and energy stimulating, preserving the gastrointestinal tract.

Because of my extended misfortunes, my pets are greatly compromised. But to those of you who lack the financial means as I do, choose a brand of commercial food (for example Dad's econ-o-mets) that is less advertised and supplement your pet's diet with herbs/foods such as garlic, onions, cayenne pepper, honey, parsley. Add cod liver oil, wheat germ and feed whatever vegetables and pasta they will eat. In Volume II, I will be more specific, for time does not allow for details.

Conventional veterinarians say that raw onions cause a life-threatening disease inducing hemorrhage and shock syndromes. In the eleven years I have been using raw onions and garlic in my own dogs (daily) and patients I have never seen such claims. Dogs eat raw onions in the wild all the time. It is my opinion that what they are concluding as onions being the cause is something else. I have personally owned or cared for several dogs over eleven years and many more patients. Need it be said anymore of what I consider law by conventional standards.

The oldest dog I have treated was a thirty-year-old mixed breed female who required a venereal tumor of the vulva removed. She never had been fed dog food in her life. She was a country dog eating country food.

For those who wish to continue with conventional methods, such as radiation and chemotherapy, I fight for your right to chose as well, but we who don't want it have had no choice for ourselves or our pets.

Selected Herbs for Some Conditions

Instead of toxic chemicals, I have used the following with success. Volume II will contain a detailed discussion of this topic.

1.   Heart/lung - congestive heart failure, cardiomegaly, cardiomyopathy, etc
   a. instead of digitalis (a deadly toxin) - "H" formula (by Nature's Way) containing cayenne, Hawthorn berries, vitamin E (water soluble) and lecithin or dandelion, honey, apple cider vinegar and cayenne
   b. instead of lasix (a nephrotoxin - destroys kidneys) for fluid in lungs (pulmonary edema) or anywhere in body is Burdock, cornsilk or parsley and garlic
   c. instead of aminophylline - bronchial dilators for lung expansion and ease of breathing - same as b. but also comfrey and anise
   d. Super Garlic (by Schiff) restores and maintains blood pressure (high or low)

2. Liver
   a. Chaparral (been removed for consumption by FDA) - excellent for purification
   b. Black Cohosh
   c. Milk thistle, Red Clover, Burdock
   d. Sarsaparilla
   e. Super Garlic
   f. Cayenne

3. Kidney/stones - bladder
   a. Couchgrass (dissolves stones)
   b. Burdock (diuretic)
   c. Cornsilk
   d. Red Clover (blood purifier)
   e. Super Garlic
   f. Cayenne

4. Blood Disorders
   a. Brewer's yeast (preferably grown on sugar beets or molasses not those as by-product of beer)
   b. Super Garlic
   c. Apple cider vinegar
   d. Cayenne
   e. Black Cohosh

f.   Burdock

g.   Pau d'Arco

5.   Muscles and Bone
   a.   "H" Rheum-aid and Bone Flesh and Cartilage (BF&C) by Nature's Way
   b.   Others in Volume II

6.   Skin
   a.   Super Garlic
   b.   AKN by Nature's Way
   c.   FruitAloe (see back of book)
   d.   Kelp
   e.   Raw wheat germ
   f.   Many others

7.   Nervous System
   a.   "B & B" by Nature's Way
   b.   Combination of chamomile, scullcap, passion flower, honey, hops
   c.   Garlic and cayenne

8.   Gastrointestinal Tract
   a.   Lemons - lemon water
   b.   Aloe vera (FruitAloe) or pure aloe
   c.   Slippery Elm
   d.   Catnip
   e.   Peppermint and spearmint
   f.   Cascara
   g.   Others

9.   All Conditions - if severe, must be monitored by a professional, experienced in clinical signs and treatment.

10.   Steroids - Are killers and depress the immune system (the entire body). Herbs such as sarsaparilla, wild yam and yucca used without the side effects of conventional preparations.

Conclusive Comments:

I regret to say that time, urgency of patients, and shoe-string budget has not permitted me to put on paper all that I wish to share, but I hope that what I have managed to record helps you, the reader, with the listening ear, to hear what I am saying.

Blood Transfusions and Organ Transplants:
Who Are We to Choose Who Lives and Who Dies?
And Are They Really Necessary Anyway?

1.   Blood transfusions are commonly done in veterinary medicine.

2.   Both transfusions and organ transplants were performed in animals for their efficacy prior to their use in humans.

3.   In the more than 4,000 patients I have seen over the last thirteen years (while I owned and managed my own clinic and emergency facility in Washington, D.C. for five of those years), I witnessed and treated many a shattered and mutilated body in need of blood transfusions, according to the standards of conventional medicine.

4.   What do you think indigenous cultures (who are dependent on the land) do when they have such cases? There are no Mt. Sinai hospitals — no Johns Hopkins Universities — no NIH's — **just the healers of the earth — the same molecules of which you are made.** The hemoglobin molecule of a plant and the hemoglobin of man is almost identical except man has an iron component where the plant has magnesium. Dwellers of the land did and still do just as I did and do — restore the damaged organs to normal functions (within minutes and hours) by nourishing those organs almost destroyed - such as the spleen, kidney and liver. The bone marrow also can be naturally stimulated to its restored function. To impose a forced injection of someone else's bodily parts into yours is unnatural, therefore requiring anti-rejection drugs.

5.   Despite man's ignorance and arrogance and his desire to control, I thank God that people have still been saved — not by God's best way but a way, using transfusions and transplants.

6.   After seeing what I have seen, and the recoveries I have witness in the countless numbers of patients, there is no doubt that herbs and diet, devoid of harmful agents, can bring life to a bleeding and dying body - man or beast. Therefore, I choose to believe the following words of my God:

> "He causeth the grass to grow for the cattle, and herb for the service of man: that he may bring forth food out of the earth"

> Psalm 104:14 King James Version

7.   Fight for your choices! Let's not allow government and the powers that be to make the choices for us that will cost the lives of ourselves and our loved ones. At least, by the Freedom of Information Act, we deserve the restoration of the sovereign will to treat the only real essence that belongs to us — our bodies. To the Christian we are owned by our Saviour who bought us with the price of His own blood.

8.   Please, again, this is a personal choice — hoping it is yours also but so be it if not.

9.   Just think about the sacredness of your health and the right to know all the information available that has been successful before you submit to the knife on that operating table or receive that blood that may be contaminated with HIV. STOP AND THINK!

Holistic Approaches I Do Not Endorse

1. There are many and varied approaches classified as holistic medicine — I do not subscribe to all of them.

2. There are many I know very little or nothing about - their origins, uses, and their effectiveness.

3. One of my clients has written a testimony in which she mentions my approach as "voodoo" — for her it was meant as a compliment. She is a dear person, I respect her and we have discussed the issue. Because of my personal spiritual orientation I am not comfortable with such practices as voodoo and witchcraft.

4. Let me make it very clear to the reader that I firmly do not stand in the position of judging the hearts of people for whatever choices they make for their own spiritual fulfillment in their lives. I can only share mine and tell you what has worked to bring me into perfect spiritual peace and harmony with the God of this universe Who created me.

5. Not even God touches your will to choose given exposure to all the information you need.

6. Part of my mission, I believe, is to help anyone I can, who wishes to hear what I have to share, to improve the health of their pets or themselves based upon my experience and findings.

Anecdote

Because of the vast numbers of herbs and plants used around the globe, diversed by cultural, medicinal, and spiritual backgrounds, it would be impossible for anyone to be completely knowledgeable about their efficacy, safety, and usage. Those plants of which I know little or nothing about or with which I have limited or no experience or those I just prefer not to use, I cannot porfessionally, in good conscience, endorse.

The only products that I can fully endorse are those herbs and herbal combinations I have personally prepared as tonics, salves, or poultices and other preparations that I develop according to the clinical signs and assessment of each patient. In my experience there is no singular cookbook recipe to meet the needs of each individual who, by nature, is always different than the next.

Memorials - To Those Whose Spirits Will Forever Be in My Heart

These two special creatures of God spurred my desire to share my knowledge:

Cody — That gentle giant of a Shepherd is responsible for the motivation of this book. His pain, his agony complicated by that dreaded disease called Demodex mange showed me just how vulnerable we have made not only them, but ourselves as well. Cody showed me it was not too late to treat the most wretched levels of this disease but that I do need proper facilities and conditions such as warmth, good shelter, bathing equipment, good lighting, and, of course, an almost perfect diet and the best quality of herbs available — to be able to repeat and maintain the required treatments and dietary management and then the process will reverse. Because of Cody, Sweat Pea now lives — destined to have died more than one year ago (see Sweat Pea's story). What really killed Cody was a lack of proper facilities due to my own financial situation. His death was not in vain.

Cindi — A beautiful, heart warming, smiling, special Dalmatian, afflicted with end-stage kidney disease. By the time I assumed Cindi's case she was quite compromised — yet immediately even with a change of diet (taken off all commercial preparations) and regular herbal infusions, she started turning around to a better quality of life. Sadly, no one could be home with her and there were no herbal clinics in which to admit her. The one day I stayed with Cindi in her own environment she showed tremendous improvement. Lack of this care revealed an immediate turn for the worse. Cindi received intravenous solutions of glucose and vitamins with oral herbal combinations to make her comfortable and she died peacefully at home with dignity. Again, had I the facilities I am confident Cindi would have lived. (see testimony under Kidney and Liver Conditions)

Ahmed — (see documents) A proud independent cat that suffered from a horrible flesh-eating, invading tumor called Rhabdomyosarcoma. The cancer invaded the muscles of his jaw and side of his neck and destroyed the many ducts to his salivary glands. He could no longer eat, only drool with his mouth open. Thank God for His herbs, diet ,and sunshine. Twelve-year old Ahmed lived two more years and may have lived longer had not his owner died of cancer leaving Ahmed to be cared for by people outside of the family.

151

Biddie — (see documents) That spitfirey little Terrier. Showing much promise of recovery just after one to two days from a horrific literally flesh-eating disease called Toxic epidermal necrosis (TEN), an affliction usually terminal to both people and dogs. Herbal treatment, though not in time, helped to bridge the gap of life into death more smoothly without long lasting agony, but death in slumber.

Christa Star — (see story) My beloved horse, a champion of courage, fortitude, and loyalty. She taught me much about how well the body can recover time and again from insult after insult. How the will to live with tender love and care dominates over the push of death.

Danielle — My beautiful blue-eyed kitten who taught me that commercial foods do incite horrible skin lesions and heart disease and depravity of general well being. Lost to me due to financial circumstances.

Deja — (see documents) A patient, kind, gentle, mixed collie who withstood the hardships of having a huge flesh and bone eating cancer called Fibrosarcoma. With Deja's cooperation, she has shown that **malignant cancer can be changed to a benign piece of tissue by just changing diet, using vegetables, fruits, and herbal poultices as well as using oral infusions of the same** — a scientific wonder but routine in the centuries old use of herbs and proper diet.

Fluffy — (see testimony) Nobody controlled "Fluffy." She was born the leader of the pack, the household, and whatever else needed leadership. She was one of the joys (with her housemate Tom) in the Dennis household. Suffering from a tumor on the sternum over her heart, Fluffy showed me just how powerful raw unfiltered honey was "alone" in strengthening her heart.

Gigi — (see documents) A dear geriatric Standard Poodle who suffered from liver disease greatly accentuated by prolonged use of steroids, Gigi showed me that even the most severe blood work results given a will to live can turn around unbelievably. Again, lack of facilities contributed to proper care in time for Gigi, my deepest regret.

Made-It — A little eight-week-old female Boxer who had been crushed by its mother leaving some neurological damage and displacement of the shoulder and shock. "Made-it" was to make it — adequate facilities are important.

Peet — (see Story) The little ball of fur who started it all. She hardly ever left my side. She was truly an example of inner strength, exhibiting a will to live no matter how afflicted her body. And she made it, recovering from right- and left-sided congestive heart failure (with severe pulmonary edema) and crippling arthritis. Her heart was completely restored — no arrythmias — no pulmonary edema — no evidence of progressive liver damage — living from then eleven years old to sixteen years. She died from pyometra (an infected uterus which causes kidney shutdown in dogs) not heart failure. We were in the mountains where facilities were unavailable.

Rosie — (see documents) She was the life of two little girls and their father, who sought me out by referral. Their docile black lab was dying of lung cancer. She had been on cough suppressants and morphine-like derivatives leaving her knocked out and sluggish; yet she still had terrible, round-the-clock gagging. Rosie was so far from me, in Baltimore, Maryland. She did improve with diet and herbal combinations, but she needed closer monitoring and increased frequency of treatments, in short, a few days of intense hospitalization. She was laid to rest as best for all concerned, but her improvement in her quality of life gave definite promise to recovery had other factors, such as earlier treatment and a hospice facility, been provided.

Taka — (see documents on blood analysis, dated January 9, 1985, for Ruth Sockwell)
Taka was my very first case of diabetes. She was presented in ataxic (staggering) state which, within minutes of her examination, led to a type of coma called ketoacidosis (which is a life-threatening condition in diabetics — humans, dogs, and cats). Taka was restored within three days to an active, vibrant dog using only diet and herbs. Foods such as Jerusalem artichokes, stringbeans, and carrots naturally contain insulin. One or any combination of these was always included in her diet of prepared food that never included commercial dog food. Copious amounts of garlic (organic) was used. A glucose level of 324 was reduced to 63 without any negative clinical effects; because her glucose level was 63 instead of the expected range of 90 to 110. But clearly, the patient was no longer in danger of the life-threatening levels of glucose in her blood stream.

Taylor — (see testimony) A courageous, lovely collie who started out being the runt of the litter. He drank anti-freeze (which is reported to taste like Kool-Aid) causing immediate destruction of his kidneys. Taylor's willingness to adapt to his new diet and herbal treatments showed that terminal conditions or those thought terminal, have hope if caught in time. Chances were slim that he would live even beyond twenty-four hours. Again for Taylor, I had no facilities. Owners are emotionally involved and also cannot make minute-by-minute adjustments in treatment according to clinical signs — that's why hospitals are important or at least the opportunity for the physician to be present with the patient.

Their stories will be recorded in completion in Volume II. Through their sufferings and afflictions I have learned much to help those after them. If I have inadvertently left out any patient whose story would help you understand the plight of our (man and beast) journeys to better health, they will be included in Volume II.

Because animals are important to God, they are important to me.

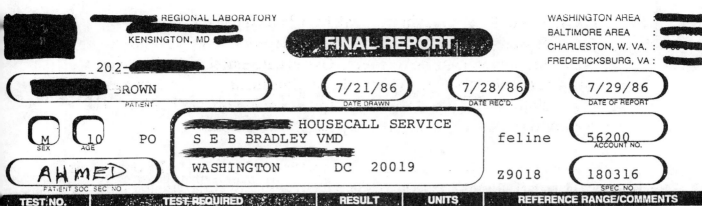

REGIONAL LABORATORY
KENSINGTON, MD

FINAL REPORT

WASHINGTON AREA :
BALTIMORE AREA :
CHARLESTON, W. VA. :
FREDERICKSBURG, VA :

202-

BROWN	7/21/86	7/28/86	7/29/86
PATIENT	DATE DRAWN	DATE REC'D.	DATE OF REPORT

HOUSECALL SERVICE
S E B BRADLEY VMD

WASHINGTON   DC   20019

M   10   PO
SEX   AGE

AHMED
PATIENT SOC SEC NO

feline   56200
ACCOUNT NO.

Z9018   180316
SPEC NO

TEST NO.	TEST REQUIRED	RESULT	UNITS	REFERENCE RANGE/COMMENTS

CLINICAL HISTORY: Submitted as tissue directly ventro-posterial-lateral to left ear; involved striated muscle. Patient presented on July 3, 1986 with large, firm, moderately circumscribed mass situated in the above location approximately 8cm in length and 6cm in width. History includes duration of what seemed only to be 7-10 days when noticed. Patient experiences no pain on deep or superficial palpation. Aspiration was totally negative. Upon incision (lateral) firm tissue of striated muscle origin bulged through opening. Only after external and internal treatment was the mass reduced to operable size and became well delineated. Underlying attachment became less. Patient was active pre and post operative.

GROSS: Specimen consists of two fragments of formalin fixed oval nodular fatty subcutaneous masses, the largest of which measures approximately 2.5x3.5x2cm in greatest dimensions. There are portions of hair bearing skin tissue attached to the specimen. Representative sections submitted in two cassettes.

MICROSCOPIC: Sections are covered on one surface by stratified squamous epithelium with adnexa. Present in the subcutis is a neoplastic mass consisting of well differentiated rather uniform fusiform cells which are quite randomly arranged. They have some tendency to form parallel bundles, and individually to interlace. Mitotic figures are rare. Present in the section is a portion of serous salivary gland and ducts which has been extensively infiltrated by the tumor. The tumor appears to be a rhabdomyosarcoma. It is bordered in part by normal appearing skeletal muscle which has been extensively invaded and in part destroyed by the tumor.

DIAGNOSIS: RHABDOMYOSARCOMA

AHMED
see
memorials

V.M.D., Ph.D.

Biddie, our female Jack Russell Terrier, could make your heart swell with joy as she sped across the fields just for the sheer fun of running. Her assertive barks and hunting prance enriched our lives with an appreciation for God's gifts to us. Imagine the letdown when we returned home one day and she emerged from the back yard, listless and swollen, with an angry rash on her underside. Her stay at the animal hospital and later with specialists provided no relief, although the doctors tried everything their training suggested. Finally, after valuable time was lost in lengthy tests, she was diagnosed as having Toxic Epidermal Necrosis, a rare and fatal disease which has no known cure.

At the time we were deciding to put her down, a friend happened to overhear our sad plight and suggested we contact Doc Bradley. Having exhausted the prevalent standard procedures, and realizing we were dealing with a hopeless case, we welcomed the positive attitude imparted by Doc. She immediately prescribed herbal remedies, both internal and external, for our poor Biddie, and, after loving administrations and prayer, darned if she didn't begin to come around !

Every sign of improvement was intently noted and rejoiced over, and our constant attention and loving care seemed to be fruitful. However, following a dose of antibiotics which we suspect contained a harmful preservative, she again lapsed, never to recover, and died in her sleep.

We believe that, had Doc seen Biddie soon enough, her style of faithful, natural healing could very well have saved our beloved pet. Although we lost our dog, our lives have been enriched in coming to know this dedicated doctor and loving friend.

But God never shuts a door without opening a window. Through Biddie's tragic illness we came to know Doc's style of treatment in the wonderful healing power of nature's medicine - *herbs*.

Fran was affected with chronic pain in both hips to the point that sleep was all but impossible; the pain even traveled down her legs and made any car transportation extremely uncomfortable.

A traditional doctor had prescribed anti-inflammatory drugs which were quite ineffective and didn't get to the root of the problem. Yet, several weeks on an herbal regimen have resulted in a remarkable reduction of pain to slight occasional discomfort. Even riding in a car has returned to being a pleasurable event.

Fran had also developed a "frozen" shoulder due to overly strenuous exercise causing a flare-up of a calcium deposit in the joint. Again, herbal applications and physical therapy seem to have alleviated the pain. The option of cortisone shots was undesirable - she doesn't want steroids in her body. Yes, the pain did last longer by going the natural route, but she feels healthier in the long run without any unnatural residues in the system. Herbal remedies as an alternative to "one pill for one bug" medicine have gained a foothold in our lives. Our minds and eyes have opened to the greatest pharmacy there is - Mother Earth !

Mayo, Maryland

11/2/94

![veterinary internal medicine logo]

date: _8/10/94_

client: ▬▬▬▬▬▬▬▬▬▬

Veterinarian: ▬▬▬▬▬▬▬

Client Discharge Information and Instructions

our pet, _Little Bit (Biddie)_ is now returned to your care. If you have
ny questions or there are any unusual developments, then please contact your
wn veterinarian or Dr. Hitt.

roblems diagnosed for your pet are: _Toxic Epidermal Necrosis (TEN)_
idiopathic (unknown cause) – poor prognosis

xercise for your pet should be normal / (special): _obviously she is painful_
and gentle handling with a blanket may be helpful

ood and water for your pet should be normal / special: _____

edications are none / unchanged / prescription / (dispensed):

drugs	instructions
Clindamycin 75mg	1 capsule twice a day orally
Baytril 20	1 tablet twice a day orally
Baby aspirin	1 per day with food

lease (call) / schedule an appointment with your veterinarian in _1_ days.
lease **schedule** an appointment at AVIM in ____ days or on _____.

omments: _The prognosis is poor. Animals and people die from TEN._
About half the cases can be identified as initiated by a drug, cancer,
or liver failure. About 1/2 are idiopathic. TEN is thought to be
some form of hypersensitivity reaction but does not respond to
steroids or antihistamine. We have tried imuran, prednisone, diphen-
hydramine with no significant improvement. Supportive care of fluids, vitamins,
nutrition and antibiotics have only helped keep her stable but not better.

Today she is the worst we've seen since sunday morning. I truly wish
I had a better scenario for you and Little Bit. This is a rare disease
and almost always fatal, cases that I am familiar with have died.

_____ Sincerely,

971-2127

Alexandria, VA 22310

CASE NO.:   X87-1072

OWNER:

SPECIES: Canine

IDENTIFICATION: Deja

MICROSCOPIC DESCRIPTION:
The specimen consists of a partially necrotic hypercellular mass which is
composed of interlacing tracts of poorly differentiated fibroblasts
surrounded by collagen. The mass lies adjacent to a zone of mature dense
fibrous connective tissue, compatible with a fascial plane.

DIAGNOSIS: FIBROSARCOMA, FASCIAL PLANE OF SKELETAL MUSCLE

COMMENT:
This is a highly aggressive neoplasm which has a distinct potential for
local recurrence and distant metastasis.

DVM, DACVP 16Nov87

*Deja- see memorials
also photos

Most significant case
to show actual
pathology of malignant
cancer converted to benign
tumo using herbal diet
in just 2 months*

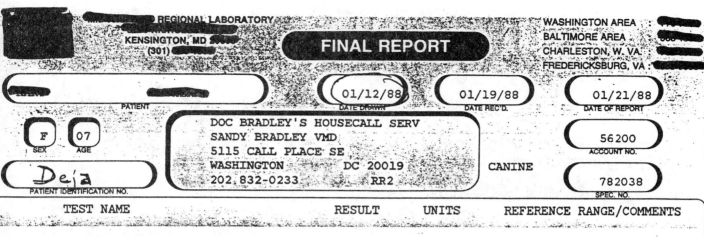

REGIONAL LABORATORY
KENSINGTON, MD
(301)

FINAL REPORT

WASHINGTON AREA
BALTIMORE AREA
CHARLESTON, W. VA
FREDERICKSBURG, VA

01/12/88	01/19/88	01/21/88
DATE DRAWN	DATE REC'D.	DATE OF REPORT

PATIENT

F	07
SEX	AGE

Deja

PATIENT IDENTIFICATION NO.

DOC BRADLEY'S HOUSECALL SERV
SANDY BRADLEY VMD
5115 CALL PLACE SE
WASHINGTON   DC 20019
202 832-0233   RR2

CANINE

56200
ACCOUNT NO.

782038
SPEC. NO.

TEST NAME	RESULT	UNITS	REFERENCE RANGE/COMMENTS

BIOPSY TISS GROSS&MICRO ANIMAL

CLINICAL HISTORY: Submitted as left leg. Entire lateral aspect
of carpal joint and lateral metacarpal joint.
Owner first noticed small swelling over a year
ago. Former vet took biopsy recommended watching
for growth over elbow. Continual growth lead to
attempts of surgical excision not all removed,
probably would re-occur. First of Nov. 87 chest
x-rays neg. One week later growth increased.
Last of Nov. amputation recommended. Later
x-rays reveal one questionable large spot.
Immediate amputation is recommended end of Dec.

GROSS: Specimen submitted in one container and contains
two pieces of formalin fixed raised rough
tannish white subcutaneous tissue, the larger
of which measures approximately 1x2.5x1.4cm in
greatest dimensions. The larger piece has a
strip of pale white hair bearing skin tissue
on one surface. Representative sections of the
larger piece is submitted in one cassette "A".
Representative sections of the smaller piece
is submitted in one cassette "B".

MICROSCOPIC:
88-00797
Sections are covered on one surface by stratified squamous epithelium with adnexa. Present
in the subcutis is a circumscribed but non-
encapsulated neoplasm composed of well differentiated fibroblasts arranged in interlacing
parallel bundles. The tumor is rather cellular.
The tumor cells are uniform and produce a
moderate quantity of collagen. Rare mitotic
figures are present. There is no well defined ✳✳✳
evidence of malignancy.

DIAGNOSIS: FIBROMA CELLULARE

VMD, PHD

Clinical Laboratory

July 8, 1994

We met Dr. Sandy Bradley about twelve years ago when everyone else had given up on our cat (Tom - Thomas Anthony) who had been injured very badly in some type of accident. His paw was infected and his ear was so mangled and infected that even the Animal Rescue League recommended that we have him put to sleep. We didn't want to exercise this option without trying further to save our son and grandson's beloved pet. We asked several people if they could recommend a good veterinarian. Finally, someone at the Animal Rescue League recommended Dr. Bradley to us, saying that in the field of veterinary medicine, she was excellent. Immediately, an appointment was made and indicated to her that we wanted her to make every effort possible to help Tom survive, even if we had to have a three-legged one ear cat. She was able to pull him thru this crisis without the loss of any of his parts. Our second crisis with Tom was when he was hit by a car and managed to crawl home where we found him under the porch half dead. Fortunately, with Dr. Bradley's skilled help, Tom is very much alive and enjoying being spoiled and loved by the Dennis family and with all his parts intact. Thus started our long relationship with her.

Fluffy Marie, our very stubborn mixed Calico and Persian cat was our only female. When she got ill, Dr. Bradley was the one we wanted to treat her, for we felt very confident that Fluffy would receive excellent care. When she recommended that she be spayed, we agreed immediately.

Dr. Bradley treated both our cats with herbs, using conventional methods when necessary, both thriving very well.

Although we were sorry for the misfortune Dr. Bradley had to endure, we enjoyed the fact she could treat our animals in our home. The animals seemed more comfortable being examined and getting their shots in an environment they were used to, as neither liked riding in a car or being in their carriers

Dr. Bradley helped us to save a poor little kitten that came to us half dead and so traumatized that it took over a year for him to make a sound. Now he is beginning to meow like a cat. Well four years have passed and Dusty Rose is now well and happy in the Dennis Household. Dusty is a Russian Blue.

In the summer of 1992, we experienced great losts in our lives that left many empty spaces. In July we lost Grandmother DeMouy and grandbaby Rachel within three weeks.

Fluffy grieved after Grandmother, not eating very well and moping around. Dr. Bradley came to administer to her and in the course of her examination she discovered that Fluffy had a tumor around her heart. Dr Bradley operated on her and worked diligently for several days to save her. However, Fluffy

(4)

died in September, 1992, after being
with us for twelve years. We
don't know who cried more Doc
or us. It was very comforting to
know that someone cared about
your pets as much as you do.

submitted by

████████████

Wash. D.C.

SPECIMEN #	TYPE	PRIMARY LAB	REPORT STATUS				
184-017-0186-0	S	VB	FINAL	PG 1		03 B	

ADDITIONAL INFORMATION

CX PED L FAX RESULTS TO 20
2-889-9569

CLINICAL INFORMATION

SPECIES - CANINE

PHYSICIAN ID.   PATIENT ID.

PATIENT NAME		SEX	AGE (YR./MOS.)
▓▓▓▓▓		F	

PT. ADD.

ACCOUNT

ANIMAL CLINIC OF ▓▓▓▓▓   081093
DR. ▓▓▓▓▓   VJ
                                       VV
WASHINGTON   , DC
202-   VAA

DATE OF SPECIMEN	DATE ENTERED	DATE REPORTED	
07/03/93	07/04/93	07/05/93	9709

TEST		RESULT		LIMITS	
DIAG.MULTI-CHEM) PROFILE I					
CALCIUM	↓	6.2 L MG/DL		9.0 - 11.5	VI
PHOSPHORUS	↑	10.6 H MG/DL		2.7 - 5.7	VI
GLUCOSE, SERUM				50 - 120	VI
SPECIMEN WAS TOO HEMOLYZED FOR ANALYSIS.					
PLEASE RESUBMIT AT NO CHARGE.					
BUN				5 - 24	VI
SPECIMEN WAS TOO HEMOLYZED FOR ANALYSIS.					
PLEASE RESUBMIT AT NO CHARGE.					
URIC ACID		0.8 MG/DL		0.0 - 1.0	VI
CHOLESTEROL		144 MG/DL		137 - 275	VI
TOTAL PROTEIN		9.0 G/DL		4.9 - 9.6	VI
ALBUMIN	↑	6.0 H G/DL		2.1 - 4.0	VI
BILIRUBIN, TOTAL	↑	10.2 H MG/DL		0.0 - 0.6	VI
ALKALINE PHOSPHATASE	↑	1020 H IU/L		20 - 200	VI
LDH	↑	4260 H IU/L		20 - 250	VB
SPECIMEN WAS TOO HEMOLYZED FOR ANALYSIS.					
PLEASE RESUBMIT AT NO CHARGE.					
CHEMISTRY RESULTS REPEATED.					
SGOT (AST)		160 H IU/L		25 - 105	VB
SODIUM		112 L MEQ/L		139 - 153	VB
POTASSIUM		4.0 MEQ/L		3.7 - 5.2	VB
CHLORIDE		76 L MEQ/L		103 - 121	VB
CREATININE, SERUM		1.4 MG/DL		0.5 - 2.0	VB
SGPT		140 H IU/L		- 10 - 75	VB
GAMMA-GLUTAMYLTRANSFEPTIDASE		0 IU/L		0 - 10	VB
TRIGLYCERIDES		226 MG/DL			VB
CANINE NORMALS: 20-80 MG/DL					
DATA INSUFFICIENT FOR OTHER SPECIES.					
AMYLASE, SERUM		416		0	VB
SPECIMEN WAS HEMOLYZED. RESULT MAY BE					
ADVERSELY AFFECTED.					
BUN/CREATININE RATIO					
CALCULATION NOT PERFORMED DUE TO NON-				DED TEST	
GLOBULIN, TOTAL		3.0			
A/G RATIO		2.00 H		58	
CBC WITH DIFFERENTIAL					
WHITE BLOOD COUNT		7.8		.0	VB
RED BLOOD COUNT		6.18		50	VB
HEMOGLOBIN		16.6		.0	VB
HEMATOCRIT		51.3		.0	VB
MCV		83 H			VB
MCH		26.8 H		.0	VB
MCHC		32.3		.0	VB
POLYS (PERCENT)		76			VB
BANDS (PERCENT)		0			VB
LYMPHOCYTES		22 %		12 - 30	VB
MONOCYTES		0 L %		3 - 10	VB

Handwritten notes: "Gigi" - see Memorials Severe liver disease worsened by continuous use of steroids - greatly improved w/ herbs & diet Before & after Blood test despite hemolysis

RESULTS ARE FLAGGED IN ACCORDANCE WITH AGE DEPENDENT REFERENCE RANGES

WESLEY BUSINESS FORMS · WINSTON-SALEM, NC 27109 · (919) 989-9101

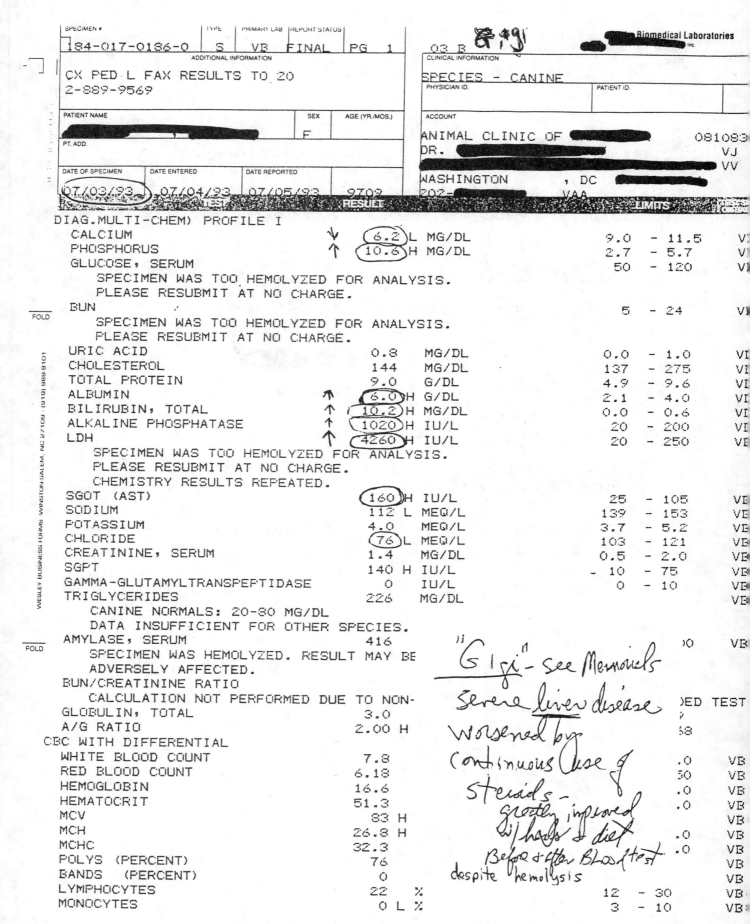

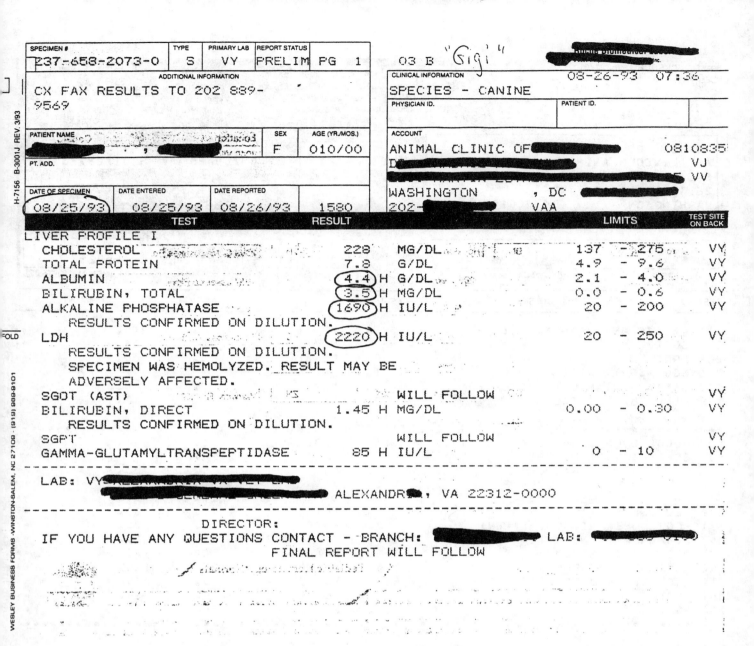

SPECIMEN #	TYPE	PRIMARY LAB	REPORT STATUS				
237-658-2073-0	S	VY	PRELIM PG 1	03 B "Gigi" 4			

ADDITIONAL INFORMATION

CX FAX RESULTS TO 202 889-9569

CLINICAL INFORMATION — 08-26-93 07:36

SPECIES - CANINE

PHYSICIAN ID.   PATIENT ID.

PATIENT NAME	SEX	AGE (YR./MOS.)
	F	010/00

ACCOUNT

ANIMAL CLINIC OF ▨   0810835
D▨   VJ
                              VV

PT. ADD.

WASHINGTON   , DC
202-   VAA

DATE OF SPECIMEN	DATE ENTERED	DATE REPORTED	
08/25/93	08/25/93	08/26/93	1580

TEST	RESULT		LIMITS	TEST SITE ON BACK
LIVER PROFILE I				
CHOLESTEROL	228	MG/DL	137 - 275	VY
TOTAL PROTEIN	7.8	G/DL	4.9 - 9.6	VY
ALBUMIN	4.4 H	G/DL	2.1 - 4.0	VY
BILIRUBIN, TOTAL	3.5 H	MG/DL	0.0 - 0.6	VY
ALKALINE PHOSPHATASE	1690 H	IU/L	20 - 200	VY
RESULTS CONFIRMED ON DILUTION.				
LDH	2220 H	IU/L	20 - 250	VY
RESULTS CONFIRMED ON DILUTION.				
SPECIMEN WAS HEMOLYZED. RESULT MAY BE				
ADVERSELY AFFECTED.				
SGOT (AST)		WILL FOLLOW		VY
BILIRUBIN, DIRECT	1.45 H	MG/DL	0.00 - 0.30	VY
RESULTS CONFIRMED ON DILUTION.				
SGPT		WILL FOLLOW		VY
GAMMA-GLUTAMYLTRANSPEPTIDASE	85 H	IU/L	0 - 10	VY

LAB: VY▨   ALEXANDR▨, VA 22312-0000

DIRECTOR:

IF YOU HAVE ANY QUESTIONS CONTACT - BRANCH: ▨   LAB: ▨
            FINAL REPORT WILL FOLLOW

RESULTS ARE FLAGGED IN ACCORDANCE WITH AGE DEPENDENT REFERENCE RANGES

WESLEY BUSINESS FORMS -WINSTON-SALEM, NC 27108 - (919) 969-9101

H-7156   B-3001J   REV. 3/93

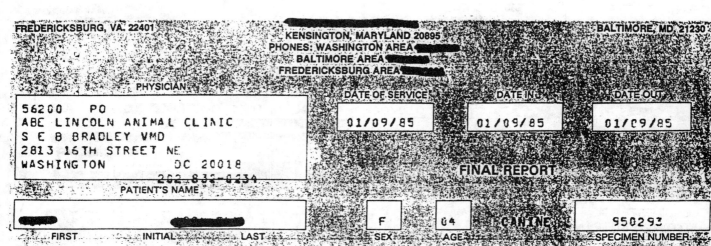

PHYSICIAN	DATE OF SERVICE	DATE IN	DATE OUT
56200 PO ABE LINCOLN ANIMAL CLINIC S E B BRADLEY VMD 2813 16TH STREET NE WASHINGTON DC 20018 202 832-0234	01/09/85	01/09/85	01/09/85

FINAL REPORT

PATIENT'S NAME

FIRST	INITIAL	LAST	SEX	AGE		SPECIMEN NUMBER
▓▓		▓▓▓	F	04	CANINE	950293

TEST NO. "TAKA"	TEST REQUESTED	RESULT	UNITS	NORMAL		COMMENT	
214	LACTIC DEHYDROGENASE (LDH)	528.	MU/ML	0.	200.		**
267	SGOT	84.	MU/ML	20.	64.		**
268	SGPT	60.	MU/ML	0.	30.		**
046	SGOT/SGPT RATIO	1.4					
173	GAMMA GLUTAMYL TRANSPEPTIDASE	6.	MU/ML	0.	9.		
128	BILIRUBIN, TOTAL	0.3	MG/DL	0.	0.5		

*************** RESULTS OUTSIDE ESTABLISHED REFERENCE RANGE *******************

507	BLOOD COUNT, WHITE CELLS (WBC)	19.8	THOUSAND	6.	17.		**
506	SCHILLING DIFF. (BLOOD SMEAR)						
	BANDS	13.	%	0.	3.		**
	SEG.NEUTS.	81.	%	60.	77.		**
	LYMPHS	6.	%	12.	30.		**
200	GLUCOSE FASTING SERUM *very high*	(324.)	MG/DL	70.	100.		**
131	BLOOD UREA NITROGEN (BUN)	27.	MG/DL	10.	20.		**
047	BUN/CREATININE RATIO	30.		5.	20.		**
277	URIC-ACID (SERUM)	2.1	MG/DL	0.	1.		**
240	ALKALINE PHOSPHATASE	144.	MU/ML	25.	130.		**
214	LACTIC DEHYDROGENASE (LDH)	528.	MU/ML	0.	200.		**
267	SGOT	84.	MU/ML	20.	64.		**
268	SGPT	60.	MU/ML	0.	30.		**

****

ROUPS REPORTED: 1010

DO IT YESTERDAY!

"TAKA" *see momsurds* — *Before+after*
BLOOD results

First case of
diabetic dog in Ketoacidic crises
completely reversed
by diet & herbs

LOEB VMD, PHD

MEDICAL LABORATORIES

KENSINGTON, MARYLAND 20895
PHONES: WASHINGTON AREA
BALTIMORE AREA
FREDERICKSBURG AREA

```
56200    PO
ABE LINCOLN ANIMAL CLINIC
S E B BRADLEY VMD
2813 16TH STREET NE
WASHINGTON        DC 20018
202 832-0234        -
```

DATE OF SERVICE	DATE IN	DATE OUT
07/13/85	07/13/85	07/15/85

FINAL REPORT

PATIENT'S NAME

		F	05 CANINE	333848
CHART		SEX	AGE	SPECIMEN NUMBER

TEST NO.	TAKA TEST REQUIRED	RESULT	UNITS	REFERENCE RANGE/COMMENTS	
0735	MICROFILARIA, EXAM & IDENTIFY				
	SPECIES	NO MICROFILARIA SEEN			
0507	BLOOD COUNT, WHITE CELLS (WBC)	14.	THOUSAND /1.X	6.	17.
0504	BLOOD COUNT, RED CELLS (RBC)	7.65	MILLION	5.5	8.5
0502	HEMOGLOBIN	19.	GM%	12.	16.5 **
0501	HEMATOCRIT (HCT)	52.9	VOL%	37.	50. **
5024	MEAN CORPUSCULAR VOLUME (MCV)	69.1	CUU		
5025	MEAN CORPUSCULAR HEMOGLOBIN	24.9	PG		
5026	MCHC	36.	%		
0506	SCHILLING DIFF. (BLOOD SMEAR)				
	BANDS	1.	% was 13	0.	3.
	SEG.NEUTS.	72.	% 81	60.	77.
	LYMPHS	23.	% 23	12.	30.
	MONO.	1.	%	0.	12.
	EOS.	3.	%	0.	6.
	PLATELET	ADEQ			
	ANISO	SL			**
	POIKILO	SL			**
	OTHER	SL POLY			
5200	GLUCOSE FASTING SERUM	63.	MG/DL 324	70.	100.
					** SAMPLE ON CLOT
0131	BLOOD UREA NITROGEN (BUN)	51.	MG/DL 27	10.	20. **
0170	CREATININE	1.	MG/DL .9	0.8	2.
5047	BUN/CREATININE RATIO	51.	30	5.	20. **
0154	CHOLESTEROL	134.	MG/DL 207	125.	250.
0272	TRIGLYCERIDES	27.	MG/DL 73		
0277	URIC-ACID (SERUM)	0.3	MG/DL 2.1	0.	1.
0139	CALCIUM	10.3	MG/DL NS	9.	11.3
0241	PHOSPHORUS	5.1	MG/DL 3.6	2.2	7.

NS = Not sufficient

WALTER F. LOEB VMD, PHD

SCIENCE IN THE SERVICE OF MAN THROUGH

Research - Clinical Diagnostics - Biological Products

Oct. 21, 1994

"For The Love of Taylor"

Taylor our Collie, was born on a cold Sun. afternoon in Feb., 1988. Shannon, his mother couldn't have her puppies naturally, so they had to be taken by emergency surgery. My husband and our 2 sons and I were with her through out her ordeal the sorrow of the puppies she lost at birth (11 puppies) and the joy of the 3 puppies who were alive when we left the vets office late that night. The next morning only 1 puppy remained. "Taylor our little miracle" From the time Taylor came home he was special. More of a human then a dog. Although we have had many dogs, Taylor was truly a gift from God. Shannon was unable to nurse or clean him, while I fed him from a bottle, Dusty his grandmother cleaned him and tried to nurse him. Even Patches, our cat, loved him.

On Nov., 6, 1990, Taylor had a seizure. After taking him to the Vet and having blood test we were told that Taylor was in kidney failure and would only live 24-38 hours. His Creatine level was 8.7 and his BUN level was 175. Our vet suggested we put him to sleep as he would suffer and have an agonizing death, with continuing seizures. Our vet is wonderful and we had no cause to doubt him. We decided to return to the vet within 48 hours to put him to sleep. The next day I remembered hearing about Dr. Bradley. I didn't know anything about her, but we knew we had to try and save our beloved dog. A few hours after calling Dr. Bradley, she arrived at our house loaded with herbs, spices, vitamins and other natural ingredients. She made gallons of a special tonic made with garlic and other natural ingredients. She was confident that she could flush out the toxics and restore the kidneys. After meeting and talking to her, I was too. Dr. Bradley is a wonderful Christian, she is kind and caring and compassionate. She came to our home almost daily, and called several times a day on the occasions when she was not available to come, and always let me know she would be there whenever I needed her. She traveled many miles to different counties when she could not find an herb that was unavailable in Charles County. She never asked us for a cent of money. She took him off the special diet he was on and treated him with her remedies.

2

During the time she was caring for him he showed signs of improving, the only signs were weight loss and his gums were pale, but outwardly he seemed to be the same dog. His appetite was good, he still functioned and he was still playful. On Nov., 26, 20 days after his seizure Dr. Bradley took a blood test to see if his readins had improved. His Creatney level was up to 21.3. It was medically impossible for Taylor to be alive.. It was a miracle. After much thought and prayer we decided to leave Taylor in Gods hands. On Nov., 29, he was eating Yougart and Ice Cream. On Nov., 30, Taylor had a terrible heartbreaking seizure, his second in 24 days. Although he came out of the seizure and seemed fine my decision was made. Taylor would be put to rest. Dr. Bradley came to our house and put in to sleep in my arms. Dr. Bradley cried along with our family. What would have been a terrible experience for us was turned into a learning and beautiful experience, ~~by~~ this wonderful lady. I have since determined that Taylor was born with bad kidney;s and that this was meant to be for him. It was taken out of our hands. I know if we had been aware of this medical problem at birth, Dr. Bradley could have prolonged his life. We are forever grateful to her for all that she did and for letting us keep Taylor until we knew it was time to let him go. Once again, we witnessed a mirale.

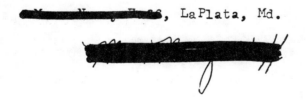

████████████, LaPlata, Md.

Testimonies — How They Came about and Why Are They Important?

How They Came about

In the early 1980's I was the only practitioner using any form of alternative medicine in Washington, D.C. By some, the approach was not welcomed at all. As a result, there was an attack on my license. **Some of my clients strongly volunteered to come to my defense by writing letters** of testimony to the source of the attacks.

From that point on, my decision was to maintain a file of outstanding cases, in the words of owners, as part of the documentation to substantiate my work. **As the years went by and I began to think more about publishing my work**, in order to help others that I could not personally reach, **I requested clients of selected cases to verify what they had witnessed (in their own words)** as to how the herbal and dietary management approaches helped their pets. Since the herbal formulas are sold for human consumption, many of my clients, voluntarily started using them for themselves with astounding results. I merely adjust the dosages for the animals, since most domestic pets (dogs and cats) have a metabolic rate that is approximately three times greater than ours.

Why Are Testimonies Important?

From the beginning of historical recordkeeping, written testimonies of eyewitness accounts have been viewed as a measure of authenticity. In a courtroom, the eyewitness account of a creditable citizen is valuable. I have several eyewitness accounts of many diseases. These accounts together with certain methods accepted as scientific data present strong evidence that herbology and careful dietary management can make a difference in the course of pathological conditions - namely, slowing them down, stopping them, reversing them or all of the above in sequential order.

With God's help, I believe, my work has shown this to be true. **Having a practice of more than 4,000 clients over a period of six years is not a situation that any responsible person or body of persons can ignore.**

Testimonials:
Kidney and Liver Disorders
(in Chronological Order)

April 24th, '85

Dear Dr. Bradley—

Enclosed are the copies of Emily's test results.

She seems to be doing quite well. She has a good appetite and loves the chicken liver, brown rice & broccoli mixture she's been getting.

Since Emily's eating so well, I've been putting the herbs in her food, and that's been very successful. She doesn't seem to notice. This way she's getting them all instead of half of it flying all over me & the floor when I did it with the syringe.

I'll be in touch soon about her next appointment.

Oh yes, haven't even given her the hops because they didn't have that one — so she's eating on her own!

So glad to know you're there.

Sincerely—

BALTIMORE
FREDERICKSBURG AREA
WASHINGTON, MARYLAND
PHONE: WASHINGTON AREA 770-7100
SOUTH CAROLINA
WEST VIRGINIA

PHYSICIAN	DATE OF SERVICE	DATE IN	DATE OUT
49262 TT	04/15/85	04/15/85	04/15/85
ANIMAL CLINIC			
DVM			
WASHINGTON DC		FINAL REPORT	
202 244-			

PATIENT'S NAME				F	17	FELINE	147157
FIRST	INITIAL	LAST		SEX	AGE		SPECIMEN NO.

TEST NO.	TEST REQUIRED	RESULT	UNITS	REFERENCE RANGE	
5044	GLOBULIN	5.1	GM/DL		
5045	A/G RATIO	0.6			
0243	POTASSIUM SERUM	3.4	MEG/L		SAMPLE CN CL
0253	SODIUM (SERUM)	144.	MEG/L		
0150	CHLORIDE SERUM	113.	MEG/L	96.	109.
0142	CARBON DIOXIDE (SERUM)	23.	MEG/L		
0240	ALKALINE PHOSPHATASE	16.	ML/ML	1.	75.
0214	LACTIC DEHYDROGENASE (LDH)	351.	MU/ML	0.	400.
				SAMPLE CN CLS	
0267	SGOT	66.	MU/ML	20.	40.
0268	SGPT	48.	ML/ML	0.	36.
5046	SGOT/SGPT RATIO	1.4			
0173	GAMMA GLUTAMYL TRANSPEPTIDASE	2.	ML/ML		
0128	BILIRUBIN, TOTAL	1.3	MG/DL	0.1	1.

****************** RESULTS OUTSIDE ESTABLISHED REFERENCE RANGE ******************

TEST NO.	TEST REQUIRED	RESULT	UNITS	REFERENCE RANGE	
0206	GLUCOSE FASTING SERUM (P PLSMA	147.	MG/DL	60.	90.
0506	SCHILLING DIFF. (BLOOD SMEAR)				
	BANDS	16.	%	3.	1.
	LYMPHS	11.	%	20.	55.
0131	BLOOD UREA NITROGEN (BUN)	41.	MG/CL	10.	30.
				SAMPLE CN CL	
0170	CREATININE	(3.4)	MG/CL	0.8	2.
0154	CHOLESTEROL	143.	MG/CL	38.	170.
0246	PROTEIN, TOTAL (SERUM)	8.	GM/CL	5.2	6.6
0132	ALBUMIN	2.9	GM/CL	1.7	2.4
0150	CHLORIDE SERUM	113.	MEG/L	96.	109.
0267	SGOT	68.	ML/ML	20.	40.
0268	SGPT	48.	ML/ML	9.	36.
0128	BILIRUBIN, TOTAL	1.3	MG/CL	0.1	1.

. . . .

BUN
CREATININE } indicators for kidney damage

SGOT
SGPT } indicators for liver damage

VMC, PHD

MAY 86
Cyth. Dca 85

Washington, D.C.
August 13, 1985

Washington, D.C.   20012

Dear Ms. ████████:

It has come to my attention that you are experiencing
some dissatisfaction with the veterinary practice of
Dr. Sandi Bradley. As a client of Dr. Bradley's, and
as one who appreciates and thinks highly of her, I feel
compelled to contact you.

I have a beloved 18 year old cat, who, in April of
this year became ill. As a tax practitioner, that is
the most busy time of year for me, and I therefore
contacted nearby veterinarians who could accommodate my
erratic schedule. The diagnosis, by both Drs. Rudolph
Fanari and Dennis Bailey was of kidney failure - "the
beginning of the end." They pulled her through for 3
days until after the 15th of April, with antibiotics and
subcutaneous fluids, and for this I am most grateful. She
was still, however, far from well yet. When it came to
discussing long-range treatment and prognosis, neither
doctor was optimistic.

I have practiced a wholistic lifestyle for myself and
my pets for over 10 years. Our health, vigor, and youthfulness
at our respective ages affirm the validity of such an approach.
I am no trendy dilletante. Holistic nutrition and herbology
have been a personal avocation for a decade. As mainstream
society has not provided me with information, I have sought
it independently, owning nearly 200 volumes on health,
nutrition, and herbalism and in consultation with wholistic
medical practitioners.

Therefore, with regard to treatment of my cat's
kidney problems, I attempted to dialogue with Drs. ████████
and ████████ about appropriate vitamins and herbs to treat
her condition. Both admitted that they had minimal
knowledge of this approach, and therefore could not assist
me. Dr. ████████ prescribed a high protein "prescription"
catfood, concurred with me that vitamin C might prove
useful, and advised me that little else could be done.

I still wonder if the prognosis would have been as dismal had I not given my cat's age. But, in all fairness, I must state that both Dr. ██████ and Dr. ██████ were kind, warm persons whom I liked, and who were, I know, assisting me to the best of their abilities.

Nonetheless, given my wholistic approach to healing, their recommendations were insufficient for me, as I wished to treat my cat wholistically and strongly believe in the efficacy of such treatment. I knew through my own research that a high protein diet is detrimental to kidney problems, due to the stress of filtering the toxins, or to any disease for that matter. I was aware of a few herbs and vitamins which would be useful. But I felt the need to work with a professional, whose knowledge surpasses my own and who could combine "conventional" veterinary treatment with my treatment preferences of herbs and vitamins, and who was sympathetic to and knowledgable about such treatment approaches. It was at this point that Dr. ██████ referred me to Dr. Bradley.

I immediately contacted Dr. Bradley. We had a lengthy conversation regarding my cat's condition, and my treatment preferences. I knew then that I had found the person who would become my permanent veterinarian. I forthwith transferred my cat from Dr. ██████ care to Dr. Bradley's. The "conventional" treatment - antibiotics and fluids - continued, supplemented by the vitamins and herbs I so desperately felt were important. Shortly thereafter, my cat returned home, where I continued to treat her. She was soon entirely well, remains so, and as always, is assumed to be half her age.

Were my cat to have died, had I followed only the treatment recommended by the allopaths, I would have agonizingly felt that not all that was possible had been done. But, had my cat died after the treatment which Dr. Bradley and I used, I could have rested easy, knowing for myself that everything possible, and most efficacious for healing, had been done.

Obviously what I've been leading up to here is that Dr. Sandi Bradley is important to me. I feel that she understands and is open to my views on treatment, in addition to being a very patient and concerned veterinarian. Contrast this with the fact that when using strictly allopathic vets, I often frustratingly felt that I was speaking another uncomprehended language when discussing nutrition, vitamins, and herbs. I would do no less for myself, and would only seek the services of a wholistic physician, were I to be ill.

I choose and prefer to use a veterinarian with approaches such as Dr. Bradley's. Others may not. The essentially important issue here is that the option remains available for us all to make such a choice.

Humans are not being encouraged to be assertive consumers of medical care - to obtain second opinions, for example. It is unfortunate that we don't often enough exercise our rights as patients - speak up for ourselves, question our medical practitioners, and assert our needs. So too with veterinary care. I asserted my rights of choice by removing Emily from Dr. ████████ care and taking her to Dr. Bradley. I questioned treatment approaches and made my choice. All others can certainly do the same. And if that means some will choose practitioners with treatment approaches different from Dr. Bradley's, then so be it.

What is important here is the availability of competent, sensitive veterinary practitioners with a variety of treatment options from which we can choose that one most suited to us. To deny that range of choices to us would be to make the Humane Society something far less than humane.

I would be glad to speak with you further about this matter. I can be reached at ████████

Sincerely,

cc: Dr. Sandi Bradley

August 12, 1985

Abe Lincoln Animal Clinic
Dr. Sandra Bradley
2813 16th St. N.E.
Washington D.C.   20018

Dear Dr. Bradley,

    It is with much pleasure that I write to you regarding my two cats. When I called your office in May, our Veterinarian had diagnosed our two cats as being in renal failure. Their BUN levels were dangerously high. The Vet's treatment consisted of pushing sub-cutaneous fluids and changing their diet. Beyond the fluids their comment was, "this is all we can do". We brought Mickey and Michi home with the fluids and proceeded to push fluids twice daily as prescribed. However, we were not satisfied that this was enough. It was during this time that were heard of you and your holistic approach to medicine. After describing their symptoms you prescribed several herbs and vitamin C. We followed your regime twice daily. Approximately two weeks later we observed the cats were developing more energy, and most especially increased urine output. The results were really remarkable. After several months on a maintenance program, they are enjoying continued good health. Thank goodness we found you in time to reverse almost permanent damage. We are indeed so grateful that you are such a caring and conscientious Vet. Your love for the animal world is truly inspiring. Just keep up the good work.

                    Sincerely,

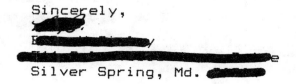

                    Silver Spring, Md.

P.S. Am enclosing a copy of Michi's BUN, so that you can compare two reports, before and after your treatment.

MEDICAL LABORATORIES

BALTIMORE AREA
FREDERICKSBURG AREA

SOUTH CAROLINA
WEST VIRGINIA

KENSINGTON, MARYLAND 20795
PHONES: WASHINGTON AREA

PHYSICIAN	DATE OF SERVICE	DATE IN	DATE OUT
88518 FN3	03/05/85	03/07/85	03/07/85

ANIMAL HOSPITAL

SILVER SPRING   MD 20904
301

FINAL REPORT

PATIENT'S NAME	SEX	AGE	OTHER	SPECIMEN NUMBER
FIRST INITIAL LAST	M	10		065041

TEST NO.	TEST REQUIRED	RESULT	UNITS	REFERENCE RANGE /COMMENTS
023	URINALYSIS (MACROSCOPIC)			
	COLOR	AMBER		
	APPEARANCE	HAZY		
	SPECIFIC GRAVITY	1.028		
	PH	6.		
	PROTEIN	2+		
	GLUCOSE	NEGATIVE		
	KETONES	NEGATIVE		
	BILIRUBIN	NEGATIVE		
	BLOOD	2+		
321	URINALYSIS (MICROSCOPIC)			
	WBC	5-10	HPF	
	RBC	20-35	HPF	
	AMORPHOUS SED	TRACE		
	BACTERIA	2+		

**************** RESULTS OUTSIDE ESTABLISHED REFERENCE RANGE ********************

023	URINALYSIS (MACROSCOPIC)			
	PROTEIN	2+		
	BLOOD	2+		
321	URINALYSIS (MICROSCOPIC)			
	RBC	20-35	HPF	
	BACTERIA	2+		

****

GROUPS REPORTED   0300

Recorded
Reported 3/8

VMD, PHD

BALTIMORE AREA ████████
FREDERICKSBURG AREA ██████   ████████ **MEDICAL LABORATORIES**   SOUTH CAROLINA ████
                                                                         WEST VIRGINIA ████

KENSINGTON, MARYLAND 20795
PHONES: WASHINGTON AREA ████

PHYSICIAN	DATE OF SERVICE	DATE IN	DATE OUT
88518 N301 ████████ ANIMAL HOSPITAL SILVER SPRING MD ████ 301	03/19/85	03/19/85	03/20/85

FINAL REPORT

PATIENT'S NAME	SEX	AGE		SPECIMEN NUMBER
MICHI ████████ FIRST INITIAL LAST	F		FELINE	090302

TEST NO.	TEST REQUIRED	RESULT	UNITS	REFERENCE RANGE /COMMENTS	
131	BLOOD UREA NITROGEN (BUN)	49.	MG/DL	10.	30.	**

******************* RESULTS OUTSIDE ESTABLISHED REFERENCE RANGE *******************

| 131 | BLOOD UREA NITROGEN (BUN) | 49. | MG/DL | 10. | 30. | ** |

****

FINAL REPORT

████████ VMD, PHD

MEDICAL LABORATORIES

KENSINGTON, MARYLAND 20795
PHONES: WASHINGTON AREA

PHYSICIAN	DATE OF SERVICE	DATE IN	DATE OUT

88518   N301
ANIMAL HOSPITAL

SILVER SPRING   MD 20904
                     301 384-1223

DATE OF SERVICE: 03/19/85

DATE IN: 03/19/85

DATE OUT: 03/20/85

FINAL REPORT

PATIENT'S NAME	SEX	AGE		SPECIMEN NUMBER
MICKI	M	10	FELINE	090319
FIRST INITIAL LAST				

TEST NO.	TEST REQUIRED	RESULT	UNITS	REFERENCE RANGE /COMMENTS	
131	BLOOD UREA NITROGEN (BUN)	57.	MG/DL	10.	30.	**

****************** RESULTS OUTSIDE ESTABLISHED REFERENCE RANGE ******************

131	BLOOD UREA NITROGEN (BUN)	57.	MG/DL	10.	30.	**

****

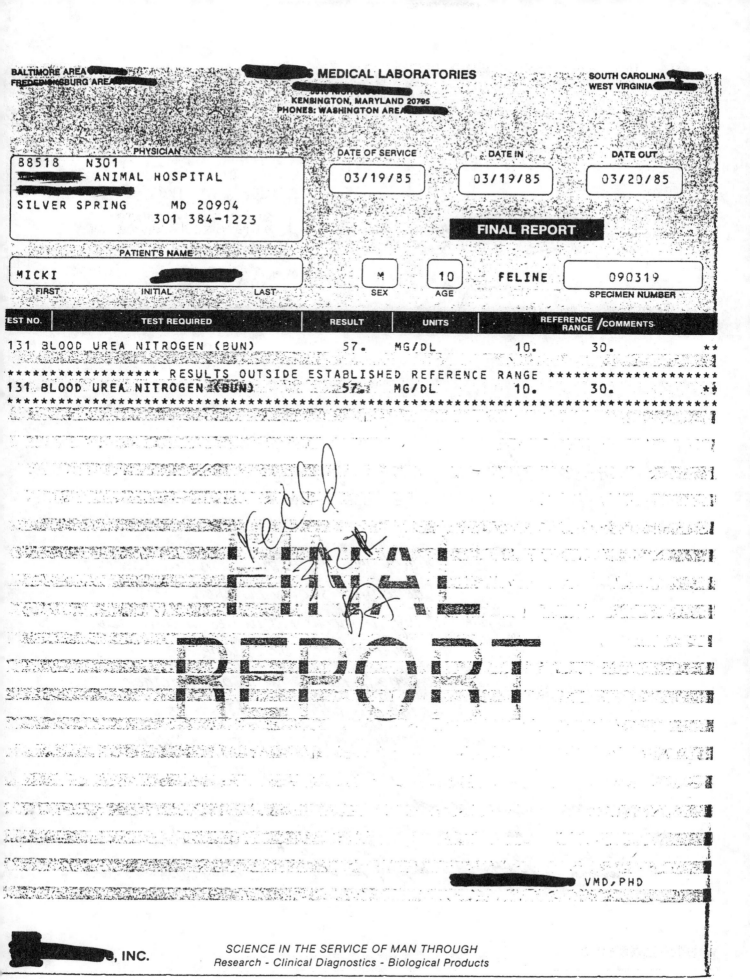

VMD/PHD

Dr. Michael Fox informed owner
He agreed with the diagnosis of
Kidney + Liver pathology

Rec'd 12/90

We love,
because he first loved us.
I JOHN 4:19

It is a time of beauty, as the earth lies sleeping
beneath a snowy blanket...
a time of joy, as the world unites once again
in a celebration of love.
It is a time to reach out to one another
in the spirit that is Christmas
and to rejoice in the gifts of good times,
good friends, family, and life.

Dear Dr. Bradley,
Thank you for helping Tiger this past year. He
is well and happy. May you have a very merry Christmas
and a healthy and happy New Year. Love + Peace, Kiki + Tiger

REGIONAL LABORATORY
ROCKVILLE, M
FINAL REPORT

CLIENT SERVICE
WASHINGTON AREA :
BALTIMORE AREA :
CLINTON, MD :

MIDDLETON, FRIEDERIKE	04/11/90	04/11/90	04/12/90
PATIENT	DATE DRAWN	DATE REC'D.	DATE OF REPORT

			DOC BRADLEY'S HOUSECALL SERV		F	56200
M		18	SANDY BRADLEY VMD			ACCOUNT NO.
SEX	AGE		STAR RT #2 BOX 2167 RIPLEY	FELINE		
SANDY BRADLEY			LA PLATA MD 20646	6:26AM		Y602820
PATIENT IDENTIFICATION NO.			301 753-9091	HH03		SPEC. NO.

TEST NAME	RESULT	UNITS	REFERENCE RANGE
CHEM-SCREEN - VET			
GLUCOSE	52	MG/DL	60 - 90
BLOOD UREA NITROGEN	39	MG/DL	10 - 30
CREATININE	1.7	MG/DL	0.8 - 2.0
BUN/CREATININE RATIO	22.9		5 - 20
SODIUM	157	MEQ/L	141.0 - 157.0
POTASSIUM	5.1	MEQ/L	4.0 - 6.0
CHLORIDE	119	MEQ/L	98 - 130
CALCIUM	11.8	MG/DL	8.6 - 10.8
PHOSPHORUS	2.8	MG/DL	2.4 - 8.1
URIC ACID	1.5	MG/DL	0.0 - 2.1
TOTAL PROTEIN	9.4	GM/DL	5.2 - 6.6
ALBUMIN	3.1	GM/DL	1.7 - 2.8
GLOBULIN	6.3	GM/DL	3.2 - 5.1
A/G RATIO	0.5		
SGOT	72	IU/L	20 - 40
SGPT	137	IU/L	0 - 36
SGOT/SGPT RATIO	0.5		
GAMMA GLUTAMYL TRANSPEPTIDASE-GGTP	0	IU/L	0 - 9
ALKALINE PHOSPHATASE	34	IU/L	0 - 75
LDH	244	U/L	0 - 400
TOTAL BILIRUBIN	0.2	MG/DL	0.1 - 1.0
DIRECT BILIRUBIN	0.1	MG/DL	0.0 - 0.4
TRIGLYCERIDES	83	MG/DL	6 - 58
CHOLESTEROL - SERUM	225	MG/DL	
IRON	138	MCG/DL	68 - 215

SPECIMEN HEMOLYZED.

Kidney & Liver Disorders

* * * * * SUMMARY OF RESULTS OUTSIDE ESTABLISHED REFERENCE RANGE * * * * *

GLUCOSE	52	MG/DL	60 - 90
BLOOD UREA NITROGEN } *Kidney*	39	MG/DL	10 - 30
BUN/CREATININE RATIO	22.9		5 - 20
CALCIUM	11.8	MG/DL	8.6 - 10.8
TOTAL PROTEIN	9.4	GM/DL	5.2 - 6.6
ALBUMIN	3.1	GM/DL	1.7 - 2.8
GLOBULIN	6.3	GM/DL	3.2 - 5.1
SGOT } *LIVER*	72	IU/L	20 - 40
SGPT	137	IU/L	0 - 36
TRIGLYCERIDES	83	MG/DL	6 - 58

* *

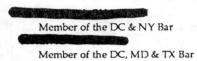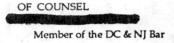
GOD, CINDI and DOC

This is a testimony to the powers of God, and how they worked to bring Doc Bradley into our lives to heal my beloved Cindi.

For over nine years, I was blessed by the most loving, gentle, beautiful dog that one could ever hope for. She was Cindi, God's gift to me. I was given a choice of the litter, and just as I was wondering, how do you select a puppy, Cindi reared her spirited little head above all the other pups and said, "You're mine!"

Cindi was my companion--an overweight, boldly black and white Dalmatian, with flopping black ears and appealing black marked eyes. Cindi loved people. She attracted people by her distinct markings, but captured them by her heart. Cindi had a passion for life. I was not always good to Cindi, but Cindi was <u>always</u> good to me.

In September, 1992 after returning from vacation, I noticed that Cindi was listless and did not possess her usual energy and voracious appetite. Her sudden disinterest in food was most confounding, because she loved to eat.

By October, I learned that Cindi had end-stage renal disease. Her vet told me that Cindi was not expected to live much longer, her kidney's were barely functioning. He could offer no hope. His treatment was to give her intravenous infusions of fluids, medication, change her brand of dog food, and observation so that we would know when it was time to put her to sleep. Cindi was getting worse, both from her illness and her treatment.

In November, God brought Doc into our lives. She confirmed that Cindi had severe kidney disease. But she gave hope that Cindi's condition could be reversed with proper nutrition, care and treatment.

By the time Cindi encountered Doc, she was very, very sick. Cindi was not eating or drinking enough to survive. She would go into convulsions. Her eyes would run with mucous. Despite her grave condition, Cindi valiantly maintained her spirited passion for life. Her favorite pastime was going for walks or taking rides with me. She continued to relish these activities, no matter how frail or ill she was.

Doc Bradley was a most amazing physician. She came to my home to care for Cindi. Doc relied principally on herbs and natural foods to treat Cindi. She ordered Cindi off all commercial dog food and made special preparations of tonic and medicines. What little Cindi would eat, Doc required be prepared with fresh and carefully selected foods.

Doc instructed me on how to care for my precious animal. Because we humans are particularly dull under stress, Doc understood the importance of frequent and persistent follow-up. Doc would call at least once and sometimes as often as two and three times a day. I had never encountered a physician so caring and who provided so much needed support.

When Cindi did not respond as she had hoped, Doc came to my home and spent twenty-four hours, round the clock, caring for Cindi. Cindi rallied. She came to life. She turned around. But the kind of intensive care that Cindi needed was not available on an ongoing basis. Cindi stabilized briefly and began to again decline. (The fact that Doc did not have a clinic in which to treat patients like Cindi was sad to all of us. I saw how the intensive care that Doc gave Cindi can make the difference between life and death for an animal, or the difference between a natural, peaceful death and an unnatural, agonizing death--as in the case of Cindi.)

Doc continued to treat Cindi, and never once gave up hope. Even on the day Cindi died, Doc was calling on all God's resources to restore her to health. It was not, however, God's Will that Cindi live any longer. Cindi died on December 22.

It **was** God's Will that Cindi live fully, joyfully and peacefully. With God's help, through the compassionate wisdom and skill of Doc Bradley, Cindi was able to live her remaining days in peace, comfort and joy, and she was able to die a natural death at home. You see Cindi, never gave up hope. Doc never gave up hope. And neither could I. God brought hope through His able ambassador-physician, Doc Bradley.

Through God, Cindi and Doc, I learned several truths. First, our animals deserve the same values that we accept as essential for our own health. Even the most committed junk-food junky would consider it foolish to spend a lifetime eating from only two or three food sources, no matter how many vitamins and minerals were packed in. That, however, is exactly what we do to our animals. We condemn our animals to an early grave by feeding them over a lifetime a diet from very limited food sources. We are killing them when we feed them nothing but canned or dry food, even when we change brands. Our animals, just like we, need a variety of fresh and nutritious foods in order to live well.

My dog's illness and death could have been prevented. Cindi, because of her breed, had an inherent kidney weakness. Although she had her share of table scraps, most of her diet consisted of commercially prepared canned or dry foods. That kind of diet in just nine years, contributed to the destruction of her kidneys which were constantly working overtime to process foods that depleted her body instead of building it up. The diet that I fed Cindi put in motion a degenerative disease process.

Doc Bradley came into our lives at the time when Cindi's disease had progressed to near death. This leads to the second truth that I learned through God, Cindi and Doc. No matter what the prognosis, God has provided a way of restoration. As a physician, Doc committed her life to the study and practice God's way of restoration. Her chief medicine are the herbs that God has given us for food. Her consistent treatment plan are Biblical principles of correct living which, in our present and confusing world, are largely forgotten, ignored or condemned.

I saw first-hand what proper treatment and care, nutrition and herbs did to turn Cindi's disease process around in just 24 hours. Had I been committed to caring for Cindi on an ongoing basis as Doc had done, or had Doc had the clinic and facilities to care for Cindi along with her other patients, I believe that Cindi would have recovered.

Since becoming Doc's client, we have become best friends. I have seen first-hand many other evidences of Doc's skill as God's physician in the lives of animals as well as herself. There is Sweat Pea, who was dying from a malignant tumor. When I first saw Sweat Pea over a year ago, she had no hair, was foul-smelling, bony and pitiful to look at. She was weak and in pain. All hope had been given up on this poor dog, and she was scheduled to be put to sleep. Through Doc's care, Sweat Pea is a different dog. Her hair is restored, she's gained weight, the foul odor is gone. And of course, she still lives. Even though she has not completely recovered, to all appearances, Sweat Pea is a healthy dog, who like Cindi, has a passion for life.

Doc herself is a living testimony to the power of healing according to God's laws. I have witnessed her miraculous recovery from shingles within three weeks. I also witnessed her recovery from carbon monoxide poisoning, from a serious foot infection after stepping on a rusty nail, and from the flair-up of a herniated disc. All these conditions were resolved through her faith in God's power to heal and the use of natural medicines and remedies.

Finally, through God, Cindi and Doc, I learned to accept the sanctity of all God's creation. I said at the beginning of this Testimony that God brought Doc in my life to heal Cindi. Yet, Cindi died from her illness. True healing brings about restoration of the spiritual nature even though the physical nature may die. Cindi, through Doc's intervention restored Cindi's spirit even though her body was lost.

Conventional medicine and practice offered no alternative except to "put her down" when the time came. Cindi most likely would have spent her last days in an animal clinic, isolated, frightened and away from me. Her last days would have been agonizing. Most assuredly, she would not have died peacefully and naturally at home with her beloved "companion". I am truly grateful that Doc provided the means for Cindi to die in the same spirit by which she lived, and to experience the peace of dying naturally in loving and familiar surroundings. I am most grateful that the quality of life that Doc's care provided allowed me to say "goodbye".

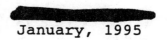

January, 1995

Takoma Park, Maryland
February 4, 1995

Dear Dr. Bradley:

I would like to express my deep appreciation for the herbal remedies you advised for Bandit.

As you may recall, Bandit is my 16-year-old dog. Bandit, a small, slim dog, had been rapidly losing weight, was experiencing vomiting and diarrhea, and was very lethargic. I feared she was dying.

Two other veterinarians diagnosed Bandit's liver and kidney diseases and prescribed an expensive diet of canned food and a canned nutrient supplement. Their prescription diet did not seem to be yielding results. One of the problems was that nothing I did could induce Bandit to eat it. She became very upset when I force feed her.

One of the veterinarians also prescribed fluids be injected under Bandit's skin over several days to keep her hydrated since she wasn't taking in and retaining enough fluids. These treatments were painful to Bandit and left her uncomfortably bloated.

I felt I was doing something inhumane by forcing my frail pet to eat something she found so unpalatable. I also worried that something in a can could not be fresh and might have lost all the nutritional and medicinal value Bandit so badly needed. Bandit's quality of life at this point was so poor, I gave up hope and began preparing myself for her death.

Fortunately my neighbor discussed Bandit's situation with you and you generously offered your assistance to us.

Bandit experienced an incredible turnaround in just a week after taking the tonic you prepared and following the natural diet high in protein but low in animal protein you recommended. Her appetite has returned, her eyes are clearer, she is alert and energetic, and has even gained weight! I can't believe how she has responded—some days she's like a puppy again.

I think your wholistic remedies have made all the difference. Bandit and I have had 16 great years together and I look forward to many more. Thank you.

Sincerely,

Dear DR. Bradley,

    We just wanted to write and express our thanks and gratitude for helping us to save our cat. Although i have been in the natural foods ind. for close to 10 years and helped a lot of people overcome some pretty bizarre circumstances i really lacked experience with animals. You really came through for us in an other wise sad situation. Had it not been for your compasionate professionalism we would have lost MAX! The regular vets had exhausted every thing they knew how to do , and really did not know what to do. So we really have been made believers all over again. Seeing max recover right before ours eyes served to reiterate my strong belief in herbal medicine as well as hom. medicine. You really are a true healer!

THANKS AGAIN

PARKERSBURG, WEST VIRGINIA

GENERAL CONSULTANTS, INC.
MEDICAL LABORATORY
(304)

R.E. LAWRENCE-BERREY, M.D.   **PAGE 1**
PATHOLOGIST-DIRECTOR

1/20/95
2:39   RSBURG, WV 26101

D: 010741   NAME: SEX: AGE: 0
ARD: ROOM: ATTENDING DR: ADMITTED: / /

EQ: 741   DATE DRAWN: 1/20/95   TIME DRAWN: 8:45
REVIEWED BY: LH
COMMENT: VET. HOSP.----FELINE"MAX"   DOB AUG,1990 FAY*

IST	LOW	RESULT	HIGH			UNITS	--EXPECTED--	
T PROFILE								
GLUCOSE		113		[	*]	MG/DL	75	116
BUN		125 →		[	]>>	MG/DL	8	26
CREATININE		10.3 →		[	]>>	MG/DL	0.6	1.4
CALCIUM				[	]>	MG/DL	8.4	10.2
PHOSPHORUS				[	]>>	MG/DL	2.7	4.6
TOTAL PROTEIN		7.6		[	*]	G/DL	6.4	8.2
ALBUMIN	3.8			<[	]	G/DL	3.9	5.0
TOT BILIRUBIN		0.3		[*	]	MG/DL	0.3	1.3
ALK PHOS	17			<[	]	IU/L	30	80
LDH	35			<[	]	IU/L	46	94
SGOT (AST)		21		[	*]	IU/L	12	26
SGPT (ALT)		20		[	*]	IU/L	4	31
CHOLESTEROL		181		[	*]	MG/DL	132	200
ECTROLYTES								
SODIUM		160 →		[	]>	MMOL/L	136	146
POTASSIUM		4.2		[	*]	MMOL/L	3.5	5.0
CHLORIDE		129 →		[	]>>	MMOL/L	100	110
CO2	11			<[	]	MMOL/L	23	30

**Testimonials:
Heart and Lung
(in Chronological Order of <u>Occurrence</u>
in Practice)**

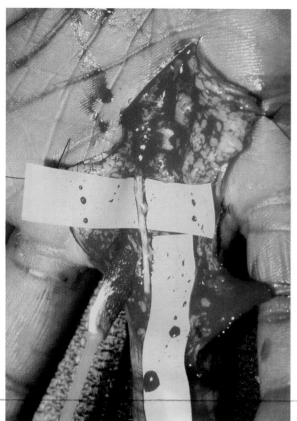

Above: Reconstructed nerve by transplantation performed at Johns Hopkins University Hospital.

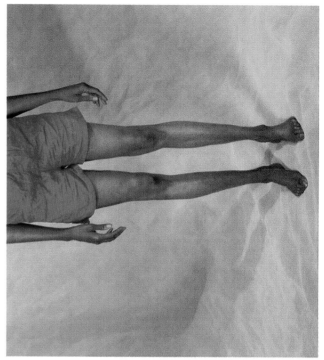

Below: July 1993—Within one month rotational and distortion reversed to near normal. Total function of leg restored.

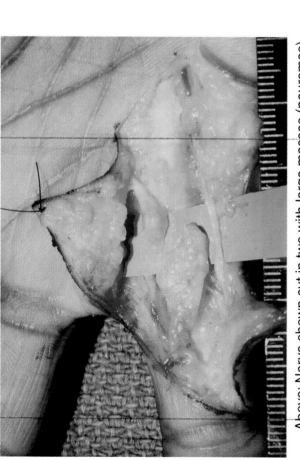

Above: Nerve shown cut in two with large masses (neuromas) on both ends as a result of a poor surgery.

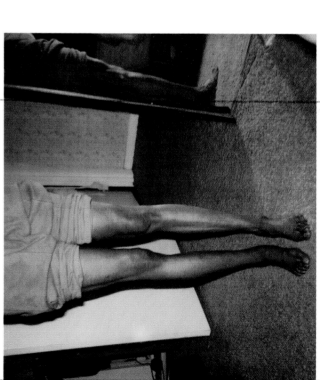

Below: June 1993—Twisted knee, leg and swollen ankle.

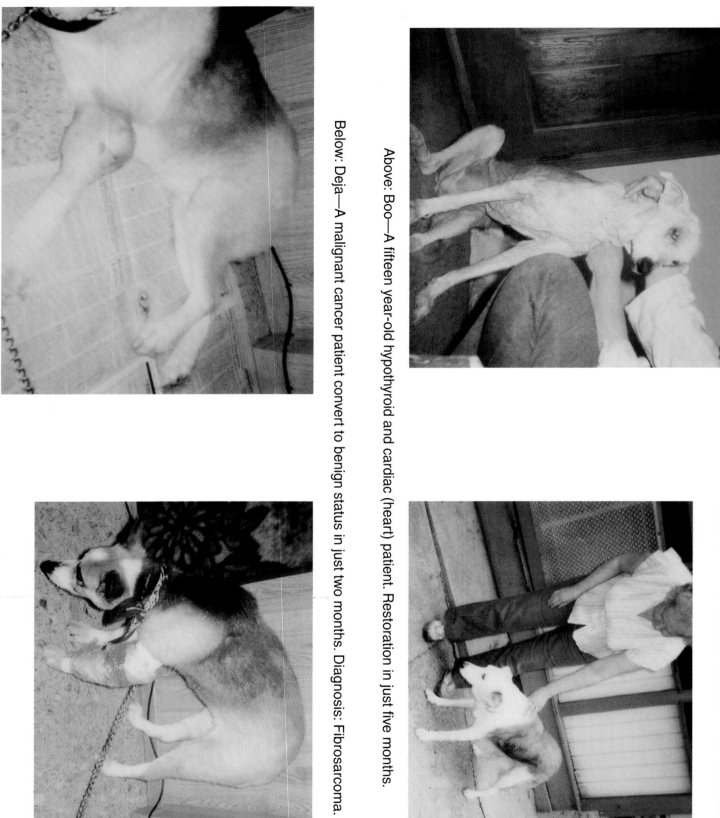

Above: Boo—A fifteen year-old hypothyroid and cardiac (heart) patient. Restoration in just five months.

Below: Deja—A malignant cancer patient convert to benign status in just two months. Diagnosis: Fibrosarcoma.

August 22, 1985

Dr. Sandra Bradley
Abe Lincoln Animal Hospital
2813 -16th Street, N. E.
Washington, D. C. 20018

Dear Dr. Bradely,

Sitting here this evening I realized how many times Toby
needed to be spanked and was scolded several times regarding
his ill-behaved ways. During one of my "Stop Toby" or "Toby
You Are a Bad Boy", I experienced a flash back that reminded me
that Toby almost was not here for the reprimands. It seems to
be so long ago but the truth is that it was just recently that
due to your patience, understanding and professional training
that my Toby still lives.

When I brought him to you with numerous medical problems,
i.e., a terrible cough, a retained testicle that surfaced, a
hernia in his rectum area, routing scratching of his mouth and
dental care, I felt overwhelmed that due to Toby's age 13 and
his being so small (15 lbs.) that he would be unable to handle
what would be needed to correct his problems. Later when you
completed your diagnoses, surgery and post treatments, I realized
that there were many other problems - heart trouble, lung disease,
trachea problems and a growth under his tongue. This added to
my frustrations and soon I shared my fears with only God.

The stress and sleepless nights caused many mental pressures
on me and my mother while Toby was home recuperating (restlessness,
not eating, diarrhea and biting at his stitches which eventually
opened exposing raw places and caused bleeding). His recuperation
period was so frustrating to me and my mother that I returned him
to your facility for care.

Remaining in your care for a week allowed me to accept the
fact that Toby's time may be near but I prayed. Routine contacts
with you allowed me to follow his progress and soon he was home.
His progress after that time was remarkable and within a week or
two he,was the same old Toby. Here I am again saying "Stop Toby",
Toby You Are a Bad Boy" and "Toby I'm Going to Spank You".

I may not be as intuned to God as you appear to be but I
feel that my prayers were answered by God through you. I feel
that many other Veterinarians would have suggested that I put my

dog to sleep. Many family and friends suggested that I put him
to sleep while he was sick or recuperating but I refused to
discuss it and thank God it didn't cross your lipe. THANKS AGAIN.
Enclosed is a photo of our miracle.

Yours sincerely,

P.S. My mother says THANKS too. Toby's diet and natural herb
      treatments are being continued. We will see you soon for
      Toby's routine shots.

To Whom it MAY CONCERN:

In the Winter of 1989 my 13½ year old Springer Spaniel named Mac became seriously ill. The diagnosis of his weakened condition was heart murmur & heart congestion Along with severe Bladder stones. My delemma was that conventional veternarians could only prescribe an operation to Remove the Bladder stones or a special high sodium diet which sometimes helped the condition. Both methods were contraindicated because of my dog's Advanced Age And congested heart. (I tried the special high sodium diet for three days with almost disasterous results!.. Mac stopped eating the high sodium which was harming his fragile heart & circulation).

I discovered Dr. Sandy Bradley who, at least, offered some hopeful alternatives consisting of herbs and natural foods to Aid my very weak dog. I gave Mac these herbal concoctions with both hope and skepticism. With "nothing to lose", I followed Dr. Bradley's treatments and advice.

Today, Almost nine months later Mac is still With us! His heart has improved.! Although other problems like cataracts and the general ageing process has taken its toll; I still consider Mac's

Condition much better than I would have expected considering his extreme weakness in January. Some of the remedies I gave Mac were exotic to the average modern American and some were common (e.g., garlic, parsley, honey) I will continue to give my dog these natural foods and food supplements. I hope to keep my ancient puppy for a while yet.

Sincerely,

WASHINGTON, DC 20015

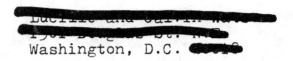

Washington, D.C.

June 27, 1993

To Whom It May Concern:

We have had our 13 year old Cocker Spaniel, Nikki, under
Dr. Sandy Bradley's care for several years and we are happy
to see he is responding favorably to her treatment with
natural herbs and foods. He had a weak heart beat and
suffered with nasal drainage.

He had been treated by a veterinarian at the Brentwood
Animal Hospital. Lab tests were made and medicine prescribed
at quite a cost with little curative results.

Since her treatment, his condition has reversed, he is much
more lively and is acting and looking much younger than before
her treatment began.

She makes herself available and if she is not in when we call,
she always returns our call and is very generous in making
suggestions over the phone of how we can cope with whatever
condition exists. She is always willing to make house calls
if she feels it is warranted.

Dr. Bradley truly has an interest in the well being of all
animals and is knowledgeable in the care and treatment of
them to a surprising degree. We have been most appreciative
what she has done for our dog Nikki to make his life more
enjoyable.

Sincerely Yours,

████████ ANIMAL HOSPITAL, Inc.   PAGE: 1

Brentwood, MD ████████
301-████████

CLIENT ID: 64208
INVOICE: 6948

████████
████████
Washington, DC ████████

PATIENT ID:	NIK	SPECIES: CANINE	WEIGHT:	SEX: MALE
PATIENT NAME:	NIKKI	BREED: SPANIEL, ENG. COCKER	BIRTHDAY: 05-90	

RE-EXAMINATION		$	12.00
CULTURE AND SENSITIVITY			60.00
Cefa-Tabs 200 mg (Antibiotic)	35		28.25
Processed by Donna, Thank You!			0.00
PATIENT SUBTOTAL:		$	100.25

CONTINUAL ACCUMULATION OF TARTAR O████████████████ SSURE AND
INFLAMATION OF GUM TISSUE AND █████████████████████████ ECOMES
VERY ODOROUS AND INFECTION C██████████████████████
AND MANTAIN FRESH BREATH, A████████ AL CHECK UP AND ██████████
ESSENTIAL. IF YOU HAVE ANY█████████████ EASE FEE███████ TO█

RETURN IN ONE WEEK FOR RE████████████

REMINDERS: MAY 04 91   VACCINATION████████
            MAY 04 91   PARVOVIRUS ████████
            MAY 04 91   DHLP BOOSTER█████
            MAY 04 91   CORONA BOOSTER███
            MAY 04 91   RABIES CANINE ████
            MAY 04 91   BORDATELLA BOOSTER
            SEP 11 91   FECAL EXAMINATION-FLO█
            SEP 11 91   Heartgard Refill
            MAR 11 92   HEARTWORM EXAMINATION

TOTAL INVOICE:	$	100.25
PAYMENT - VISA:		100.25
BALANCE DUE:	$	0.00

In order to better serve our clients & their pet needs we now provide
Professional Grooming & Quality Boarding. Give us a call (301 ████████

APR 10 1991

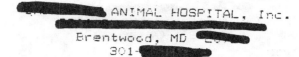

ANIMAL HOSPITAL, Inc.

Brentwood, MD

301-

PAGE: 1

CLIENT ID: 64208
INVOICE: 7060

Washington, DC 20018

PATIENT ID: NIK   SPECIES: CANINE   WEIGHT: 31.00 lbs.   SEX: MALE
PATIENT NAME: NIKKI   BREED: SPANIEL, ENG. COCKER   BIRTHDAY: 05-80

Cefa-Tabs 200 mg (Antibiotic)   35 $ 28.25

                           PATIENT SUBTOTAL: $ 28.25

REMINDERS: MAY 04 91   VACCINATION EXAMINATION
              MAY 04 91   PARVOVIRUS BOOSTER
              MAY 04 91   DHLP BOOSTER
              MAY 04 91   CORONA BOOSTER
              MAY 04 91   RABIES CANINE 1 YEAR BOOSTER
              MAY 04 91   BORDATELLA BOOSTER
              SEP 11 91   FECAL EXAMINATION FLOTATION
              SEP 11 91   Heartgard Refill
              MAR 11 92   HEARTWORM EXAMINATION

                           TOTAL INVOICE: $ 28.25
                           PAYMENT VISA: 28.25

                           BALANCE DUE: $ 0.00
                                        ==============================

In order to better serve our clients & their pet needs we now provide
Professional Grooming & Quality Boarding. Give us a call (301

 **ANIMAL HOSPITAL, Inc.**
Brentwood, MD
301-

PAGE: 1

CLIENT ID: 64208
INVOICE: 6746

Washington, DC

PATIENT ID:	NIK	SPECIES: CANINE	WEIGHT:	SEX: MALE
PATIENT NAME:	NIKKI	BREED: SPANIEL, ENG. COCKER	BIRTHDAY: 05-80	

MAR 11 91	EXAMINATION-COMPREHENSIVE		$	20.00
MAR 11 91	CBC, SMA14-K9 (BLOOD TO LAB)			55.00
MAR 11 91	X-RAY 12 X 14 (2 VIEWS)			60.00
MAR 11 91	FECAL EXAMINATION-FLOTATION			9.00
MAR 11 91	HEARTWORM EXAMINATION			18.00
MAR 11 91	✓ Lasix Injection			12.00
MAR 11 91	✓ Baytril Injection			12.00
MAR 11 91	Lasix tablets 12.5 mg	20		6.00
3/18 MAR 11 91	✓ Baytril-20 Antibiotic	30		14.00
MAR 11 91	✓ Neobacimyx (Trioptic-P)			8.25
MAR 11 91	✓ Aminophylline tablets 100 mg	30		6.50
MAR 11 91	Heartgard Chewables 51-100 mg			23.65

4/1 4/10 *Cefa-Tab*

PATIENT SUBTOTAL: $ 244.40

CONTINUAL ACCUMULATION OF TARTAR ON PETS'S TEETH CAUSE ... ... ARE AN
INFLAMATION OF GUM TISSUE ... ... LOOSEN TEETH ... ... BECO ...
VERY ODOROUS AND INFECTION CAN ... ... TO KEEP TEETH HEALTH ...
AND MANTAIN FRESH BREATH, ANNUAL DENTAL CHECK UP AND SCALING IS VE ...
ESSENTIAL. IF YOU HAVE ANY QUESTION - PLEASE FEEL FREE TO ASK US ...

RETURN IN ONE WEEK FOR REEXAMINATION.

REMINDERS: SEP 11 91   FECAL EXAMINATION-FLOTATION
             SEP 11 91   Heartgard Refill
             MAR 11 92   HEARTWORM EXAMINATION

TOTAL INVOICE: $ 244.40
PREVIOUS BALANCE: -125.00

BALANCE DUE: $ 119.40
PAYMENT - MASTERCARD: 119.40

BALANCE DUE: $ 0.00
=================

IMPORTANT: For our Washington D.C. clients! Please use the 301 prefix
when dialing our hospital. These calls will still remain local calls.

12 45 Monday

MAR 18 1991   ███████ ANIMAL HOSPITAL, Inc.   PAGE: 1

                     Brentwood, MD ██████
                     301 ██████████

                                          CLIENT ID: 64208
                                          INVOICE: 6817

    ████████████████
    ████████████████
    Washington, DC ██████

PATIENT ID: NIK   SPECIES: CANINE   WEIGHT: SEX: MALE
PATIENT NAME: (NIKKI)   BREED: SPANIEL, ENG. COCKER   BIRTHDAY: 05-80

        RE-EXAMINATION ' $ 12.00
        Baytril-20 Antibiotic   27   13.60
        ELECTROCARDIOGRAM (EKG)   60.00
        Processed by Barb, Thank you!   0.00

                         PATIENT SUBTOTAL: $ 85.60

    CONTINUAL ACCUMULATION OF TARTAR ON PETS'S TEETH CAUSES PRESSURE AND
    INFLAMATION OF GUM TISSUE AND EVENTUALLY LOOSEN TEETH. BREATH BECOMES
    VERY ODOROUS AND INFECTION CAN EASILY OCCUR. TO KEEP TEETH HEALTHY
    AND MANTAIN FRESH BREATH, ANNUAL DENTAL CHECK UP AND SCALING IS VERY
    ESSENTIAL. IF YOU HAVE ANY QUESTION, PLEASE FEEL FREE TO ASK US.

REMINDERS: MAY 04 91   VACCINATION EXAMINATION
            MAY 04 91   PARVOVIRUS BOOSTER
            MAY 04 91   DHLP BOOSTER
            MAY 04 91   CORONA BOOSTER
            MAY 04 91   RABIES CANINE 1 YEAR BOOSTER
            MAY 04 91   BORDATELLA BOOSTER
            SEP 11 91   FECAL EXAMINATION
            SEP 11 91   Heartgard Refill
            MAR 11 92   HEARTWORM EXAMINATION

                         TOTAL INVOICE: $ 85.60
                         PAYMENT - MASTERCARD: 85.60

                         BALANCE DUE: $ 0.00
                                          ================

IMPORTANT: For our Washington D.C. clients! Please use the 301 prefix
when dialing our hospital. These calls will still remain local calls.

CONSULTATION REPORT

Routine Small Animal ECG   Dr. ▓▓▓   **Code** 46173

Date 11/23/93   **Time** 4:24 PM   **STRIP#** 3326302   First Time

Veterinarian ▓▓   **Phone** (410) 547-8384   **Fax** (410) 547-8390

Client ▓▓   **Patient** Cash   **Breed** Domestic Shorthair

Sex Male   **Age** 1 years, 6 months   **Wt:** 11.2 lbs. 5.0 kg

---

HISTORY AND PHYSICAL FINDINGS
  VITAL SIGNS: Normal
  GENERAL SIGNS: Lethargy
  CARDIOPULMONARY SIGNS: Murmur (V/VI)
COMMENTS: Three weeks ago had tar poured on him and the owners put mineral spirits on him (turpentine)

ECG FINDINGS:
HEART RATE: 180
RHYTHM: Sinus Rhythm
P-QRS-T: S-T segment: elevated
ECG INTERPRETATION: Sinus rhythm with S-T segment elevation.

ECG AND CLINICAL ASSESSMENT: S-T segment elevation is seen in Cash. This may be associated with myocardial hypoxia. The T-wave is also enlarged, a change that has been associated with myocardial hypertrophy. I do note that we have a very loud murmur in this young cat.

DIAGNOSTIC RECOMMENDATIONS: I would recommend chest radiographs in this patient to complete the cardiac database. I we see significant changes I would recommend an echocardiogram to fully define heart size and function.

THERAPEUTIC CONSIDERATIONS: for Cash Isner
It is difficult to make recommendations for cardiac medications based on the ECG alone at this stage. If, however, you wish to discuss this further, please call me.

▓▓▓▓▓, B.V.M. & S., M.R.C.V.S.,Diplomate A.C.V.I.M. (Cardiology)\nmk

▓▓ Animal Clinic
▓▓
Baltimore, MD ▓▓

OUR DIVERSE STAFF OF SPECIALISTS ARE AVAILABLE ON SATURDAYS AND SUNDAYS FOR ECG AND IMC EVALUATIONS.

11-23 "93" Veterinarian

Patient (Cash)

Code 6123

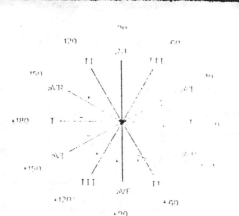

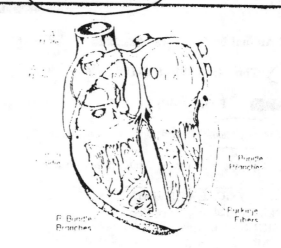

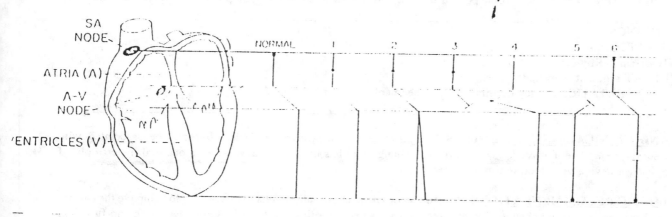

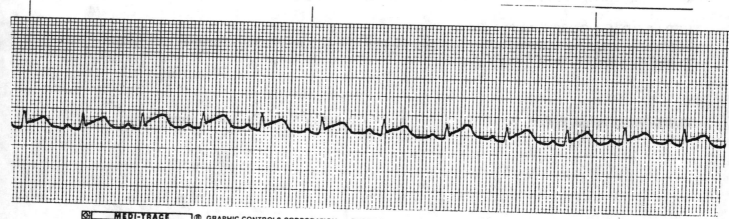

© MEDI-TRACE ® GRAPHIC CONTROLS CORPORATION   BUFFALO. NEW YORK

PRINT

INCORPORATED

FLORAL PARK. NEW YORK 11002 0208

ATTORNEY AT LAW

BALTIMORE, MARYLAND 21201

(301)▮▮▮▮▮
TELECOPIER ▮▮▮▮

June 10, 1994

Dr. Bradley
P.O. Box 4001
Upper Marlboro, Maryland 20775

Dear Dr. Bradley,

This will set out the course of treatment for my dog,
Rosie, after she became ill in the summer of 1993.

Rosie started coughing sometime in August 1993. The
coughing became progressively worse and my son took her to the
▮▮▮▮▮▮ Dog & Cat Hospital in October 1993. Being a young adult
he did not tell me what the vets told him, however, when I took
Rosie to the same vet in November 1993 the she showed me several
tumors in Rosie's lung on an x-ray and informed me that Rosie had
lung cancer. The vet talked about doing such things as biopsies
and chemotherapy, however, since Rosie was 14 1/2 years of age at
that point I did not deem it advisable to proceed in that way. I
enclose Academy's estimate. Instead, I asked for medication which
would suppress the coughing and result in as little pain for Rosie
as possible. The first medication, torbutrol, was small pills
which completely suppressed the cough but left Rosie a little
groggy looking. The pills cost $60.00 for a 10-day supply.
Because of the expense I requested a more inexpensive medicine and
the vet supplied another which cost $30.00 for a 10-day supply.
This medicine suppressed the cough somewhat (not as well as the
first) but did not leave Rosie as groggy as the first. In order
to secure a bulk source of the medicine so as to reduce the expense
I started calling various Animal Rights groups which eventually
referred me to the ▮▮▮▮▮▮▮ Animal Hospital where I
inadvertently discovered you. You examined Rosie and supplied me
with a gallon jug of an herbal concoction to give Rosie several
times per day. You also directed me to change Rosie's diet from
what she had been eating (Gravy Train) to a stew of vegetables
and/or fish and meat with rice, etc.

For the month following our first visit with you Rosie
seemed to improve dramatically. Her cough was not much in evidence
and she looked better and seemed a little more lively. Thereafter,
from January to late February she slowly declined until
approximately early March when she sporadically stopped eating.
You visited Rosie every few weeks, examined her, and adjusted her

liquids and also adding diet supplements of various herbal products. I believe that your intervention provided Rosie with an improved quality of life until her disease overtook her and I also believe that with earlier and more frequent contacts Rosie may have lasted a good deal longer. As it is, she was just short of 15 years old at the time of her death.

I thank you for your efforts and wish you well

Very truly yours,

CL:ll

ESTIMATE

ANIMAL HOSPITAL - BALTIMORE, MD. 21206

PHONE: (301)

PRODUCER NO.		No.
COMPUTER NO.		DATE

NAME: La Mesa Rosa

	PROFESSIONAL EVALUATION	
2500	EXAM - COMPREHENSIVE	
2510	EXAM - FOLLOW-UP	15 9
2497	EXAM - INPATIENT / DAY	
2498	EXAM - INPATIENT / INTENSIVE CARE	
2501	EXAM - EXTENDED	
2514	EXAM - AFTER HOURS	
2506	EXAM - HEALTH CERTIFICATE	
2508	EXAM - RABIES	
2511	EXAM - SPECIALIST	
2502	EXAM - AVIAN / EXOTIC	
2516	OFFICE VISIT - BRIEF	
2495	REFERRAL - ULTRASOUND	25
2513	TELEPHONE CONSULT - SPECIALIST	
2515	TELEPHONE CONSULT - LONG DIST.	
	X procedure 15	

	IMMUNIZATION	
0106	RABIES	
0104	DHLPPC BOOSTER	
0109	DHLPPC SERIES	
0114	DHLPPC SERIES / LITTER	
0101	MEASLES	
0112	LYME BOOSTER	
0113	LYME SERIES	
0111	BORDATELLA	
0102	PARVOVIRUS	
0151	FVRCP BOOSTER	
0150	FVRCP SERIES	
0153	FVRCP SERIES / LITTER	
0110	LEUKEMIA BOOSTER	
2529	LEUKEMIA SERIES	
2523	FELINE PERITONITIS BOOSTER	
2522	FELINE PERITONITIS SERIES	
2531	FERRET DISTEMPER	
2530	FERRET RABIES	

	PARASITE CONTROL	
2554	COCCIDIA (1st day injection)	
2557-60	HOOKWORMS S / M / L / XL	
2561-64	ROUNDWORMS S / M / L / XL	
2569-72	WHIPWORMS S / M / L / XL	
2565-68	TAPEWORMS S / M / L / XL	
2671	PROFILE - SUPERCHEM / CBC	
3585	PROFILE - THYROID	
3584	RETICULOCYTE COUNT	
3609	SKIN SCRAPING	
	TOXOPLASMOSIS	
	T4	
3610	URINALYSIS - COMPLETE	
3613	URINALYSIS - PARTIAL	

	DENTAL PROCEDURES	
2715	ULTRASONIC SCALE / FLUSH	
	POLISH / FLUORIDE TREAT.	
2718	EXTRACTIONS	
2716	ENDODONTICS	
2723	GINGIVECTOMY	
2724	TOOTH CLIP	

| | **SUB TOTAL** | 54.75 |

	RADIOLOGY	
2573	SURVEY - 2 VIEWS	
2575	ADDITIONAL VIEW(S)	
2576	BARIUM SERIES - 6 VIEWS	
2577	CONTRAST MEDIA	
2578	POST-OPERATIVE VIEW(S)	
2583	OFA	
2588	REFERRAL	
2574	SPINAL SERIES - 6 VIEWS	

	PROFESSIONAL SERVICES	
3614	ANAL SAC EXPRESSION	
3615	ANAL SAC INFUSION	
2579	ARTIFICIAL INSEMINATION	
2580	ASPIRATE MASS	
2581	ASPIRATE ABDOMEN / THORAX	
2730-33	BANDAGE S - M - L - XL	
2734-35	BANDAGE - PADDED S - L	
2582	BLADDER FLUSH	
2737	BLOOD TRANSFUSION - CANINE	
2736	BLOOD TRANSFUSION - FELINE	
2738	BLOOD TRANSFUSION - PUPPY	
2739	BLOOD TRANSFUSION - KITTEN	
2744	CATHETER - INTRAVENOUS	
2745	CATHETER - JUGULAR	
2742	CATHETER - URINARY	
2743	CATHETER - URINARY OBSTRUCTION	
2740	CAST APPLICATION	
2741	CAST REMOVAL	
2584	CLIP / CLEAN WOUND	
2585	CYSTOCENTESIS	
3623	EAR CLEANING	
3622	EAR IRRIGATION	
2587	EAR SPLINT	
2750	ECG - INITIAL	
2752	ECG - STAT	
2751	ECG - REPEAT	
2753	ECG - LEAD II	
2758	ENEMA - DSS	
2757	ENEMA - WARM WATER	
2586	EMERGENCY ASSISTANT PER ½ HR.	
3571	EYE - CORNEAL STAIN	
3776	EYE - CORNEAL SHIELD	
3735	SPLINT	
2746	THORACIC TUBE PLACEMENT	
2747	THORACOCENTESIS - EVACUATION	
2748	TRANSTRACHEAL WASH	
3581	VENIPUNCTURE	

	ANESTHESIA	
2540-43	INHALATION / HR. S - M - L - XL	
2536-39	INTRAVENOUS S - M - L - XL	
2546-47	LOCAL S - L	
2548-49	PREANESTHETIC S - L	
2550-53	SEDATION S - M - L - XL	

| | **SUB TOTAL** | |

	SURGERY	
0001	DISPOSABLES	
0000	SURGICAL PACK(S)	
2590-91	SPAY / NEUTER - CANINE	
2592-93	SPAY / NEUTER - FELINE	
2606-07	SPAY / NEUTER - OTHER	

	HOSPITALIZATION	
2768	INCUBATOR / DAY	
	WARD OCCUPANCY / DAY	
2673	– SMALL	
2674	– MEDIUM	½d. 13.50
2675	– LARGE	
2676	– EXTRA-LARGE	
2681	– AVIAN / EXOTIC	
2679	– FELINE	

	BOARDING	
2682	AVIAN / EXOTIC / DAY	
	CANINE / DAY	
2666	– SMALL	
2667	– MEDIUM	
2668	– LARGE	
2669	– EXTRA-LARGE	
2665	FELINE / DAY	

	GROOMING	
2649-52	BATH - CANINE S - M - L - XL	
2655-58	BATH & DIP - CANINE S - M - L - XL	
2647	BATH - FELINE	
2648	BATH & DIP - FELINE	
2654	MEDICATED SOAK	
2653	SPRAY / POWDER	

	AVIAN	
3640	BAND REMOVAL	
3616-18	BEAK RESHAPE S - M - L	
3619	PEDICURE	

RE-EXAMINATION

SUTURE REMOVAL

CLIENT EDUCATION MATERIAL

RECORD RECALL

DISCHARGE CONSULTATION

LABORATORY PENDING

| | **SUB TOTAL** | |

SUB TOTALS	555.95
DEPOSIT	
TOTAL	
PREVIOUS BALANCE	
SUB TOTAL	
CREDIT	
TOTAL	
PAYMENT	
TOTAL AMOUNT DUE	

Special Instructions

PAID BY:
CASH ☐   CHECK ☐   CREDIT CARD ☐

OWNER'S SIGNATURE:
X

PAYMENT RECEIVED BY

ATTORNEY AT LAW

BALTIMORE, MARYLAND 21201

(301)
TELECOPIER

July 8, 1994

Dr. Bradley
P.O. Box 4001
Upper Marlboro, Maryland 20775

RE: Rosie

Dear Dr. Bradley,

Per your recent request, enclosed is a copy of Rosie's medical records from Academy Dog and Cot Hospital. If I can be of further assistance, please call my office.

Thank you for your consideration in this matter.

Very truly yours,

CL:ll

Enclosure

531 N. Curley Street
Baltimore, MD. 21205

January 17,1994

Dear Doc Bradley:

We want to thank-you again for your help and treatment of CASH, our 2 year old Classic American Short Hair. My husband and I are sure that CASH would have died or had to be put to sleep without your help.

On October 31,1993, CASH had tar dumped on his back and hind legs. We watched him suffer by pulling out his hair and crying for a day. We called a Vet and asked if we could use mineral spirits to remove the tar from him and after they had assured us that it would be safe as long as CASH was thoroughly shampooed and rinsed afterwards, we preceded. CASH must have suffered a heart attack from the trauma but he revived and as far as we could tell was none the worst. In less than a week, we watched him become more and more lethargic, his eating and playing habits changed completely he no longer acted as our CASH. We became concerned and took him to the Vets. CASH was diagnosed as having a severe heart murmur (4.5), and was kept for testing. My wife listened to his heart at this time and heard a swishing sort of sound and knew something was not right. CASH's EKG tests came back and the Vet, Dr. Little confirmed our fear, CASH had a heart condition and would need care and medication for the rest of his life.

This is when we met you and you told us of an herbal treatment using herbs and healthy foods that would help CASH, without testing and drugs. You told us to put CASH on a cooked diet, consisting of chicken or turkey, boiled as though making soup, add river rice, carrots, green beans and any other fresh green vegetable and cook, he also could have tuna, salmon or mackerel. You also advised us to give him a capsule of garlic oil and one H Formula (Hawthorn berries, Cayenne, Natural vitamin E and Lecithin) capsule daily for his heart. CASH was not thrilled at first with his diet and least of all with having pills put down his mouth, but after a few weeks on the diet and pills we noticed that his hair was starting to look brighter and his eyes seemed to shine again. He still wasn't quite up to par, but a lot better than before.

After several weeks of treatment we made an appointment and brought CASH in for a check-up, CASH was by this time more like his 'ole' playful self, his eyes were bright, he was alert, his coat was shiny and starting to fill back in and most importantly, CASH no longer had a heart murmur. We were so happy, my wife cried on the way home, had it not been for you, we would have lost a very special friend and companion.

We can not thank you enough!! We now are firm believers in your methods of treatment and are grateful that you shared them with us.

Sincerely,

P.S.
Our 10 month old kitten, George, is on the same diet and garlic pill as CASH and they both would have thanked you in person for helping them but neither can write yet.

 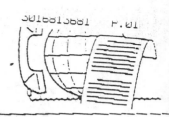

Business Services Center

Fax Transmission

TO: _____ Dr. Bradley _____

FAX NUMBER: _____ ███████ _____

SENDER'S PHONE: ███████   FAX: _____

FROM: ███████   DATE: 11/4/94   # OF PAGES: 4

If you have any difficulties with this transmission,
please call the Business Services Fax Operator at: _____

NOTES: <u>Client's comment:</u>

" Emily " is eating well and it feels she is
putting on weight.

_____

<u>Doc Bradley's comments</u>

a) Emily's new diet is chicken, turkey, fish with pastas + vegetables + grains — (No longer cat food)

b) on product called <u>Green essence</u> — a dried vegetable juice supplement — Store Stamp
contains ① young barley leaf extract
② maltodextrin   ⑨ garlic extract
③ carrot   ⑩ shiitake mushroom
④ coix extract   ⑪ lecithin
⑤ wheat germ extract   ⑫ spinach
⑥ Aloe   ⑬ Broccoli
⑦ Brown rice   ⑭ celery
⑧ Alfalfa   ⑮ green pepper
                              ⑯ Kelp

#190 SILVER SPRING, MD ███

FAX (301)███

LOW PRICE EVERY

Thank You For Using ███████ Customer Fax S█

Routine Small Animal ECG   Dr. ██████   Code 41168

Date 09/02/94   Time 9:14 AM   STRIP# 4244463   First Time

Veterinarian ██████   Phone (301) 449-1610   Fax

Client ██   Patient Emily   Species Feline   Breed Domestic Shorthair

Sex Female   Age 12 years   Wt: 7 lbs.   3.2 kg

HISTORY AND PHYSICAL FINDINGS
   VITAL SIGNS: Normal
   GENERAL SIGNS: Panting; Weight loss, lbs.
   CARDIOPULMONARY SIGNS: Murmur (II/VI); Mucous Membranes (Pink); Abnormal Heart Sounds
   (Irregular Rhythm)
RADIOGRAPHIC FINDINGS: Date taken: 09/02/94, No Lasix was given prior to radiographs.
   Thorax: Cardiomegaly (Mild, right atrium); Bronchial (Mild, Dorsal)
LABORATORY FINDINGS
   HEMOGRAM(CBC): Pending
   CHEMISTRY PROFILE: Pending
COMMENTS: open mouth breathing and panting for the last four days.

ECG FINDINGS:
HEART RATE: 283
RHYTHM: Sinus Tachycardia
ECG INTERPRETATION: Increase in heart rate consistent with hyperthyroidism or cardiomyopathy.

DIAGNOSTIC AND THERAPEUTIC ADVICE

I would suggest doing a T₄ to exclude the possibility of hyperthyroidism, although she fairly young to have that. Therefore, I suspect that we should treat her for cardiomyopathy with 7.5mg of diltiazem BID or TID and 2.5mg of Inderal BID or TID. I would also add 25mg of Theo-Dur BID and 6.25mg of Lasix SID. If she does not improve dramatically from this within two or three days, please contact us with the idea of more aggressive therapy.

██████ D.V.M., Diplomate A.C.V.I.M. (Specialty Cardiology)\cwc

Dr. ██████
██████ Animal Hospital
██████
Camp Springs, MD ██

██████ SPECIALISTS ARE AVAILABLE EVERY
SUNDAY FROM 9 A.M. TO 1 A.M. EASTERN.

VETERINARY ██████████ MEDICAL LABORATORY, INC.
DIVISION OF ██████████

Baltimore, Maryland 2████

Baltimore ██████████ / Washington Area ██████████
Annapolis ██████████ / Virginia ██████████

████████ ANIMAL HOSPITAL (R-12620)   ████ EMILY
          (62.A)   ID: ██████████   BREED: DSH
TEMPLE HILLS MD   20748-0000

(T4 called in 9/3/94)

SPECIMEN COLLECTED: 09/02/94
COMPLETED REPORT: 09/03/94 04:41 AM

ANIMAL'S NAME	DATE	AGE	SEX	LAB NUMBER	LABORATORY REPORT
████ EMILY /FELINE	09/02/94	12	F	R94343631	

HEMATOLOGY:

RBC	7.66	M/CMM (5.00-10.00)	WBC	7.9	K/CMM (	5.5-19.5
HGB	12.8	GM/DL (8.0-15.0)	BANDS	0	% (	0-3
HCT	36.1	% (24.0-45.0)	POLYS	39	% (	35-75
MCV	47	FL (39-55)	*LYMPHS	56	% (	20-55
MCH	16.7	PG (12.5-17.5)	MONOS	1	% (	1-4
MCHC	35.3	G/DL (30-36)	EOSIN	4	% (	2-12
			BASOS	0	% (	0-2
			ATYP LYMPH	0	% (	0-0

COMMENT:
Slight Anisocytosis
Clumping of platelets precludes an accurate count
    however, the platelet estimate appears adequate.
The results of this CBC have been confirmed by
    review of the smear.
SLIGHT RBC CRENATION.

PLATELETS —————————————————— NT   K/CMM   (200-800)

CHEMISTRY:

LDH	238	IU/L (80-340)	GLUCOSE	72	MG/DL (	60-160
*AST (SGOT)	91	IU/L (10-60)	BUN	23	MG/DL (	15-38
*ALT (SGPT)	399	IU/L (10-80)	CREATININE	1.1	MG/DL (	0.7-2.2
*ALK PHOS	179	IU/L (20-90)	BU/CR RATIO	20.9	(	7-30
*TOT. BILI	0.4	MG/DL (0-0.2)	URIC ACID	0.3	MG/DL (	0.1-1.5
*DIR. BILI	0.1	MG/DL (0-0.1)	CALCIUM	9.6	MG/DL (	8.2-10.8
*IND. BILI	0.3	MG/DL (0.1-0.2)	PHOSPHORUS	4.8	MG/DL (	3.8-6.4
TOT. PROT.	6.7	G/DL (5.8-8.4)	SODIUM	152	MEQ/L (	147-156
ALBUMIN	3.4	G/DL (2.4-4.2)	POTASSIUM	3.7	MEQ/L (	3.6-5.0
*GLOBULIN	3.3	G/DL (3.5-5.0)	CHLORIDE	119	MEQ/L (	112-129
A/G RATIO	1.03	(0.4-1.2)	*CO/2	9	MEQ/L (	17-24

CHOLESTEROL ————————————————— 148   MG/DL   (70-270)
AMYLASE ————————————————————— 751   IU/L   (400-1500)

(*** REFERENCE VALUES ***)
(A NEW NORMAL RANGE FOR AMYLASE HAS BEEN)
(ESTABLISHED DUE TO A CHANGE IN METHOD.)

SIGNATURE   DATE REPORTED

VETERINARY DIAGNOSTIC SERVICES

DIVISION OF ██████████ MEDICAL LABORATORY, INC.

Baltimore, Maryland ██████████

Baltimore (██████████) / Washington Area ██████████
Annapolis ██████████ / Virginia ██████████

██████████ ANIMAL HOSPITAL (R-12670)   ██████ .EMILY
                            (62, A)   ID: ██████   BREED: DSH
TEMPLE HILLS MD 20748-0000

SPECIMEN COLLECTED: 09/02/94
COMPLETED REPORT: 09/04/94 04:52 AM

ANIMAL'S NAME	DATE	AGE	SEX	LAB NUMBER	LABORATORY REPORT
██████.EMILY /FELINE	09/03/94	12	F	R94348383	

CHEMISTRY:
  *THYROXIN — T4 ———————————————————— 13.4 UG/DL   (1.1-3.9)

Doc Bradley's comments:

① Emily's results for T4 for the thyroid was 13.4
   normal is (1.1-3.9)

② therefore Emily does have hyperthyroidism
③ also her liver enzymes are elevated:
        a) SGOT = 91   NORMAL
                               10-60
        b) SGPT = 399   10-80
        c) ALK Phos = 179   20-90

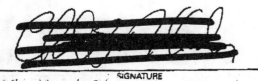

SIGNATURE   (COMPLETED)   09/04/94 4:52 AM

                                                            DATE REPORTED

Fax Cover Page

To: _Doc Bradley_____

Fax# (301) ███████_____

_____

From: ███████_____

Fax# ███████

_____

Comments: #of pages including cover page 3___

_____

_____

should you have any problem with transmission, please call (215) 343-4036

Singer (Binky)

History

    7 year old (whelped April 4) Weimareiner. Problem with
right knee in July '94. Veterinarian (Karen) advised 1
aspirin 2 times a day. Took about 1 month untill the leg
appeared to cause no discomfort.

    We got Singer at 12 weeks old. About a week or two
later, as I held him, I noticed that his heartbeat was so
irregular, it was occasional. I am an RN., so I also noticed
that it was bounding. Resting my hand on his chest, it
felt as if the heart was pounding against his chest. This
is not normal (or good). Our vet at the time (Karen) said
that dogs with big chest cavities often have irregular heartbeats.
Singer has always been a "couch potato", and considered
dumb, uncoordinated and clumsey. He Falls a lot.

                    August 14, 1994

    While riding in the back seat of truck (not padded),
dog yelped in pain and cried. Quick hand exam could find
no area of injury or discomfort. Same thing happened 2
more times during the 8 hour trip. Singer got progressively
worse over the next couple of days until he began having
trouble assuming the position to defecate. He could squat
to urinate (his usual position), but his rear legs shook
violently. No crying or reaction of pain on manual exam.

                    August 18, 1994

    Call to Vet (Karen) to report symptoms over the phone.
Vet called in a prescription for steroids. I did not begin
these medications.

    Instead I gave him Arnica 30c and ST. Johns Wort tincture
2X a day for the next 4-5 days without any noticeable improvement.
My husband then began the steroids as prescribed. He continued
these for approximately 10 days with no improvement. I
went to the AHG symposium, August 26-29, in Capon Bridge
WV and took 2 classes with Doctor Bradley who gave me a
private consultation about singer. I thought that he had
hip dysplasia. Doctor Bradley listened to his symptoms
of falling and not being able to assume the poop position
and said that the dog did not have hip dysplasia. Singer
is a bout 100 lbs. and Doctor Bradley said she thought singer
had Congestive Heart Failure, and went over the symptoms
with me. Singer had all of them except Cyanosis. On August
31 we left our home in Pennsylvania for our property in
West Virginia again. On the trip down in the truck, Singer

became crying and upset when we got out of the truck for
gas. He became extremely Cyanotic; blue lips, nose, gums,
purple tongue, very disturbed respirations, panting, puffing
out his lips, falling down. He stayed upset and cyanotic
for some time after we got back in the truck. On arrival
in Grantsville we went to the health food store and purchased
items suggested by Doctor Bradley. We started Singer on
Honey, Cayenne pepper and garlic right away. Within 2 days
he felt much better. I brewed up some tonic with fresh
burdock root and red clover blossoms at the farm because
the health food store in wv didn't have all the ingredients
that Dr. Bradley recommended. By the middle of the week
Singer felt so good he was throwing himself around the yard
like a puppy. He was up and down the mountain with me and
only once did I notice some shortness of breath when he
had been climbing over fallen trees on an old logging road.
I checked and his lips and gums were very pale but not cyanotic.

     Once we returned to PA I started Singer on the H formula
and BF&C, 2 capsules each, 2X a day. I called Dr. Bradley
and told her about his condition. She said that because
of his size, increase H formula to 3 capsules, 3x a day.
Give cayenne and honey any time he gets cyanotic, and give
lots of honey through the day. Singer was put on the following
formula:

In 1 gallon warm water, simmer;
     Burdock root
     sassafras
     Lecithin (about $2 worth)
     red clover
     organic apple cider vinegar
     brewers yeast
     kelp
cook over low heat for 45 minutes. Take off of heat and
add:(
     cayenne pepper
     honey
     blackstrap molasses
give 1 cup, 2X a day

     Singer responded very well, his energy increased, we
noticed that he got off the couch a lot more, was "perky",
no signs of cyanosis. You could no longer feel his heartbeat
when he leaned against you. In fact you had to search a
pulse or use a stethoscope. His heartbeat is very regular.
Singer developed pneumonia a couple of weeks later, but
after treatment for that his lungs remain clear. Although
still under treatment for a nerve disorder (myelin sheath
deterioration), his CHF is very well controlled.

Submitted by
of Phila. Pa.

Ted's Recovery

The first time that I heard Ted, my 10 year old female West Highland Terrier coughing was in the summer of 1994. The cough particularly alarmed me because her littermate just died earlier that summer and had a cough that sounded exactly like the cough I was now hearing. The frequency of the cough increased dramatically in the fall, from once weekly to several times hourly in the matter of a few months.

Several different vets examined Ted that fall. They were all in agreement that there was not much that could be done. Two echocardiograms were performed, the latter by a cardiologist. His diagnosis was that Ted has an enlarged heart and a genetic lung condition called pulmonary fibrosis.

The cardiologist recommended antibiotics to rule out a possible infection and prescribed Theophylline, a pill to help her breathe more easily. He suggested a bronchoscopy to more closely examine the lungs, but the procedure would not provide a cure. The coughing persisted for weeks and did not improve. The cardiologist recommended the use of over-the-counter cough suppressants. Her symptoms were being relieved but the condition itself was not being treated. For instance, no treatment was recommended for her enlarged heart.

When Doc Bradley first examined her, Ted had been under the care of the cardiologist for about a month and had shown little or no improvement. Doc suggested that there could be a treatment for Ted's condition if I was willing to try some specific herbal remedies and change her diet from the prescription heart diet dog food to natural foods.

At this writing, Ted has been on a natural diet and herbal treatment for one month. During this month I have seen an impressive decrease in the frequency of Ted's coughing. At the start of the new regimen, she was coughing about 5 times each hour. Now Ted sometimes has days when she has only 5 coughs in an entire day. Doc correctly predicted that she will cough more on days when her routine is different and she's under stress.

Doc Bradley has re-examined her and has already noted a slight improvement in her heart. She has closely monitored Ted's progress and recommended that Ted continue with the herbal treatment and natural diet so that she may continue to heal from within. She suggested that I record her daily progress. Doc remains available and is very supportive.

I still struggle to accept that my dog has serious health problems. I have had her since she was a puppy. She is family. With God's help, Doc's guidance, and lots of love, Ted now has a start at recovering from a condition that was diagnosed by other veterinarians as virtually untreatable.

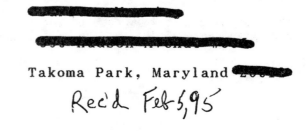

Takoma Park, Maryland

Rec'd Feb 5, 95

Patient: ████████   Date: 11/30/94

Diagnosis: Diffuse pulmonary disease
Rule out infection / fibrosis / allergic — pulmonary fibrosis, it's not
Hypertension   not edema

---

1) Lanoxin (0.125 mg) (0.25 mg)   (5) Aminophylline (100 mg)
                                              Theophylline
                                              Theo-Dur

                                              3/4 tablet twice daily

---

2) Lasix (12.5 mg) (20 mg) (50 mg)   6) Cardizem (30 mg)

---

3) Tenormin (25 mg) (50 mg)   7)

---

4) Vasotec (1.0) (2.5) (5.0) (10) (20 mg)   (8) Chloramphenicol 250 mg
   Enacard   1/2 tablet 3x a day

                                         (DO NOT HANDLE TABLETS WITHOUT GLOVES)

If any blood work has been drawn prior to starting Vasotec - you must call for the
results prior to starting Vasotec. If a serum digoxin test is to be done - it must be
done 6 hours after the morning dose of Lanoxin/Cardoxin to obtain high peak blood levels.

Additional recommendations: Call tomorrow afternoon for results of
blood work. Depending on results may need cushings work up

See regular veterinarian: Recheck here:

Signs of heart failure: cough   tongue turns blue   fainting
                         excessive panting labored breathing   abdominal fluid
                                           can't sleep (restless)
If these are happening, there may be fluid build-up. An extra dose of Lasix can be
given and/or you may wish to call for help.
Signs of Digitalis (Lanoxin, Cardoxin) toxicity: appetite loss   vomiting
                                                  depression   diarrhea
If any of these occur, STOP Digitalis. Call us within 24 hours. It is rarely an
emergency. We will simply stop the drug, and restart at a lower dose.

In an emergency in evenings and weekends, please call the above phone numbers. If the
emergency veterinarian cannot help, ask the receptionist to have Dr. ████████ return
your call.

Feb. 8, 1995

My 60 pound mix-breed Eicho had been sick for about 10 days.
She was very lethargic and showed signs of abdominal discomfort,
as well as had no appetite. At 2yrs. of age, she is normally bouncing
the walls with energy and has a voracious appetite. After becoming
tired of conventional veterinarians that didn't care what was wrong
with her, I decided to try the natural route of healing. I was at the
health food store trying to make heads or tails of all the formulas
and roots and so on, when I was referred to Doc Bradley.

I called her on Jan. 29 with my concerns and she proceeded to tell me

what she felt I should do. Her treatments and results go as follows.
I first spoke to Doc Bradley on a Sunday morning. I was not happy
about calling her on most people's day off, but Eicho had already lost
10 pounds in 10 days and my feeling was that she needed immediate
attention. Doc Bradley asked of Eicho's symptoms and I told her of
her lethargy, redness in the eyes, apathy and weight loss. She seemed
especially concerned about the redness in her eyes because apparently
that can indicate a heart ailment.

That day over the phone she instructed me to mix a solution involving
lemons, honey and distilled water. We made an appointment for her to
come out the next morning. That first evening after only honey, lemon
and water, I could see a noticeable difference in her eyes as well as
her atitude. I made her a large helping of chicken soup and she devoured it.

Doc Bradley came to see us around 10:15 on Monday morning. She checked Eicho over and treated her with penicillin and B-complex. She also provided me with a gallon jug of a tonic she put together the previous evening; explaing about the ingredients and how often to give it to Eicho.

Before Doc Bradley left, she gave me a list of items I should get that would improve as well as maintain my dog's health. Within a few hours of Doc Bradley's visit I could see a significant change in Eicho's condition. She was getting more alert and seemed not to be in pain anymore. Best of all, her spirits were improving.

In the next couple of days, the progress was amazing. By Tuesday she was willing to play a little bit and even enjoyed our walks. By Wednesday she was almost completely healed. She was once again running around the house with her toys and chasing squirrels outside. Here we are exactly one week after our visit with Doc Bradley and I doubt Eicho even remembers being ill. Thanks to Doc Bradley's new diet consisting of pasta, rice, chicken, fish, vegetables, etc and of couse her knowledge and concern, I have my companion back.

Actually, I believe Eicho is on her way to becoming healthier than ever. Thank you Doc Bradley!

Submitted by ▆▆▆▆▆▆▆▆
Waldorf, Md.

Heart disease is a frequent problem especially in older dogs. In can also be a problem in young dogs. The most common form of heart disease, congestive heart failure, results when the heart fails to pump blood efficiently. Congestive heart failure usually results in a "seepage" of fluids from the blood vessels into the tissues of the lungs or abdomen thus causing "congestion" in these areas.

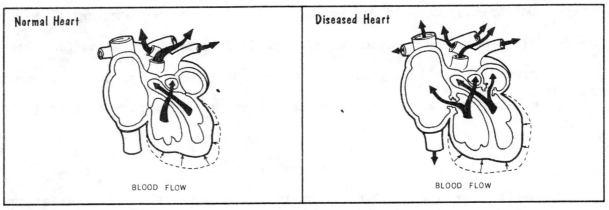

When the heart begins to fail, it will attempt to compensate, or "make-up" for the inefficiency, by: (1) dilating — the chambers of the heart enlarge in an attempt to handle a greater volume of blood, (2) increasing its rate (tachycardia) — the heart speeds up to pump more blood, (3) enlarging (hypertrophy) in an attempt to pump more blood (the larger the pump, the more volume of blood it can handle).

However, these compensatory mechanisms cannot keep pace with the failure of the heart and this leads to the most common signs associated with this form of heart disease: coughing, irregular and rapid breathing, weight loss, abdominal enlargement, and sometimes fainting.

Congestive heart failure can be controlled by use of medication, diet, and reduced exercise. Digitalis (digoxin) is a drug used in treating congestive heart failure. Digoxin helps the heart become a better pump by increasing the force of its muscular contractions and also by slowing its rate.

When used as directed, digoxin can help your dog live a much longer life; however, it does require precise, individualized dosing. Your veterinarian must adjust the dosage of digoxin to the needs of your dog. This dosage will be influenced by such things as the age and condition of your pet and the severity of the heart disease. You may have to visit the veterinarian several times so that he may adjust the dosage.

You can help a great deal by watching your pet to determine how well he is doing with the medication. First you should observe your pet to see if the signs of heart disease are diminishing. As you recall, these are:

☐ **Coughing** ☐ **Abdominal enlargement**
☐ **Irregular and rapid breathing** ☐ **Fainting**
☐ **Weight loss**

If these signs persist, it may indicate that the heart disease is not being controlled and an adjustment in the medication by your veterinarian may be necessary. Once an animal is being given heart medication, even though these signs may be present, you should never increase the amount of medication unless on the advice of your veterinarian.

Since digoxin is a potent drug and dosage adjustment is critical, you should also observe your pet for signs of overdosage. Overdosage can result from giving too much medication or changes in drug metabolism or both. Overdosage can make your dog sick. Signs of overdosage are:

☐ **Nausea**
☐ **Vomiting**
☐ **Diarrhea**
☐ **Refusal to eat (more than one meal offered)**
☐ **Weakened condition**
☐ **Depression**

These signs are early warning signs of overdosage and are not serious if detected early. If you notice these signs of overdosage in your pet, you should stop all medication and call your veterinarian. He will tell you when to restart the digoxin and prescribe an adjusted dosage. Never give any more medication than is prescribed by your veterinarian!!!

By adhering to the professional advice of your veterinarian and with your own careful attention, your pet will be able to live a more comfortable and longer life.

Testimonials:
Feline AIDS
Feline Heart Failure
Leading to Embolism and
Bilateral Paralysis.

To Whom It May Concern,

     This is a brief summary of my personal experience with the
services of Dr. Bradley. I would like it to be noted that if I was
to share all that Dr. Bradley has done for me, I would be able to
write a book. So it takes great effort to condense my experience.
     My cat Bandit was Dr. Bradley's first patient. Bandit was
diagnosed with FIV related illness. FIV(feline AIDS), As we all
know there is no known cure for AIDS, however, my veterinarian
at the time said that Bandit may live a few months longer if he
responded to the antibiotic, in addition she said they could do
a biopsy to determine the exact nature of his elevated liver enzymes.
She suspected a cancerous tumor. She explained that FIV was the
feline's version of AIDS, and Bandit was vulnerable to all the
opportunist illness that HIV victims would be. In addition, there
was Bandit's observable symptoms,which reinforced her suspicion
of cancer. Badit's symptoms are as followed; observable symptoms
included, severe weigh loss (5lbs), sunken eyes, no appetite,
severe vomiting (4-6xdaily), extreme weakness. Symptoms reported
from test results runned by ██████ Animal Hospital; blood test
found FIV, elevated liver enzymes, x-ray shoowed inlarged heart.
Extensive test where run, the above where of the main concern of
my veterinarian at the time. Knowing Bandit's condition I was
encouraged to have him put to sleep, As I explianed that I did not
have the hundreds of dollars that it would of cost for a biopsy
and surgery, it is important to add that I was still given a gloomy
prognoses for Bandit, she explained that there was no cure,
my only hope was to prolong his life for a brief period of time.
Bandit was 8years at the time, which was also a factor to be considered. Despite the fact that Badit is a cat, I though of him as
family, after all he had been my faithful companionfor 8 years.
So putting him to death was out of the quetion. So he was put on
a variety of antibiotics, there was no response on Bandit's part.
In fact his condition appeared to be more critical as he had to be
hand feed, and what little I got down he vomited back up. He was
no longer able to take his-self to the liter box, he released himself wherever he laid. My grief may of clouded my common sense
but I was still unable to have him put to death. In my desperation
I searched out for additional help, as I was told by my veterinary
there was nothing she could do and that he should be put down. That
was when I was given Dr. Sandy Bradley's number, after I expained
my situation to a worker at the local Humane Society.
     Dr. Bradley came out right away, I explained what I was told
by my vet. and explained Bandit's condition. After she examined
Bandit he was put on a herbal combination and a natural diet of
chicken, rice and vegetables. She expained the ingredients of the
herbal combination and what their functions where. Bandit showed
immediate improvement. Within a week, he was eating on his own,
and keeping it down. He no longer had that sunken face look, He
looked perky and had a brightness that I had not seen for a long
time. To my amazement, he started playing and acting like his old
self. Slowly he gained weight and continued to have an increased
appetite. It has been three years, he plays, eats and shows no sign
of discomfort. I had had much guilt about not putting him to death
in those early days, but now I thank God that I didn't. To see so
much life in Bandit overwhelms me with joy, like I said he

is family. As for Dr. Bradley, she treated Bandit like he was family
and not just a cat who did not deserve to fight for life because
he wasn't a human being. Dr. Bradley called to check on Bandit and
ask questions to see how I was doing with giving him his medicine
and how his new diet was going. She monitored his progress closely,
and gave me the guidance and direction I needed. She not only helped
Bandit, but she helped me deal with his illness and provided me with
the much needed hope for his recovery.

Simone was was Dr. Bradley's next patient. Simone collapsed
one day without warning. She was three years old and until she
collapsed we nerver expected anything was wrong with her. I called
Dr. Bradley panic stricken, Simone was an all white cat so it was
easy to see that her gums, eye lids, and ears had lost all calor.
She would not walk, and just cried when we picked her up. She was
also breathing very rapidly. I was given instructions over the
phone to give her some "H", which is an herbal combonation for the
heart and to get fluid in her as she showed signs of dehydration.
I made plans to take Simone to see Dr. Bradley the next day. Needless
to say I did not make it. Simone became critical on the way. I
stopped at ███████ Veterinarian Hospital, as Simone was breathing
through her mouth and her eyes started looking strange like she was
about to pass out, of course I thought she was going to die right
then and there. At ███████ they rushed her to the x-ray machine after
I was told on a scale of 1to6 for having a heart murmur, Simone had
a 5 1/2. The x-ray showed that her heart had ballooned. The Vet.
at ███████ immediately discussed putting her to death. I explained
that I was on my way to see my Vet who was still another 30 minutes
away. The vet. at Squires did not thank she would make it. At that
time I had her call Dr. Bradley. It was decided to put Simone on
oxygen and she was given a dose of digitalis in hopes of stablizing
her so she could be moved. The vet. at Squire explained that Simone
will never fully recover because her heart was severely inlarged.
Simone was released to Dr. Bradley, as the vet would not release
her to me because of her condition. She said She would only
release Simone to another vet. or a heart specialist she could refer me to, as Simone would need to be on oxygen if she was to survive.
Through the guidance of Dr. Bradley, Simone was sent home with me
as it was her belief that the animals do better with their owners.
I also wanted Simone with me if she was going to die. I am very
attached to all my animals. In the mean time Simone had had
additional complications. She developed a saddle emboli, as a
result she lost the use of everything from the waist down. Her
legs would not move at all the skin color was blue. Dr. Bradley
instructed me of what to do and how often to administer medication
and fluids. She explained that Simones condition was critical and
that we were going to need faith and administer her medication hourly.
My husband and I would give her medication every hour on the hour
for three days. Dr. Bradley called constantly and did not mind
my calls in the middle of the night. Dr. Bradley had given us a
animal carrier to keep Simone as she did not want her to move and
we used heating pad and foods that were good for the heart, along
with herbs. Simones recovery was not as instantaneous as Bandit's
but I knew from my experience with Bandit that it was important not
to give up hope. So I didn't, Dr. Bradley was always supportive
and she provided sound advice that did not always sound so sound,

but I followed her advive and directions. So I gave Simone herbs
when Dr. Bradley said to, I massaged her legs and kept her confined
to her carrier. Well Simone surpassed all my greatest expectations.
I think she surprised Dr. Bradley too. Simone regained total use
of her legs, her heart rhythm as normalized. Next week will have
been one year since she first collasped, Today Simone plays she
has good color and a normal heart beat. To look at Simone you
would never believe that she was the same weak kitty who could
not walk or hold her own head up for any significant amount of
time. I can't say enough about Dr. Bradley's expertise with
using alternitive methods to help animals heal that might other
wise die. I know for a fact if I had not used Dr. Bradley's
services I would not be enjoying Bandit and Simone.
    Words can not express my gratitude, but I hope sharing my
experience willmake a difference. Dr. Bradley, saved two very
special pets, who I care about like a family member. She also
saved me hundred of dollars that I just did not have. She worked
with us in all aspects of treating my animals. She also got us in
volved with the treatment of our animals and that was something
that no other vet. has ever done. She also gave me a new
respect for diet and the natural approach to healing diseases. As
a result my husband and I got a family physician who shares simular
philosophies as Dr. Bradley. We figured if it worked for our
animals it could work for us. Dr. Bradley has made a very big
impression on our lives and it has brought so many positive
results to my family's well being.

If you would like any further information please feel free to
contact me.

Hollywood, Md. 20636

This is my follow up letter regarding my experience with herbs and Dr. Bradley's approach to holistic pet care. My cat Bandit is no longer with me, but I was able to have him in my life for three years longer then predicted by my mainstream veterinarian, who felt at the time Bandit should of been put to sleep as he was very sick and showing no signs of improving on antibiotics. My heart told me I needed to try everything possible before making that kind of decision. That's when I sought alternative medicine and found Dr. Bradley. Bandit rapidly improved once he was put on a wholesome diet and herbs. He had a quality of life with no sings of suffering until the last two weeks of his life. As for Simone, she is doing great! you would never believe almost two years ago she was unable to walk because of complication to a sever heart problem. I was told by the mainstream veterinarian that to try and save Simone was unlikely and that if I did she would never be the same, meaning she would have no quality of life. Well! she plays and walks, runs, and appears normal. She is still on herbs for her heart, but other than that she requires no additional help for her to have a happy life. I am very grateful for Dr. Bradley's wisdom of herbs and healing, my cats mean everything to me, and to have them sick and suffering was like having a child sick and suffering. I thank God for people like Dr. Bradley and the plants and foods that are available to bring about well being.

Sincerely,

Rec'd Nov, 3, 1994 (SB)

██████ VETERINARY CLINIC

• UPPER MARLBORO, MARYLAND 20772 • (301)██████

██████, D.V.M.
██████, D.V.M.
██████, D.V.M.
██████, D.V.M.

Dr. Bradley,

"Simone" has been in an oxygen cage since shortly after arrival. Her breathing is still rapid although not as labored. The FeLV/FIV test was negative. (Ag test).

Treatment thus far has consisted of digoxin, 0.04 mg PO and 12.5 mg aminophylline SQ at approximately 10 AM.

Enclosed also are the additional radiographs.

Good luck with this case.

Sincerely,

██████, DVM

Referenced to ██████s cat

**Testimonials:
Diabetes
(also See "Taka"
under Memorials)**

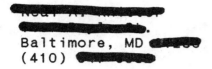

Baltimore, MD ████████
(410) ████████

July 17, 1994

To Whom It May Concern:

This testimonial is an attempt to chronicle my experience employing non-conventional veterinary care, largely under the guidance of Dr. Sandy Bradley at whose request this is being written.

By way of introduction, in mid-year 1992, my cat Joanna (then 13 years old) developed a skin problem which my traditional vet began treating as an allergy to dust. Although shots improved her skin and coat, the overall problem continued. In fall of 1992 my vet also switched my cat from Science Diet C/D to D/D (a lamb/rice mixture) on the chance her problems might also be food-related. This was supposed to be for a several months' trial period. However, Desert Storm intervened with my primary vet serving overseas. During the course of his absence several different vets rotated at the clinic to maintain his practice. None of the substitute vets could recommend anything other than continuing Joanna's bi-weekly allergy shots. A couple of times, due to the severity of her skin rash, antibiotics were also prescribed. This whole situation did not change when my primary vet finally returned from Desert Storm, for he himself was ill and forced into retirement.

In November of 1993, Dr. Sandy Bradley happened to be the vet on hand when I brought Joanna in for yet another allergy shot. While Dr. Bradley gave my cat her shot due to her immediate need, she also began to enlighten me to the possibility of a non-conventional approach to using herbs and natural supplements. However, it was advised that, due to the length of Joanna's problems without appreciable results, a full battery of tests be performed to better understand her general physical condition.

The results of these major tests were surprising. Given her advanced age (now 14 years old) Joanna was in very good shape - with one serious exception: She was badly diabetic which was straining her heart as well. It would appear that the entire time Joanna was being treated for allergies, we were really only treating a secondary illness; the real problem was that her immune system was so badly depressed from the attempt to fight the diabetes. At this time, Joanna's blood sugar was in the high 400's.

Dr. Bradley and I discussed options. I did not wish to subject my cat to a regimen of insulin shots and decided to try an herbal solution based on Dr. Bradley's success with other diabetic animals. This included terminating the prescription diet Joanna had been on in favor of a diet based on rice, carrots, potatoes, string beans, fish and chicken - all cooked "from scratch" by yours truly. To this were added herbal compounds: "PC" (for pancreas) consisting of cedar berries, uva ursi leaves, licorice root, mullein leaves, cayenne and golden seal; "H" (for heart) with hawthorn berries, cayenne, vitamin E and lecithin; as well as sarsaparilla, cod liver oil, brewer's yeast and garlic. While a natural approach takes longer for results than conventional medicine we did observe in succeeding weeks a general improvement in Joanna's attitude and energy level. Her blood sugar count had remained basically the same. We continued the allergy shots.

In mid-December '93 Dr. Bradley ended her affiliation with my clinic. We continued to remain in touch by phone (as we do today) as we live in different cities. Shortly after this (Christmas) Joanna started having a real problem again with her rash and serious loss of hair. A new primary vet had now assumed direction of the clinic, one who knows Dr. Bradley and is open to a combined conventional/natural approach. Antibiotics were required to get Joanna's rash under control once more and I returned her to the Science Diet D/D (lamb/rice) food she had been on before. I subsequently learned she was allergic to chicken! So much for good intentions. I did continue all the supplements recommended by Dr. Bradley. Joanna's attitude and energy level once again improved noticeably; her sugar however remained in the 400's and she was generally degenerating, having lost two pounds in six weeks. My 14 year old cat, who had once weighed 15 lbs, now weighed slightly more than 8 lbs. Her skin and coat had improved under the regular allergy shots, but I could no longer delay insulin treatment. The allergy shots were now stopped.

On Feb. 22, 1994 we started with 2 units/twice a day of "R" insulin. A week later her blood sugar had increased to 530! We then switched to 3 units of "NPH" insulin along with one glucotrol pill twice a day. My primary vet did not hold much hope for these pills as they had shown no appreciable success in cats; I however, wanted to try anything I could to help my long-time companion. At this time I also added alfalfa and zinc to her diet based on my reading of human diabetic "testimonials" in Shaklee materials. I know the favorable results I had when I became a member of this company and began a life enriched by healthy supplements. I hoped they would have a positive affect on Joanna also. I kept Dr. Bradley informed as to my decisions and she was also anxious to see if there would be an improvement.

One week after starting the new insulin, glucotrol pill and additional supplements, on March 4, 1994 Joanna's sugar had dropped from 530 to 275. Encouraged, I proceeded to add yet more Shaklee products to my cat's diet (a multi-vitamin/ mineral, an instant protein mixture and another mixture which helps stimulate natural insulin). One week later (March 12, 1994) blood sugar was down to 179 and Joanna's weight up to 8.6 lbs.

On March 19 we eliminated 1 insulin shot a day — leaving 1 shot of 3 units and 1 pill in the morning; 1 pill only at night. On March 26, sugar was up (273) and weight slightly down, 8.5 lbs. We decided to try doubling the evening pill to see if it could pick up the slack. On April 9 Joanna's sugar was an amazing 56 and weight 8.8 lbs.

After consultation with both my primary vet and Dr. Bradley, I decided to try what would have been unthinkable earlier — to eliminate both shots, with two pills twice a day. March 15: blood sugar had risen to 174; weight 8.3 lbs.

March 22: blood at 177; weight 8.0 lbs. One possible side affect of the glucotrol is depressed appetite (clearly the problem here). While the sugar level could have been accepted, the weight reduction definitely could not. We therefore resumed a 1 shot + 1 pill/2 pill regimen. One month later (May 27, 1994) Joanna's blood sugar was 96 and holding with weight also improving. After an often rocky road over approximately 6 months, Joanna was now considered stable. Her skin and coat are healthy without additional medication and she acts younger than her years. The big question is what caused the big improvement. The correct insulin was necessary — for a time at least. Joanna did not do as badly as we feared she might have during the two weeks in April '94 when we tried eliminating all shots. I can foresee trying again sometime in the future. Joanna will soon be 15 years old and the trauma of her daily shot is something I'd prefer to forgo. The biggest variable appears to be the glucotrol pills which up to now were largely unsuccessful in cats. What caused them to work in Joanna's case? I can see no other explanation than crediting the combination of herbal supplements suggested by Dr. Bradley and the Shaklee products I added. Given time the herbs and vitamins may improve Joanna's health to the point where I can eliminate that last shot. However, even if that does not happen, one small shot of 3 units is not bad when you consider a "normal" dosage of insulin for a diabetic cat would be one-to-two units per pound of body weight. In Joanna's case, therefore, she could expect to be receiving 8 to 16 units (or more) a day.

My primary vet is amazed how Joanna has improved so drastically and (I might add) unexpectedly, given her severe diabetic condition when it was finally diagnosed. Dr.

Bradley is happy we could augment conventional treatment with natural supplements and receive results far beyond our expectations. And I? I'm just happy to have my old girl around for a few more years yet.

Baltimore, MD

Dear Doctor Bradley;

Sorry, for the delay in my writing to you. But it seems that the days do not have enough hours for me to do all the work I have to do! With my home, yard etc. and my job 1 acre of land to cut grass, and look after 32 duplexes plus about 35 older people keeps me hopping, but it is good for my mind to keep busy right now, and the money I can also use of course!

I really appreciate all your phone calls you have given me, and help you have offered to me. "Thank You".

Bunny, so far seems to bee doing fine. She has her off days, but not too often! Bunny never was a real active dog ever since she came into our home & lives at the age of 6 month old. She was more of a sleeper! Than a run about.

I really do not know what you wish for me to write to help others on your work. (Book.) To understand Bunny's Condition. But here goes, I hope it helps you......

Bunny, is our 10 year old beloved gentle white Toy Poodle. She became a Diabetic Feb 3/84. She seemed depressed, and withdrawn after her first few injections (Insulin) and change in her diet. (Eats ¼ cup 4 times a day now.) She used to love to eat, and sort of stopped eating right away!

She also has the start of eye cataracts. She is on 2 Insulin injections - A.m & p.m. 8.30   8.30
daily.

After much reading about Natural Health for dogs and cats. I got in touch with Dr. Seddy Bradley, long distance, by phone, and with her tend guidance via phone, We put Bunny back on the road again of being her old self.

I give Bunny at least 2 Eye Bright capsules a day for her eyes. So far her cataracts have not progressed. I give her also the capsules super garlic - 2 of these. ———>

"Daily" she eats a low fat diet, Chicken, carrots, sometimes baked Potatoes, eggs, Rye Bread toasted.

l also give her cod-liver oil or Flax seed oil.

1 Vitamin c 500 milligrams

1 Teasp of Nutritional yeast. (mixed in a bit of milk)

1 teasp of granular Lecithin. (she does not like it)

l truly-believe that all this is very helpful to Bunny, to live a better life.

15 years ago l had another little poodle, with Diabetes, And l did not have (Monique) the knowledge of all the above mentioned and her life Was shortened l believe, also she became blind with in weeks of being diagnosed With Diabetes, and had many Insulin reactions, at least 1 a month, and later into her Diabetes at least one a week. Bunny, so far has not have had one !!

Also the same Veterinarian, that has treated my-Monique, is treating Bunny now.' This might be of interest to you, he also increased his knowledge l believe.

...Well. Dr. Bradley, l hope this letter is O.K. by you. If not sorry. but as promised you did hear from me !!

Take Care,
Many thanks,

~~Signature~~

Good luck in publishing your Book.

~~Signature~~

Testimonials:
Thyroid Problems
with Skin Disorders
and
Miscellaneous Skin Disorders

Dear Dr. Bradley,

This is to thank you for the kind attention you gave to our dog Peek-A-Boo when she so unfortunately lost her fur. We appreciate how you took extra time to show us how to mix and apply the healing mixture that helped her miserable skin condition. Following your advice about proper diet and the use of the proper herbs truly did work an amazing cure and total regrowth of her beautiful coat--looking even better than before--a constant amazement to all.

We have learned from this just how herbs and diet can help us as well.

Thanks again!

Sincerely

~~[signature]~~

Chevy Chase, Maryland   20815

June 27, 1993

To whom it may concern:

Dr. Bradley was referred to me by Mr. ██████████. I was very impressed with the results that Mr. Ackerman had with Dr. Bradley's treatment for his dog. Consequently, I arranged for her to treat our dog, Rafe. When Dr. Bradley first saw Rafe, he was in very poor condition. He had lost most of his fur and his skin was very dry, flaky, itchy and full of raw skin sores from excessive scratching. Also, his eyes were dull and listless and he had an irregular heart beat.

After approximately three months of treatment, Rafe showed remarkable improvement in all of these areas. In particular, his fur rejuvenated from a scraggly\mangy coat to a thick, shinny and beautifully healthy looking one. Thus, the results are clearly satisfactory.

Prior to Dr. Bradley's treatment, we had taken Rafe to several Veterinarians and a skin disease specialist. He showed no improvement under their care.

In addition, Dr. Bradley is very courteous, professional and conscientious as demonstrated by her consistent follow-up efforts to insure Rafe's future good health. Therefore, I highly recommend Dr. Bradley and I am confident that her expertise in the field of Herbal Medicine will continue to benefit many families and their pets.

Sincerely,

Baltimore, Md. 21230

Dear Dr. Bradley ~   12/15/93
     WONDER OF WONDERS!

     That applies to you ... as well as to Simon's progress!

     What I can't figure yet is how you came up with
the solution BEFORE we knew the problem: Simon's
rump, raw from chomps against fleas? To relieve
boredom? In response to stress? Symptomatic of
allergy? Who knew for sure?

     But what I do know is that he chomps no more
... that his relief is matched only by mine ... and
that you ~ and what I ~~affectionately~~ reverentially
called your 'voo doo' ~ made history of the misery!
     THANK YOU, THANK YOU, THANK YOU.

     But how can I thank you? Would you like a
plant from my form greenhouse? A dinner at my
museum-ship-row house? Attendance on New Year's
Eve for you & your guests, to experience the fireworks,
showering right down on your head, as you sit on
the harborside deck of my house? Any or all of the
above? Please advise (727-1880, very early or very
late easiest times to reach me).
                                         appreciatively

Note: No one knows your
      first name, at IHAC!

Muscle and Bone Disorders
(in Chronological Order
Seen in Practice)

July 22, 1985

Dr. Bradley
Abe Lincoln Animal Clinic
Washington, DC.

Dear Madam,

During the years that you have been treating Dutchess, her health has been very good.

In the first six months, her rib muscle on the left side, as you know, was swollen; we rubbed her down with the herbs, as you instructed, twice a day. The muscle returned to its normal size in about five weeks, and she is doing fine now.

Respectfully,

The May Family.

May 12, 1993

To Whom This May Concern,

I am in favor of Dr. Sandy Bradley reopening her case
against ~~████████████████████~~

Dr. Bradley has been serving the needs of my pet dog for
nearly eight years. When I first got my dog, Dr. Bradley
had a wonderful, well equipped clinic that served the needs
of all pets. I sincerely hope that she will someday have a
clinic that the concerned community of pet owners can
patronize with trust.

In 1987 my small mixed terrier was attacked by two german
shepherds. When I was unable to reach Dr. Bradley right
away, I took my dog for emergency treatment at another
clinic. After keeping her for two days I was informed that
she needed an orthopedic surgeon, and would possibly lose
her damaged leg. I was then able to reach Dr. Bradley. She
examined my dog's leg, checked her X-rays, and used all
natural remedies to help mend my dogs broken bones.

Although the other vet warned that my dog's leg might have
to be amputated, with Dr. Bradley's excellent holistic
approach, my dogs leg has been normal for almost five years.
She still chases squirrels on a daily basis, and runs as
fast as she did as a pup!

I sincerely hope that Dr. Bradley is able to get a much
needed animal clinic like she once had. I'm certain many
animal owners would patronize her business, I know I would.

Sincerely,

~~████████████████████~~

See Princess Tela
Cases with a
story completed for Vol I

This is a short note to thank Dr. Bradley for coming to our rescue <u>Halloween night last year.</u> Oct. 93

My ~~five~~ (5) y.o. male toy poodle (Zacchaeus) had a reoccurrence of a slip disk in his lower back, that basically arrested his mobility.

Four months prior to this incident, he was disabled in the same manner. He could not walk, sit or raise his hind leg to urinate. Because of the pain he'd get from trying to move, he would stand motionless for hours in one spot. Lying him down on his side so he could rest would be a challenge. He had to be carried outside several times a day so he could relieve himself.

Taking him to a modern day veterinarian, he was not certain about the prognosis without x-rays, so a shot of steroids & some pain pills were given, to be taken twice daily. The vet suggested surgery if the problem did n't go away. He got better several days later.

But, once again without any visible signs or symptoms it happened again.

One morning much to my surprise when Zacchaeus was not on the bed, but standing in the middle of the floor motionless I knew what was wrong.

My beautician came over later that morning and suggested that I call Dr. Bradley. She has used Dr. B. for years for her four dogs. So we call Dr. B. & she returned my call later that day, & assured me she would take care of Zacchaeus.

As she promised, Dr. B. came that night, examined him and recommended a herbal tea blend of over _?_ herbs. This was given him at least three times daily, starting that night, along with White Oak Bark for pain, which I had on hand for myself.

The next evening I could see the difference. He was trying to move & he was able to lie down on his pillow w/very little discomfort. I still continued to take him outside physically because of my step, but later that night he walked to the door himself.

When Dr. B. called to check up on him Two (2) days later, he was about 85% better and barking. But I limited his jumping. I will recommend Dr. B's blended herbal teas to any one who has Pets of any charterization as well as for them self.

I am very glad to see that someone has the time and knowledge to go back to basic where you won't have any side affects. Thank God for Dr. B.

~~Signature~~

Bryans Road, MD.
5/27/94   20616

Dear Doc. Bradley,

I wanted to write you
and thank-you for all you have done;
I think your wonderful; it isn't very
often that one meets a Vet (or any
(other kind of doctor) that really cares
about what they do. I'm sure when
they first started they all cared; but
they have seemed to loose it, and
you did not.

I remember when you
were recomended to me by a friend;
You have helped my pets and you
even eased my heart when you
came to look at our family dog
whom I thought was dieing; you
gave him some kind of shot and
made up a tonic that I gave to
him everyday, and within the
week he went from a dog who
would not even get up off the floor

To his old playful self. It hurts
when an animal that you've
grown attached to becomes so ill
that you think its going to die,
and I am so greatful that you
were here to help.
       The tonic you told me
to mix up because our dog was
scratching so bad that he caused
a sore on the side of his face worked
great. Who would of thought that
lemon juice, menthol rubbing
alcohol, pesoxide, olive oil and
apple cider vinegar would stop
him from scratching, and the
sore on the side of his face healed
beautifully; by the way; it also
helped me, I put it on my
poison ivy and it stopped
that from itching too, thanks!
       I want to truely thank
you for everything, for my dog
and my cats.
       You even paved a friends
dog, I don't know how you do

what you do, on how you know,
its a God given talent and your
great at what you do.
        I hope life treats you
very well and that all you do ends
with great succes. May God Bless
you and keep you safe.
        Thank-you so very much,
for everything.

                Sincerly
                ~~Miss Ashley Schaefer~~

**Testimonials:
Heartworm Disease
(With and Without
Other Complications)**

June 3, 1993

Dear Sirs:

I am writing this letter to let you know how glad I am
that I found Dr. Bradley. I was given her name by a friend of
mine that had used her services before.

I have a dog that at the time had delivered 8 puppies in
March. She was still bleeding and the vet that I took her to told
me that it was my fault because I had not brought her into them
while she was pregnant. I had tooken her in when I thought she
was late in delivering her puppies. She had a very hard delivery,
she actually refused to help out the first three puppies that
were born. I had to take care of them so that they would live.

I took her into the vets when the puppies were about 3 weeks
old, they had to stay overnight because they needed to check out
the reason for her bleeding. They could not find a reason that seem
to make sense to me.

A week later I went down stairs to see the puppies because
they were a little nosie and everyone of them were alive. That was
at 1:30 p.m. then at 3:30 p.m. my oldest daughter came home from
school and went down to see the puppies. She started screaming beca
one of the puppies was not moving. I went to check this out and the
puppy was dead. We got rid of the dead puppy.

Two hours later another puppy started to get sick, she was
having trouble breathing, and she looked very sick. I called the
vet and told them that we had a puppy that was sick and that we
also had a puppy that had died two hours earlier. I was told that
I needed to bring in the died puppy only after I had gotten to the
vet. They checked the rest of the puppies out and gave different
reason as to way the puppies were getting sick: the delivery had
been to hard on them(this was 4 weeks after they had born), they
could possibly have the parvo virus, or they could have another
virus all together. They gave me medicine for that one puppy and
another puppy that was starting to get sick. (I had 7 puppies at th
time that could get sik.) In fact by the end of the night I had
three puppies sick, and the puppy that I had taken to the vets
was dead. (She had died within an hour of getting her home.)

I called Dr. Bradley and she came right out to the house.
She stayed with me for 4 hours and looked after the puppies. We
had the time had two of the three puppies that were sick that looke
like they could die. Dr. Bradley gave them her nature medicine which
was simply to give them some lemon severl time within the next 4
hours. They were not allowed to drink or eat for next couple of days
She keep tabs on them and when necessary I called her and she told
me what to do to help them. I only lost one of them three puppies
that had come down sick. The worst puppy lived and to this day she

is doing beautiful.

Dr. Bradley has been able to do what no Dr. was willing to do, she gave these puppies a chance to live. I believe that if she had been unable to care for them they would have died.

Pepper, the mother dog, also had a sever case of heartworm, she was to go into the hospital and receive the medication to start ridding her body of the worms. The treatment was expensive and I was unable to care for Pepper through the vets. While she was they Dr. Bradley check Pepper out. She gave her a mixture that she was to drink, or eat over her food. Pepper was so bad that she was not even given the possible clean bill of health from the vets with their treatments. I gave Pepper the treatments the Dr. Bradley gave me, it was something that I was able to make-up when I needed it and it was inexpensive. Pepper to this day is very health and she has delievered her second litter of puppies. This time her litter was 9. She had only one heartworm that could be found when her blood was tested this year. That worm was so hard to find that it took two blood samples to find.

Dr. Bradley's way of practicing medicine is different but she has been given a gift of healing. I would not take my animals to another vet now that I have seen her work first hand.

Dr. Bradley thank-you for helping all the animals that you come in contact with.

Sincerely your,

My "peek-a-poo", Shasta Lynn, is about 5 years old, and is a very lovable little dog. She plays well with children and loves to haver he tummy and back scratched. Once a year she goes to the vetinarian for her shots and kenneling. In October 1993 when we picked Shasta up from the vetinarian we were told that she had heart-worm. The vetinarian had determined this during her routine physical. They had taken a blood smear. The vetinarian stated they would confirm how serious the heart-worm was by drawing blood prior to treatment. The treatment was up to 4 shots of arsenic over a two day period. After six-weeks, Shasta would return for another blood test to determine if the treatment was working.

I knew a lady in Port Republic whose dog had had the arsenic treatment. Somehow the arsenic had gotten on leg tissue and as the tissue died, it sloughed off. Eventually the dog had to be put to sleep because they could not stop the spread of whatever was causing the dog to lose his flesh and skin.

My daughter told me about Dr. Bradley. Dr. Bradley had treated her two dogs, Katie and Pepper, for heart-worm and they were cured. She told me that Dr. Bradley did not use arsenic, but treated the dogs organically. Naturally I got in touch with Dr. Bradley and explained the situation.

Dr. Bradley examined Shasta Lynn in my home. She gave me a tonic that she had made. I could see clover flowers floating in it! Shasta was to get 6cc's twice a day. It was very difficult to get Shasta to take the tonic, so we began putting it in her food. Dr. Bradley also showed me the commercial dog food I was feeding Shasta had steriods and other ingredients that neither she nor I wanted Shasta to have. Dr. Bradley asked me to stop feeding Shasta the commercial food and fix her a "stew" with lots of vegetables, some garlic, and use only fish, chicken, or turkey. On occasion I could give Shasta beef -- but only as a treat. This was similar to what my Daddy had fed our dogs when I was growing up. In addition, I was to give Shasta about 1500 miligrams of garlic. We put this in her food.

I did not notice that Shasta was not real active before we began this treatment. She still barked at passerbys and ran around the yard chasing a thrown ball. However, after a few days, Shasta was behaving like a puppy with more energy than I'd seen in a long time. She began romping with the cat, chasing birds, and could jump half-way up the screen door. When she came in the house, she ran around from room to room rather than plopping under the table. In December, Dr. Bradley gave us another container of tonic, and asked us to add Cod Liver Oil to it. In (March) of this year, Dr. Bradley drew blood from Shasta for the lab to test for heart-worm. The report came back negative. Sometime this month (June) Dr. Bradley will draw another specimen of blood for further testing.

I am not sure if the vetinarian diagnosed Shasta's heart-worm correctly because we were unable to draw blood from her on Dr. Bradley's first visit. But I do know that my dog is healthier thanks to Dr. Bradley's treatment.

DATE	DR.	RECEP.	OWNER	CASH	CHECK	CREDIT CARD	TOTAL FEE	PATIENT
		INITIALS			PAYMENT RECEIVED			

1. PROFESSIONAL EVALUATION — FEE
- ☐ Initial Examination
- ☑ Regular Examination — 20
- ☐ Comprehensive Examination
- ☐ Re-Examination
- ☐ Avian/Exotic
- ☐ Presurgical
- ☐ Health Certificate

2. EMERGENCY FEE

3. HYPODERMIC INJECTIONS
- ☐ Antibiotics
- ☐ Allergy Shots
- ☐ Antiinflammatory
- ☐ Analgesic
- ☐ Vitamins
- ☐ Other:

4. MEDICATION (PHARMACY Rx)
- ☐ Prescriptions

- ☐ Prescription Diet ( )
- ☐ Heartworm Preventive
- ☐ Multiple Vitamins
- ☐ Flea Control Products
- ☐ Other:

5. IMMUNIZATIONS   1 2 3 4 5
- ☐ PUPPY ☐ KITTEN ☐ FERRET
- ☑ Canine Bordetella (B-Vac)
- ☑ Distemper/Hepatitis/Parvo/Parainfluenza (DHPP) — 8
- ☐ Feline Distemper/Rhino/Calici (FVRCP)
- ☐ Feline Leukemia Vaccination (FELV)
- ☑ Rabies (RAB) — 17
- ☐ County License Fee (Intact/Ster./Sr.) — 15
- ☐ Other:

4. PARASITE CONTROL   S   M   L
- ☐ Hookworms   1   2   3
- ☐ Roundworms   1   2   3
- ☐ Tapeworms   1   2   3
- ☐ Coccidia   1   2   3
- ☐ Whipworms   1   2   3
- ☐ Other:

7. OUTPATIENT PROCEDURES
- ☐ Eye
- ☐ Ear Flush
- ☐ Anal Sacs
- ☐ Wound Preparation
- ☐ Bandages/Wrap/Dressing Change
- ☐ Nail Trim
- ☐ Wing Clip/Beak Trim
- ☐ Euthanasia
- ☐ Other:

8. ANESTHESIA
- ☐ Premedication
- ☐ General (Injections)
- ☐ General (Injections & Inhalation)
- ☐ Local
- ☐ Sedative

9. SURGERY
- ☐ Operating Room
- ☐ Surgical Pac
- ☐ Electrosurgery
- ☐ Cryosurgery

SOFT TISSUE

ORTHOPEDIC

OTHER

10. RADIOLOGY
- ☐ Survey Films & Interpretation
  Number of Views
- ☐ Special Studies & Interpretation
  Organ System
  Number of Views
- ☐ Certified Rad Interpretation

11. LABORATORY
- ☐ Fecal Flotation   Pos (Neg)
- ☐ Fecal (Direct)   Pos   Neg
- ☐ Urinalysis   Norm Abnor
- ☐ Culture & Sensitivity
- ☐ Fungal Culture
- ☐ Gram Stain
- ☐ Heartworm (Filter)   Pos (Neg)
- ☐ Heartworm (Occult)   (Pos) Neg
- ☐ Blood Count ☐ (RBC) ☐ (WBC) ☐ (HCT) ☐ (Dif)
- ☐ Thyroid Profile
- ☐ BUN - Kidney   Norm Abnor
- ☐ SALT. - Liver   Norm Abnor
- ☐ Chemlary Profile 1 2 3 4 — 77
- ☐ Glucose — 75
- ☐ Needle Aspirate
- ☐ Ear Mite Check
- ☐ Allergy Testing
- ☐ Leukemia Virus Test (Feline)   Pos   Neg
- ☐ Skin Scraping   Norm Abnor
- ☐ Schirmer Tear Test   Pos   Neg
- ☐ Fluorescein Dye
- ☐ Vaginal Smear
- ☐ Histopathology (Biopsy)
- ☐ Cytology
- ☐ Proban Screen ☐ Pro-Spot Screen
- ☐ Hemabartonellosis ☐ FIP
- ☐ Other:

12. ELECTROCARDIOGRAM
- ☐ Stat

13. DENTAL CARE
- ☐ Anesthesia
- ☐ Ultrasonic Scale ☐ Polish
- ☐ Extractions   @$
- ☐ Antibiotic Injections
- ☐ Oral Hygiene (Dispensed)

14. FLUID THERAPY
- ☐ I.V. Catheters & Infusion Sets
- ☐ I.V. Fluids
- ☐ S.Q. Fluids   Liters
- ☐ Blood Transfusions
- ☐ Respiratory Therapy

15. BATHS   S   M   L
- ☐ Regular Bath   C   F
- ☐ Medicated Bath   C   F
- ☑ Bath/Dip (Flea & Tic) C   F   50%
- ☐ Bath/Dip (Mites)   C   F
- ☐ Other:

16. HOSPITALIZATION
- ☐ Dr. Supervision & Nursing Care
- ☐ Intensive   Days @ $ Day
- ☐ After Hours Nursing   Days @ $ Day
- ☐ Hypodermic Injection

17. BOARDING   S   M   L
- ☑ Canine   13 Days @ $ 6   Day
- ☐ Feline   Days @ $ Day
- ☐ Bird   Days @ $ Day
- ☐   Days @ $ Day

TOTAL CHARGES — 174

DEPOSIT

BALANCE DUE

CASH	CK	MC	VISA	INITIAL:

PAYMENT IS DUE WHEN SERVICE IS RENDERED.
DEPOSIT IS REQUIRED ON ALL INPATIENT SERVICES.

HOME CARE INSTRUCTIONS
- Please CALL nurse to report progress in ____ day
- Heartworm/urine/fecal test requested in ____ day
- Revaccination recommended
- Reworming recommended
- Suture removal in
- Re-exam required in ____ days (Please schedule appt)
- Follow-up Blood work, ECG, X-Ray
- Keep patient warm 80° 85° 90° F
- Additional Comments:

SPECIMEN #	TYPE	PRIMARY LAB	REPORT STATUS		
077-017-2056-0	S	VB	FINAL	PG	1

03 C

CLINICAL INFORMATION   03-21-94   08:56

ADDITIONAL INFORMATION

L FAX RESULTS TO
202-889-9569

SPECIES - CANINE

PHYSICIAN ID.   PATIENT ID.

PATIENT NAME	Location	SEX	AGE (YR./MOS.)
████████ , SHASTA		F	010/00

PT. ADD.

ACCOUNT

ANIMAL CLINIC OF ██████████   0810835
DR. ████████████████   VJ
████████████████ ██ AVE ██   VV
WASHINGTON   , DC ██████
202-██████████   VAA

DATE OF SPECIMEN	DATE ENTERED	DATE REPORTED	
03/18/94	03/19/94	03/21/94	7626

TEST	RESULT	LIMITS	TEST SITE ON BACK
CANINE OCLT HEARTWORM ANTIGEN	(NEGATIVE)		VB

DIRECTOR: ████████ DVM ████ DACVP
IF YOU HAVE ANY QUESTIONS CONTACT - BRANCH: ████████ LAB: ████████
LAST PAGE OF REPORT

Note:
Dr. ████ is a colleague of Dr. Bradley
Follow-up (blood tests were submitted via her hospital

H-7156 B-3001J REV. 10/93

WESLEY BUSINESS FORMS -WINSTON-SALEM, NC 27109 - (919) 969-9101

Rev. 10/93

Testimonials:
G.I. (gastrointestinal) Disorders

To whom it may concern: June 8, 1994

Our 7 year old Doberman had serious stomach/intestinal discomfort
for some time as a result of several operations and residual
adhesions.
Dr. Bradley prescribed a tonic of natural ingredients to be
fed at meal time. This tonic has substantantially alleviated
our Dobermans discomfort and he is again active and healthy.

Col. USAF (Ret.)

To whom it may concern:

I am writing this letter in behalf of Dr Sandy Bradley, my cat's doctor. He is 16 years old & had suffered from food poisoning from store bought cat food. He was sick for a year & a half. During that time Dr. Bradley was out of business. I went to several other vets & he was also put in the vet hospital (~~   ~~) & no doctor could find out what was wrong with him. After that ordeal, my cat was still sick & they wanted to kill him. I refused to believe he had to die, because they could find nothing really wrong with him. Twink was so sick - I could find no help & out of about $800.00. Finally, Dr Bradley called. I was so happy because I knew she could help him. Throughout his lifetime he has had mini illnesses & Dr. Bradley cured them with little medicine & herbs. Since Dr. Bradley lost her Clinic, it has been very difficult for me & Twink. I can't find the help he needs from other vets around town. My old cat & I have suffered needlessly because she was out of business.

over

please help Dr. Bradley to re-establish
her business any way you can. It would
do her clients & their pets a great service &
I am sure you will be blessed in doing so.

Thank-you very much

~~Sylvia K. Little~~
~~520 H St. N.E.~~
Wash. DC 20002-6705
~~202-4545~~
wk H~~oward Univ. Hospital~~
~~St.~~

Rec'd Oct. 12, 1994

Katie is our four year old Elkhound mix. She was a stray dog some friends took in. They had Katie spayed and vaccinated. At about two years old, when we got her, we put her on a good maintenance diet. This consisted of half a cup of dry and a quarter can of canned food twice a day. During this time we were rather liberal with rawhide chews. After about eight months she developed digestive problems. Symptoms consisted of vomiting white froth and diarrhea with mucous in it. Katie normally bright and active, began to act lethargic. A visit to the veterinarian was in order. With fecal test and temperature normal, we decided to treat her conservatively. The vet treated her with anti-spasmodics. Water was allowed in small to moderate amounts, but no food, in order to let Katie's digestive tract rest. Three days later, Katie continued to vomit and was straining to defecate. A barium series ruled out any intestinal blockages. Lab tests were negative, with the exception of slightly elevated liver values and the need for some subcutaneous fluids to replace fluid loss. Katie remained off food despite having to watch her adopted sister, Raven being fed regularly. Katie was unable to hold down small amounts of baby food or canned intestinal diet. At this time we also tried aloe vera juice, but this was vomited as well. Two weeks later, on the advice of Dr. Bradley and a ninety two year old kennel owner, I started Katie on small amounts fresh squeezed lemon juice and honey. To our surprise Katie's energy level zoomed. Then she had no bowel movements for three days . The vomiting stopped. The first food we started Katie on was boiled oats with slippery elm powder mixed in. Slippery elm is a demulcent that coats the intestinal tract. Katie finally had a formed bowel movement with barium in it. Besides the oats , the next food we tried with Katie was boiled, peeled potatoes mixed with applesauce. All is well with Katie to this day, although we continue to feed her slippery elm powder twice a day.

~~Mary Richmont~~

January 2, 1995

Testimonials:
Neurological
Seizures (Epilepsy)
With Other Complications

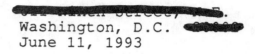

Washington, D.C.
June 11, 1993

To Whom It May Concern:

I have been associated with Dr. Sandy Bradley for more than 10 years, during which time she has had my dog Sacha as her patient. Our association began when Dr. Bradley was at the Abe Lincoln Clinic.

My dog is a retriever mix, who is now more than 13 years old. Over the years, but particularly in the last year and a half, Dr. Bradley has treated her for a variety of ailments, including dry skin, seizures, and ear, joint, and respiratory problems. Dr. Bradley became Sacha's primary veterinarian about a year and a half ago, when she was kind enough to come to my home on a Sunday afternoon when Sacha was suffering seizures. She stabilized her, examined her, recommended changes in diet and herbal supplementation, referred her to a consulting veterinarian for tests, and monitored her progress closely in the ensuing weeks.

Sacha is today an alert, healthy dog who appears much younger than her 13 and a half (at least) years. I attribute her good health to Dr. Bradley's diet recommendations, to the tonic that she prepares for me to add to Sacha's food, to the herbal supplements that she has prescribed, and to the attention she gives to tailoring her care to the particular needs of her patient. I am also happy that Dr. Bradley attempts to avoid using drugs and other substances that might harm Sacha.

In my years of dealing with Dr. Bradley, I have seen her many times go out of her way to help pets and their owners: making special home visits; assisting with obtaining certain foods and products; reducing the charges for what often becomes expensive pet care, at her own personal sacrifice.

I would also like to note that over the years I have been greatly impressed by her personal integrity and her genuine concern for animals.

Sincerely,

~~████████████████~~
My name is ~~████████~~
I am writing you this letter concerning
Doctor Bradley. I feel you are making
a mistake in fact I know you are
as far as Dr. Bradley is concern. If you
have a pet or know someone who loves
animals they would tell you the same
thing and if you really get to know
Dr. Bradley and see the care she give
to pets you will fell the same way.

Pets get sick the same way
people do, but we have hospitals
that is open to us 24 hrs a days.
but if we don't have the money
or insurance they will turn people
away. I feel if there is a doctor
that care enough to take someone's
pet in no matter how late it is
they should me able to stay open
and do there job, I think a lot of
people will agree with me that love
-you-

animals and people.

When I first met Doctor Bradley
my dog Toby was hit by a car his
pelvis bone was broken and he was
in shock, it was about 10:00 clock.
When I found him a man & lady was
with him he had bitten the man
on his hand when I got there. I
bought Toby home and call all over
trying to get help finally the animal
rescue came out. They told me that
most people would put the dog asleep
if there pelvis bone is broken, because
of the expense and that there was not
much hope, they offer to take Toby in
Upper Marlboro until a vet open
the next morning, but I didn't want
Toby to go that far. I can't really
remember how I got Doctor Bradley
number but I think one of the
man told me about her and I call.
He talk to her and told Dr. Bradley
Toby's condition, so she told me
to bring him right over.
Toby & I went over there
with Toby all I had was Twenty-five

Dollar I thought that Dr. Bradley would turn me away since I didn't have enough money but she didn't.

Dr. Bradley took Toby and started working on him right when I got there and no question ask about money. While she was working with him she explain to me that Toby was in serious condition but she would do her best, he was in to bad of shape for her to operate that same night, but she did operate on him as soon as he was strong enough. Dr. Bradley told me that she was going to used herbs for Toby and I said ok.

About two or three days later Dr. Bradley call me because she was worried about Toby he wasn't eating so she ask me what kind of food did he like so I told her chicken she went out and bought Toby some chicken and she called me back very happy & please because Toby eat the chicken so well.

I felt bad because I wasn't able

to give her any money but she
kept telling me don't worry about
that. I asked Dr. Bradly if she
would take a post dated check and
she did, I still wasn't able to
pay her all of her money only pay
her a little at a time and beside
that I really just finished paying
her this month since 7/11/84 is
when Toby got bit.

Dr. Bradley knew Toby was getting
home sick so she suggested that I
bring him home and she told me
that it would be a while before
Toby would be walking but to give
him the herbs she give me for him
but within a week. Toby was
walking + doing very good. Dr. Bradly
would call me to check on Toby and
everytime she call I was able to give
her good news, Toby was even going
up the steps before we ever thought
he would be.

All of the care she give to Toby
Dr. Bradly only charge me half price
for getting Toby well, and that was

Time and equipment.

Toby have been sick twice since then he had the same symptom that his uncle had because I had a Yorkshire that came from the same breed that Toby came from and he died at the Vet which I felt that more could had been done if the Doctor was there and not just a helper because if I would have known that the lady didn't know what to do I wouldn't had never left Mitch there and went to work.

So when Toby started having the same symptom I took him around to Tailwagger Animal Clinic on Oglethorpe St. N.W. which is in walking distance from me but they didn't give me much hope they give me a list of Animals hospital I could have took him to.

So I came home and had my mother to take me over to Dr. Bradly's she took care of Toby and he was back to normal. Dr. Bradly found a tumor on Toby's brain and also found out that

he had a bad heart. The Doctor
felt that way Toby had a brain
tumor also at Sailwagger.

Dr. Bradley also told me to
give Toby some more tests. Toby
is doing fine for a dog that should
have been dead three times.

I could write much more but
I hope that I can get my point
across to you because I really feel
and know for a fact that Dr. Bradley
is a very good Doctor and honest
women and will do know harm to
anyone or give them false hope about
anything. I have ~~proof~~ proof of everything
I have said, including my mother,
Mr. Bates, my sister, my children
and plenty of friends who seen
Toby sick also the Doctor at
~~████████~~.

Thank you
~~██████████████~~
~~███████~~

Testimonials:
Miscellaneous Disorders

I first met Dr. Sandy Bradley in the early 1980s. Since that time, I have witnessed several rather miraculous instances of wholistic veterinarian medical treatment. She has saved many animals that were considered untreatable by the conventional veterinarian community. Her method of treatment involves a profound spiritual approach to each animal and its medical condition, a system of natural herb medications for internal and external application, and perhaps most importantly, an intense love and sense of caring for all living things. In this brief paper, I would like to discuss some of Sandy's work that I have witnessed over the years.

At some time in the late 1980s, Sandy acquired an approx-imately twenty year old buckskin horse named Crista, who had earlier been diagnosed as having liver disease, emphysema, heart disease, arthritic joints, and upward fixation of one of her hind legs. I use the word "acquired" because most of the animals in Sandy's care and ownership are there because a former owner or vet was unable to successfully treat the animal by conventional means. These animals were expected to die, and they certainly would have died without Sandy. Once being brought to Sandy, Crista enjoyed a level of care and medical "doting over" that she probably had never known before. The horse went, in short order, from a decrepid, illness ridden old mare to a lively, strong horse ready to ride all day and come back for more. She was a pleasure horse, healthy, and with a feeling of usefulness once more. She is still living and thriving.

Meshi came along some time after Crista, and came with a diagnosis of severe pneumonia. Once in Sandy's care, this beautiful buckskin with line-back began to appear as if she had never known a day of illness in her life. She had almost died a matter of weeks before, and again, was expected to die soon from the pneumonia. Today, approximately four years after her arrival, she is considered a low maintenance horse; fat, sassy and happy, and I am convinced that Meshi will be with us for the duration.

Spring Wind, a prideful Appaloosa, was presented to Sandy with leg problems. The former owner told Sandy that the only problems were concerned with the ferrier having cut Spring's hooves too close to the feet. The horse was almost completely lame, and for more reason than close-cut feet. Sandy can discuss the additional medical problems by diagnosis and definition, I unfortunately cannot. I do know that the horse came in limping and once treated, went to her new owner and home running around with her head up and "living" up to her name.

Iron Fortress, a big, long-legged thoroughbred bay, was ~~sold~~ adopted to Sandy by ~~a former owner~~ Equine Rescue League who was ~~convinced~~ told that Iron would be destroyed without Sandy's care. He had been diagnosed with severe arthritis in the hind leg joints, and again, additional diagnosis beyond my understanding. Sandy was told by Iron's former vet that if he survived, it would be with regular pain killers. Of course, Sandy has an answer for pain killers of the conventional variety, in the form of the natural herb tonics and applications that vary per animal and medical condition. Sandy was also told by the depart- ing vet that Iron should never be ridden again, after having been a winning english jumper. Iron is mine now, and he loves brisk rides.

Many dog owners, of course, have brought their pets to Sandy when all else had failed. "Sweet Pea", a shepherd currently in her care, presented with symptoms of lymphosarcoma and demodex mange. For the past year, Sandy has worked tirelessly to save the dog's life, and Sweet Pea has almost died several times. She lives today because Sandy has refused to give up on her. I last saw the dog one day before the time of this writing, and not only had the hair grown back, but she was running around, playfully greeting visitors, and barking at anything that moved.

Cody, another shepherd with demodex mange just as severe as Sweet Pea's diagnosis was eventually put to sleep by his owners. They were unable to endure his suffering, and that was understandable. I am however convinced that Cody would have survived if Sandy had had more time to continue his teatment, since he was showing more and more signs of improvement. The major problem with treating such conditions seems to be the back-and-forth of remission, during which times owners must endure their pet's suffering, and sometimes, as in Cody's case, decide that their pet has suffered enough and must be given a chance to rest. It was a very sad and frustrating time for the owners and no less so for Sandy.

Perhaps one of the more notable cases involves my own cat, Sheba, whom I found upon returning home from work one day with a gaping hole in her stomach area. When I saw it, I was so horrored by it that I did nothing but stare at it for several minutes. I had no idea where it came from...no clue as to what caused it. Sandy was notified; she came, she saw, she conquered. It was one of those natural herb concoctions I mentioned earlier that did the trick. Within a week, the hole was gone and the hair had grown back. It looked then as if she never had a problem at all, and I am still in awe at the severity of the injury against the unbelievably short time of complete treatment and resolution.

Last, but by no means least, is the story of Ceyenne. As a kitten, he was brought to Sandy by a mailman who had just witnessed him being hit by a car. To refer to his spinal injury as severe would be understatement, in fact, when he was brought to Sandy, his hind-legs were pointing east, and his forelegs were pointing west. He also exhibited symptoms of coma and brain damage. Sandy put ceyenne pepper under his nose, and administered liquid ceyenne extract to his system, and within less than ten minutes, shook his head and was concious and alert. Again, as I am not a doctor I am unable to explain the method of approach to his back, but as an observer, I can say that the results were remarkable. I did not see Ceyenne for about a month after his arrival, but when I did, I could not believe it was the same cat. He was sitting up and alert, and trying to walk. At that time the best he could do was crawl, dragging his hind-legs. The next time I saw him, he could move the hind-legs some. He was already acting as if nothing had ever happened, as far as he knew. A matter of weeks later, the cat was running around around, jumping onto and off of things,

and just being an agile cat. I was not sure that Sandy was going to
be able to save this one when she told me about him the day following
his injury. Anyone who saw Ceyenne then would have expected there to
be no medical treatment under the sun that could save him.

Now, it is two years later, and while his walk is still a
bit wobbly, and many of his head movements slow, his running gaits
are strong and quick, and appear quite normal. He jumps as he wants,
and is a very friendly cat who seems to be enjoying life quite a bit.
This jet-black cat, reserved yet nutty, should never have lived long
enough to grow from kitten to cat following that injry he suffered.
He should never have lived long to have a son, Ceyenne Jr., the
spitting image of him, follow him around learning the ropes, and
without Sandy, he certainly would not be here today.

One thing that is important to note is that each animal
mentioned here, and others not mentioned, seemed convinced that
Sandy was their mother. Who wouldn't thrive in a mother's care?
I believe that what happens between Sandy and her patients, before
the treatment even begins, has a great deal to do with the success
of each case. Her attitude is the key to her medical approach and
rapport with the animals. She can, and has, walked up to a full-
grown Rottweiler, sickened by a super-mammary teet condition, with
a leash in her hand and a smile, and bring the owner-less dog in
without even a hint of ͜incident. A professional dog trainer (Rottweiler
specialist), remarked later on that he probably
would not have approached the dog himself. She
did successfully treat the dog, and gave her to ͜a mechanic who needed

a watchdog to guard his lot.

Each animal mentioned here was treated with natural herbs
and other forms of treatment too technical for my non-medical mind
to explain. However, I would indeed without hesitation or reservation,
recommend any pet owner who needs help, and any vet to compare notes
with Dr. Sandy Bradley. She is a new-world craftswoman who really does
believe that we are all God's creations.

William H. ████, █.█.
████ ████████ ████
Washington,D.C. 20002
(███)███-████

June 26, 1993

To Whom it may concern,

I ~~████████████~~ can verify that
Dr. Bradley has treated my dog
since he was a puppy, and for
many times when I didn't have all
the money at the time. I am pleased
with the way she practice natural
medicine it has helped my dog on many
occasions as well as my self. I have
known Dr. Bradley for ten years and when
my dog get sick on when I do know whats w
I can call her anytime and she will com
over or tell me over the phone what to do
and I Really like that.

Thank you

~~████████████~~

July 14, 1994

SPECIAL THANKS TO DR. BRADLEY

I am writing this letter in regards to a special holistic veterarianarian who save my cat - Groover. Groover is a 17 year old Norwegian Forest Cat. He became real sick when he was 10 years old. One day he stopped eating, and drinking. He became very weak as the days progressed. He could hardly make it to his litter box. I finally had to carry him to his box. He became very anemic. I took him to an animal hospital. They gave Groover a physical, did blood tests, and gave him Cortisone shots. Groover did not get better. They suggest exploratory surgery, but said that he had a 50:50 chance of surviving the operation. They were very puzzled with his condition. After alot of prayer, we decided against the surgery and took Groover home. We were impressed to go to the health food store and seek out a remedy. We inquired at the store if they knew of a good veterinarian. They suggest that we contact Dr. Bradley. We called Dr. Bradley. She was getting ready to go out of town, but said that she would cancel her plans if Groover needed her assistance. She immediately came over to our apartment. After a few injections of vitamin B and some herbs given orally, Groover was up walking on his own. Groover had an infected paw which was not noticeable. I believe that God answered our prayers in sending Dr. Bradley to us. Our paths were meant to cross. We have learned alot from each other. I feel this will be a friendship that will last a lifetime.

What strikes me most about Dr. Bradley (beside her wealth of practical and useful information) is her great concern and compassion towards animals. She provides animal health care through careful dietary planning and nutritional supplementation. She is an excellent veterinarian that blends her practice with the latest scientific research with traditional non surgical treatments whenever possible. She not only helped Groover through this medical crisis, but she provided him with a personal nutritional program.

Forever Grateful,

I HAVE THREE CANINE FRIENDS AND DOC BRADLEY'S KNOWLEDGE OF NATURAL REMEDIES HAS BEEN USED TO TREAT THEIR VARIOUS AILMENTS FOR THE PAST SEVEN YEARS.

EXAMPLE #1:

JUDAH BEN-HUR, AN AIREDALE-DOBIE MIX, WAS RUN OVER BY A CAR AT THREE MONTHS OF AGE. JUDAH HAD CRACKED RIBS, A BADLY BRUISED SHOULDER BLADE AND INTERNAL BLEEDING. DOC PROMPTLY TREATED HIM WITH NATURAL REMEDIES. THE ONLY CONVENTIONAL MEDICINE USED WAS PENICILLIN. ALSO, WITHOUT USING ANY BANDAGES OR SPLINTS, DOC'S NATURAL CARE HAD JUDAH UP AND RUNNING, WITH A SLIGHT LIMP, IN ONE WEEK.

EXAMPLE #2:

JESSE, A GERMAN SHEPHERD, WAS DIAGNOSED WITH AN ARRHYTHMIC HEART AT THREE MONTHS OF AGE. HER CIRCULATION WAS VERY POOR. DOC WOULD NOT GIVE HER ANY VACCINATIONS UNTIL THE CONDITION WAS BROUGHT UNDER CONTROL, AS NOT TO STRESS HER HEART. AFTER BEING ON AN HERBAL COMBINATION CALLED "H" FOR APPROXIMATELY FOUR TO SIX MONTHS, THE CONDITION WAS CORRECTED AND HER CIRCULATION WAS GOOD. JESSE WAS THEN ABLE TO RECEIVE THE REQUIRED VACCINATIONS. THE HEART CONDITION HAS NOT RETURNED.

EXAMPLE #3:

MIRIAM, A GERMAN SHEPHERD MIX, WAS FOUND BY A FRIEND ON THE MEDIAN STRIP OF A FOUR LANE PARKWAY. SHE WAS IN A DEPLORABLE STATE - BALD DUE TO MANGE AND SEVERE INTESTINAL PARASITES. SHE LOOKED SO BAD THAT MY HUSBAND THOUGHT SHE WAS A SICK CAT. XRAYS SHOWED THAT SHE HAD RECOVERED FROM A BROKEN FOOT. MIRIAM WAS APPROXIMATELY SIX WEEKS OLD. FOR HER SKIN, DOC PRESCRIBED DAILY BATHS WITH ORGANIMALS SHAMPOO AND DIP. FOR THE PARASITES, GARLIC AND CAYENNE WERE GIVEN IN
CONJUNCTION WITH A CHICKEN/VEGETABLE AND RICE STEW TO SUPPLEMENT THE KIBBLE. WITHIN A MONTHS TIME, MIRIAM'S COAT GREW IN AND THE PARASITES WERE GONE. SHE LATER DEVELOPED RICKETS, SHOWN IN HER BADLY BOWED LEGS. DOC PRESCRIBED GOAT'S MILK (VITAMIN D) ALONG WITH AN HERBAL COMBINATION CALLED "BF&C". WE TOOK HER OFF ANY PET FOOD OR SNACKS WITH ADDITIVES AND PRESERVATIVES. MIRIAM STAYED ON THIS FROM FOUR TO SIX MONTHS AS HER BONES STRENGTHENED.

OVER THE PAST TEN YEARS OR SO, DOC BRADLEY HAS TREATED ALL MY FRIENDS WRAPPED IN FUR PRIMARILY WITH HERBS FROM THE SIMPLE THINGS SUCH AS INTESTINAL WORMS TO THE COMPLEXITIES OF BROKEN BONES.

███████ ██████, WASHINGTON, D.C.

7-11-94

HERNDON, VA. 22091

JUNE 25, 1993

TO WHOM IT MAY CONCERN:

I HAVE HAD DR. SANDY BRADLEY AS MY PETS' VETERINARIAN SINCE JUNE OF 1988. MY DOG HAS HAD A NUMBER OF MEDICAL PROBLEMS WHICH DR. BRADLEY HAS CONSISTENTLY TREATED SUCCESSFULLY WITH THE USE OF VARIOUS FORMS OF DIET MANAGEMENT WITH HERBS. OVER THE NUMBER OF YEARS THAT I HAVE KNOW "DOC" SHE HAS ALWAYS PROVIDED QUALITY CARE WITH MINIMUL REIMBURSEMENT. SHE HAS MAINTAINED A GOAL TO RE-OPEN HER OWN CLINIC DESPITE HER ON-GOING PROBLEM WITH HER RIGHT HAND. I HAVE ALWAYS KNOWN "DOC" TO BE AN HONEST CHRISTIAN PERSON WHO BELIEVES THAT HER FAITH IN GOD WILL SEE HER THROUGH LIFE DESPITE ITS OBSTACLES. I BELIEVE IN HER FAITH BUT I ALSO BELIEVE THAT SHE HAS BEEN DEALTH WITH UNFAIRLY AND UNJUSTLY BY HER ATTORNEY, ███████████ IF ███████████ WOULD GIVE HER THE MONEY THAT IS DUE HER SHE WOULD HAVE THE OPPOR-TUNITY TO GET ON WITH THE PROFESSION THAT SHE SPENT SO MANY YEARS AND SO MANY DOLLARS TO PURSUE.

IT IS VERY SAD THAT PERSONS WHO DO NOT HAVE FINANCIAL MEANS TO FIGHT BACK CAN SO EASILY BE IGNORED. SURELY THERE SHOULD BE SOME WAY TO INVESTIGATE WHETHER MR. LIGHTFOOT PAID HER THE PROPER MONIES. SURELY THERE IS SOME AVENUE THAT COULD LEAD TO A FAIR RESOLUTION.

ALTHOUGH I CANNOT PROVE THAT "DOC BRADLEY" HAS BEEN TREATED UNJUSTLY BY MR. LIGHTFOOT, I CAN ATTEST TO HER CHARACTER. SHE IS HONEST AND TRUSTWORTHY. SHE IS PROFESSIONAL IN HER WORK AND DEDICATED TO HER CHOSEN PROFESSION: THE CARE OF ANIMALS.

SINCERELY,

D█████████

**For Cancer Cases
See Memorials**

**Actual Reversal from Malignant
to Benign - Documented**

See "Deja" Color Plate

**Articles and Information Revealing
Dangerous Contaminants in Our Foods
and Their Effects on Our Bodies
and What You Can Do About It**

**1) Issues you may investigate and
find out for yourself.**

**2) Information that may be informative
and offer helpful aids that may
improve your health no matter
what level you are.**

FOOD & WATER
I N C O R P O R A T E D

December 21, 1994

Dr. Sandy Bradley
605 Hudson Ave #219
Tacoma Park, MD 20912

Dear Dr. Bradley,

I am writing to confirm our arrangements that you may reference/quote, with appropriate citations, any of the materials sent to you from this office in your upcoming book, *Let the Mockingbird Sing Herbal Praise (from the old barn)*.

We would appreciate receiving a copy of the book for our library. Also enclosed please find the membership information and action alerts we spoke of today. Please feel free to contact us if you require more materials or have any other questions.

Good Luck with your book.

Sincerely,

Michele Kirchner
Executive Assistant

The government's next radiation experiment?

Radiation-exposed meat: We're all the guinea pigs.

In the wake of the E.coli outbreak, the government would like the meat industry to be a part of their next radiation experiment: meat irradiation. And the effects could be devastating to the meat industry and consumers.

Why is meat irradiation an experiment? Because it has never been proven safe. In fact, the former head of the FDA's own scientific review panel on radiation-exposed foods recently reported that the available studies "were not adequate...to evaluate the safety of any product, especially a food product such as irradiated foods." Thus, she concluded, radiation-exposed foods have been approved and promoted "based on politics, not science."

Exposing meat to radiation destroys essential nutrients. **Worse, studies have shown that radiation-exposed foods contain dangerous residues–some of which can cause cancer.**

And what about consumers? They understand that only unhealthy and unsanitary meat products require radiation treatment. In a recent editorial against the use of meat irradiation, *Meat & Poultry* magazine warned the industry that "American consumers have shown a huge unwillingness to accept irradiated food products." They're right. No one wants to be a part of this experiment.

FOOD & WATER, INCORPORATED – 1-800-EAT-SAFE

Summary

Early this year in the Pacific Northwest, three children died and hundreds of other child
and adults became seriously ill as a result of eating hamburgers contaminated with E. cc
bacteria. In the wake of this tragedy, many in the food industry and government, includi
Mike Espy, the new Secretary of Agriculture, have called for irradiation of meat as a
"solution" to the problem.

However, irradiation is not the food-safety panacea that some of its supporters would ha
us believe. The widespread use of irradiation could pose numerous threats to human hea
and the environment, and the long-term health effects of consuming irradiated food migl
be as bad or worse than the effects of eating contaminated beef. Conspicuously absent
from the recent dialogue about irradiation has been any informed, rational discussion of
these arguments against irradiation.

Meanwhile, the beef industry operates plants with conditions reminiscent of Upton
Sinclair's *The Jungle*. Production lines run at breakneck speeds, forcing slaughtering errors and making the workplace hazardous for employees. Deregulation drastically cut th
number of inspectors and their authority to enforce food safety laws. Furthermore, the
USDA has avidly pursued the goal of raising profits in the meat industry, at the expense
beef safety. In short, there's a glaring need for reform.

If we are to honestly and adequately address this serious problem, we have to look at the
root causes and strive to change them. Informed consumers will not accept Espy's approach of looking for quick-fix, band-aid "solutions" like irradiation that create new
problems and merely cover up old ones.

The E. coli Outbreak: Understanding the Causes

The E. coli bacteria responsible for the Pacific Northwest disaster has been traced to a batch of contaminated hamburgers processed by Vons Companies of Arcadia, California and sold to the public by the Jack in the Box fast-food chain. Health experts believe that the meat most likely became contaminated during slaughtering when E. coli from a cow's burst intestines or fecal matter came in contact with the meat. As the Government Accountability Project (GAP), a government watchdog group, has pointed out,

such contamination can only occur when there has been a mistake in slaughtering.

When a cow is slaughtered, workers are suppo to use utmost caution to ensure that consumabl meat is not exposed to intestinal fluids or fecal matter. The intestinal tract should be tied at bc ends—throat and anus—and removed carefully ensure that it does not burst. Surfaces that com in contact with meat should be cleaned off to remove any traces of fecal matter or dirt, and meat that comes in contact with contaminants should be trimmed off of the carcass. However slaughterhouses don't always meet these stand-ards.

COMMON FOOD ADDITIVES!

Additives listed below are among those most commonly found <u>in both pet and people</u> food.

1. SODIUM NITRATE and SODIUM NITRITE · Chemical preservative and color fixative. In an infants intestine, nitrates are converted to nitrites which combine with hemoglobin to cause an asphyxiating disease called methemoglobinemia. (Chemical Feast, by James S. Turner) Nitrosamines, which include nitrates, can produce mutagenic changes, and by similar pathogenic processes, these agents are carcinogenic and teratogenic as well. Sodium nitrite is converted to nitrous acid, which is mutagenic in a variety of lower organisms. In recent years, cases of illness and deaths were traced to excessive amounts of sodium nitrite added to fish, by sellers who hoped to prolong even further, the shelf life of their products. Sodium nitrite is used to keep the color of the meat bright and appealing to the adult who makes the purchase. (Consumer Beware, by Beatrice Trum Hunter) Of the two compounds, sodium nitrite is the more toxic. However, sodium nitrate readily converts to sodium nitrite. Nitrites have induced severe arthritic symptoms. Sodium nitrate and sodium nitrite have decreased liver storage of Vitamin A and Carotene, inducing deficiency symptoms. Sodium nitrite fed regularly to rats, induced permanent epileptic like changes in their brain activity. Nitrites may be carcinogenic, mutagenic and teratogenic, as well as toxic. Nitrosamines have been shown to act throughout the body, and produce cancer in a wide range of organs and in many species. Critics charge that less hazardous additives can be substituted, that would serve the same functions as sodium nitrate and sodium nitrite. (Food Additives and Your Health, by Beatrice Trum Hunter) Nitrite is one of the few food additives that is definitely known to have caused deaths in the United States. Nitrite is one of the most toxic chemicals in our food supply. Its toxicity is due to its ability to disable hemoglobin, the molecule in red blood cells that transports life giving oxygen. Nitrate (Potassium and Sodium) Potassium Nitrate, well know for gunpowder and fireworks, is also know as saltpeter and niter. Sodium nitrate is also called chile saltpeter. (Caveat Emptor).

2. MSG (Monosodium Glutamate) when fed to rats in doses comparable to amounts in baby foods, rats suffered brain and eye damage from the chemical. Some rats showed a significant loss of weight, when compared to controls. A product can remain on the market until definitely proven dangerous. (The Chemical Feast, by James S. Turner) MSG has been put into animal feed, since it induces cattle, swine, poultry and sheep to eat more. MSG is used to suppress oxidized flavor which may develop during storage. Federal legislation specifically prohibits the addition of any material to food which causes "damage or inferiority" to be "concealed in any manner" or which can make a food appear better or of greater value than it is. Nonetheless, the FDA permits wide latitude in the use of MSG, a substance which helps disguise inferior food quality. MSG has caused epigastric fullness, belching, distention, numbness, general weakness, palpitation, cold sweat, viselike throbbing in the head. Lab experiments revealed brain damage, stunted skeletal development, marked obesity and female sterility in mice, showing that effects are more than transitory. Brain lesions and nerve cell deaths are also noted. A most concentrated source of sodium. (Consumer Beware by Hunter)

3. BHT (Butylated Hydroxytoluene) Various experiments & control studies have demonstrated damaging effects, including metabolic stress, depression of the growth rate, loss of weight, increase of liver weight, damage to liver, increase of serum cholesterol, baldness, and fetal abnormalities such as failure to develop normal eyes in offspring. BHT produced deleterious deviations from normal cellular behavior. Researchers suggest that detoxification of these phenols occurs in the liver, and changes in this organ represent an attempt to meet stresses placed by ingestion of these umphysiological substances. BHT has caused tingling sensations of face and hands, extreme weakness, fatigue, edema, chest tightness, difficult breathing and severe allergies. (Consumer Beware, by Beatrice Trum Hunter) BHT seems to be more toxic than BHA. Adverse effects also include damage to kidneys, increase in phospholipids, and storage of BHT in tissues, fats and organs, with slow excretion of it. BHT is banned in Sweden and Australia. BHT was banned from baby food in Great Britain, and reduced to half in other foodstuffs. Scientists reported that when pregnant mice were fed diets containing large amounts of BHA and BHT, offspring frequently suffer major changes in brain chemistry, and show abnormal behavior patterns. (Food Additives and Your Health, by Beatrice Trum Hunter) BHT is much cheaper than BHA, but its use is limited because it is less stable at high temperatures used to pasteurize food. Eastman Chemical Products, a major producer of antioxidants states that "BHA &/or BHT are not found to provide significant improvement in the stability of vegetable oils." There is fragmentary evidence that natural antioxidants such as Vitamin E retard aging and increase an animal's life span. BHA and BHT have NOT been adequately tested, accumulate in body fat, and are actually superfluous in many of the foods in which they are used. (Eaters Digest, by Michael F. Jacobson) BHT was originally developed to prevent color film from deteriorating. BHT is insoluable in water, therefore concentrations are cumulative.

4. BHA (Butylated Hydroxyanisole) retarded growth of weaning albino female rats and caused weight loss in adult animals. BHA inhibits contraction of smooth muscles of the intestine in the ileum area. (Food ADDITIVES and Your Health, by Beatrice Trum Hunter) BHA is a petroleum product used as an antioxidant. Safety testing of both BHA and BHT was done by the industry desirous of marketing products with this additive, and not by a source of independent research.

THIS INFORMATION IS BROUGHT TO YOU AS A PUBLIC SERVICE BY

NATURAL PET FOODS

, DIRECTOR

, NEW YORK 11743   TELEPHONE (

Irradiation Is Back!

The U.S. government and the meat industry are attempting to breath life into the once dying food irradiation industry. In late February 1994, Mike Espy, Secretary of the U.S. Department of Agriculture (USDA), and the American Meat Institute announced their support for a petition seeking approval of beef irradiation. They believe that zapping dirty meat with radiation will "solve" the meat contamination problem. Consumers must take action now to ensure that *all* forms of food irradiation are stopped.

Beef Is Just the Start

The irradiation industry has long been struggling to find any segment of the food industry willing to participate in its radiation experiment. Due to strong consumer opposition, the fruit, vegetable, and poultry industries have all rejected irradiation. Now it's the beef industry's turn, and we must take immediate action. If beef irradiation is widely adopted, hundreds of nuclear facilities will be constructed across the country and *all* forms of food irradiation will likely follow.

The Dirtiest Meat in the World?

No other country in the world has adopted the widescale use of meat irradiation. In fact, South Africa is the *only* country in the world that allows meat irradiation--and nearly all of it is used for military rations. Instead of using irradiation to cover up dirty meat problems, the USDA and the meat industry should prevent meat contamination in the first place by cleaning up filthy meat plants, halting sloppy slaughtering practices, and putting inspection back on the side of consumers.

Call or Write:

Burger King
1-800-937-1800
P.O. Box 520783 GMF
Miami, FL 33152

Since fast food meat will be the first target for irradiation, call Burger King and let them know that you are aware of the dangers of irradiation and strongly oppose the technology. Ask them to join McDonald's by issuing a statement which assures their customers that they will not expose their food products to radiation.

American Meat Institute (AMI)
J. Patrick Boyle, President
(703) 841-2400
P.O. Box 3556
Washington, DC 20007

AMI is the meat industry's largest trade organization. For more than a year, James Marsden, AMI's vice president, has been recklessly promoting meat irradiation in the media and to members of the meat industry. Consumers should write or call the head of AMI, Mr. Boyle, to let him know that you do not want to be a part of the government's food irradiation experiment and that you are outraged by James Marsden's promotion of the technology. Also, ask him or his representative why no other country, with the current exception of South Africa, allows the irradiation of meat? Is the U.S. meat supply the dirtiest in the world? Why else would it need radiation treatment?

Food Irradiation Raises Concerns

Irradiation has given us what "The San Francisco Bay Guardian" has labelled "The New Hot Potato." Nuclear radiation is used to prevent sprouting in potatoes and onions.

The National Nutritional Foods Association (NNFA) has taken an official position on the issue of food irradiation (treating or processing with gamma ionizing, or radionuclide radiation). It "opposes the concept of food irradiation and endorses the position that further government or commercial food irradiation be discontinued, or that at least immediate steps be taken to adequately inform consumers as to which products in the marketplace have been subjected to this process." Among the areas for concern listed by the NNFA are safety, nutritional losses and the consumer's right to know.

— Already, certain foods are being irradiated. They include white potatoes, wheat, wheat flour, garlic, onions, garlic powder and some herbs and spices.

Recently, irradiation of pork was approved by the FDA. Irradiation of fruits and vegetables is now being proposed, as is the construction of irradiation centers throughout the country.

Among some of the charges made against the use of irradiation in foods, according to the Coalition to Stop Food Irradiation, are the following:

• Gamma or ionizing radiation produces deleterious or uncharacterized effects on nutrients; fat- and water-soluble vitamins, essential amino acids, nucleic acids and enzymes are depleted or destroyed.

• Irradiation produces radiolytic chemical by-products in foods. These free-radical medicated chemical by-products have not been tested for long-term, latent toxicity.

• The largest animal feeding study done to date resulted in extraordinarily high incidences of both sick animals and elevated death rates.

• Irradiation may convert a wide variety of "economic poisons" (herbicides, insecticides, pesticides and fungicides, as well as GRAS additives: colorants, antibiotics, steroids, preservatives and stabilizers) to chemical by-products (Unique Radiolytic Products, U.R.P.'s), which may pose unidentified toxicity risks to consumers.

The FDA proposes to permit irradiated foods to be sold to retail consumers without any informational labels.

Irradiation may encourage nuclear proponents to justify their position by tying food processing to the nuclear arms race. Irradiation would help resolve the up-to-now thorny problem of how to dispose of nuclear waste, the Coalition points out.

• Legislation, such as H.R. 696, proposed by Washington State Congressman Sid Morrison, and S. 288, its Senate companion, will institutionalize food irradiation and drastically change the existing law (21 U.S.C. 321 (s), Section 201), which protects consumers from food additives and food irradiation.

More complete information on irradiation, including whether it will have the positive economic impact its proponents claim for it, is available from The _____, Inc.

Beltsville, Md. 20705

Coalition To Stop Food Irradiation, 1227 10th Avenue, San Francisco, CA 94122; (415) 566-5235 or 566-CSFI.

The coalition was co-founded by Jeff Reinhardt and Denis Mosgofian. Reinhardt has appeared before some of the NNFA regional organizations and at the NNFA Convention in June in Las Vegas to discuss irradiation and its possible consequences.

The Coalition for Food Irradiation, Washington, DC, on the other hand, holds that the FDA's decision to permit irradiation of pork to prevent trichinosis "is an important step toward increased food safety," according to Dr. Harry C. Mussman, Coalition chairman and executive vice-president for scientific affairs for the National Food Processors Association. The Coalition is composed of over 25 companies from the food industry.

Mussman cites also the usefulness of irradiation in "helping solve world hunger crises" by reducing food spoilage and waste. Irradiation, it is claimed, prolongs shelf life.

Among other statements made by Mussman in his paper, "Tech-Aid," are that the American Medical Association has endorsed food irradiation; irradiation does not make food radioactive; and that because irradiation involves no heat, the process keeps the quality closest to that of fresh foods. He adds: "Minute losses of niacin, thiamin, riboflavin and vitamin C have been noted with food irradiation, but the losses are nutritionally insignificant."

Commenting on some of these points in a letter to the editor of *The Sciences,* The New York Academy of Sciences in New York, Noel F. Sommer, lecturer and postharvest pathologist at the University of California at Davis, stated: "There is considerable evidence to indicate that certain diseases of harvested citrus fruits would be more active after irradiation." Sommer also said that "irradiated fruit clearly exhibited increased susceptibility to the damaging effects of chilling injury. . .; that it is doubtful that any fresh (living) commodity's shelf life would be increased by more than a few days by using irradiation to control rot organisms." Regarding nutrition, Sommer indicated that irradiation "causes destruction of vitamin C."

At the very least, it seems that the issue of irradiation should be studied thoroughly before consumers are forced to eat foods that have been irradiated. It appears that consumers already have enough concerns about threats to their health from "outside" pollutants. Why add internal toxicity from nuclear sources to the toxic substances already festering within them: fluoride, insecticides, fungicides, PCBs, thorium, chlorine, *ad infinitum?* □

Who is Food & Water, Inc.?

Food & Water is the only nonprofit, public interest organization working nationwide to educate consumers, government officials, and food industry executives about the environmental and health risks posed by food irradiation. Food & Water was founded by a family physician in 1986. We have recently broadened our focus to address the health and environmental hazards of pesticides and genetically engineered foods. Food & Water depends upon contributions from members and donors.

What has Food & Water accomplished?

As a result of Food & Water's efforts, thousands of food wholesalers and retailers and more than 80 major food industry corporations in the U.S. have issued "no irradiation" statements. The list of participating companies includes General Foods, Kellogg's, Kraft, Gerber, Borden, Campbell Soup, Pepsi, Coca Cola, McDonald's, Quaker Oats, Perdue and A&P Supermarkets. Food & Water has played a leading role in stopping the construction of food irradiation plants in Arizona, Oklahoma, Alaska and Hawaii. Food & Water also provided educational materials to legislators who banned the sale of irradiated food in New York, New Jersey, Maine, and Cleveland, Ohio.

What can I do to help?

Support Food & Water's work with a contribution, and join our Safe Food Network. Use the reply form (on back) to become a member of Food & Water or to make a tax-deductible contribution. Members receive Food & Water's quarterly newsletter, *Safe Food News*, which provides up-to-date information on food safety issues. They also receive timely updates and periodic Action Alerts describing how they can take part in critical food safety battles. Food & Water members provide the grassroots support that makes Food & Water's campaigns successful.

What are the environmental dangers associated with food irradiation?

Food irradiation's potential environmental dangers stem, for the most part, from the use of radioactive isotopes in the process. Workers can be exposed to radiation on the job, and entire communities can be exposed in the event of a leak from the plant. Plus, radioactive materials would have to be transported to irradiators around the country, putting thousands of people at risk of exposure to radiation in the case of a traffic accident. Significantly, multiple accidents of these types have occurred in the U.S. and other countries.

At a time when food poisoning from the salmonella and E. coli bacteria is on the rise, can irradiation make food safer?

Food irradiation can kill most of the salmonella and E. coli bacteria present in food, but so can proper cooking, which carries none of the environmental or health risks associated with irradiation. Moreover, doses of radiation that are adequate to kill salmonella and E. coli are not enough to kill the bacteria that causes botulism. However, such doses would kill the bacteria which signal spoilage through a foul odor. Thus, with irradiation, we would not be able to rely on the usual warning signs that tell us when food is dangerous to eat.

Who is responsible for food irradiation?

Food irradiation was developed in the 1950s by the Atomic Energy Commission (now the Nuclear Regulatory Commission) as a part of the "Atoms for Peace" program, which was established to seek potential uses for the byproducts of nuclear weapons production. Today's food irradiation industry is a private, for-profit business enterprise with ties to the U.S. nuclear weapons and nuclear power industries. The FDA approved irradiation for various foods during the deregulation of the 1980s. The food irradiation industry, like other nuclear industries, is regulated and licensed by the Nuclear Regulatory Commission.

What is food irradiation?

Food irradiation is a process whereby food is exposed to as much as 300,000 rads of radiation—the equivalent of 30 million chest x-rays—in order to extend the shelf life of the food and kill insects and bacteria.

Could eating irradiated food be dangerous to my health?

Yes. High-quality studies supporting the long-term safety of irradiated foods have never been done, as even the Food and Drug Administration (FDA), which has approved the use of irradiation on most foods, admits. However, we do know that irradiation results in the creation of new chemicals, called radiolytic products, in food and that some of these radiolytic products are known carcinogens or mutagens. Studies have suggested that irradiation may be linked to cancer and birth defects. Additionally, it is known that irradiation destroys nutrients essential to human health.

What foods are being irradiated?

At the time of this writing (January 1994), dried spices, some fresh fruits and vegetables, and a small amount of chicken are being irradiated in the U.S. However, all fresh fruits, vegetables, pork, poultry, nuts, teas, and spices have been approved for irradiation by the FDA, so irradiation of these foods could begin at any time. In addition, the USDA is currently seeking approval for the irradiation of beef.

How can I tell if food has been irradiated?

The FDA requires that irradiated whole foods, such as fresh tomatoes or chickens, be labeled with a radura symbol (see figure, below), and a written warning that the food has been treated with radiation. However, if those tomatoes or chickens are used as ingredients, say for a can of soup or a TV dinner, no label of any kind is required. Irradiated foods prepared in restaurants, schools, and other public institutions need not be labeled either.

THE ISSUE OF PESTICIDES

DO YOU UNDERSTAND WHAT THEY ARE? DO YOU UNDERSTAND WHAT THEY DO—TO YOU AND THE PESTS? IS THERE ANOTHER AND BETTER WAY TO RID THE PESTS AND STILL PROTECT YOUR HEALTH? WHY AREN'T WE MADE AWARE OF OUR GOD-GIVEN CHOICES? WHAT CAN WE DO ABOUT IT?

I will use 3 articles from three different sources that may help you to understand this life and death dilemma that not only we as Americans face, but the world at large. The status of our health has been in the hands of a few. We are told—even with recent bills being passed in Congress—that regulations are being put in place to create and monitor safer chemicals for food and industrial use. The question is can we trust these promises given the records of the past? Let's look at the definition of pesticide: Any substance, as a chemical poison, used to destroy weeds, insects, rodents, or other noxious plants or animals. I invite you to closely examine my comments on excerpts of the following articles. After thorough examination ask yourself the following questions:

These pesticides were an issue more than 10 years ago. Are they still part of our food chain and why? Do I care—for myself, my children, my family? If I do—how and where can I find out the Truth? What can I do about it? What will I commit to do to help make a change for safer food and water supply for America or wherever I live?

These are the articles for examination:

I. Pesticides in 15 Common Foods May Cause 20,000 Cancers a Year (Tomatoes, Oranges, Wheat Among Those Posing Worst Risk), subtitles: Pesticides—Treated Foods with High Cancer Rates; Pesticides in Foods Linked to Cancers, written by Michael Weisskopf, staff writer of Washington Post 5/21/87

II. Pesticides Listed by NAS as Cancer Risks issued by The Packer, Sat., May 23, 1987, subtitles: Regulating Pesticides in Food—The Delaney Paradox

III. Problems Associated with Food Contaminates (see article).

Between radiation on our produce, hormones, antibodies and chemical growth additives given to our livestock before slaughter then artificial colorings, artificial flavorings, and preservatives after slaughter—not to mention all or some of the above in everything you drink, including water—everyday—DOES THE BODY HAVE A CHANCE? DAILY INSULTS BY POUNDS OF POISONS!

Article #1

1. According to the National Academy of Sciences a report was released confirming public fears of chemicals sprinkled liberally on U.S. farmland.
2. A two year study by a special committee of the Academy's National Research Council reported 15 foods treated by a handful of pesticides pose the greatest risk of cancer. Many of these pesticides are listed in article #2 and supports article #1. These 15 foods were listed as the following in order of importance: tomatoes, beef, potatoes, oranges, lettuce, apples, peaches pork, wheat, soybeans, beans, carrots, chicken, corn and grapes. JUST THINK ABOUT IT! All the foods we are told to be nutritious and feeding our bodies to be stronger and better instead leads to illness and slow or rapid death.
3. Weisskopf goes on to say that the EPA focused on 28 of the 53 pesticides believed to be carcinogenic or potentially cancer causing. Article #2 states 90% of the risk stems from these pesticides—most were registered before 1978. "More than 80% of those analyzed exceeded the EPA threshold of "acceptable cancer risk for a pollutant."
4. A comparison was made to cigarette smoking which was expected to cause 120,000 cases of lung cancer that year, stating that the risk was small. But, "You can volunteer not to smoke." He further states "The public has no way of protecting itself against pesticides."
   This is my precise concern. We have no way to protect ourselves—because we (most of us) don't control what or how we grow our food (plant or animal). Therefore, we don't control the quality of the substances put before us as "food" to eat.
   Please refer to definitions for food, poison, etc.
5. The articles also states that the committee's projection of cancer risks were probably underestimated because not all but nearly half of the known or suspected carcinogens were studied. Also there were no estimates done on the effects of pesticides on drinking water!
6. The article cites 10 of the most commonly used chemicals (some of which are cited in article #2) which are responsible for 80% of the cancer risk from pesticides. These are linuron, zineb, captafol, captan, maneb, permethrin, mancozeb, folpet, chlordimeform and chlorothalonil. The article, quote, "All of them exceed by hundreds of times the EPA's acceptable risk standard endorsed by the academy committee."
7. Another shocking statement, "Tomatoes treated with four of the most dangerous chemicals account for 15% of the total dietary cancer risk for pesticide residues under the worse-case analysis," the report said.
8. Weisskopf's article further states that all pesticides in the U.S. must be registered by the EPA. It's charge is to balance the crop benefits (of each chemical) verses it's health risks. However, health assessments have been impeded due to the lack of health data and chemical residue data particularly for the older registrants.
9. The article goes on to say for the first time since 1972, there was a bill seeking to reform pesticides regulations that would require manufacturers to submit a full health data within 10 years that the bill was passed.
10. Further, every registered pesticide was to have legal limits specifying how much residue can be present in food sold between states. These limits were to be set by the EPA.
11. In 1958 there was a legislative provision which required EPA to prohibit any cancer causing additives in processed foods called the Delaney Clause. To the best of my knowledge this provision has been overturned recently. What this means is that where a known carcinogen was required to be pulled from processed foods that we eat, instead it can now be left there.

12. Weisskopf reports that because of this there is a tougher standard to pesticides in processed foods than raw which represented 80% of the cancer risk, according to the study.

13. Another alarming conclusion—the article states "From the standpoint of consumption, the source of exposure—raw commodity versus processed food seems irrelevant."

Commentary: If this article represents true statements and conclusions then the health and welfare of the American people are in the hands of people who are either truly deceived as to the destructive nature of poisons (no matter how small the amount) or they don't care believing that profit gains and mind control of an ignorant populous is more gratifying than constructing a concerted effort to approach the problems of pests and safety control for the optimal benefit of all American citizens. Obviously, the power of the dollar—the power of power is more desirable than the health of you and your families.

The equation is easy—the sicker the food you consume, the sicker you become, the bigger the pharmaceutical and medical bills—not to mention the by-product of funeral escalations. As a physician myself, now learned of the consequences to that which is not recognized, by the body, as food (in part or whole) is directly related to all sources of disease—congenital or acquired. Diseases with which we are born have somehow been created by the poor nutrition of the ancestor who passed down the gene for it. A clear example close to this is the effects on the newborn from mothers who drink or smoke during their pregnancies. Alcoholic beverages nor nicotine is a food to your body. Disobedience to the dietary laws to protect us have been broken over and over again. We are resistant and rebellious to the use or thought of the word "disobedience." Yet, we are well aware and accept the Truth that if we are disobedient to the laws of gravity than there may be serious or fatal consequences to breaking that law. Case in point, jumping off a forty story building insures any human being their death when they reach the bottom. Why can't we respect God's spiritual laws of health as we respect His physical laws of science? This is my professional opinion drawn from my 17 years of clinical experience and spiritual orientation.

Article #2 specifically mentions certain pesticides cited in The Farm Chemicals Handbook. Among these are fungicides, herbicides and insecticides—some of which are the following for public inspection. According to this article there are approximately 8 fungicides. One of them listed is O-Phenylphenol which is a post-harvest chemical used in wax and applied commercially to fruits and vegetables while in transit to market to reduce spoilage. Impregnated fruit wraps and dips into crates, hampers and the like are used also.

Five others are mentioned in article #1.

1. Zineb—on fruits and vegetables especially potato seeds pieces; tomatoes
2. Captan—for weed control in citrus and apple orchards
3. Maneb—for control of early and late blights on potatoes, tomatoes and many other diseases of fruits and vegetables
4. Mancozeb—cleared for use as a seed treatment for potatoes, corn, peanuts and tomatoes
5. Folpet—on fruits, berries, vegetables and ornamentals

Some of the herbicides listed are:

1. Linuron—used for selective weed control in carrots, celery, post-transplanted parsnips and potatoes

2. Glyphosate—used on beans, green peas, apples, asparagus, citrus, corn, grapes, nut crops, pears, and avocados
3. Pronamide—on direct seeded or transplant lettuce (all types), endive and escarloe
4. Metolachlor—on peanuts, pod crops, and white potatoes

Some insecticides included:

1. Permethin—been used under emergency exemptions (whatever that means) on celery, lettuce, cabbage, tomatoes, potatoes, grapes, green beans
2. Acephate—tolerances and labels now exist for use on celery, head lettuce, bell peppers, dry and succulent beans
3. Parathion—has a wide range of application of many crops against numerous insect species (a restricted-use pesticide in the U.S.)
4. Cypermethrin—active against a wide range of insect pests

Commentary: If hundreds of health food stores and industries can provide foods (produce, meats, dairy and others) throughout the country without unnatural and poisonous preservatives, why can't we have foods available at our local supermarket and grocery stores? The technology is here, but the desire by the powers that be is not!

Article #3 (see article)

1. Read about the safety of the farmer and farm hands and how many diseases can be linked to their poor health and even deaths. One of today's examples is the chemical exploitation on farm hands harvesting grapes.
2. Observe how bacterial contamination, animal drugs, antibiotics, directly effect how you feel by what you eat and the constant battle between the controlled individuals and the individuals that control.
3. Please read the article entitled Common Food Additives in both pet and people food. This document demonstrated, more than 15 years ago, these same 4 poisons (nitrates, MSG, BHT, and BHA) are still in your foods just as much or more than they were 15 years ago—producing even more dangerous diseases and conditions because of the collective addition of newer and more numerous chemicals. Over the years these mounds of chemicals produce an accumulative effect. How many cancers a year are related now to not only pesticides, but the myriad of chemical upon chemical? Where will it end? Don't think for one moment it doesn't matter. What are we going to do about it? Together, as people who care, we stand—scattered, as people who don't care we fall and perish! Fight for the right to your health of your loved ones. Fight for the choice of eating live wholesome foods and not just handed poisonous toxic substances passed off as good nutrition.

In conclusion: The answer to why there is such a struggle to maintain standards of good health care and food provision is that there is a spiritual battle between what God (Yahweh) wants for us and how His enemy, Satan is determined to kill, steal, and destroy our rightful heritage to good health and prosperity for all of God's children.

"Beloved, I wish above all things that thou mayest prosper and be in health, even as thy soul prospereth." 3 John 2 King James Version

For Safe Food

301 Sixteenth Street, N.W., Washington, D.C. 20036

PROBLEMS ASSOCIATED WITH FOOD CONTAMINANTS

FARMER AND FARMWORKER SAFETY

An estimated 45,000 human pesticide poisonings (including household accidents) occur annually, including 3,000 cases admitted to hospitals and about 200 fatalities.

A 1986 study in Kansas showed the relative risk of non-Hodgkin's lymphoma (NHL) increased significantly with the number of days of herbicide exposure per year. Men exposed to herbicides more than 20 days per year had a sixfold increased risk of NHL relative to nonfarmers. Frequent users who mixed or applied the herbicides themselves had an eightfold increase. Excesses were associated with the use of phenoxyacetic acid herbicides, specifically 2,4-dichlorophenoxyacetic acid.

If you farm in Iowa, the changes of dying from multiple myeloma (a cancer affecting the bone and bone marrow) is about 48 percent greater than that of the general population. People living in counties with high herbicide use were 60 percent more likely to die of leukemia.

In a California study, children born of agricultural workers were found to have deformed limbs at a rate of 5.2 per thousand, 13 times the rate among the general population.

BACTERIAL CONTAMINATION

The Centers for Disease Control have estimated that foodborne infections kill some 9,000 persons in this country every year.

ANIMAL DRUGS

FDA officials believe that as many as 90 percent or more of the 20,000 to 30,000 new animal drugs estimated to be on the market have not been approved by FDA as safe and effective. It is estimated that as many as 4,000 of these new animal drugs may have potentially significant adverse effects on animals or humans.

Adequate regulatory methods are currently not available for over 70 percent of the animal drug residues that may occur in meat, milk, and eggs.

Most approved animal drugs were cleared for marketing years ago on the basis of safety evaluations now considered inadequate.

Copyright 1986, Center , CSPI.
Reprinted/Adapted from **Nutrition Action Healthletter**
(1875 Connecticut Ave., N.W., Suite 300
Washington, D.C. 2009-5728.
$24.00 for 10 issues).

During 1984, violative levels of sulpha drugs were found in more than 6 Percent of all hogs tested.

Ninety-five percent of the vets surveyed by the magazine Animal Health and Nutrition admitted to giving chloramphenicol to livestock. (This drug causes a human disease called a plastic anemia, which is irreversible, untreatable, and inexorably fatal. Approximately one in 40,000 human beings has a generic susceptibility to chloramphenicol).

Thirty percent of vets admitted to having used it for the past ten years. Although FDA banned the oral form of chloramphenicol in early 1986, after being severely criticized by a House committee for stalling, it still permits other forms of the drug.

In early 1986, USDA's Food Safety and Inspection Service caught almost 100 feedlots misusing hormone implants in cattle. Zeranol and estradiol were implanted in the brisket and other edible portions of carcasses rather than the ear. In other cases, multiple pellets were used. USDA inspectors first detected cattle lots with misplaced hormone implants in January, 1986, but waited six months to take action.

ANTIBIOTICS

Antibiotics routinely fed to animals increase the prevalence of drug-resistant bacteria. Antibiotic-resistant bacteria that infect people are difficult to treat with antibiotics.

In 1977, the FDA announced its intention to ban the use in animal feed of antibiotics that are especially important in treating human infections, specifically penicillin and tetracycline. In 1978, Congress told the agency that before it proceeded with any restrictions it should conduct additional studies. According to Lester Crawford, then Director of FDA's Center for Veterinary Affairs, "...I think scientific opinion has changed over the past six years so that at the present time there is support for FDA's original position...Resistant organisms are what we are worried about in this particular case. Resistant organisms can result from a very small amount of antibiotics ingested by the animal and may not even produce measurable amounts of the drugs in the meat." FDA, under pressure from industry, rejected a recent petition for an immediate ban of these antibiotics.

USDA

Estimates that 15-20 percent of the poultry, 75 percent of the hogs, 95-100 percent of the veal calves, 25-33 percent of the turkeys and 60 percent of the cattle are fed penicillin or tetracyclines in their feed.

FOOD SAFETY

A Toronto study showed that 86 percent of non-occupational exposure to persistent toxic chemicals comes for food, as compared to only 10 percent from drinking water and 4.5 percent from the air.

Between 78 and 82 percent of chemicals in commerce have no toxicity information available; 80 percent of food additives have below minimal toxicity information available; and 64 percent of the pesticides and inert ingredients of pesticide formulations have below minimum toxicity information available, according to the National Academy of Sciences.

PESTICIDES

Of the $3 billion worth of pesticides sold in the U.S. each year, only a fraction - in some cases less than 1 percent - of the material actually reaches target pests. More than 99 percent winds up in the environment to contaminate land, water, and air and the social and environmental damage from pesiticides cost society another $1 billion annually. Despite a tenfold increase in insecticide use since 1945, losses of crops from insect pests have increased 7 percent to 13 percent.

The groundwater of Long Island, which is the only source of drinking water for 3 million people, has been contaminated with aldicarb (Temik) and other pesticides (carbofuran, chlorothalomil, dacthal, dinoseb, oxampyl (vydate), and 1,2 - dichloropropane).

Before World War II, only seven species of insects and mites were known to be resistant to chemical insecticides. By 1984, at least 447 species were resistant to one or more insecticides.

CONSUMER PREFERENCE

In a 1985 study done for the Food Marketing Institute, 75 percent of a U.S. random sample of consumers thought insecticide and herbicide residues were a serious hazard in the food supply.

A 1984 study found that 70 percent of the respondents said they would be willing to buy fruits and vegetables that were not completely insect-free if farmers would use fewer pesticides, and 56 percent said they would be willing to pay more for pesticide - free food.

* Citations available upon request.

9/86

Pesticides on Board

It can happen on the ramp, in the hanger, upon landing, or when passengers are waiting to disembark. A flight attendant or agricultural official suddenly begins to spray an aerosol can of pesticide. Or, passengers are exposed unknowingly as the spray is released through the jets' ventilation systems. Despite high risk to chemically sensitive individuals, asthmatics, etc., passengers are given little or no warning that the spraying is about to occur. At high altitude, they become sitting ducks for a range of toxic side effects that could cause serious damage.

On a 1988 flight to Australia, New Yorker Irene Kleiner suffered injuries to her eyes and face after a stewardess emptied two cans of insecticide over the passengers. The spraying began a half hour before landing, while Kleiner was asleep. Her eyes and face swelled, turning red and itchy. The next day, a doctor told her she was allergic to the pesticide. He gave her a written letter warning that she must not be sprayed again.

But between Australia and New Zealand, Kleiner and her husband were subjected to another spraying! This time, Kleiner was confined to a hospital. Her $35,000 lawsuit against

Quantas Airways lost on appeal in New York federal court. Now Quantas is releasing the pesticide through their airplanes' vents.

What exactly is being sprayed? According to the EPA and airline spokespersons, d-phenothrin is used most commonly. Sold under the brand name Sumithrin, it is a synthetic pyrethroid insecticide manufactured by Sumitomo Chemical Company, Ltd., of Osaka, Japan. (Warning labels on pesticide cans state that it is a violation of federal law to apply a registered pesticide in a manner inconsistent with its labeling. Sumithrin's label claims that it is "Hazardous to humans. May be fatal if swallowed or absorbed through the skin. Harmful if inhaled. Do not get in eyes, or on clothing. Avoid breathing vapors. Wear protective clothing and rubber goggles," etc.)

The application of pesticides in passenger compartments and cargo holds is required by law in many countries. But there are no FAA regulations governing such use on airlines; the spraying occurs under the jurisdiction of the USDA Animal and Plant Health Inspection Service (APHIS). According to Charles Havens, director of APHIS port operations for plant protection, the treatment is approved by the World Health Organization for soft-bodied insects, like mosquitos, that are usually implicated in transmission of human diseases.

Toxicologists argue that no insect control is achieved by spraying passengers. An insect would have to be directly hit by the spray to be killed; insects inside luggage would probably not be affected at all. They call the spraying a "token" procedure to mollify agricultural department regulations.

While it is known that pyrethroids adversely affect the nerves, liver, and skin, the inert ingredients in a can of pesticide are cause for as much or greater alarm than the product itself (see story, page 14). These toxins include known or suspected carcinogens and neurotoxins like DDT, xylene, toluene, and trichloroethylene. However, because inert ingredients are considered trade secrets under the Federal Insecticide, Fungicide, and Rodenticide Act, they are exempted from disclosure. Actually, any chemist can analyze the ingredients and duplicate them. Concerned scientists believe the real reason companies don't identify the inerts is because they are known to be dangerous, and contents can be changed at will to include petroleum distillates, etc., without responsibility being assumed for their use.

What can flyers do to protect themselves? Write letters to the airlines demanding your rights to be informed of the chemicals used in flight. Also, write letters to local newspapers to help educate others and bring attention to the situation. —A.M.C.

U.S. Pesticide Use on the Rise

2.23 Billion Pounds in 1993

In 1993, total U.S. pesticide use reached an estimated 2.23 billion pounds, up from 2.15 billion pounds in 1990, according to the Environmental Protection Agency's (EPA) June 1994 report, "Pesticide Industry Sales and Usage: 1992 and 1993 Market Estimates." The study, which presents an overview of the U.S. pesticide industry for 1992 and 1993, reports that U.S. pesticide user purchases account for one-third of the total world market in dollar terms, and one-fourth of the total volume of active ingredients.

During recent years, use of active ingredients in the U.S. has remained relatively stable at 1.1 billion pounds. The volume of pesticides used for agricultural purposes also remained steady at approximately three-fourths of the total use. The EPA attributes the stabilization to "lower application rates due to the introduction of more potent pesticides, more efficient use of pesticides, and lower farm commodity prices."

Other findings include:

- Pesticides were used on more than 900,000 farms and in about 69 million households in the U.S.

- Annual pesticide user expenditures totaled approximately $8.5 billion in 1993.

- Farmers' expenditures on pesticides equal about 4.2% of total farm production expenditures, up from 3.9% in 1991.

- Herbicides are the leading type of pesticides, in terms of both user expenditures and volume used. Atrazine and metolachlor are the two most widely used pesticides in U.S. agricultural crop production.

- More pesticides and pesticide uses have been registered during the past year than in any year since 1975. In 1993, EPA registered 21 new uses and 20 new chemicals. In 1990, 8 uses and 8 new chemicals were registered. The EPA attributes the increase to improvements in the registration process and industry's expedient submission of data.

[Reprinted from: Pesticide Action Network, North America Updates Service, August 1994.]

Pesticides: The Hidden Threat of 'Inerts'

You would think that pesticides that cause cancer, birth defects, and damage to our immune, nervous, and reproductive systems are enough trouble. But we, as citizens and consumers, don't even know the half of it. As it stands now, when the government and industry address health risks, they're only concerned with the active ingredients in pesticides. Other ingredients, some of which are even more toxic, are completely ignored, though they make up 30 - 99% of a pesticide formula. And to add to the confusion, these ingredients are called "inerts."

Therefore, everyone who uses pesticides, eats food that has been treated with pesticides, lives, works, and plays where pesticides are used, are made vulnerable to numerous unknown health hazards.

An inert ingredient is defined as any ingredient in a pesticide product that is not aimed at killing some target organism. It does not mean that the ingredient is benign to humans or other living organisms. Inert ingredients include everything from contaminants, emulsifiers, and solvents to surfactants, preservatives, dyes and anti-volatility ingredients. Inerts include such toxic chemicals as benzene, formaldehyde, and asbestos.

When the EPA evaluates the health risks of pesticides, inerts are disregarded. Testing of pesticides for chronic toxicity is required only for active ingredients. In 1991, only 1% of the EPA's resources were devoted to inerts. Of this limited amount of testing done on inerts, none of the studies examine the synergistic effects of pesticide ingredients, that is the effects of the inerts in combination with the active ingredients and with each other. However, the synergistic effects often can be even more toxic than the sum of the effects of the individual ingredients.

Unfortunately, the lack of data concerning the toxicity of inerts is only part of the problem. Currently, pesticide manufacturers are allowed to sell pesticide products without listing inert ingredients on the labels. In fact, many chemical companies (e.g., Monsanto and Dow) may not know what inert ingredients are in the products they sell since they purchase them from an inert manufacturer and then send the list of these ingredients "blind" to the EPA (in an unopened envelope). The EPA also may not even know what the inert ingredients are since these lists often do not contain information identifying the exact chemical makeup. The chemical manufacturers may also list alternative chemicals that are sometimes used in place of the usual inert ingredients found in a pesticide product.

Even when the inert ingredients are known to the EPA and the chemical companies, the public is still kept in the dark. According to the EPA, inerts are considered trade secrets, and therefore citizens have no rights to this information. This policy of corporate rights over citizens' rights is not only morally disgraceful, but the motivations for allowing it to continue are highly questionable. Despite pesticide manufacturers' claims that secrecy is necessary in order to protect company interests, the company labs are able to determine which ingredients are used in the competitor's products, rendering trade secret protection useless. Therefore, everyone who uses pesticides, eats food that has been treated with pesticides, lives, works, and plays where pesticides are used, are made vulnerable to numerous unknown health hazards.

So what is known about inert ingredients? Of the approximately 1800 "inert" ingredients found in about 20,000 products, about 50 have been categorized as "toxicologically significant." That is, they have been shown to cause either cancer, nerve damage, adverse reproductive effects, birth defects in humans or laboratory animals, or other long-term health effects. Fifty inerts are "potentially toxic" with a high priority for testing. These are chemically and/or structurally similar to known toxic chemicals. Approximately 250 ingredients are "innocuous," and include ingredients such as water, coffee grinds, corn cob grits, etc. The remaining 75% of inert ingredients are of "unknown toxicity." There have been no studies on how these substances affect human health or the environment.

The inerts issue is another example of how pesticides are considered innocent until proven guilty. It is these unknown dangers that provide consumers with another reason for strongly opposing the use of pesticides on the food supply, in the workplace, at home, and in all other areas of the environment. Relying on research and registration of inerts is not the answer, given how slow the EPA has been in registering active ingredients and that government regulations have chronically failed to protect public health in the past (See Safe Food News, Winter 1994). The inerts issue provides another compelling reason for the elimination of toxic pesticides from our food supply and for the promotion of sensible alternatives.
—R.A.R.

98% FREE OF CANCER-CAUSING CHEMICALS

Buyer Beware: Chinese Garlic

Garlic producers were relieved when the Department of Commerce announced on July 11th that a tariff would be immediately imposed on Chinese garlic imports.

Two letters filed by attorneys on behalf of the California fresh garlic industry document that fresh-peeled garlic from the People's Republic of China is being irradiated.

The tariff was sought by the Fresh Garlic Producers Association after the 1993 season, when Chinese garlic was selling as low as 6¢ a pound in the U.S. During that time, U.S. prices fell 20-40¢ a pound.

But consumers also have reason to applaud the tariff, which deals a crippling blow to Chinese exporters of garlic. Two letters filed by attorneys on behalf of the California fresh garlic industry document that fresh-peeled garlic from the People's Republic of China is being irradiated. FDA and Customs laws were violated by U.S. importers of the product, as none of the fresh-peeled garlic was properly labeled as irradiated under FDA regulations. Because the FDA has determined that the distribution of improperly or excessively irradiated food products poses a significant risk to the public, consumer avoidance of irradiated produce concerns the food industry. Therefore, it is feared that some U.S. importers will seek to conceal the fact that Chinese garlic has been irradiated. California growers fear that once the U.S. public discovers that any garlic was ir-radiated, the image and credibility of the entire industry will be damaged, plummeting sales.

Another concern is that irradiation extends the shelf life of Chinese fresh-peeled garlic. Usually, Chinese garlic sprouts more quickly than its U.S. counterpart, which gives the U.S. product a longer shelf life. With irradiation, distributors of Chinese garlic can claim that their product has a longer-than-normal shelf life and will not sprout (a condition that renders the garlic commercially undesirable.) Thus, the Chinese garlic, unlabeled as having been irradiated, would gain an unfair economic advantage over the un-irradiated domestic variety.

California Congressman Don Edwards corresponded with the Chinese Ambassador to the U.S. regarding the issue, asking him to verify whether "Chinese garlic may be irradiated to arrest growth of the bulb so that it does not sprout before reaching the marketplace. This appears to be most probable for garlic shipped late in the season." The ambassador's reply stated that the Chinese had used irradiation on a small amount of garlic for research only, and that the treated garlic had never been exported. "It is groundless to say that there is irradiated Chinese garlic exported to any countries, including the U.S.," Ambassador Li Daoyu concluded.

However, a California garlic producer visited the province of Shandong in China, where a significant amount of fresh garlic is exported to the U.S. He toured 2 of 3 irradiation facilities located there. At the first, in the provincial capital of Jinan, he saw approximately 100,000-120,000 pounds of fresh garlic on the floor either ready to be irradiated, or having recently been irradiated. The manager of the Jinan plant told him that when garlic is being harvested in Shandong, a large number of trucks are always lined up outside the facility, waiting for their cargo to be irradiated.

They also hastened to inform their contacts that the containers in which the garlic would be sold in stores bore no labeling for irradiation, so that "downstream" purchasers would never know.

In the port city of Quindao, the producer witnessed a large amount of dehydrated garlic, as well as white onions and pepper, on the floor of another irradiation plant. He was told that "virtually all product irradiated at this facility was destined for export." At no time at either facility was the need for compliance with FDA regulations concerning irradiation discussed.

Other testimony collected by the law firm found China exported container loads of fresh garlic and fresh-peeled garlic, at 40,000 to 45,000 pounds per container. The exporters assured their U.S. contacts that the garlic had been irradiated in China, and therefore would not spoil through sprouting. They also hastened to inform their contacts that the containers in which the garlic would be sold in stores bore no labeling for irradiation, so that "downstream" purchasers would never know.

In light of the garlic situation alone, ignorance of food treatment prior to sale can be dangerous to the public health.

—*A.M.C.*

Freeze! Plum Police

A California group of farmers, activists, and church groups recently joined in protest of a California law which prohibits the sale or distribution of slightly blemished plums. The group, which attempted to deliver blemished plums to the poor, called the California law a "national disgrace" since it allows nearly 10 percent of the nation's plums—about 52 million pounds—to rot or be fed to cows.

California Department of Food and Agriculture officials have threatened the group with a $1.6 million fine for violating the state's fruit and vegetable cosmetic laws. "We've got murderers and rapists walking the streets, and tens of thousands of people starving to death in Rwanda, and I'm being visited by the plum-compliance officers," said Dan Gerawan, who grew and packed the plums.

Burnt-hair Burger? Wet-dog Chicken?

The government and irradiation industry's latest concerted propaganda campaign to fool the public into accepting meat irradiation as the "solution" to the E.Coli problem has been missing a few very significant facts. For example, what about the carcinogens created in meat exposed to radiation? Where are we going to put the dozens or even hundreds of new nuclear irradiation facilities? Who is going to pay for the $10 million facilities? How will a nuclear accident at these facilities affect the safety of the meat supply and/or consumer confidence in the meat industry? What about the nuclear waste generated?

But, from the consumer acceptance standpoint, none of the factual omissions can be as damaging as the taste test research that has been conducted on irradiated meat. *The Economist* re-

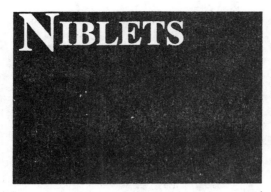

NIBLETS

cently reported that a meat-company scientist privately conceded "that customers in a taste test were able to identify the irradiated product in every case, since irradiation sufficient to kill the bacteria produces 'off flavors.'" The flavor? According to this scientist, "a burnt-hair taste—especially in beef." Perhaps this is a step up from the "wet-dog" taste that is said to exist in irradiated chicken. But it's all a matter of taste.

Government Ethics, I
Earth To Washington, Come In Washington

Remember Michael Taylor? He's the attorney who represented Monsanto and then became the Food & Drug Administration (FDA) regulator who signed the FDA's decision to approve—without consumer labeling—the use of, you got it, Monsanto's bioengineered bovine growth hormone (BGH) to stimulate milk production in dairy herds. Well, Mr. Taylor recently left the FDA to head the USDA's Food Safety and Inspection Service, the agency that oversees the inspection of the meat and poultry industries.

Given his past, one might expect some criticism of his previous cozy relationship to industry and apparent conflict of interest in the BGH case. Not so—at least in Washington. The *Washington Post* went as far as to call Mr. Taylor "A People-Oriented

Lawyer" whose "focus is the well-being of people, not animals or industry" in its article announcing his new position. Only in Washington could a corporate-lawyer-turned-regulator be considered a "people's lawyer." Give us a break.

Government Ethics, II
Bad Fish At The FDA

Food & Drug Administration seafood inspector Roberto Vaccaro was recently convicted of taking bribes to allow contaminated seafood into the United States. According to the U.S. Attorney's office in Newark, N.J., Vaccaro's conviction included eight counts of bribery and one count of importing seafood previously rejected by the FDA. Vaccaro could receive up to 130 years in prison and $250,000 in fines.

Eleven other federal employees and seafood importers also pleaded guilty or were convicted for similar offenses. For example, seafood importer Thekkedajh Peethamb Menon was convicted for re-importing more than 31,000 pounds of shrimp that were earlier found to contain salmonella and were rejected by the FDA when Menon initially imported them.

Another lesson in the importance of knowing where your food comes from.

(Source: *Supermarket News*, 6/13/94)

Cheeri-oops

Cheerios aren't so cheery when you find out what's been in them for the past year. Those toasted Os were found to be in violation of food safety regulations because they were contaminated with Dursban, an insecticide that is toxic to the nervous system. A Minnesota chemical application company, Fumicon, under contract with General Mills, decided to cut their costs by spraying a cheaper but illegal pesticide on the oats used in Cheerios. Not surprisingly, this went on for over a year before the FDA detected the illegal residues. Nobody knows how many other cereal products have been contaminated.

The response from our guardian government? The Food and Drug Administration (FDA) and the Environmental Protection Agency (EPA) quickly announced that this is not a public health issue, but simply a regulatory problem. In other words, pesticides are supposed to be "part of a complete breakfast".

BIG BURGER		1.79
BABY BURGER		.99
BARBER BURGER	CRISPY, YET MOIST!	1.69
BOW-WOW WINGS	MOIST, YET CRISPY!	1.29

its passage. To me, this represents a certain contempt for grassroots activism and the public. If we are striving for an honest culture and real reform in our country, shouldn't we begin by being honest with our constituents and supporters? If Food & Water sends out an action alert, you can bet that we've done our homework and there is a very, very good chance of a victory—if there's not, we'll tell you.

Ironically, the same thing is happening in the legislatively-oriented pesticide campaign. A huge coalition of groups are calling on grassroots leaders to stimulate calls supporting the "Waxman Bill." Besides the serious drawbacks of the bill itself—it calls for a flimsy five to eight year "phaseout" of carcinogenic pesticides (see SFN Toolbox, Fall 1993)—the chances of Congress actually passing it are zero. Again, I called several

leaders of this legislative effort and, without hesitation, everyone said that there is "no way" that the Waxman Bill will pass anytime soon. In fact, despite having some of the largest and most well-financed organizations supporting this effort, there are only about 30 co-sponsors of the bill in the House—out of 435.

We all lose from activist malpractice.

These actions represent activist malpractice. These campaigns and initiatives mislead the public and, perhaps worse, give false expectations. The result will be an increasingly cynical public that becomes even more reluctant to get involved in the essential work for social and environmental justice. In other words, we all lose from activist malpractice, even if

we're not directly involved in these campaigns.

We don't need focus groups and polls to tell us that the public is deeply concerned about the real problems that confront us. But instead of the same old legislative strategies and the same old defeats, activist leaders need to find the creative energy to go farther, inspire the public, secure a victory in a manner that is possible and, by all means, *be honest*.

Food & Water does not relish the task of criticizing our peers, but we refuse to be accomplices in efforts that we believe are misleading and ineffective. Besides, someone has to speak up and offer constructive criticism. The public doesn't need any more "practice" calling Congress, leading activist groups need more creative and effective strategies to secure the victories the public so rightfully expects.
—M.C.

Ever since I visited a radiation sterilization plant, when I was involved with the sterilization of medical devices, I was aware of how easily a bomb could be slipped into a package to be irradiated. This could easily happen in those type facilities and they are quite controlled, but the thoughts of how easy it would be to slip a bomb into a drum of spices or a bale of cocoa powder or even in a chicken is really alarming. Products like spices, gums and cocoa powder would arrive in the U.S.A. and go directly to the irradiation plant. The sacks or bales are never opened before treatment. Perfect for a terrorist operating from outside the country.

Think what would happen if a bomb went off in Vindicator while the cobalt rods were up? The blast would spread radiation dust for miles around even as far as Tampa if the wind was right. The radioactive particles would blast out through the ventilators that are so needed to remove ozone radiation generates.

Morris Warren
Bowie, MD

I am writing to thank Michael Colby for coming to Johnson State College to speak on food safety activism. I enjoyed his talk on food irradiation as well as other topics. I was very impressed with the tactics F&W uses to

reach your goals. I am a firm believer in getting to the root of the problem rather than going through the bureaucracy's red tape. Please keep up the great work. He made a lot of people think twice about what they put into their bodies who might not have known they have a choice.

Angus Anderson
Johnson, VT

It is indeed a pleasure to help support an organization that is doing so much good in protecting our food supply and insuring that the public receives the information it needs to remain healthy.

My check for $3,000 is enclosed.

Hopefully, the Garden of Eatin' Foundation will be able to make another contribution before the year is over.

Al H. Jacobson
Los Angeles, CA

Can you please include in one of your issues information on how to remove residues of pesticides from lettuce, celery, carrots, apples, etc.

Beatice R .Savin
Philadelphia, PA

Dear Ms. Savin,

Unfortunately, there is no way to remove pesticide residues from food that has been grown with these harmful chemicals. This fact has been demonstrated by a recent USDA study which found that even after fruits and vegetables were washed and peeled, 60 percent were still contaminated with residues (see Safe Food News, summer 1994).

The only way to ensure the safety of our nation's food is to stop using pesticides to grow it. Purchase foods that are produced without chemicals, demand safe foods where they are not available, and hold food companies responsible for the crime of selling toxic chemicals instead of nutrition.
—R.R.

Please send correspondence to:
Letters
Safe Food News
Food & Water, Inc.
RR1, Box 114
Marshfield, VT 05658

Fax:
(802) 426-3711

URGENT BGH ACTION ALERT!

Stop Bovine Growth Hormone (BGH) ACTION 2

Your first call worked!

In a previous issue we asked you to call Land O'Lakes, one of the largest dairy processors and retailers in the U.S., and let them know that you strongly object to their use of bovine growth hormone (BGH). Your efforts—and the efforts of tens of thousands of others who also called—have paid off. Land O'Lakes has taken its first small step in the right direction: They are now offering a new BGH-free line of milk in a few midwest states. They even named the milk "Superior"!

We must continue.

Now we must keep up the pressure and encourage Land O'Lakes to get BGH out of *all* of its products. Land O'Lakes has shown that—when pressured enough—they will respond to consumers. But they are still using BGH in the rest of their products. They're hoping that their new "Superior" line will appease consumers, and they're just waiting for this issue to go away. BGH is a dangerous, genetically engineered hormone that poses serious health hazards to both cows and humans. Only the chemical companies that have developed BGH will benefit from its use. This is a crucial time to remind Land O'Lakes that we will still refuse to buy their BGH products.

Keep the pressure on. Call Land O'Lakes again.

Let them know that you appreciate the first small step the company took to provide a BGH-free line of milk, but that you will still not purchase any of its products (butter, cheese, sour cream) until they are *all* certified BGH-free. In addition, let them know that you will ask your supermarket manager to stock only dairy products which are labeled BGH-free.

LAND O'LAKES 1-800-328-4155
9-12am & 1-3pm Central Time. Ext. 2 to speak directly to a person.

For more information contact Food & Water, Inc. 1-800-EAT-SAFE

☐ *Yes*, I called Land O' Lakes. Here are some comments about the call. (Use reverse side if necessary.)

NAME

ADDRESS

TELEPHONE

and mail to: Food & Water, Inc. RR1 Box 114, Marshfield, VT 05658

Yes, I would like to make a tax deductible contribution to help Food & Water send more of these action alerts.
(Contributions of $25 or more includes Food & Water membership.)
___ $10 ___ $15 ___ $25 ___ $35 ___ Other

☐ Payment enclosed. Please make checks payable to Food & Water, Inc.
Charge my ☐ VISA ☐ MC

Account No. _____ Exp Date _____

Signature _____

Telephone

ANSWERS TO QUESTIONS ABOUT

FOOD IRRADIATION

FOOD & WATER.
INCORPORATED

FOOD & WATER.
INCORPORATED

Depot Hill Road
RR1 Box 114
Marshfield, VT 05658

(cut and mail)

YES! I want join Food & Water, Inc. in its efforts to stop food irradiation in the U.S. and to ensure the availability of safe, nutritious food. Here is my tax-deductible membership contribution (minimum $25 individual, $15 low-income, $40 non-profits, $50 cooperatives, $100 stores and businesses). Please enter my subscription to *Safe Food News*.

☐ $25   ☐ $100   ☐ $500
☐ $50   ☐ $250   ☐ Other

Please make checks payable to Food & Water, Inc.

NAME

ADDRESS

TOWN   STATE   ZIP

TELEPHONE (DAY)

TELEPHONE (EVENING)

Credit Card Contributions
☐ MasterCard   ☐ VISA
Exp. Date
Signature

Food & Water, Inc. is the only nonprofit, grassroots organization working nationwide to prevent food irradiation and to promote safe, nutritious food. For a copy of our latest financial report, write us at the address below.

For more information call toll-free

1-800-EAT-SAFE

Food & Water, Inc.
Depot Hill Road
RR1 Box 114
Marshfield, VT 05658
(802) 426-3700

FOOD & WATER
I N C O R P O R A T E D
A Non-profit Organization
Depot Hill Rd. • R.R. 1, Box 114 • Marshfield, VT 05658-9702
(802) 426-3700 • 1-800-EAT SAFE

DECLARATION OF OPPOSITION TO
"NEGLIGIBLE RISK"

I, _____, oppose "negligible risk".

PLEASE WRITE SIGNATURE

I oppose the government's "negligible risk" policy which allows the deaths of an "acceptable" number of American children by condoning the presence of pesticide residues in our nation's food supply.

I oppose allowing the sale of fresh vegetables, fruits, herbs, spices, grains or foods of any origin which contain pesticide residues of any type for any reason whatsoever.

I hereby exercise my right to be informed if I am being required to consume foods containing pesticide residues of any kind, in any quantity, because of the government's "negligible risk" policy.

I exercise my right to be advised if I'm being forced to purchase foods containing pesticide residues, either by the bag, box, package or item, without my knowledge and/or consent.

I exercise my right to be warned of any side effects or dangers, regardless of how minimal those dangers may be perceived by others, of any and all ingredients containing pesticide residues in pre-packaged foods prior to my purchase and consumption of those foods.

I hereby hold the local, state and federal governments, food industry, grocery stores and their executives personally, individually and collectively responsible for any disease or affliction, including cancer, birth defects, allergies or other which might result, now or in the future, from being forced to consume pesticide residues without my knowledge and/or consent.

PLEASE PRINT OR TYPE IN BLUE OR BLACK INK

NAME _____ PHONE: ( ) _____

ADDRESS _____

CITY _____ STATE _____ ZIP _____

PLEASE LIST ONE OR TWO PRIMARY PLACES YOU SHOP FOR FOOD
SUPERMARKET • GROCERY • DELICATESSEN

NAME OF GROCER _____

ADDRESS _____

CITY _____ STATE _____ ZIP _____

NAME OF GROCER _____

ADDRESS _____

CITY _____ STATE _____ ZIP _____

Would You Like To Make A Personal Comment?

Send me: ❏ 25 ❏ 50 ❏ 100 ❏ 500 ❏ Other _____ additional Declarations to distribute.

**This Declaration Is Part Of A National
Citizens'   mpaign To Stop Pesticides
★ One American Voice Can Make A Differer
Information Made Available For Review By
The Food Industry And The U.S. Congress**

Printed on recycled paper with soy-based ink.

What is "Negligible Risk?"

"Negligible risk" is an unethical government policy, lobbied for by food companies, that allows an "acceptable" number of people to contract cancer from exposure to pesticides in food. According to this policy, the risk from the use of a pesticide is considered "negligible" and therefore "acceptable" if it doesn't cause cancer in any more than one in every million people from each crop use of each pesticide. The risk assessment process does not take into account the increased vulnerability of children and the elderly, it ignores the dangers of "inactive" toxic ingredients in pesticides, and it assesses risk as if we're exposed to only one pesticide during our lifetime. This means that each year tens of thousands of people contract cancer from pesticides as a result of this policy. Every day 1,400 people die from cancer. Enough is enough.

The food industry and the government are protecting corporations and their chemicals, not people. Sign this Declaration to voice your objection to the morally bankrupt notion that thousands of cancer deaths by pesticides are "negligible" or "acceptable."

This Declaration Is Part Of A National
Citizens' Campaign To Stop Pesticides
★ One American Voice Can Make A Difference ★
Information Made Available For Review By
The Food Industry And The U.S. Congress

Please Read & Respond Today
A National Citizens' Campaign to Stop Pesticides

Americans, particularly children and the elderly, are being ravaged by the effects of toxic pesticides. With one in three Americans now getting cancer, it's time for consumers to unite and put an end to the unnecessary use of toxic chemicals in the food supply.

This Declaration is part of a vital ongoing citizens' campaign to stop pesticides—an effort to protect the health of all children, consumers, farm workers, and the environment. Your signature will be part of many presentations before major food companies and the U.S. Congress declaring opposition to growing the national food supply with carcinogenic pesticides. Regional organizations are joining in a nationwide effort to get harmful pesticides out of the marketplace.

Please read and sign the enclosed Declaration of Opposition to Negligible Risk. Fold the declaration so the Food & Water name and address can be seen and place a first class stamp in the box provided.

Thank you for your participation. You can order additional copies of this declaration at the bottom of the comments section (see reverse). Please feel free to make as many copies as you wish and distribute them to your family and friends.

Together, we will stop toxic pesticides. We will!

Copyright By Food & Water, Inc © 1994
1-800-EAT-SAFE

IMPORTANT: Declaration of Opposition to "Negligible Risk" policy which allows the deaths of an "acceptable" number of American children by condoning the presence of pesticide residues in our nation's food supply.

PLACE
STAMP
HERE

FOOD & WATER
INCORPORATED
Depot Hill Rd. • R.R. 1, Box 114
Marshfield, VT 05658-9702

Help Stop Pesticides
Sign & Mail Today

FOOD IS MEDICINE

Ezekiel 47:12 …Their fruit will serve for food and their leaves for healing. NIV

Psalm 104:14 He causeth the grass to grow for the cattle, and herb for the service of man; that He may bring forth food out of the earth. KJV

Genesis 1:30 And to every beast of the earth and every fowl of the air, and to everything that creepeth upon the earth, wherein there is life, I have given every green herb for meat; and it was so. KJV

Apple—contains pectin with other fruits like pineapple (contains bromelain) helps with pancreatic insufficiency; helps lower cholesterol, control diabetes by regulating blood sugar and relieves diarrhea.

Banana—Vitamin B₆ increases immunity to infections, colds, flu and reduces inflammation; high in potassium and stops muscle cramps and stomach stress.

Beans—Vitamin E (in soybeans and limas) little or no gas if not chemically prepared helps fight heart disease—anti oxidant; Vitamin B—in red and white beans, lima, and soybeans known to help with some birth defects such as spina bifida

Bran—helps fight cancer as soluble fiber; lowers LDL; Magnesium helps prevent convulsions by regulating heartbeat therefore helping to decrease risk of heart attack.

Carrot—Beta carotene boosts every system especially immune system, therefore fights carcinogens; lowers cholesterol; calcium pectate lowers cholesterol; helps with diarrhea; far more calcium than cow's milk.

Celery—lowers blood pressure by helping to stop vaso constriction; insoluble fiber helps to maintain good digestive system thus preventing constipation and gallstones.

*Cruciferous vegetables (called this because they all have flowers with four petals that botanical historians describe as resembling the crucifix or Cross—there are 12 of these vegetables). Broccoli, Kohlrabi, Cauliflower, Kale, Turnip, Radishes, Rutabaga, Cabbage, Watercress, Brussels Sprouts, Mustard Greens, Horseradish—Vitamin C, Beta carotene, indoles, many others, slows growth of cancer cells; enhances and strengthen immune system—the entire body's protective agents. Is inhibited and destroyed by chemicals.

Garlic—allicin rich, helps fight all types of cancer (organically grown); helps relieve asthma; control hyper and hypotension according to body's need; prevents blood clots; lowers cholesterol; fights fleas and ticks; removes intestinal parasites; immune system builder; natural antibiotic—contains sulfur compounds.

Ginger—helps nausea. motion sickness and vomiting; good for the stomach, indigestion, intestinal disorders, joints, muscles, circulation, coughs, asthma, and decreases blood platelet clumping, sore throat discomfort, and cleanses kidneys and bowel.

Onion—greatly reduces platelet clumping; much like garlic contains sulfur; contains over 150 compounds which aid in body's defenses.

Orange—Vitamins C and A, choose oranges that don't look waxed—they have been picked green before the acid can turn to fructose—this is why most people can't tolerate them; they are sprayed with an orange color to look more appealing; if picked green they may cause "joint-like" arthritic pain; green oranges have very little Vitamin C because the citric acid has had no time for conversion to natural fructose sugar; some are also sprayed to prolong shelf life and colored with a dye and waxed, the spray is a fungicide. Organically grown oranges helps fertility in production of healthy sperm; fights heart disease and carcinogens.

Peppermint—calms stomach, helps reduce gas pains.

Pumpkin seeds—High potassium, helps reduce prostate enlargement and regulates testosterone levels; helps fight intestinal parasites.

Spinach—Beta carotene; high in iron, protects against cancer by boosting immune system; Magnesium—helps migraines; potassium-helps regulate blood pressure.

Strawberries—fights carcinogens; decreases cholesterol; increases fertility; protects against colon and rectal cancer.

Comments: This is just a short sampling of foods that heal. I urge you to do your own reading. Try them yourself, but high heat and over cooking destroys the life giving enzymes necessary to carry out your bodily functions.

Be mindful that foods that are contaminated with pesticides and irradiation will not only prevent the desired results of repair, rebuilding and restoration of your cells, but poisonous to your system—adding to the detriment of your condition. If the chemical content is above the threshold that your body can tolerate, it will promote disease and the death of your immune system. On the other hand, if these healing foods are available with minimal contamination, the benefits will out weigh the detriment.

If You Care, Take Time To Find Out The Truth!! And Follow It! Yeshua Christ said, "I am the way, the TRUTH, and the life. John 14:6 (NIV)

As a disciple (a follower of a particular teacher—The Webster Reference Dictionary) of Yeshua Christ I am committed to taking care of this temple (my body), according to what He has provided as my Creator—every **green herb** (every **plant** that is **medicinal** and **healing**) to me and the animals under my guardianship, to us it shall be for **food**. Unadulterated by the tamperings of mankind which then become a synthetic substance. A substance no longer a creation of The Creator, but an unnatural creation of the created being—mankind.

Let's go back to basics! **THERE IS A CURE.** The simple gifts of the earth—not synthetics from a test tube!

IT WAS NOT CONVENTIONAL MEDICINE THAT REVERSED MY PAIN, SUFFERING AND TWISTED BODY, BUT THE POWER OF PRAYER, HERBS, AND A NUTRITIONAL DIET GIVEN TO US ALL BY THE ALMIGHTY GOD OF THE HOLY SCRIPTURES

As for me and my house, we will serve the Lord, God Almighty.

What say ye?

Documents Proving My Painful Experiences Seeking Social Services, Medical Assistance, Welfare, and Social Supplemental Income (SSI)

1) Necessity to seek medical and welfare assistance due to prolonged - often misdiagnosed and unsuccessfully treated conditions

2) Attempts to seek disability Social Supplemental Income as advised

    Note: The welfare system as it exists today is not designed for those who wish to help themselves but instead induces, promotes, and perpetuates the stripping of one's dignity.

    a.   I was not allowed to work or earn more than $300 to $400 per month though my room rent was $200 — received only a $190 monthly check.
    b.   I was not allowed to work unless I had children.
    c.   I was not allowed to have phone consultations — it was considered work -- forced to wait <u>five</u> months on decision for disability.

<u>Conclusion</u>:

Propagation of the poor is often by the hand that offers to feed them.

** HELP US TO REDUCE FRAUD SO THAT WE CAN PROTECT PROGRAMS WHICH HELP PEOPLE **

FRAUD STATEMENT

The application which you just completed gives us information which determines your eligibility for benefits and gives your consent to match that information with the records of public and private agencies and businesses. If you give us information that is not true - or do not give us all the required information we requested about you and your household - or do not report changes promptly (within 5 days of the change), you are breaking the law and you could be prosecuted for welfare fraud. The law requires that we read to you or have you read what constitutes welfare fraud and what the penalties are if you commit such fraud.

Article 27, Section 230A of the Annotated Code of Maryland states that:

(a) Any person who fraudulently obtains, attempts to obtain, or aids another person in fraudulently obtaining or attempting to obtain money, property, food stamps, medical care or other assistance other than Medicaid to which he is not entitled, under a social, health, or nutritional program based on need, financed in whole or in part by the State of Maryland, and administered by the State or its political subdivisions is guilty of a misdemeanor. For purposes of this section, fraud shall include:

(1) Wilfully making a false statement or representation; or
(2) Wilfully failing to disclose a material change in household or financial condition; or
(3) Impersonating another person.

(b) Upon conviction, after notice and the opportunity to be heard as to the amount of payment and how the payment is to be made, the person shall make full restitution of the money, property, food stamps, medical care or other assistance unlawfully received, or the value thereof, and shall be fined not more than $1,000 or imprisoned for not more than three years, or both fined and imprisoned.

1. Did you read or have read to you your application? Yes ☒   No ☐

2. Do you understand that your signature on the application authorizes the Department of Social Services to look at the records of Federal, State, local and private institutions and compare them with the information you have given? Yes ☒   No ☐

3. Do you want to change or add anything on your application at this time? Yes ☐   No ☒
(If yes, please do so now.)

4. Did you truthfully answer under penalty of perjury all the questions to the best of your knowledge? Yes ☐   No ☐

5. Do you understand your responsibility to report all changes in your circumstances (within 5 days of the change) to the Department of Social Services?   Yes ☒   No ☐

6. Do you understand your application may qualify you for benefits, and therefore, by wilfully giving any false information, your application could be used against you in a fraud prosecution? Yes ☒   No ☐

7. Do you understand that by giving false information that you can be fined and/or imprisoned for welfare fraud?
Yes ☒   No ☐

I hereby acknowledge that all of the above information was read by me or to me and understood by me.

X _Sandy Bradley V.M.D._
Signature of Applicant/Recipient   Signature of Spouse (if both signed application)

Br R+ 2 Box 2167 Ridge Rd La Plata, Md. 20646   _12-26-89_
Address   Date

_12-26-89_   _Charles County_
Signature of Agency Representative   Date   Department/District

MARYLAND MEDICAL ASSISTANCE PROGRAM
NOTICE OF ELIGIBILITY FOR MEDICAL ASSISTANCE STATE ONLY

☐ Retroactive Eligibility ☒ Current Eligibility

Date of Notice: _2-23-90_

Case Number: _33203_

Dear _M's Bradley,_

This is to notify you that based on the application you filed on _12-26-89_ you have been determined eligible for Medical Assistance State Only. The period and basis for your eligibility are checked below.

☒ You are eligible for coverage effective _12-1-89_ through _2-28-90_ because your income and resources are within the limits allowed.

☐ You are eligible for coverage effective _____ through _____ based on your income and incurred medical expenses. The income considered for the period _____ through _____ is as follows:

SOURCE	AMOUNT	DEDUCTIONS

The total income is $_____ The total amount of deductions is $_____. The net income is $_____ The amount allowed for ____ person(s) is $_____. Therefore, you have $_____ more than is allowed. However, the amount of medical expenses considered is $_____ and qualifies you for coverage. The medical expenses considered in establishing your eligibility remain your obligation and will not be covered by the card.

Within a short time you will receive a red and white plastic card for each eligible person. You must show this card and any other health insurance membership cards to the providers of all health care services you have received or will receive.

Effective _3-1-90_, you will not receive further assistance unless you reapply and are determined eligible. The decision is based on COMAR 10.09.25 _11B_

If you do not agree with this decision, you have the right to request a hearing. The procedures for requesting a hearing are on the back of this letter. You also have the right to reapply after the expiration of your current eligibility.

Sincerely,

~~_____~~

ELIGIBILITY TECHNICIAN

M.A.# 0803320347 0

Charles County

DEPARTMENT OF SOCIAL SERVICES

_934-2700_

TELEPHONE NUMBER

~~_____~~

DHMH 4220 (4/85)

MARYLAND MEDICAL ASSISTANCE PROGRAM
NOTICE OF CURRENT INELIGIBILITY DUE TO EXCESS INCOME

☐ Medical Assistance   ☒ Medical Assistance State Only

Date of Notice: 12-17-90

Case Number: 33203

Dear M's Bradley :

This is to notify you that based on the application you filed on 12-3-90 , you have been determined ineligible for the period 12-1-90 through 2-28-91 because your income is more than is allowed. The decision is based on COMAR 10.09. 25 . 07 . D

The income considered for the period is as follows: 3 months

SOURCE	AMOUNT	DEDUCTIONS
Earnings	$ 1527.99	$ 150.00

The total income is $ 1527.99 . The amount of deductions is $ 150.00 . The amount allowed for 1 persons is $ 1152.00. You therefore have $ 225.99 more than is allowed. This is called "Excess Income."

You may become eligible if you receive medical services before the end of the above period for which you must pay yourself without reimbursement from health insurance or other sources. These expenses must be as much as the amount of excess income. Currently your medical expenses total $ —0— . Enclosed is a sheet which tells you how to keep records of your expenses. If your medical expenses equal the amount of your excess income within the time period specified above, you should immediately report to your local Department of Social Services.

This decision is based on your circumstances as described at the time you applied.

If you do not agree with this decision you have the right to request a hearing. The procedures for requesting a hearing are on the back of this letter.

Sincerely,

_____
Eligibility Technician

Charles County
Department of Social Services

_____
Telephone Number

DHMH 4213 (4/83)

MARYLAND MEDICAL ASSISTANCE PROGRAM

NOTICE OF ELIGIBILITY FOR MEDICAL ASSISTANCE STATE ONLY

☐ Retroactive Eligibility   ☒ Current Eligibility

Date of Notice: _3/8/91_

Case Number: _33,208_

Dear _M's Bradley_

This is to notify you that based on the application you filed on _2/28/91_, you have been determined eligible for Medical Assistance State Only. The period and basis for your eligibility are checked below.

☒ You are eligible for coverage effective _2/1/90_ through _8/31/91_ because your income and resources are within the limits allowed.

☐ You are eligible for coverage effective _____ through _____ based on your income and incurred medical expenses. The income considered for the period _____ through _____is as follows:

SOURCE	AMOUNT	DEDUCTIONS

The total income is $_____. The total amount of deductions is $_____. The net income is $_____. The amount allowed for_____ person(s) is $_____. Therefore, you have $_____ more than is allowed. However, the amount of medical expenses considered is $_____ and qualifies you for coverage. The medical expenses considered in establishing your eligibility remain your obligation and will not be covered by the card.

Within a short time you will receive a red and white plastic card for each eligible person. You must show this card and any other health insurance membership cards to the providers of all health care services you have received or will receive.

Effective _8/31/91_, you will not receive further assistance unless you reapply and are determined eligible. The decision is based on COMAR 10.09.25 _11 B_

If you do not agree with this decision, you have the right to request a hearing. The procedures for requesting a hearing are on the back of this letter. You also have the right to reapply after the expiration of your current eligibility.

Sincerely,

_____
ELIGIBILITY TECHNICIAN

Charles County
DEPARTMENT OF SOCIAL SERVICES

_____
TELEPHONE NUMBER

DHMH 4220 (4/85)

Continuing Your Food Stamps

Case Number_____

STATE OF MARYLAND
DEPARTMENT OF HUMAN RESOURCES
INCOME MAINTENANCE ADMINISTRATION

Date (MARCH 26, 1991)_____

18-08033203   04-91   08   LF   103

Name.

SANDY   BRADLEY
ST RT 2 BOX 2167
RIPLEY RD

Address.   LA PLATA   MD   20646

Dear__MS. BRADLEY_____

We are writing to tell you that your household will not get food stamps after ___APRIL 30, 1991_____ unless a member of your household completes a new application and is interviewed again. We've set your interview for ___TUESDAY, APRIL 9, 1991 at 1:30 p.m.___ If your age or health make it impossible for you to come in for the interview, and you are unable to find someone to come in for you, call us at ▓▓▓▓▓▓ bet. 2 & 4 p.m. and we will make other arrangements for your interview.

When you get the application, you don't have to complete the entire form right away. To begin the application process, you can complete the first page, tear if off and mail or bring it to the food stamp office located at:

_____

If you can't mail or bring in the first page, someone else can do it for you.

If we receive the first page of your aplication by_____

_____

and find that your household is still eligible, you'll continue to receive food stamps without a break. If we receive your application after that date, your benefits may be late.

Please call and let us know if you can not get your application to us on time. If you were sick or have another good reason and qualify, you'll get all the food stamps you missed. If we decide you didn't have a good reason for applying late, you can appeal our decision by asking for a fair hearing.

NOTICE

If all members of your household are now receiving Supplemental Security Income (SSI) or plan to apply for SSI you may reapply for food stamps at the social security office instead of filing your application at the food stamp office.
If you choose to do this, the social security office must also receive your application by the date shown on the left. They will send it on to the food stamp office for recertification processing.

Sincerely,

▓▓▓▓▓▓▓▓

DHR/IMA-FS 44 (Rev. 8/82) Previous edition may be used.

WHITE — Client Copy   •   CANARY — Record Copy

When you no longer have insurance or no longer have credit or even an address you become a "vagrant" as I was told by Greater S.E. Hospital & could not receive occupational therapy for my hand in 1987

SANDY BRADLEY

Category & G. T. No. __GPA-33203__

State of Maryland — Department of Human Resources
INCOME MAINTENANCE ADMINISTRATION

EVALUATION FOR DETERMINATION OF DISABILITY

Charles Co.   Department of Social Services

__P. Box 1010__
Mailing Address
__La Plata, MD. 20646__

Caseworker's Name and Telephone Number

RECEIVED
JUN 27 1991

DIRECTIONS

TO THE APPLICANT: Use these directions to complete Part I of the form before giving it to the examining physician or Medical Facility
(NOTE: If you need help completing the form, someone else may help you or contact your caseworker for assistance):

1. Read the statement as to why you are applying for assistance.
2. Fill in your name, address, date of birth and telephone number.
3. State the type of work you do most often.
4. State the type of work you did on your last job. When did you stop working and why did you stop?
5. Describe the other work you have done.
6. State your current medical problem(s) which keeps you from working, *how* it keeps you from working, and if it has worsened.
7. List *all* your other medical problems and the date (month and year) each problem started.
8. Read the statement. Sign and date the form in the spaces provided.

PART 1. *(NOTE: PLEASE PRINT ALL ANSWERS, LEAVE NO BLANK SPACES, BE SURE TO SIGN AND DATE FORM)*

1. I have applied to the State for temporary assistance. I think I am unable to work because of a medical problem.

2. Name __Sandy Bradley V.M.D.__   Date of Birth __2-13-47__
   Address __Rt 231 Middle House #2__   Telephone No. (__301__) __932-9353__ (neighbors)   NONE PRESENTLY
   __Benedict Md. 20612__

3. My usual occupation is (if you have never worked, write "none" in the space below; if homemaker, write "homemaker" in the space) __Veterinarian - self employed - Doc Bradley's House Call Service__

4. I last worked as (describe kind of work and give reason and date you stopped working) __April 15, 1991 - unable to use hand w/instruments__ About
   __severe pain back - standing sitting - driving → ↓ income → unreliable transportation → No phone → No work__
   NECK + legs

5. I have also done other work (describe) __ownership a Veterinary Hospital from Jan 1981 to Mar 16, 1986__
   Part-time supplementary work as Pizza driver; commercial cleaning; substitute teaching; supervisor - store restaurant

6a. I am now disabled due to (describe disability) __Herniated disc at L-5, mild degenerative osteoarthritis__
   __3th vertebral facets at L3 L4 L5 (bone scan) residual effects from hematoma left back and__
   __spreading & neuromatous scar tissue & severed nerve & right hand__
   b. My disability keeps me from working (how) __can not stand a sit long - driving long periods & bending -__
   __HAND - had Tinel's syndrome in palm - hyperesthesia; numbness__
   c. Since my last application, my condition has worsened. ☑ yes ☐ no If yes, how? __HORSE ACCIDENT after auto accident__
   __precipitated a bulging disc to a herniated DISC at L-5__

7. The following is a list of all my other medical problems and the date (month and year) each problem began:

Problem	Date	Problem	Date
(1) iatrogenic severed nerve (R) hand	25-86	(2) nerve transplantation (repair)	3-19-86
(3) whiplash / bulging disc auto accident	6-12-86	(4) herniated disc (Dr. Mar-90) hematoma left back → vagospasms	3-?-90 7-3-89

8. TO EXAMINING PHYSICIAN OR ADMINISTRATIVE OFFICIAL OF MEDICAL FACILITY: Please complete the following statement, Part II, regarding my medical condition. I authorize you to release to the State any information regarding my medical condition. I understand this information is required by the State to determine my eligibility for General Public Assistance.

__Sandy Bradley, V.M.D.__
Signature of Applicant

__5-31-91__
Month/Day/Year

DHR/IMA 402 Side 1 (5/88) Destroy all previous editions.

_7/1_ _Charles Co_ **Department of Social Services**

NOTICE OF DECISION

AT ☑ Application/Reapplication
☐ Extension of Payment Period

Case Name & Address

Date of Notice _7-1-91_
Category & Case No. _33203_

Dear _M's Bradley_,

READ THE SECTIONS CHECKED: THEY APPLY TO YOU

YOUR GENERAL PUBLIC ASSISTANCE CHECKS HAVE BEEN:

☑ Approved for the months of _7/91_ through _12/31/91_. You can expect to receive your first check on or about _7/5/91_. Because you are eligible for General Public Assistance, you are also eligible for Medical Assistance. Your Medical Assistance card will be mailed to you. GENERAL PUBLIC ASSISTANCE PAYMENTS ARE MADE BASED ON A MENTAL OR PHYSICAL IMPAIRMENT SUPPORTED BY MEDICAL FINDINGS WHICH PREVENT OR RESTRICT AN INDIVIDUAL'S ABILITY FOR SELF SUPPORT. PAYMENTS ARE MADE FOR A LIMITED NUMBER OF MONTHS AT WHICH TIME THEY AUTOMATICALLY STOP.

THEREFORE, if no other changes occur in your circumstances, the check for _12/91_ is the last you will receive. Authority: COMAR 07.03.04.02B(1) and COMAR 07.03.04.01C(1) (2).

☐ Approved as a one time only check for _____ which you can expect to receive on or about _____. THIS IS THE ONLY CHECK YOU WILL RECEIVE. Your Medical Assistance card will be mailed to you.

☐ Disapproved. You are ineligible for General Public Assistance which you applied for on_____ because_____

_____ according to COMAR 07.03.04 _____.

If your circumstances change, you have the right to reapply.

If you have any question or disagree with our decision, please call or come in immediately. You have the right to discuss this with us and to file an appeal if you aren't satisfied. PLEASE SEE SIDE 2 AND SIDE 3 OF THIS LETTER FOR INFORMATION ABOUT YOUR APPEAL RIGHTS.

☐ You may be eligible for a Non Public Assistance Medical Assistance card. If interested, call_____.

☒ Your monthly check has been computed as follows:

1. Amount for ___1___ (number of eligible) persons..............................$_205.00_

2. Amount Deducted

    (1) Net Earnings counted (gross monthly earnings—$55 = net earnings)$_____

    (2) Social Security (monthly benefit—$25) .... $_____

    (3) For_____ .... $_____

3. Total deducted from check.................................$___—0—___

4. Amount of check ....$_205.00_

YOU HAVE THE RIGHT TO FILE AN APPEAL, SEE SIDE 2 AND SIDE 3 FOR DETAILS.

YOUR FOOD STAMPS HAVE BEEN:

☑ Approved for the months _____7/91_____ through _____12/91_____. Your first allotment will be _____105_____ which is for the month(s) of _____7/91_____. Your allotment for the remaining months will be _____105_____ for ___1___ persons in your household. In the month of _____ you will need to reapply to continue to receive Food Stamps.

☐ Disapproved. You are ineligible to receive Food Stamps which you applied for on _____ because_____

_____per Food Stamp Manual_____.

If you want to discuss this decision on your Food Stamps, call_____.

☑ YOU MUST let us know of any changes in money you receive, employment, family group, living arrangement, medical condition, address and/or telephone number within 5 days of the change. Any one of these changes may affect your need for financial assistance or eligibility for Food Stamps. Information may be mailed or telephoned to the agency worker.

☑ If you do not agree with this decision on Assistance Payments, and/or Food Stamps, you have the right to an agency conference to discuss the decision with your worker's supervisor. You also have the right to appeal to the State Income Maintenance Administration:

   (1) The amount of your check and/or amount of your Food Stamps.

   (2) The length of your payment period for General Public Assistance, and/or your certification period for Food Stamps.

   (3) The decision to disapprove your application for General Public Assistance, and/or Food Stamps.

Our agency will assist you in making an appeal. If you wish to file an appeal you must do so within ninety (90) days from the date of this letter. You may request an appeal by writing or calling the agency at the telephone number given below. Your personal representative, lawyer or a friend can assist you in filing an appeal.

PLEASE SEE SIDE 3 FOR MORE INFORMATION ABOUT APPEALS

If you have any questions about the above, telephone the number below.

Sincerely yours,

_____
Worker

_____
District

_____934-6659_____
Telephone Number

JOSEPH L. SHILLING
STATE SUPERINTENDENT OF SCHOOLS

JAMES S. JEFFERS
ASSISTANT STATE SUPERINTENDENT
IN VOCATIONAL REHABILITATION

P.O. BOX 17011
BALTIMORE, MARYLAND 21203-7011
TELEPHONE:
TDD 339-4550
FOR DEAF ONLY
923J   1-800-492-4283
ext. 4521

DISABILITY DETERMINATION SERVICES

MARYLAND STATE DEPARTMENT OF EDUCATION
DIVISION OF VOCATIONAL REHABILITATION

July 1, 1991

MS SANDY BRADLEY
RT 231 MIDDLE HOUSE 2
BENEDICT MD   20612

SOCIAL SECURITY NO.:   160 40 4416

Dear   MS BRADLEY,

Your Social Security disability claim has been forwarded to the Disability
Determination Services for review. However, in order to complete your claim,
more information is needed regarding Your back, hand, concussion and intestinal
problems.

Please call ▓▓▓▓▓▓▓▓▓▓▓▓▓▓▓▓▓▓▓▓▓, the claims examiner, immediately at
the number above so that we may obtain the necessary information. We
encourage you to call during the hours of 9:00 AM to 3:30 PM.

Sincerely yours,

▓▓▓▓▓▓▓▓

The Disability Determination Services

DDS-23 (1/89)

MARYLAND MEDICAL ASSISTANCE PROGRAM
NOTICE OF TERMINATION FOR NON-FINANCIAL REASONS

☐ Medical Assistance   ☐ Medical Assistance State Only

Date of Notice: _9/3/91_

Case Number: _33203_

Dear _Ms. Bradley_

You are currently certified for the period _3/91_ through _8-31-91_ This is to notify you that you are no longer eligible effective _9-1-91_ for the reason(s) checked below:

☐ You did not submit a completed and signed application for a determination of your continued eligibility (applicable only to persons terminated from SSI).

☐ You failed to appear at the Local Department for the required interview.

☐ You did not provide the information/verifications required to determine continued eligibility.

Specify: _____

_____

☑ Other - Specify: _You are now Receiving Public_ General _Assistance, you will Receive a medical_ _Card through this program._

The decision is based on COMAR 10.09. _____

If you do not agree with this decision, you have the right to request a hearing. The procedures for requesting a hearing are on the back of this letter. You also have the right to reapply.

The Welfare system, medical
assistance programs not the
disability programs are
designed for those who really
want to help themselves -
needing temporary assistance only.
These programs are designed
for the recipient to lose
all self-respect, dignity and
honor. I know
I've been there!

Sincerely,

_____
ELIGIBILITY TECHNICIAN

_____
DEPARTMENT OF SOCIAL SERVICES

_____
TELEPHONE NUMBER

Documents to Verify Retained Attorney for
Two Cases: Auto Accident
and Medical Malpractice Case

LAW OFFICES

A PROFESSIONAL CORPORATION

WASHINGTON, D.C.

MARYLAND OFFICE

LANDOVER, MARYLAND 20785

VIRGINIA OFFICE

FALLS CHURCH, VIRGINIA 22046

WRITER'S DIRECT DIAL

June 18, 1987

TO WHOM IT MAY CONCERN:

Please be advised that our firm represents Dr. Sandy Bradley for injuries she sustained from an automobile accident and an improperly performed operation.

Both of these cases are meritorious and Dr. Bradley has an excellent expectation of winning substantial settlements.

At this time, of course, we cannot predict the amount of the award or the settlement date.

If I can be of any further assistance on Dr. Bradley's behalf, please do not hesitate to call me.

Very truly yours,

Letter of Disappointment
to Department of Justice on My Behalf

*The following letter is by a well-respected veterinarian
who testified as an expert witness at my trial -- believing and
urging that the case would be investigated and evaluated fairly.
<u>It was not</u>.*

U.S. Department of Justice
U.S. Attorne█████████████████
District of Columbia
Judiciary Center
████████████████

Washington, D.C. 20001   October 18, 1991

Dear Mr. Stephens

I have known Dr. Sandy Bradley VMD casually for 8 years and more
extensively for the last 2 years when I was asked to serve as an
expert witness on her behalf. I believe that I was chosen for this
because of my reputation and visibility in the Washington Area
Veterinary community.

I attended Ohio State University undergraduate and Veterinary School.
I served three years in the United States Army as a Veterinarian, most
of that in animal research. I have been in private practice in Maryland
since 1977.

Some aspects of Dr. Bradley's case continue to trouble me when I look at
them in relation to myself and other members of the Veterinary Profession.
A career in Veterinary Medicine is a rather large investment in time [8 years
of college], money, and financial and personal risk and sacrifice. Veterinary
Medicine is very rewarding mentally, emotionally and acceptable financially.

Veterinary Medicine is a profession that requires excellent small motor
manipulation of your fingers in 95 % of it's career applications. Most
Veterinarians choose Veterinary Medicine because they want to"handle" animals.
Depriving any Veterinarian of the use of his/her hands is an incredible
depravation mentally, emotionally, and financially.

I was shocked that her depravation was not in my opinion given the importance
that it deserved. I am concerned for the future of all Veterinarians in light
of this decision.

I hope that all relevant allegations surrounding her case will be investigated
and evaluated fairly.

                        Sincerely,

                        ████████████████████████
                        ████████████████████ D.V.M.

How Can Poverty Be a Blessing?

What the Fate of Evil Has Meant for Bad, God Has Made Good

In my opinion, no one without good reasoning skills would purposely desire to be impoverished unless they were convinced that their mission in life was to serve some ultimate purpose in doing so. There are two basic reasons why I have not reached the goal of financial stability after my injuries. First, is that there is virtually no job market or opportunities for a practicing wholistic veterinarian, especially if you have an objective restricted to herbology and dietary management, as I do. Secondly, had the attorney I hired been forthright in the handling of my case for the "permanent" damage incurred, I would not have the financial problems that I have today.

The cascade of events involving the misdeeds of my attending physician as well as the firm I retained led to a series of lessons and discoveries which not only changed my life but <u>strengthened my abilities to cope</u> with life's disappointments and challenges.

While in this interim of now eight years, I had been unable to perform surgeries. I have not had access to hospitals or clinics for the express purpose of practicing naturopathic medicine, but I have discovered that more than ninety percent of surgeries (in my opinion) are not necessary and that diet change is more than eighty percent of the battle. Having more than 4,000 clients has provided me with irrefutable observations including my own personal healings.

Despite all the injustice Yeshua instructs us to pray, "Forgive us our trespasses <u>as we forgive</u> those who trespass against us" Matthew 6:12 King James Version.

> "You intended to harm me, but God (Yahweh) intended it for good to accomplish what is now being done, the saving of many lives."
> Genesis 50:20 (NIV) New International Version

Documents to Verify
Joint Efforts between
Myself and Other Organizations
Who Have Endeavored
to Serve the Community
(in Chronological Order)

August 16, 1985

Dear ▮▮▮▮▮▮▮▮▮▮▮▮

    I am writing this letter to you on behalf of Dr. Bradley who is a customer of our's and who refers several of her patients to us.

    Dr. Bradley has been referring clients to us for approximately 18 months, we have, on occassion, referred customers to her for services, several of our staff members are established clients with Dr. Bradley, including myself.   To my knowledge, those patients of Dr. Bradley's who patronize our shop are highly satisfied with the services which Dr. Bradley renders. Personally, I will go on record stating that I find Dr. Bradley to be a fine professional woman who cares deeply for the animals s.. treats and for the animals' owners. She is a generous person who : believe strives daily to practice her profession as consciencio..ly as possible.

    As a professional woman myself, who is involved in a small business built on the belief that the American public does indeed have the right to choose from many different options, I encourage you to further explore Dr. Bradley's holistic/natural approach as one of these viable options.

    I will be glad to meet with you on a personal basis if you have any questions or comments.

Sincerely,

▮▮▮▮▮▮▮▮▮
Sales Manager
▮▮▮▮▮▮▮▮▮▮

cc:Dr. Bradley

Washington, D.C. 20017
April 24, 1993

To Whom It May Concern:

For more than a decade I used the veterinary services of Dr. Sandra Bradley. I first took my pets to her hospital on the basis of the high recommendations I had received, both as to her proficiency and as to her obvious love of animals. On this first visit I was deeply impressed by the clinical cleanliness and odorless atmosphere of her place.

With a DVM degree from the University of Pennsylvania and licenses to practice in four jurisdictions, there is no question about Dr. Bradley's competence. Many of her customers, especially in North East Washington, feel that this area has lost a valuable asset.

Any agency that can help Dr. Bradley reestablish the veterinary service to which she has given, and wants to continue giving a dedicated, warm, and personal relationship to animals and to the owners who love their pets will be doing a service of justice and humaneness.

Yours truly,

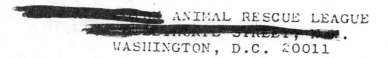

ANIMAL RESCUE LEAGUE
~~BALTIMORE STREET, N.~~
WASHINGTON, D.C. 20011

March 22, 1988

To Whom It May Concern:

As a clerk for the Rescue League, one of my duties
is to assign our new pet owners to a veterinarian thats in our
program for spay and/or neuter. Dr. Bradley's office was located in an area that was very convenient to the majority of
our customers' in the upper northeast and northwest area, somewhat in the middle of the upper D.C. area. Dr. Bradley was
doing a great job in her field and for the League since she
started back in 1981 as a staff member then on to her private
practice. She has made well over $7,000. per year in our low-
cost spay/neuter program fund, that doesn't include other services and referwals.

Speaking on a personal level, I met Sandy Bradley in
April 1983, when I started work at the League. She has always
been a very warm and gentle person. I later found her to be a
good Vet. when I had an emergency with my dog, she was the first
Vet. that came to mind. She ever so gently cared for my young
dog as well as calm me down and all was well. Since she is no
longer in practice, we have had to reschedule over 30 clients
that were booked in advance for spay in 1986. This isn't an
easy task, especially for the regular clients that came to
know and love her, and trust their pets to her. It was a very
sad and wastful thing to have happened to her and to this day,
we are still getting calls from clients that are looking for
Dr. Bradley.

Thank you for your time.

Sincerely,

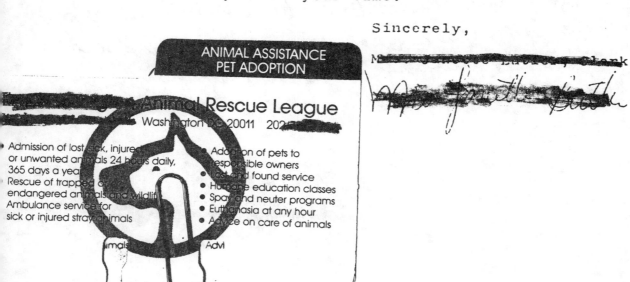

ANIMAL ASSISTANCE
PET ADOPTION

Animal Rescue League
Washington D.C. 20011   202

- Admission of lost, sick, injured
  or unwanted animals 24 hours daily,
  365 days a year
- Rescue of trapped or
  endangered animals and wildlife
- Ambulance service for
  sick or injured stray animals

- Adoption of pets to
  responsible owners
- Lost and found service
- Humane education classes
- Spay and neuter programs
- Euthanasia at any hour
- Advice on care of animals

It's about Priorities — Why I Have Been Successful?

I am committed to the belief that just as there are physical laws of the universe such as gravity there are spiritual laws such as the consequence of original sin (disobedience to God's ways.)

I refuse to allow anyone to make me feel ashamed that I have made a conscious decision to accept the Holy Spirit of Yeshua (Jesus) Christ as Lord of my life and Saviour of my soul. Saved from what, you say? Saved from total and eternal separation from the God I love, the Father who sent Him. The Son, Yeshua, is God clothed in earthly flesh who offered this flesh in death, shedding His blood for my sin (disobedience) passed on in the genes from the original earthly father of the human race, Adam.

Because God the Father loved me so much (even if I were the only one on earth) He came that I may be able to choose the truth about Him to be reconciled and never separated again from my heavenly Father. The same power (God the Father) that raised Yeshua God, the Son from the dead (grave) lives in each one of us who believes in Him. "**I am the Way, the Truth and the Life and no man comes to the Father except by me,**" says Jesus. (John 14:6) I invite anyone to explore and study this possibility as Truth as I have. If you choose not to believe as I believe then the issue is between you and your Creator and I love you still.

There will be some who will use this book to hail me as a religious looney-tune or extremist. There will be some who will claim to be Christians and distort the meanings intended. There will be some who will claim that one so nonsensical could hardly be noteworthy of any scientific achievements — certainly none that any rational mind should contemplate.

My answer to all such claims are the following:

a. I am not religious - religion, I believe is man's way to God (the True God of this universe) but true Christianity is an intimate, committed relationship with Yeshua (Jesus) Christ. His Spirit guides me in all my ways as long as I listen with my spiritual ears and follow my spiritual heart according to the ways He has instructed for us that **we may love one another as He has loved us.**

b. Many of you believe in channeling where an ancient spirit of wisdom speaks through another chosen human being. I believe these spirits do exist. **Just as one may choose that spirit as their guide I choose the Spirit of Yeshua Christ who was historically crucified, died, was buried, but defeated death so that I and all who believe this will live**

with Him eternally — Him inside us and us inside of Him wherever we are.

c.   Some may believe that the earth as they call it goddess "Gaia" is the true god; or some give reverence to many spirits. Yet still for others no god exists. I can only say that I wish you would believe as I do, but because you don't does not make me love my fellow human being any less.

I believe in the spiritual law of accountability. I believe that God (Yahweh) — my God — is a God of eternal love but He is also a God of eternal <u>justice</u>.

Would it be just for one of your children (for example — a Jeffrey Dahmer) to be permitted to slaughter and murder and eat the rest of your children until they were all dead? Doing nothing to stop him? Should his behavior be rewarded the same as your other innocent children? Any thinking person would admit to do nothing and reward him for a totally merciless, destructive behavior would certainly not be a righteous judgement on behalf of the innocent. Do we expect our God to do less? We, who were created in His image of righteousness and justice. Yet as individuals we are not to become solo vigilantes but create a government of justice in which to allow the hand of God to operate.

Many of us do not do the right and just things simply because <u>we do not seek to do them</u>. Never grow weary of doing good.

> "And let us not lose heart and grow weary and faint in acting nobly and <u>doing right</u>, for in due time and at the appointed season we shall reap, if we do not loosen and relax our courage and faint."
> Galatians 6:9 and 2 Timothy 3:13 Amplified King James

We are accountable for <u>our beliefs</u> (given the circumstances) and we are therefore, accountable for <u>the choices we make</u> based on those beliefs. I have a joy in my heart that circumstances cannot change nor man can remove, but lives there forever from Yeshua God, my God. I love Him so. He is the source of my foundation.

And I Repeat,
Is Doc Bradley Really Cured?

I challenge the establishment to show America that if it were not the herbs and dietary changes that improved the lives of my patients-clients and myself, then <u>what did</u>?

The herbs have proven themselves over and over and over again for centuries in every culture in the world. Literature and generations of knowledge passed on since the beginning of time support this. I think it quite unjust to require the presentation of anymore <u>so called</u> "scientific evidence" to prove <u>what has already been proven</u>.

Powers that be - Congress, FDA, USDA, all pharmaceutical companies, the AMA, the AVMA, I address you. <u>Now it's your turn</u> to prove that organic herbs and organic diets <u>do not work</u> - **without tampering with the evidence!**

When the issue becomes the life of your mother, your uncle, your son, your niece, you say you want everything humanly possible to save your loved ones, but you reject answers that are and have been viable and available for ages. **More that fifty years ago as mentioned before, a man named Jethro Kloss (whose techniques I have successfully used) appealed to the authorities and offered his help and wisdom. He was flatly rejected (see documents at the end of this chapter).** Today's devastation of America's health lies in the hands of the "powers that be" because truth was denied the American people.

Jethro Kloss' letter addressed to the National Cancer Research Institute fifty-five years ago has given more than enough time for the establishment to investigate the validity of his claims. Because of Mr. Kloss' work I was cured of many conditions, some diagnosed as irreversible. There is no longer an excuse for modern-day practitioners (allopaths) not to offer choices we rightfully deserve.

The term "cure" refers to the restoration of function for which that body or body part was created to do. **Whether the cure** (restored to function) **is temporary or till death** (some erroneously say permanent) **the means to achieve that goal should be the choice of the American citizen — not that of the doctor — not that of the government — not that of another party —** unless it can be <u>proven</u> beyond all doubt that that person is incapable of choosing <u>how</u> he or she wants to preserve his or her life.

1. <u>My hand</u> is no longer progressing in contraction like a bird's claw nor does it have shock impulses going up my entire arm or extreme numbness and pain nor extreme sensitivity to cold, nor the inability to perform tasks

such as abdominal or thoracic surgery (if need be).

2. <u>My leg</u> is no longer contorted and twisted; painful and dysfunctional in walking or running or jumping.

3. <u>My back</u> is strong although I am still subjected to hauling gallons of water for my livestock. On October 26, 1994, I was able to <u>transfer</u> 300 pounds of whole shelled corn, 200 pounds of oats and 180 pounds of dog food from my truck to the old barn, not alone, but with my God — Yeshua Christ. Follow-up tests have not been done since 1990, therefore the diagnosis of a herniated disc remains. I have learned to use my back brace, tons of herbal re-enforcement and determination to get the job done!)

4. <u>A nail went through my foot</u> on Tuesday, September 13, 1994. I was sent home <u>without</u> any medicine and <u>told</u> "your foot is infected." I was told to soak it, quick wipe with an antiseptic while the attendants applied a small gauze bandage and out I went. I was <u>unable to walk.</u> I did not tell them I was a doctor and they didn't ask my occupation; just this one major question — **"Do you have insurance?"** My answer was, "NO." Suddenly, no x-rays were needed, no licensed physician was called in to examine, treat, or prescribe medication for me. If I were not a physician able to assess my own clinical signs and <u>treat myself, herbally</u>, I am certain the consequences of the rapidly progressing infection would have developed into gangrene without proper intervention.

I used large amounts of garlic (organic), onions, wintergreen, Red Clover, Burdock honey applied to the wound, combined with our FruitAloe drink and the actual aloe plant, topically. This combination turned the tide.

Even though I felt better immediately, it took <u>three</u> weeks for me to walk normally again without pain. In fairness to the hospital staff, I must say I was instructed to see the doctor recommended written on the information sheet within two days if complications set in (see document dated, September 13, 1994 at the end of this chapter).

5. <u>A colon dysfunction developed from mechanical obstruction following my first horse accident in 1989</u> — I was discharged from the hospital still devoid of the ability to rid toxins by intestinal excretion (bowel movement); no better than I could several days before being admitted. The vomiting had subsided but extreme nausea remained up to the day of discharge. I was still unable to eat most foods or drink liquids. I was still ataxic (stumbling or weak gait) and unable to focus clearly. I barely had

strength to drive or take care of myself. These conditions combined with those of the herniated disc, vago spasms (described to me as vascular headaches) and the severe muscle contractions along all of my back and neck left me quite debilitated. I drove twenty miles to buy seventy dollars worth of herbs. Within forty-eight hours colon function had been restored. Purifying the blood of accumulated toxins in the colon is one of the first steps to healing, no matter what the infirmity. I used natural digestive enzymes like apple pectin, pineapple bromalein, and papaya with the natural laxatives aloe vera and cascara. Enemas were not necessary. Jethro Kloss frequently recommends enemas but I have a good measure of success without them, unless extreme toxicity is evident.

6. A terribly painful case of shingles developed due to a chronically compromised immune system. Today I still bear the pathogenic scar pattern on my belly. I was too ill to get to a hospital and was alone in the house. The hospital personnel practically confirmed the diagnosis over the phone. It was suggested that I get in immediately. The pain was so severe it would stop me dead in my tracks as if someone stabbed me in my abdomen. I never felt anything like this sudden debilitating pain. It is understandable why the condition is so crippling and even fatal to the elderly. While driving I almost caused an accident. I was forced to pull over. This pain remained for weeks. The herbs reduced the intensity of the pain greatly. I never went to a hospital. I was not inclined to go for several reasons; I had little money, no insurance, and a lack of confidence that the hospital staff would even be helpful because, traditionally, antibiotics, pain killers, and/or steroids are usually prescribed. Since that time I have discovered by recent news reports that suicides have often resulted due to the degree of pain associated with this condition.

Am I really cured? Well, all body parts in question are no longer debilitated and dysfunctional as some were medically declared permanent and irreversible. Some ailments were determined treatable but only by the intervention of modern medicine. Am I happy? The answer is YES. Then I am cured!

DISCHARGE INSTRUCTIONS FOR << SANDY BRADLEY 165215 >> (NAIL IN FOOT)

Our doctors and staff appreciate your choosing us for your emergency medical care needs. Read these aftercare instructions carefully. Please call us if you have any questions about your medical problem. We are here to serve you.

PUNCTURE WOUNDS:

You have a puncture wound. This type of wound is very common, especially in feet. Puncture wounds go deeply beneath the skin. They can cause serious problems, including:

* Infection - This often develops in 1-3 days. There will be more swelling, redness, and pain. Red streaks and pus drainage also mean infection. This needs immediate medical care.
* Deep Injury - Tendons, joints, nerves, or blood vessels can be damaged. Call your doctor or the emergency room if you have trouble moving the injured area, or unusual pain, numbness, or bleeding.
* Foreign body - Undetected small bits of clothing or footwear may remain in the wound. This will prevent healing and cause infection.

Please rest and elevate the injured area until all the pain and swelling are gone. Ice packs may be used for 1-2 days to reduce swelling. Start soaking your wound in warm water for 30-60 minutes 3 times daily. This promotes normal drainage and reduces the chance of infection. Cover the wound with a dry, clean dressing between soaks. Antibiotics may be needed to help fight infection. Call your doctor or the emergency room right away if you think your wound is infected, or if you have other problems with your injury.

TETANUS PREVENTION (TETANUS TOXOID):

You were given a booster today to prevent tetanus infection. You will be protected from tetanus for at least 5 years. Remember this date so you will not be given unnecessary tetanus shots in the future. Your booster shot may cause some swelling, pain, and tenderness in your arm. This is normal. It does not mean that you are allergic to tetanus shots. To reduce your pain you should rest your arm, apply ice packs, and take mild pain medicine.

FOLLOW-UP CARE:

Your physician today has been DR. CHARLES BRIGGS
For follow-up care you have been referred to the following doctor or clinic:
████████████████ Phone: 301-████████

Please make an appointment for further treatment in __2__ days. Be sure to tell your referral doctor or clinic that we have sent you, and bring your medicines and instructions to the office. If you had x-rays, an EKG, or lab tests today, they have been reviewed by your doctor. We will contact you at once if other important findings are noted after further review by our staff. If you do not continue to improve or if your condition worsens, please call your doctor or the emergency department right away so you can be examined.

I acknowledge receipt of these instructions. I understand that my condition may require more care and will arrange for further treatment as recommended.

Sandy Bradley, V. MD

_____	Patient or Representative Signature
Staff Signature	

Tuesday, (September 13, 1994) - 10:45 PM

(The following excerpt from <u>BACK TO EDEN</u> is reprinted with permission from BACK TO EDEN BOOKS, Copyright (c) 1992, by the Jethro Kloss Family.

"In different parts of the earth people are searching for cures for cancer and other so-called incurable diseases. The treatment for them is found in this book.

Cancer is a treacherous disease. When there is any suspicion of cancer, take a cleansing diet — fruit and vegetable juices, taken separately. Cancer cannot live in a system where all the mineral elements are present which God put there in the beginning.

If cancer is suspected, clean out the system, and get a new supply of pure blood. There are non-poisonous herbs that will purify the blood and kill malignant growths internally or externally, leaving no bad after effects. Cancer will not live in a system when the blood stream is pure.

While it may be all right to treat symptoms, the cause of a disease must be ascertained and removed before there can be a permanent cure. Practitioners, will you not try it?"

"My ambition is to give my findings to the practitioners so the people may receive the benefit of them. I have written the American Medical Association in Chicago, Illinois, and they have asked me to come to Chicago and give it to their clinic."

Not long ago a woman came to me who had cancer involving the liver, lungs, and stomach. She lived only a few weeks after I saw her. A post-mortem was held, and we found that her liver was almost entirely gone. Parts of both lungs were hardened, and the throat and stomach had growths in them. She had not been able to retain anything in her stomach for some time. Portions of her intestines were very much shrunken. Upon inquiring into what had been her diet, we found that it had been white bread, jellies, jams, soda crackers, and denatured foods.

Many times I have removed hard swellings in the breast, bowels, rectum, and vagina with hot applications, massage, and herbs.

In different parts of the earth people are searching for cures for cancer and other so-called incurable diseases. The treatment for them is found in this book.

Cancer is a treacherous disease. When there is any suspicion of cancer, take a cleansing diet—fruit and vegetable juices, taken separately. Cancer cannot live in a system where all the mineral elements are present which God put there in the beginning.

If cancer is suspected, clean out the system, and get a new supply of pure blood. There are non-poisonous herbs that will purify the blood and kill malignant growths internally or externally, leaving no bad after effects. Cancer will not live in a system when the blood stream is pure.

While it may be all right to treat symptoms, the cause of a disease must be ascertained and removed before there can be a permanent cure. Practitioners, will you not try it?

Since I have been asked many times about my experiences with cancer cases, I will give a few.

Many years ago I was asked to go to see a man who was in a charity hospital. His trouble had not been pronounced cancer. In fact, he had no outward sign of cancer—just a little swelling on the under side of his jaw which was not

(460)

**ONE PERSON CAN MAKE A DIFFERENCE
AND YOU**

CAN BE THAT PERSON

Commentaries on X-Rays

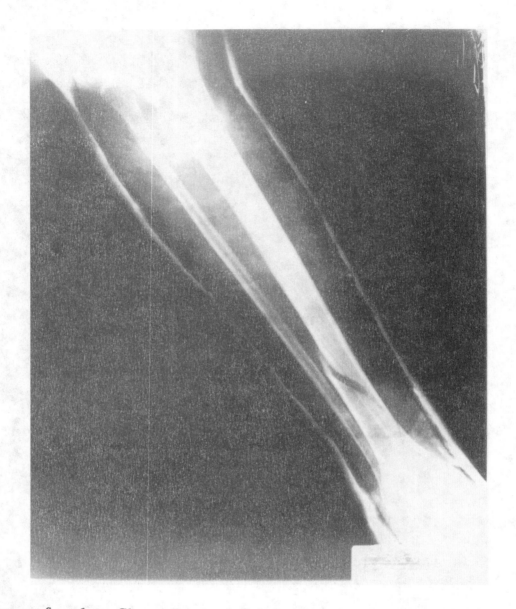

<u>Fractures of my leg</u> - Shows three spiral fractures: a) bottom of tibia (large bone), b) smaller one just below and behind in fibula (small bone), c) top of fibula.

   Fourth fracture not show here (in the ankle) - X-ray reports dated, July 1, 1992, July 29, 1992, August 19, 1992, October 21, 1992 all state alignment or position is excellent or good. How could my bones have excellent alignment when my knee, leg, and ankle were so distorted and rotated? My assessment would be that the bones may have healed in good apposition (close to each other) but clearly not properly aligned as indicated by the pictures shown in the views taken.

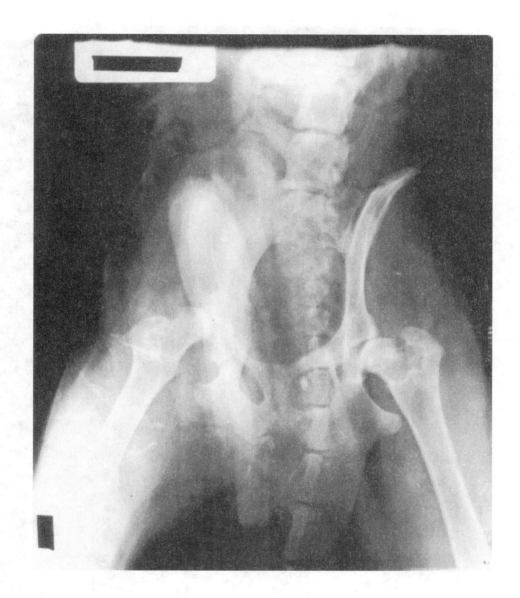

Killer - VD (ventro-dorsal view - dog lying on back) Six-month-old German
 Shepherd, "Before" photo dated, January 30, 1984 - completely crippled
 in hind legs (hip dysplasia) V-D (ventro-dorsal view) to your left is the
 dog's right leg - can plainly see that both femurs are not in their sockets
 as a ball and socket joint should be. The ligaments to hold the joint in
 place are weak. The socket portion or acetabulum is shaped more like a
 saucer than an ice cream scooper. The joint no longer fits like hand and
 glove, the femur bone will slip out of place rubbing bone against bone
 causing severe pain - the poor alignment prevents walking. This is
 largely a genetic disease worsened by diet of poor meat quality in commercial foods. (Killer climbed stairs within twenty-four hours of herbs!

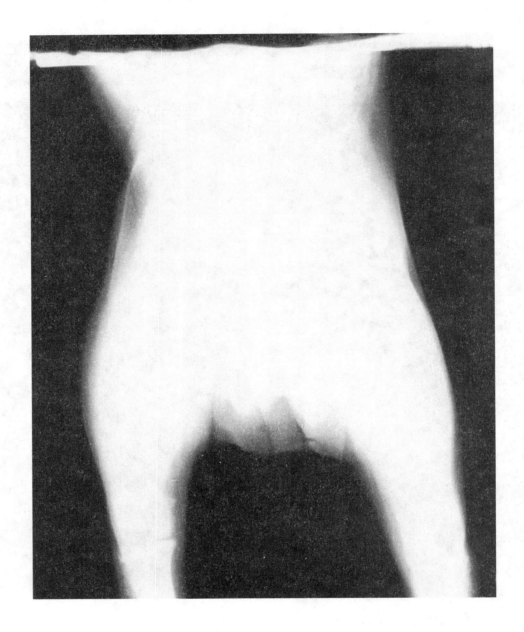

"After" photo - taken by another hospital when Killer was hit by a car seven months later on August 20, 1984. Both sockets actually remodelled, as demonstrated especially by left leg (right of picture) ball and socket joint fitting snug and tight, not wide, so that femur slides out of joint. Right leg was obviously hit. He has fractures of wing of ilium and extending into acetabelum. The heads of both femurs are no longer flattened. Killer's pain left within twenty-four hours of herbs, just as mine did. Killer still lives as of November 12, 1994.

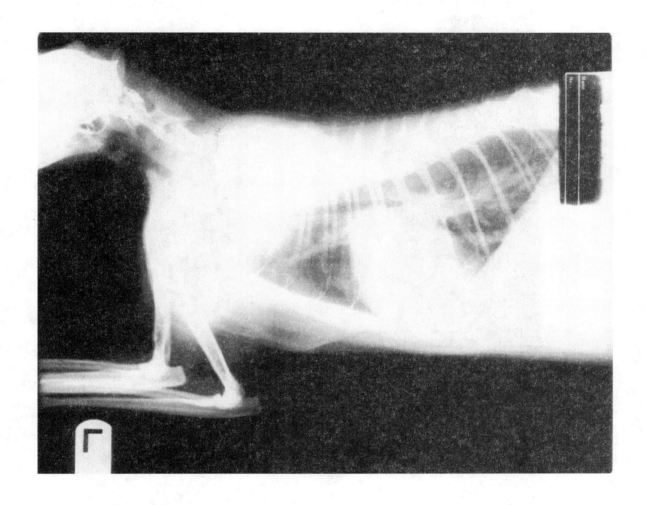

<u>Simone Ziegler</u> - (lateral - animal lying on left side) A three-year-old domestic
short hair (DSH) diagnosed by another clinic to be in severe congestive
heart failure so much so that the referring veterinarian would not release
the pet to the owner unless it was going to a cardiac specialist or myself.
She was unable to even reach me because of severe cyanosis (turning
blue) and the inability to breathe. I walked the owner through Simone's
recovery by phone.

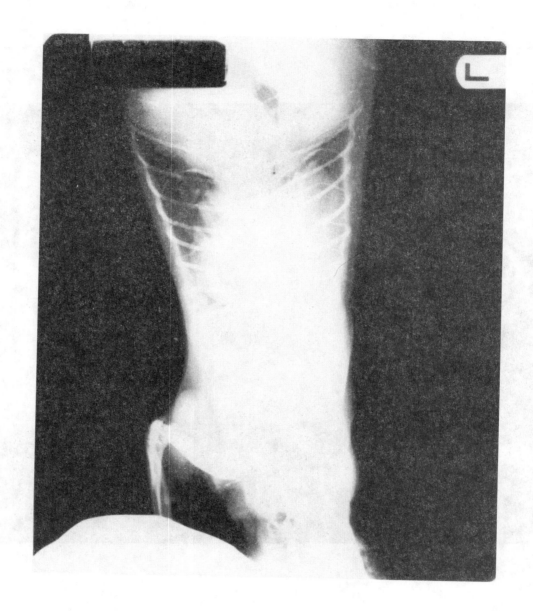

<u>Simone Ziegler</u> - DV (dorso-ventral view - cat lying on stomach). These photos (two laterals and one D-V views) demonstrate the greatly enlarged heart and extreme amount of fluid in the lungs (pulmonary edema). The referring veterinarian gave little to no hope and suggested to consider euthanasia. X-rays taken by the referring verterinarian hosital and sent to me. See letter by referring veterinarian under testimonies (Feline AIDS and Feline Congestive Heart Failure).

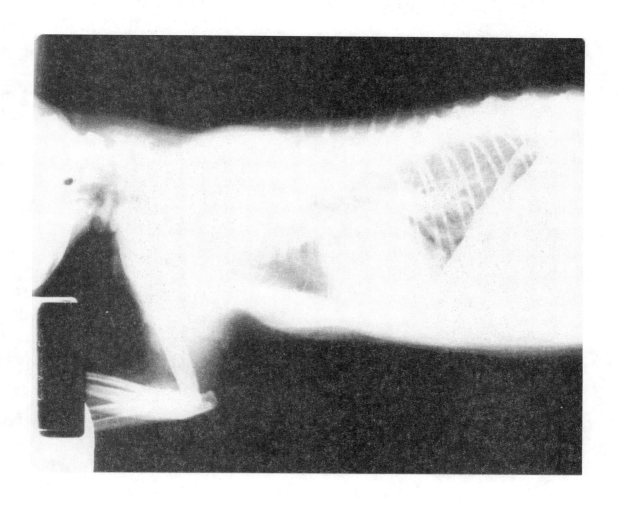

Simone Ziegler - Second lateral from referring Veterinarian.

APPENDIX

Additional Documents of My Hand, Back and Leg and Other Conditions Plus an Extraordinary Testimony

**Remaining Documents
Related to
Hand Injury
(in Chronological Order)**

E: BRADLEY, Sandy   HISTORY NO. 160-40-4416   LOCATION: Outpatient

E OF REPORT: OPERATIVE REPORT

TE OF OPERATION: 3-19-86

RGEON: Dr. Moore, assisted by Dr. Martin.

ESTHESIA: Right axillary block.   ANESTHESIOLOGIST: Dr. LaVina and Mrs. Rose.

EOPERATIVE DIAGNOSIS: Status post excision of tumor from the right ring finger with
ssible digital nerve injury.

TOPERATIVE DIAGNOSIS: Same.

ERATION PERFORMED: Nerve graft from the medial antebrachial cutaneous nerve to the digital
ve of the ring finger, radial aspect.

CEDURE: The right upper extremity was prepped and draped free. The right arm was elevated
anguinated, and the tourniquet inflated to 250 mm. of Mercury. A Brunner type zig-zag
cision was made and was incorporated into the previous scar. Skin flaps were elevated
the nerves were traced from a healthy area into the area of the previous scarring. The
ital nerve along the ulnar aspect of the finger was noted to be intact and was noted
be somewhat thinned. A rather large neuroma of the distal aspect of the digital nerve
the radial aspect of the finger was appreciated and was resected off of the flexor tendon
ath. Next, the digital nerve was exposed proximally and a smaller neuroma was also
ected from this area. The neuroma was sent to Pathology and the nerve gap was measured.
roximately a 2.5 cm. gap was appreciated with the wrist in extension and the fingers
full extension. The finger flexion with mobilization in the nerves could not easily
p the ends of the nerves and, therefore, it was chosen to perform a nerve graft. A
ll oblique incision over the medial aspect of the elbow was made and carried on down
u the subcutaneous tissue and medial antebrachial cutaneous nerve was isolated. This
dissected free and was removed for the graft. The skin was closed with subcuticular
0 Dexon sutures and Steri-strips were applied. The nerve graft was placed in the defect
, under the microscope, a fascicular pattern was appreciated, both proximally and distally,
the digital nerves, and interrupted epineural sutures were performed to sew in the nerve
ft under no tension. The tourniquet was deflated. Hemostasis obtained. The wound
thoroughly irrigated and the skin was loosely closed with interrupted #5-0 nylon suture.
patient was placed in a well padded splint and brought to the Recovery Room in satisfactor
dition.

pc
ated: 3-19-86.   Transcribed: 3-20-86.
0192   18-3490

NAME: BRADLEY, Sandy
SSN#:
ORTHOPEDIC CLINIC

DATE SEEN: April 15, 1986

Sandy is approximately one month following a nerve graft to the radial digital nerve of the right ring finger. At this time her flexion is excellent, however, her extension is somewhat limited in the ring finger. Her scar is healing well and she has minimal sensitivity along the scar. A Tinel sign is present over the MCP area.

At this time she states that last week a dog hit her right hand which caused severe pain and in the meantime she has been using DMSO castoril and other agents on her hand.

I have recommended at this time that she protect her hand from vigorous use, especially contact with animals and that once her sensitivity is diminished then she should be able to work with her animals again. In particular, I have recommended that she stop using DMSO and to use coco butter or some other approved skin lotion.

JM/TL/618/17A
DD: 4/15/86
DT: 4/20/86

Community Hospital

Washington, D.C.

Department of Rehabilitation Medicine

December 4, 1986

TO: ████████████, M.D.
               ████████████████████
               Baltimore, MD 21239

FROM: ████████████████, OTR

SUBJECT: Sandy Bradley
          Diagnosis: S/P nerve graft, radial digital nerve
                      of right fourth finger
          Treatment Request: Desensitization Therapy
          Frequency of Tx: 2 x week for 3 to 6 weeks

PROGRESS REPORT

10/20/86   Initial evaluation indicated verbalized hypersensitivity to
           touch at the base of the right fourth finger which was
           described by Dr.Bradley as "electric shock" like sensation.
           Unable to get a grip or pinch strength of the right hand
           due to the sensitivity level. Dr. Bradley was given a
           desensitization treatment with instructions in home program
           to normalize sensation, to strengthen the right hand and
           to maintain ROM and work tolerance of the right upper limb
           in general. An adjustable wrist support with sheep-skin
           lining was given to augment the use of the right hand in
           grasp and release functions.
10/30/86   Dr. Bradley demonstrated improvement in response to textures
           touching the sensitive area of the right hand. Desensitization
           Tx. given. Patient was able to tolerate Tx using different
           textures, massage and ROM for 30 minutes. Dr. Bradley indi-
           cated the difficulty in attending therapy at the frequency
           indicated above due to problems related to trying to re-
           establish   her private practice in Veterinarian Medicine.
11/06/86   Desensitization for 30 minutes produced further improvement
           in reduced hypersensitivity in the right hand. Importance of
           daily home therapy emphasized. Dr. Bradley indicated that
           the wrist support is very helpful in allowing her to use her
           right hand.
11/17/86   Continued therapy as 11/6/86 with demonstrated improvement.
12/01/86   Sensitivity level improved enough for the grip strength test
           using a dynamometer and the pinch test using the #1 bulb of
           the vigorometer. Below is a comparison of these tests with
           the results of this patients hand at the time of discharge
           on 8/13/86 when she was under Dr. Neil Green's care.

	8/13/86		12/1/86	
	Right	Left	Right	Left
Grip	60 lbs.	66 lbs.	42.5	72.5
3-point pinch	8 "	7 "	4	7

(Continued -)

SUMMARY: Therapy sessions to date indicated that this patient consistently demonstrated improvement in response to the desensitization program. However, progress has been slow due to Dr. Bradley's inability to attend therapy on a more regular basis.

RECOMMENDATIONS: Continued desensitization program with exercises and functional activities to increase over-all functional strength and work tolerance so that this patient may be prepared physically to return to her profession and handle animals as necessary.

Thank you for the referral of this pleasant and interesting patient.

NAME: BRADLEY, Dr. Sandy
HISTORY NO.: ████████████

DATE SEEN: 12/09/86

    Sandy Bradley was seen in follow-up today. Her desensitization program is coming along satisfactorily. She has a full range of motion and has minimal, if any, swelling today. However, she states that she does get swelling on occasion.

    I think one of the main problems that Sandy will encounter in the next several months is frequent cold intolerance and sensitivity in that digit during the first winter following a nerve graft of this fashion. For this reason, if it is available to her, it might be reasonable for her to seek warmer environs to prevent any severe problems from cold exposure. She will see us back in several months.

████████████████, M.D.
JRM:tmr
Dictated 12/09/86
Transcribed 12/11/86

DEC 1 8 1986
Dr. ████████
NS. █████████

NAME: BRADLEY, Sandy Dr.
HISTORY NO.:   ████████

DATE SEEN: 3/10/87

To Whom It May Concern:

Sandy Bradley was seen in follow-up today, 3/10/87, following a digital nerve graft to the right ring finger.

At this point, she is making improvement, however, she is unable to perform her full duties as a Veterinarian, especially with respect to heavy or large animals.

She is currently licensed in Washington, Maryland, and Pennsylvania, however, plans a move to Florida in the near future. I think her hand problems should be taken into consideration when requesting her to perform lengthy procedures or tests that would involve vigorous use of her right hand.

If any further information is needed, please feel free to contact my office (301)-532-4735.

JRM/tlw

dict.   3/10/87
trans. 3/12/87

Washington, D.C.

August 21, 1987

Attorney at Law

Washington, D.C.

Re: Dr. Sandy Bradley

HISTORY: This 40 year old female veterinarian had been referred for evaluation of the right ring finger. The patient had developed a mass over the volar aspect of the hand for which she underwent surgery for it's removal in February, 1986. Following surgery, she noted the loss of sensation over the radial aspect of the digit but this apparently was not addressed by the treating physician. Subsequent to this, she required further surgery for the removal of a neuroma which had developed and a nerve transplant for repair of the nerve, occurring in March of 1986. She presently complains of paresthesias in the finger, with pain over the volar aspect of the finger at the intersection of the hand. She is right hand dominant.

PHYSICAL EXAM: Shows her to be a well developed, slim female in no distress. Examination of the (R) hand shows no frank visual deformities. There is a well healed z shaped incision over the volar aspect of the ring finger. There is also tenderness over the proximal phalanx and the 4th metacarpal head with some evidence of hyperesthesia present. Attempts at grasping objects firmly are resisted because of pain. There is also an area of hypoesthesia over the radial aspect of the middle and distal phalanges. She has nearly a full range of motion in the finger, lacking approximately 5 degrees of flexion at the metacarpal phalangeal joint.

IMPRESSION: The impression is that the patient probably has another neuroma development at the repair site, responsible for the pain and hypersensitivity. The loss of sensation is probably due to the incompleteness of the difficult repair.

Re: Dr. Sandy Bradley

DISCUSSION: This patient in particular, because of her (R)
                       hand dominance, does not appear to be able to
                       function in her previous capacity, performing
                       delicate surgical procedures, restraining
                       animals, etc... It is therefore my opinion
                       that she is disabled due to 50% dysfunctional
                       loss of the hand, 5% loss of motion and 10%
                       due to pain. This disability is also felt to
                       be permanent.

_____, M.D.,P.C.

D

BRADLEY, SANDY

OFFICE NEUROSURGICAL CONSULTATION

5/31/88

REFERRED BY: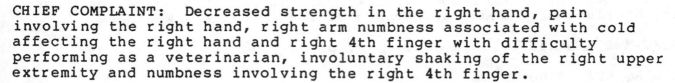

CHIEF COMPLAINT: Decreased strength in the right hand, pain involving the right hand, right arm numbness associated with cold affecting the right hand and right 4th finger with difficulty performing as a veterinarian, involuntary shaking of the right upper extremity and numbness involving the right 4th finger.

HISTORY OF THE PRESENT ILLNESS: The patient is a 41-year-old right-handed black veterinarian physician who indicates that on 1/31/86 she was seen in consultation by Dr. Ernest Martin, a local orthopedic surgeon, for evaluation of what she described as a pea-sized lesion involving the proximal interphalangeal joint of the right 4th finger. According to Dr. Bradley, she was examined by Dr. Martin and was informed that she had possibly a cyst. Subsequently, on 2/5/86, she underwent surgical intervention at Providence Hospital in the In and Out Surgical Department under local block anesthesia. During the surgical procedure, the patient reportedly told Dr. Martin that there was a dead feeling. Following surgery, she was discharged and the next day she continued to experience numbness involving the right 4th finger. She saw Dr. Martin approximately 2 days following the surgical procedure complaining of numbness involving the right 4th finger and severe pain involving the right 4th finger and entire hand. Because of the persistence of her pain, she sought a second opinion and, approximately 1 week later, she was seen by Dr. Neil Green who referred her to a Dr. Moore at Johns Hopkins University Hospital. Subsequently, according to Dr. Bradley, she underwent a nerve graft for repair of transected digital nerve of the right 4th finger no 3/9/86. Dr. Bradley also indicates that at the time of the surgery, two large neuromas were resected. Since surgery, she has been plagued by severe pain involving the right hand including primarily the right 4th finger. She has also had difficulty functioning in her work as a veterinarian. She has trouble opening a cat's mouth. She had had tremendous difficulty holding up a horse's leg and difficulty using a hoof tester. Strength in the right hand has been significantly impaired to the point where she has difficulty lifting a cast iron pot or simply functioning in her kitchen at home. She has had no problems with the left upper extremity. The patient has had one episode of involuntary shaking of the entire right forearm and hand which lasted approximately 10 minutes. The latter occurred while driving. The numbness of the right 4th finger has remained persistent as has the deep pain which involves the entire right hand, forearm and arm. Cold periods are associated with worsening of the numb sensation affect the entire right hand. She has had burning sensation involving the right 4th finger radiating proximally into the right palm and distal forearm. For the most part, the impairment that she had dealt with since her surgical procedures, according to the patient, has impacted tremendously on her ability to perform as a veterinarian. She simply cannot continue to perform thoracic or abdominal surgery at all because of the pain in the right hand and also because of the associated weakness.

PAST MEDICAL HISTORY: Negative for prior injuries.

ALLERGIES: None known.

PRESENT MEDICATIONS: None.

EXAMINATION: Dr. Bradley is alert and fully oriented. She is a well developed, well nourished black female. Cranial nerves are grossly normal. Motor testing in the left upper and both lower extremities is within normal limits. Funduscopic evaluation reveals no evidence of papilledema. Both carotid are equally palpable and without bruits. In the right upper extremity, there is a healed surgical incision involving the 4th finger on the right hand primarily overlying the distal metacarpal area and proximal interphalangeal region. The incision is in the form of a Z-plasty. She is profoundly tender on palpation overlying the surgical scar. She demonstrates hypalgesia involving the lateral aspect of the right 4th finger beginning at the metacarpal phalangeal joint. The right grip is slightly impaired. The latter is associated with complaint of severe pain involving the metacarpal phalangeal region proximal to the right 4th finger. The intrinsic hand muscles appear grossly normal. However, on performing the latter test with the right hand, the patient does complain of mild shock-like sensation involving the lateral aspect of the right 4th finger beginning at the metacarpal phalangeal joint. There is mild asymmetry involving the proximal right forearm as compared to the proximal left forearm. However, there is no evidence of fasciculations involving the musculature of the right proximal forearm. Tinel's sign is present when tapping is applied at the metacarpal phalangeal region of the right 4th finger.

DIAGNOSIS: Right painful hand syndrome secondary to traumatic neuroma formation of the right 4th digital nerve on the lateral side.
Status post nerve graft to the right 4th digital nerve.

OPINION: Dr. Bradley has indeed suffered a traumatic injury to the
right 4th digital nerve on the lateral side which is currently rather
painful and has impacted on her ability to perform in the capacity of
a veterinarian. It impacts on her ability to hold and to restrain
and also impacts on her ability to lift. Even though this finger is
not as crucial to performance of surgery as are the right thumb and
index finger or even the right thumb and third finger, the causalgia
type-like pain that she has experienced, as is elicited on the Tinel
sign and also based on the patient's clinical history, impairs
significantly on her ability to perform surgical procedures involving
the abdominal cavity and also the thoracic region. It is my opinion
that she has sustained a permanent injury to the digital nerve of the
right 4th finger which has rendered her total impairment to the hand
itself of at least 15% and this has, in turn, permanently impacted on
her ability to continue effectively as a veterinarian surgeon. She
is at a point where she will have to learn to live and deal with this
pain and its incapacitation. As far as her involuntary tremors
affecting the right upper extremity, I have referred her for an
electroencephalogram and a Magnetic Resonance Image scan.

_____,M.D.

HOSPITAL
Washington, D.C. 20010

NUCLEAR MEDICINE DEPT.
RADIOLOGY DEPT.
CT SCAN DEPT.
MRI CENTER

MRI CENTER

Washington, DC   20003

Phys. Ph #: 2025292370
Phys. Pgr #:

Exam Name: MRI BRAIN
Exam # 321A-081788

Date of Exam: 17-Aug-88
MRN: 1323201

CLINICAL HX:
    MEMORY LOSS
    FALLING ASLEEP; POSSIBLE SEIZURES

Exam: MRI BRAIN

TECHNIQUE: Axial T2 weighted images, sagittal, coronal and axial
T1 weighted images.

FINDINGS: The ventricles and sulci are normal. A single 1 to
2 mm. in diameter focus of high signal intensity is noted in the
posterior aspect of the left brachium pontis. No other intra-
axial or extra-axial lesions are identified. In particular there
is no evidence of mass in the jugular foramen. A 1 cm. in
diameter node is identified in the right carotid space on the
coronal T1 weighted images.

CONCLUSION: A single 2 mm. in diameter focus of high signal
            intensity in the left brachium pontis as described
            above. This is an entirely nonspecific finding which
            can occasionally be seen in asymptomatic patients.
            The differential diagnosis would include demyelinating
            ischemic or demyelinating disease. Please note that
            the neck has not been examined on this study and,
            thus, the neck masses described in the clinical
            history were not evaluated. If clinically indicated,
            a Gadolinium enhanced MRI may be helpful in excluding
                            (continued)

Page

Patient Name: BRADLEY,SANDY
41 F
MRN: 1323201
Ward/Clinic: MRI
Account # 83342428

 **HOSPITAL** ███████

███████, Washington, D.C. 20010
Drs. Groover, Christie and Merritt

NUCLEAR MEDICINE DEPT.
RADIOLOGY DEPT.
CT SCAN DEPT.
MRI CENTER

MRI CENTER

Washington, DC   20003

Phys. Ph #: 2025292370
Phys. Pgr #:

Exam Name: MRI BRAIN
Exam # 321A-081788

Date of Exam: 17-Aug-88
MRN: 1323201

CLINICAL HX:
   MEMORY LOSS
   FALLING ASLEEP; POSSIBLE SEIZURES

CONCLUSION: (continued)
      meningeal processes and in possibly further
      characterising the left brachium pontis findings.

         signed: ALEXANDER S. MARK, M.D.

ASM/nsc

Patient Name: BRADLEY,SANDY
41 F
MRN: 1323201
Ward/Clinic: MRI
Account # 83342428

PHYSICIAN'S COPY

...dy Bradley, DVM   AGE _____

_____   DATE 11-18-88

...erve conduction study + EMG

(R) hand + wrist

c/o   (R) Carpal tunnel Syndrome

...3 PRN. _____ M.D.

_____ B N DD#

"*Maximize
Ability &
Capacity*"
10/9/91

Suggested desensitization Program for home use:

(2) 1) Warm the hand through the use of
- Warm Water soak
- Towel Wrap
- Repetitive range of motion exercise

(3) 2) Manipulate objects with different textures
- Rice & Bean Box
- Marble bath
- Arts and crafts (wood working, wood finishing, Ceramics, etc.)

(1) 3) Fitness Exercise for over all well being

```
BTE QUEST          Maximum Strength Comparison          Static/Isometr
-------------------------------------------------------------------------
Patient ID: 160404416          Name: SANDY BRADLEY
Attachment: 162H  PINCH STRENGTH   2 point pinch   Height: 38
                                  (tip pinch)
```

	LEFT			RIGHT	

LEFT	RIGHT
1 : 117 inch-lbs.	1 : 169 inch-lbs.
2 : 132 inch-lbs.	2 : 183 inch-lbs.
3 : 125 inch-lbs.	3 : 176 inch-lbs.

LEFT	RIGHT
Average : 125 inch-lbs.	Average : 176 inch-lbs.
Coeff. Of Variation : 4.9%	Coeff. Of Variation : 3.2%

Left Is 29.0% Less Than Right

```
June 21, 1994 At 16:27 From ███████████████  TRAINING CENTER
```

```
BTE QUEST          Maximum Strength Comparison      Static/Isometric
--------------------------------------------------------------------
Patient ID: 160404416        Name: SANDY BRADLEY
Attachment: 1620  GRIP/PINCH  3 point pinch      Height: 38
```

LEFT	RIGHT
1 : 142 inch-lbs.	1 : 167 inch-lbs.
2 : 123 inch-lbs.	2 : 167 inch-lbs.
3 : 136 inch-lbs.	3 : 174 inch-lbs.
Average : 134 inch-lbs.	Average : 169 inch-lbs.
Coeff. Of Variation : 5.9%	Coeff. Of Variation : 1.9%

```
Left Is 20.7% Less Than Right
```

```
June 21, 1994 At 16:30 From ████████████████ TRAINING CENTER
```

```
BTE QUEST          Directional Strength Trials        Static/Isometri
------------------------------------------------------------------------
Patient ID: 160404416        Name: SANDY BRADLEY
Attachment: 601   D-HANDLE                Height: 38    Side: LEFT
```

CLOCKWISE	COUNTERCLOCKWISE
1 : 45 inch-lbs.	1 : 51 inch-lbs.
2 : 41 inch-lbs.	2 : 38 inch-lbs.
3 : 32 inch-lbs.	3 : 44 inch-lbs.
Average : 39 inch-lbs.	Average : 44 inch-lbs.
Coeff. Of Variation : 13.8%	Coeff. Of Variation : 12.0%

CW Is 11.4% Less Than CCW

June 21, 1994 At 16:51 From ▆▆▆▆▆▆▆▆▆▆▆▆ TRAINING CENTER

```
BTE QUEST          Directional Strength Trials          Static/Isometric
----------------------------------------------------------------------------
Patient ID: 160404416     Name: SANDY BRADLEY
Attachment: 601  D-HANDLE                  Height: 38      Side: RIGHT
```

CLOCKWISE	COUNTERCLOCKWISE
1 : 42 inch-lbs.	1 : 43 inch-lbs.
2 : 45 inch-lbs.	2 : 36 inch-lbs.
3 : 48 inch-lbs.	3 : 40 inch-lbs.
Average : 45 inch-lbs.	Average : 40 inch-lbs.
Coeff. Of Variation : 5.4%	Coeff. Of Variation : 7.2%
	CCW Is 11.1% Less Than CW

```
June 21, 1994 At 16:54 From ██████████████████  TRAINING CENTER
```

Right hand greater in strength turning objects clockwise so many pounds per inch

but here right hand just slightly less in strength than the left hand turning objects counterclockwise so many pounds per inch

fatigue with time, use and healing in this area are factors of consideration

```
BTE QUEST          Directional Strength Trials      Static/Isometri
----------------------------------------------------------------------
Patient ID: 160404416        Name: SANDY BRADLEY
Attachment: 302K  RADIAL/ULNAR DEVIATION      Height: 32    Side: LEFT
```

CLOCKWISE	COUNTERCLOCKWISE
1 : 44 inch-lbs.	1 : 51 inch-lbs.
2 : 42 inch-lbs.	2 : 45 inch-lbs.
3 : 39 inch-lbs.	3 : 42 inch-lbs.

Average : 42 inch-lbs.	Average : 46 inch-lbs.
Coeff. Of Variation : 4.9%	Coeff. Of Variation : 8.1%

CW Is 8.7% Less Than CCW

June 21, 1994 At 16:59 From ███████████████ TRAINING CENTER

```
BTE QUEST          Directional Strength Trials      Static/Isometric
--------------------------------------------------------------------
Patient ID: 160404416        Name: SANDY BRADLEY
Attachment: 302K  RADIAL/ULNAR DEVIATION     Height: 32    Side: RIGHT
```

CLOCKWISE	COUNTERCLOCKWISE
1 : 34 inch-lbs.	1 : 49 inch-lbs.
2 : 33 inch-lbs.	2 : 52 inch-lbs.
3 : 37 inch-lbs.	3 : 44 inch-lbs.
Average : 35 inch-lbs.	Average : 48 inch-lbs.
Coeff. Of Variation : 4.9%	Coeff. Of Variation : 6.8%

CW Is 27.1% Less Than CCW

June 21, 1994 At 17:01 From ████████████████ TRAINING CENTER

Here - left hand exceeds in clockwise direction involving hand + forearm - indicating possible residual disuse atrophy of right forearm

**Notations
Related to Initial
Back Injury from
Auto Accident**

2/25/87   certains his
         severe spasms

① Driving— ~~full back~~ cushions - recommend?
         — head rest? type?

② carrying groceries— >10 lbs = pain

③ bending over to take Bld in patients

④ standing up >1/2 hr. (spontaneous spasms - entire back)

(level) ⑤ Walking — lower back + hip

(uphill) ⑥ Walking — shoulder - neck pain
         + right upper & lower quadrant - back

⑦ can not handle restraint for horses well at all
         (helping a friend in Md. (obtained Md. license   to be able to
                                         do Equine Rx)

* even just using ~~this~~ left hand to hold bridle

⑧ Damp weather — severe spasms with above   especially
         activities — ~~especially~~ coupled
         ~~with activities~~

⑨ can not bend over to clip dog's & cats nails without
pain — (Housecalls)
         heat + exercises seem to control spasms
the most - but on occasion still
         no relief

To: Dr ████

pain it disturbs me.
don't want to make
trouble just get
some consolation
betw Feb + Dec. 86
- lost 50 days hard/bek

a) complained to Dr ████ on 2/12/87 of severe pain

b) He told me to see ████ as an emergency
- I was told to bend over + turn head + neck + prescribed Parafon Forte
If I had further pain - see Dr ████ the following week

c) 2/25/87 gave ████ this sheet told him of severe pain
b. did same - bend over - turn neck - recommended frequent stops & points.

Back Injury
and Other Related Injuries, etc.
(Colon Damage and Concussion)
Worsened
by First Horse Accident

CHART OF EFFECTS OF SPINAL MISALIGNMENTS

"The nervous system controls and coordinates all organs and structures of the human body." (*Gray's Anatomy*, 29th Ed., page 4). Misalignments of spinal vertebrae and discs may cause irritation to the nervous system which could affect the structures, organs, and functions listed under "areas." The effects listed are conditions or symptoms that may be associated with malfunctions of the areas noted.

Dr. ▬▬▬   7/6/89

ATLAS
AXIS
CERVICAL SPINE
st THORACIC
THORACIC SPINE
st LUMBAR
LUMBAR SPINE
SACRUM
COCCYX

Vertebrae	Areas	Effects
1C	Blood supply to the head, pituitary gland, scalp, bones of the face, brain, inner and middle ear, sympathetic nervous system.	Headaches, nervousness, insomnia, head colds, high blood pressure, migraine headaches, nervous breakdowns, amnesia, chronic tiredness, dizziness.
2C	Eyes, optic nerves, auditory nerves, sinuses, mastoid bones, tongue, forehead.	Sinus trouble, allergies, pain around the eyes, earache, fainting spells, certain cases of blindness, crossed eyes, deafness.
3C	Cheeks, outer ear, face bones, teeth, trifacial nerve.	Neuralgia, neuritis, acne or pimples, eczema.
4C	Nose, lips, mouth, eustachian tube.	Hay fever, runny nose, hearing loss, adenoids.
5C	Vocal cords, neck glands, pharynx.	Laryngitis, hoarseness, throat conditions such as sore throat or quinsy.
6C	Neck muscles, shoulders, tonsils.	Stiff neck, pain in upper arm, tonsillitis, chronic cough, croup.
7C	Thyroid gland, bursae in the shoulders, elbows.	Bursitis, colds, thyroid conditions.
1T	Arms from the elbows down, including hands, wrists, and fingers; esophagus and trachea.	Asthma, cough, difficult breathing, shortness of breath, pain in lower arms and hands.
2T	Heart, including its valves and covering; coronary arteries.	Functional heart conditions and certain chest conditions.
3T	Lungs, bronchial tubes, pleura, chest, breast.	Bronchitis, pleurisy, pneumonia, congestion, influenza.
4T	Gall bladder, common duct.	Gall bladder conditions, jaundice, shingles.
5T	Liver, solar plexus, circulation (general).	Liver conditions, fevers, blood pressure problems, poor circulation, arthritis.
6T	Stomach.	Stomach troubles, including nervous stomach, indigestion, heartburn, dyspepsia.
7T	Pancreas, duodenum.	Ulcers, gastritis.
8T	Spleen.	Lowered resistance.
9T	Adrenal and supra-renal glands.	Allergies, hives.
10T	Kidneys.	Kidney troubles, hardening of the arteries, chronic tiredness, nephritis, pyelitis.
11T	Kidneys, ureters.	Skin conditions such as acne, pimples, eczema, or boils.
12T	Small intestines, lymph circulation.	Rheumatism, gas pains, certain types of sterility.
1L	Large intestines, inguinal rings.	Constipation, colitis, dysentery, diarrhea, some ruptures or hernias.
2L	Appendix, abdomen, upper leg.	Cramps, difficult breathing, minor varicose veins.
3L	Sex organs, uterus, bladder, knees.	Bladder troubles, menstrual troubles such as painful or irregular periods, miscarriages, bed wetting, impotency, change of life symptoms, many knee pains.
4L	Prostate gland, muscles of the lower back, sciatic nerve.	Sciatica, lumbago, difficult, painful, or too frequent urination; backaches.
5L	Lower legs, ankles, feet.	Poor circulation in the legs, swollen ankles, weak ankles and arches, cold feet, weakness in the legs, leg cramps.
SACRUM	Hip bones, buttocks.	Sacro-iliac conditions, spinal curvatures. scoliosis
COCCYX	Rectum, anus.	Hemorrhoids (piles), pruritis (itching), pain at end of spine on sitting.

NECK REGION — MID-BACK — LOW BACK — PELVIS

For further explanation of the conditions shown above, and information about those not shown, ask your Doctor of Chiropractic.

#1300090

Telephone

ORTHOPEDIC SURGERY

27 February 1990

TO WHOM IT MAY CONCERN:

REF: Sandy Bradley

Please be advised that Ms. Bradley was seen in my office
on the following dates: 7/12/89, 1/18/90, 2/14/90.

DIAGNOSIS: Hematoma, thoracolumbar spine, post-traumatic.
              Lumbosacral strain.
              Cervical strain.
              Rule out degenerative arthritis, small joints,
                 of the fingers, right hand.

The patient was referred for a neurological consultation
with Dr. Rajindar Sidhu.

Sincerely,

, M.D.

MAKE CHECKS PAYABLE TO:

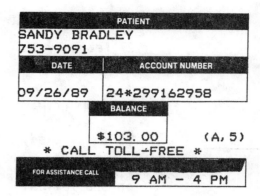

WASHINGTON, D. C. 20090

ACCT# 24*299162958

FORWARDING AND ADDRESS CORRECTION REQUESTED

STATEMENT

PATIENT
SANDY BRADLEY
753-9091

DATE	ACCOUNT NUMBER
09/26/89	24*299162958

BALANCE
$103.00

(A, 5)

* CALL TOLL-FREE *

FOR ASSISTANCE CALL	9 AM − 4 PM

SANDY BRADLEY

LA PLATA MD 20646

PLEASE DETACH THIS PORTION AND RETURN WITH PAYMENT OR CORRESPONDENCE

PRINCE GEORGES RADIODIAGNOSTICS

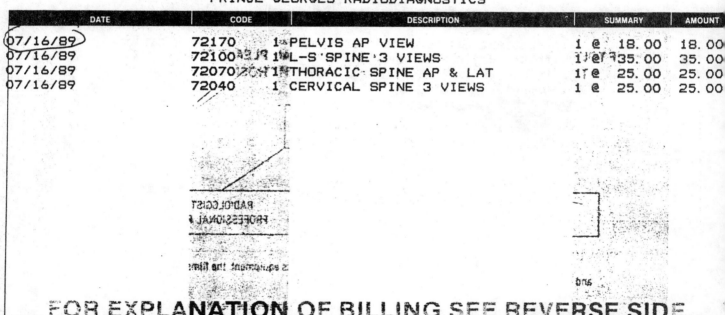

DATE	CODE	DESCRIPTION	SUMMARY	AMOUNT
07/16/89	72170	1 PELVIS AP VIEW	1 @ 18.00	18.00
07/16/89	72100	1 L-S SPINE 3 VIEWS	1 @ 35.00	35.00
07/16/89	72070	1 THORACIC SPINE AP & LAT	1 @ 25.00	25.00
07/16/89	72040	1 CERVICAL SPINE 3 VIEWS	1 @ 25.00	25.00

FOR EXPLANATION OF BILLING SEE REVERSE SIDE

PATIENT	ACCOUNT NUMBER - PLEASE PRINT ON ALL PAYMENTS AND CORRESPONDENCE		AMOUNT DUE
SANDY BRADLEY HOSP CNTR-IP	24*299162958 52-1571614	ER PHYSICIAN	$103.00
PLACE OF SERVICE	TAX ID. NO.	REFERRING PHYSICIAN	

- - - - ATTENTION - - - -

YOUR ACCOUNT IS NOW DELINQUENT.   PAYMENT IS DUE WITHIN 20 DAYS.

IF YOU HAVE RECENTLY MADE PAYMENT, PLEASE DISREGARD THIS NOTICE.

THANK YOU.

HCI

1189
BIRTH-DATE
02/13/47   164

HYATTSVILLE, MD
FEI # 52-1289729

1   5
HRADLEY, SANDY
GUAR PH:

SANDY BRADLEY
LA PLATA, MD 20646

29916295B F 42 07/17/89 07/19/89 2

1 SELF PAY   101

CASIBANG V

DETAIL OF CURRENT CHARGES, PAYMENTS AND ADJUSTMENTS

Date						Charge		Balance
07/18	001	TRAUMA AND				316.00	316.00	
07/16	001	CO2				3.92	3.92	
07/16	001	CHLORIDES-Q				3.92	3.92	
07/16	001	CREATININE				3.92	3.92	
07/16	001	POTASSIUM				3.92	3.92	
07/16	001	SODIUM				3.92	3.92	
07/16	001	GLUCOSE QTY				3.92	3.92	
07/16	001	BUN				14.32	14.32	
07/16	001	CBC				14.32	14.32	
07/16	001	CBC				14.32	14.32	
07/16	001	CERVICAL SP				35.39	35.39	
07/16	001	THORACIC SP				35.39	35.39	
07/16	001	L-S SPINE				35.39	35.39	
07/16	001	PELVIS				35.39	35.39	
07/16	001	IV SOLUTION				2.26	2.26	
07/16	001	OXY INJ 8X				3.63	3.63	
07/16	001	OXYGEN CANN				.74	.74	
07/16	001	OXYGEN TUBI				.53	.53	
07/16	001	IV-CONT C				1.41	1.41	
07/16	001	VENOTUBING.				1.27	1.27	
07/16	001	NECK LOCK				43.49	43.49	
07/16	001	SET SOLN A				1.72	1.72	
07/16	001	URINE-ROUTI				9.11	9.11	
07/17	001	TELEPHONE						
07/17	006	ORAL PRESCR				1.00		1.00
07/17	001	ADMISSION				192.00	192.00	
07/17	001	PROC(S) 6PM				63.53	63.53	
07/17	001	ROOM K326				309.00	309.00	
07/18	001	TELEPHONE S				1.00		
07/18	003	ORAL PRESCR				45.26	45.26	1.00
07/18	001	ROOM K326				309.00	309.00	

HCI ?

FINAL 08/22/89
INP.   HYATTSVILLE, MD.   1189
                             FEI # 52-1289729   BIRTH-DATE
1 S   02/13/47   764
BRADLEY, SANDY   2
GUAR PH: 29916258 F 42 07/17/89 07/19/89   2

NANCY BRADLEY   1 SELF PAY   101
LA PLATA, MD 20646

                                          CASIBANG V

07/19 001 I. SOLUTION 41131053   2.26   2.26
07/19 003 OR. PRESCR 41480218   2.43   2.43
07/19 001 CON. N. FLO 41111141   6.84   6.84
07/19 001 KIT, I. STA 41311182   3.65   3.65
07/19 001 PUFF PAD OF 41251454   10.16   10.16
07/19 001 VENO. SORE. 41351829   1.29   1.29
07/19 001 INCON. PAD 41394437   4.14   4.14
07/19 001 ADMISSION K 41392062   45.28   45.28
07/19 001 CORB HOD/YR 41355061   45.03   45.03

TOTALS   1468.47 1466.47   PAY THIS AMOUNT   2.00

29916258

HYATTSVILLE, MD HOSPITAL CENTER   2.00

FINAL 08/22/89   1189
INP.   FEI # 52-1209729   BIRTH-DATE
                                                                   02/13/47   764

1   S
BRADLEY, SANDY   29162958 F 42 07/17/89 07/19/89 2
GUAR PH:

SANDY BRADLEY   1 SELF PAY   101
LA PLATA, MD 20646

                                        CASIBANG V

SUMMARY OF CHARGES
R&C SEMI-PR 2DAYS@ 309.00   618.00   618.00
  EMERGENCY ROOM   618.00   618.00
  LABORATORY   36.55   36.55
  X-RAY   141.58   141.58
  PHARMACY   14.38   14.38
  MED/SURG SUPPLIES   84.00   84.00
  PHYSICAL THERAPY   154.00   154.00
  ADMISSION CHARGE   102.00   102.00
  TELEPHONE   2.00   2.00

SUB-TOTAL OF CHARGES   1468.47   1468.47   2.00

GUAR RELATIONSHIP: S   SEX: GUAR NO: 2.00

PROMPT PAYMENTS ASSIST IN REDUCING HOSPITAL COSTS
YOUR AMT DUE IS   1.90 IF PAID BY 09/16/89

T O T A L S   1468.47 1466.47   2.00
29162958   PAY THIS AMOUNT 2.00

M.D.

LA PLATA, MARYLAND 20646

ACCT# NEEDED TO PROCESS PMT.

STATEMENT

DATE	NUMBER
8/25/89	08102

PATIENT   08102

SANDY   BRADLEY

LAPLATA   MD 20646
165215   753 9091

DATE	DESCRIPTION	PROC CODE	CHARGE
08/18/89	X-RAY GI NO KUB	74240	60.00
08/17/89	CT,ABD.W/O CONTRAST	74150	105.00
08/16/89	X-RAY ABDOMEN	74000	16.00
08/15/89	X-RAY BCE/AIR	74280	84.00
08/14/89	X-RAY ABDOMEN FLAT & ERECT	74020	23.00
08/14/89	X-RAY CHEST	71020	19.00

DIAGNOSIS:
DEHYDRATION
DEHYDRATION
DEHYDRATION

DR ID# 506-56-3775

LA PLATA,MD 20646   MEMORIAL HOSP.

CHARGES	CREDITS	BALANCE DUE
307.00		307.00

TO CLAIM INSURANCE BENEFITS:
1. COMPLETE THE PERSONAL INFORMATION ON YOUR FORM.
2. ATTACH A COPY OF THIS RECEIPT & MAIL TO YOUR INSURANCE COMPANY

M.D., P.A.
GENERAL SURGERY

La Plata, Maryland 20646

Sandy Bradley
St. Rt. 2, Box 2167 Ripley Road
La Plata, Md 20646

OV-Office Visit HV-Hospital Visit	HCD-House Call Day HCN-House Call Night	INJ-Injection P-Physiotherapy	OB-Obstetrics CP-Complete Physical	L-Laboratory S-Surgery

DATE	SERVICE RENDERED	CHARGE	PAID	BALANCE
Patient	Sandy Birthdate	2-13-47		
Admitted	8-14-89			
Diag	Dehydration			
	Contusion (left) back			
	Hospital care 1st day admission 8-14-89			
		100.00		100.00
	2nd day care 8-15-89	50.00		150.00
	Daily care 8-16-89 to 8-18-89 for 3 days			
	at $35.00 each	105.00		255.00
Disc	8-18-89			
	No Ins.			
	1 1/2 months later			
	after 1500 lb horse's body			
	fell on top of my body			

LAST AMOUNT IN THIS COLUMN IS BALANCE DUE ⟶
Please return this statement with remittance

Admitting
for partial obstruction

Still "left hosp." very sick
recommend prune juice

PATIENT DISCHARGE INSTRUCTIONS

NAME: Sandy Bradley

ATTENDING PHYSICIANS: ▓▓▓▓▓▓

DIET: (Prune juice cbS)   INSTRUCTED BY: ▓▓▓

The following medications are to be taken:

MEDICATION	DOSAGE	HOURS
∅		

ACTIVITY: UP AND ABOUT (✓
            OTHER (AS STATED)   As instructed.

APPOINTMENTS: PHYSICIAN (✓   See Dr. in office in 1 wk
                OTHER (AS STATED)   Call for appt.

INSTRUCTIONS: Any problems, call Dr.

Horse had fallen on me 7/▓/94
① admitted 4 times to hosp
② once stated to me "You're in a stressful occupation" to explain why my back still hurt & my bowels were not moving
③ released me on prune juice
④ I was dying

```
612    0239-02   08/14/89
BRADLEY, SANDY
F   B    02/13/47    42Y
LAPLATA, MD
▓▓▓▓▓    M.D.,  ▓▓▓▓
PATIENT BILLING   277938
MEDICAL RECORD    165215
```

68 71 60

I know that it is important that I follow the instructions given to me when I leave the hospital. These have been explained to me and I understand what I will be expected to do.

SIGNATURE: X Sandy Bradley V.M.D.   DATE: 8/18/89

NSG-006

DICK WILDES PRINTING CO., INC.

Prince Frederick, Maryland 20678

EMERGENCY DEPARTMENT RECO.

		MEDICAL RECORDS #	128486	

HOSPITAL NO.	ADMITTED BY	PREVIOUS ADMISSION DATE	PREVIOUS ADMIT NAME		TYPE OF SERVICE
0007108535					

RELIG. PREF.	SOCIAL SECURITY NO.	PREOPERATIVE OR ADMITTING DIAGNOSIS		
		(INJURED BACK) LM		

PATIENT NAME (Last, First, Middle)	HOME PHONE	AGE	SEX	RACE	DATE OF BIRTH	MARITAL STATUS	VET.	ROOM NUMBER
BRADLEY, SANDY		44Y	F	B	02/13/47	S		

ADDRESS (Street, City, State, Zip) BENEDICT, MD 20612

GUARANTOR NAME (Person Paying Bill)	RELATION	HOME PHONE	SOCIAL SECURITY NO.	OCCUPATION
BRADLEY, SANDY	SELF			

ADDRESS (Street, City, State, Zip) BENEDICT, MD 20612

GUARANTOR'S EMPLOYER	PHONE NUMBER (Business)

INSURANCE I   MD MEDICAL ASST.-STATE

AN #	POLICY HOLDER	INS. REL.	POLICY NUMBER	GROUP NUMBER	F.C.	INS. EFF. DATE
01901	BRADLEY, SANDY	PATIENT	08033203470	NS/ELIG. STATE	20	09/01/91

ADDRESS (Street, City, State, Zip)

INSURANCE II

AN #	POLICY HOLDER	INS. REL.	POLICY NUMBER	GROUP NUMBER	F.C.	INS. EFF. DATE

ADMITTING PHYSICIAN	ATTENDING PHYSICIAN	ADM. DATE	TIME	
NO LOCAL (DR.)		09/24/91	1702	

IN CASE OF EMERGENCY NOTIFY (NEAREST RELATIVE OR FRIEND ADDRESS)

NAME	PHONE NO.	RELATION TO
		FRIEND (Neighbor)

ADDRESS

REQUESTED P.M.D.	BROUGHT BY:	DISPOSITION AND TIME:
☐ YES ☐ NO	☐ SELF ☑ RELATIVE ☐ POLICE ☑ RESCUE SQUAD ☐ OTHER	☐ ADM ☐ TRANS. ☐ DOA ☐ DIED ☐ OTHER ☐ REL.

INSTRUCTIONS TO PATIENT: YOU SHOULD SEE YOUR PRIVATE PHYSICIAN IN _____ DAYS FOR FOLLOW-UP _____

_low back sheet. Rx Flexeril 10 mg 30/day, Anaprox 555mg
may C-12h for pain. Followup if Dr ___ is needed_

Sandy Bradley V.M.D.

I HAVE READ AND UNDERSTAND THE ABOVE INSTRUCTIONS

PHYSICIAN'S SIGNATURE / DATE	DISCHARGE INSTRUCTIONS BY PATIENT COPY	PATIENT'S SIGNATURE

Fractures and Rotation
of Knee, Leg and Ankle

☐ OB GYN CENTER

☐ MED SURG CLINIC

NAME: _____ NO. _____

MD 20785

DATE	Medicine____ Surgery____ Gyn.____ E.N.T.____ Ped.____ Ortho.____ Other____
2/24/92 Ortho 723.80	Wt. approx 120 B.P. 120/70 "Please ? codein "Gets out of it"

×Horse fell on ×to ℝ leg 6/19/92 –
Fx leg in 3 places –
Swell leg ____ in ____

As above. LLC placed on 6/19.
Seen by Kothakotu yesterday (who felt re-realistic inclination clinically there is some external rotation. ____
SVOP.

X-ray shows spiral fx ̄c external rotation & un-displaced fx through plafon –

Imp – Spiral fx ⓇTibia.

Plan – Remove cast.
         Manipulate
         LLC
         ✓ RTC 1 wk – x-ray check 7/1/92

Inst R+C as scheduled
  G Novak R.N.
</td> |

oc Bradley's notes:
his doctor
knew my
leg needed
re-doing but
when discovered
I was in a
previous lawsuit
for my hand he
dropped me in
the middle of
the treatment

My leg was
never properly
set from this
time forward

IC 4-101 (11/90)

DEPARTMENT OF RADIOLOGY
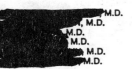
HOSPITAL CENTER

CHEVERLY, MARYLAND 20785

RADIOLOGY:
SCHEDULING:
FAX:

M.D.
M.D.
M.D.
M.D.
M.D.

PATIENT'S NAME	AGE	REFERRED BY	HOSP./E.R. NO.	ORIGIN	DATE OF EXAM	X-RAY NO.
BRADLEY, SANDY	02-13-47	ORTH CLN	10346101	ORTH CLN	07-29-92	328923

REPORT

PATIENT ACCOUNT #: 400598314
PROCEDURE CODES: 7305-9, 7306-7

INDICATION: Leg fractures.

RIGHT LOWER LEG AND ANKLE: There is a healing oblique fracture of the distal shaft of the right tibia as well as a fracture of the proximal shaft of the fibula. The position of the fragments are similar to the July 1, 1992, examination.

_____ M.D.
Radiologist

D: 07-29-92
T: 07-29-92

No MENTION of ankle progress although included to be assessed

I had to insist that X-RAYS of ankle were to be taken. There was much confusion about written orders omitted at the time of X-RAYS to be taken.

(SB)

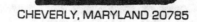

DE␣␣RTMENT OF RADIO␣␣GY
␣␣␣␣␣␣HOSPITAL CENTER

CHEVERLY, MARYLAND 20785

RADIOLOGY: ▮▮▮
SCHEDULING: ▮▮▮
FAX: ▮▮▮

M.D.
M.D.
M.D.
M.D.
M.D.
M.D.

PATIENT'S NAME	AGE	REFERRED BY	HOSP./E.R. NO.	ORIGIN	DATE OF EXAM	X-RAY NO.
BRADLEY, SANDY	02/13/47	MED CLN	10346101	ORTHO	08/19/92	328923

REPORT

PATIENT ACCOUNT #: 400598714
PROCEDURE CODES: 7305-9, 7306-7

INDICATION: Fracture.

RIGHT LEG: A fiberglass cast is in place which starts at the knee.   A
healing fracture of the proximal fibula and spiral fracture of the distal
tibia are noted.   There has been no significant change in the alignment and
position of the fracture fragments.

▮▮▮▮ M.D.
Radiologist

NO MENTION of inKle progress
(SB)

D:08/19/92
T:08/19/92

DHC 5-106A (6/92)

DEPARTMENT OF RADIOLOGY

[redacted] HOSPITAL CENTER

[redacted] M.D.
[redacted] M.D.
[redacted] M.D.
[redacted] M.D.
[redacted] M.D.
[redacted] M.D.

[redacted]
CHEVERLY, MARYLAND 20785

RADIOLOGY: [redacted]
SCHEDULING: [redacted]
FAX: [redacted]

PATIENT'S NAME	AGE	REFERRED BY	HOSP./E.R. NO.	ORIGIN	DATE OF EXAM	X-RAY NO.
BRADLEY, SANDY	02/13/47	[redacted] U	10346101	OPC	09/09/92	328923

REPORT

PATIENT ACCOUNT #: 400598314
PROCEDURE CODES: 7305-9

INDICATION: Trauma.

LEFT TIBIA: The tibial spiral fracture is satisfactorily reduced as seen through an overlying cast.

should say right tibia

for [redacted], M.D.
Radiologist

[redacted]
D:09/09/92
T:09/10/92

No mention of ankle progress
SB

DHC 5-106A (6/91)

DEPARTMENT OF RADIOLOGY

HOSPITAL CENTER

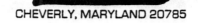

CHEVERLY, MARYLAND 20785

RADIOLOGY:
SCHEDULING:

FAX:

M.D.
M.D.
M.D.
M.D.
M.D.
M.D.

PATIENT'S NAME	AGE	REFERRED BY	HOSP./E.R. NO.	ORIGIN	DATE OF EXAM	X-RAY NO.
BRADLEY, SANDY	02-13-47		10346101	ORTHO CLINIC	10-21-92	328923

PATIENT ACCOUNT #: 4005988314 **REPORT**

PROCEDURE CODES: 7305-9

INDICATION: Fracture follow up.

RIGHT LEG: A healing fracture of the distal shaft of the tibia is
identified with good alignment and positioning of the fracture fragments.
A healing or healed fracture of the proximal shaft of the fibula is also
visualized.

for _____, M.D.
Radiologist

D:10-21-92
T:10-22-92

No mention of ankle progress

(SB)

DEPARTMENT OF RADIOLOGY
HOSPITAL CENTER

3001 HOSPITAL DRIVE
CHEVERLY, MARYLAND 20785

M.D.
M.D.
M.D.
M.D.
M.D.
M.D.

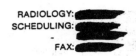

PATIENT'S NAME	AGE	REFERRED BY	HOSP./E.R. NO.	ORIGIN	DATE OF EXAM	X-RAY NO.
	02/13/47			OPC		
BRADLEY, SANDY		ORTHO	10346101		11/25/92	328923

REPORT

PATIENT ACCOUNT #: 400637443.
PROCEDURE CODES: 7305-9.

INDICATION: Fracture.

RIGHT LEG: The films in plaster demonstrate a healing spiral fracture of the distal shaft of the tibia. A fracture line is still evident.

, M.D.
Radiologist

D: 11/25/92
T: 11/25/92

Still no mention of ankle or its progress
(SB)

DISABILITY ENTITLEMENT ADVOCACY PROGRAM (DEAP)
DISABILITY REVIEW TEAM DETERMINATION

Client's Name _Bradly_ _Sandy_ _____ Date to DRT _6-24-93_
        Last   First   M.I. Date from DRT_____

MA Case Number _1639061O_ _2-13-47_ _160-40-4416_

DMAU, 311 W. Saratoga Street, Seventh Floor, Baltimore, Md. 21201
===

A.   Eligibility Period Under Consideration

_____|_____|_____

Retro Period | Pending Period | Prospective Period
===

B.   DRT Findings

    NOTE: THE CLIENT'S ELIGIBILITY IS BEING CONSIDERED FOR EACH
         ELIGIBILITY PERIOD SHOWN ABOVE.

    [✓] 1. Disabled   From _6/93_   Through _7/14_
        [ ] No Re-examination Required
        [✓] Re-examination Required
         * Specify Diary Date: _7/14_
    [ ] 2. Not Disabled
    [ ] 3. Insufficient Evidence to Determine
    Comments:_____

    *If Medical Re-review is Necessary, Date Must Be Specified.
===

C.   Basis for DRT Decision

    [ ] 1. Medical Evidence Alone
    [ ] 2. Medical & Vocational Guidelines Considered
        Specify the Vocational and/or Educational Factors Deemed
    Significant:_____
    _____
    _____

    [ ] 3. Ophthalmologist Findings:
        [ ] a. Blind, No Re-examination Necessary
        [ ] b. Blind, Re-examination Necessary
        *Specify Diary Date:_____
        [ ] c. Not Blind
    * If Re-review is Necessary, Date Must Be Specified.
===

D.   DRT Signatures

    DRT Physician_____ Date _6/25/93_
    DRT Vocational Examiner_____ Date_____
    DRT Psychologist_____ Date_____
    DRT Ophthalmologist_____ Date_____

===

DEAP DRT Review Form: Revised June 6, 1991

JUL 0 1993

Medical Documents related to Fractured leg & ankle

HEALTH CORPORATION
☐ Hospital Center
☐ Hospital
☐ Health Center

OB GYN CENTER

☐ MED SURG CLINIC

NAME: _Bradley Sandy_ NO. _____

DATE	Medicine	Surgery	Gyn.	E.N.T.	Ped.	Ortho.	Other

1-25-92
ortho
7
823380

To have cast removed + X-ray. — L.S. Shook, RN

Cast removed, Healed ē the several rotation previously described. Will leave out of cast —

RTC 1 week X-ray 12/31/92

Last RTC + X-ray
12/30/92 — L.S. Shook, RN

⬛⬛⬛⬛

12/14/92

Some pain in ankle. Will try ____

___ ____

⬛⬛⬛

7-30-92
Ortho
#

CANCELLED
CLINIC APPOINTMENT

Cat Scratch Disease
- diagnosed biopsy
- follow up treatment adjunctively
with herbs and diet

Plus an extraordinary testimonial

DEPARTMENT OF PATHOLOGY AND LABORATORY MEDICINE

[REDACTED] Hospital

,M.D. ,M.D. ,M.D.

Surgical Pathology Report

Pathology No. P90-05145

Patient:	BRADLEY, SANDY	
Birthdate:	FEB 13 47 Age: 43 Sex: F	
Hosp.No:	165215 Room No: I/O	
PreOp Dx:	Multiple lymph adenopathy.	
PostOp Dx:	Multiple lymph adenopathy.	
Clin. Hx:	Multiple lymph adenopathy.	
Specimens:	Lymph node front neck.	

Surgeon: [REDACTED] ,M.D.
Physician:

Operation Date: DEC 20 90
Date Received: DEC 20 90
Report Date: DEC 21 90

Macroscopic Examination and Description

MSC

The specimen is labeled "lymph node front neck". The specimen consists of yellowish adipose tissue measuring 1.5 cm x 0.7 cm. Cut section reveals a grayish-red cut surface. Imprints were done as well as a fragment was submitted for bacteriological studies. Four blocks, four sections.

Microscopic Description and Diagnosis

Topography	Pathology Diagnosis	
Lymph node, NOS	Lymphadenitis, chronic and acute with fibrosis.	MSC

Procedure: Excision

Microscopic Comments

Sections show some lymph node which presents marked fibrosis around the capsule. The lymph node is moderately fragmented and presents some evidence of distortion. There is numerous polysegmented neutrophils within the lymph node. This is acute and chronic lymphadenitis. The reason for the lymphadenitis must be found. If other clinical diagnosis are being considered another lymph node may be biopsied.

Benign

Pathology No. P90-05145

,M.D.
Reporting Pathologist

REPLY TO
ATTENTION OF

PATIENT IDENTIFICATION		PLEASE USE AFIP ACCESSION NUMBER IN ALL CORRESPONDENCE	
AFIP ACCESSION NUMBER		CHECK DIGIT	SEQUENCE
2310020-9		02	00
NAME		SSAN	
BRADLEY, SANDY P90-05145 SB			
SURGICAL AUTOPSY PATH ACCESSION # S			

PLEASE INFORM US OF ANY PATIENT IDENTIFICATION ERRORS

DJW/sm

_____, M.D.
Department of Pathology
_____ Hospital

La Plata, MD   20646

DATE. 06 February 1991

CONSULTATION REPORT ON CONTRIBUTOR MATERIAL

AFIP DIAGNOSIS: P90-05145   Lymph node, cervical: Cat scratch disease, bacilli
found.

The staff of the AFIP agree with your diagnosis. Microscopic examination
of the cervical lymph node reveals foci of proliferating vessels with
widened eosinophilic walls and foci of early necrosis with karyorrhexis.
Careful examination of Warthin Starry stained sections reveals many
silvered single, filamentous and branched bacilli of cat scratch disease
in collagen fibers, vessel wall and centered in areas of necrosis.

Representative Warthin Starry stained section sent under separate cover.

Thank you for this interesting contribution to the Registry of Geographic
Pathology and our study of cat scratch disease.

Department of Infectious and
Parasitic Disease Pathology

NATURE'S HERBAL HEALING

I am 88 years old with poor circulation. Four months ago,
Dr. Bradley, my dog's liscensed veteranarian came by to give Rusty
his shots and we began to discuss my circulatory problem. I told
her that I could not take the blood thinner prescribed by the
doctor because the side effects from the medication was making me
sick. Dr. Bradley suggested for me to try Kelp, Garlic, H-Formula
and Comfry. I began to use H-Formula and all of the above for the
circulation. It worked so well, that the numbness that caused my
circulatory disease was gone. I thank God for **Nature's Way** of
healing.

Mrs. Daisy B. █████████

Final Thoughts

I want the reader to remember that I am fully aware that there are certain concepts and messages that are repeated.

I experienced severe physical pain in more that eighty percent of my body, but emotional, mental, and spiritual pain occurred as well. The cure was not found in conventional medicine.

Many of you have also experienced similar or even greater pain than I. I want you to know that my heart reaches out to you and I hope to make a difference to ease some of your pain in letting you know that because I overcame with God's help you can, too.

A Few Definitions

Taken from the Webster Reference Dictionary of the English Language

So Why Shouldn't Garlic and Onions Or Any Herb Cure?

NOTE: Many of these words were chosen to show that by their definition they are medicinal in nature.

herb -

(herb, from a root meaning to eat or nourish, seen in Gr. phorbe, pasteur, fodder)
Any plant with a soft or succulent stem which dies to the root every year; any similar plant, esp. used in medicines, scents, or seasonings

drug -

Fr. drogue, origin uncertain
Formerly, any ingredient used in chemistry, pharmacy, dyeing , or the like; now any medicinal substance for internal or external use; often a habit-forming medicinal substance; a narcotic; a commodity that is overabundant, or in excess of demand on the market. -v.t. - drugged, drugging. To mix, as food or drink, with a drug, esp. a narcotic or poisonous drug; to administer medicinal drugs; to stupefy or poison with a drug; to administer anything nauseous to; to surfeit

medicine -

Any substance used in treating disease or relieving pain; medicament; remedy; the art or science of restoring or preserving health or physical condition often divided into medicine proper, surgery, and obstetrics; the science of treating disease with drugs or curative substances as distinguished from surgery and obstetrics, the medical profession; any object or practice regarded by N. American Indians as of magical efficacy

garlic -

A plant of the lily family, Allium sativum, with a strong scented, pungent bulb used in cooking and medicine; any of various species of the same genus; the bulb or a clove of any such plant

onion -

An edible bulb of a garden herb, Allium cepa in the lily family, with a strong characteristic pungent odor and taste; the plant itself

<u>sage -</u>

A shrubby menthaceous perennial, Salvia officinals, whose grayish - green leaves are used in medicine and for seasoning; the leaves themselves; any species of the genus Salvia; as S. splenens; sagebrush

<u>parsley -</u>

A well known garden <u>herb</u>, Petroselinum crispum, in the parsley family, Umbelliferae, native to Europe and widely cultivated for its leaves which are used as a garnish for foods - a, garnished with parsley

<u>rosemary -</u>

A species of green shrub, Rosmarinus officinalis, native to the Mediterranean regions and well known as a garden plant; its aromatic leaves being used as a seasoning and as the source of a volatile oil <u>used in medicines</u> and perfumes

<u>thyme -</u>

Any small aromatic subshrub of the genus Thymus as T. vulgaris and T. serphyllum whose leaves are use as a seasoning in cooking

<u>myrrh -</u>

Valuable gum resin obtained from small, spiny trees native to Arabia and E. Africa, esp. form Commiphora myrrha, used medicinally as a tonic and in dentifrices; C. Erythraea, the myrrh of antiquity, still used in incense and perfume

"And when they had come into the house, they saw the young Child with Mary His mother, and fell down and worshipped Him. And when they had opened their treasures they presented gifts to Him: gold, frankincense, and myrrh."

Matthew 2:11 New King James

Definitions Continued - Medical Categories:

allopathy -

[Gr. allos, other, and pathos, morbid] The method of treating disease by the use of agents producing effects different from those of the disease treated: opposed to homeopathy

naturopathy -

[Fr. birth, natural constitution or character] A method of treating illness or disease without drugs or surgery, using proper foods, heat, exercise, and massage to aid natural healing

homeopathy -

The system of treating disease by administering in minute quantities drugs which would, if given in larger doses to a healthy person, produce symptoms similar to those of the disease

Bibliography

Bragg, Paul C., N.D., Ph.D. and Bragg, Patricia, N.D., Ph.D.;
Apple Cider Vinegar Health System (Bragg Crusades - Health Science, Santa Barbara, CA)

de Bairacli Levy, Juliette;
The Complete Herbal Book for the Dog — A Handbook of Natural Care and Rearing (Arco Publishing, Inc., New York, 1970)

Jarvis, D.C., M.D.;
Folk Medicine (Fawcett Crest, New York, 1958)

Kloss, Jethro;
Back to Eden (Back to Eden Books Publishing Co., Loma Linda, CA, 1972 original 1939)

Pitcairn, Richard H., D.V.M., Ph.D. and Pritcairn, Susan Hubble;
Dr. Pitcairn's Complete Guide to Natural Health for Dogs and Cats (Rodale Press, Emmaus, PA, 1982)

The Webster Reference Dictionary of the English Language - encyclopedia edition (Delair Publishing Company, Inc., 1983)

Suggested Readings

Note: I do not agree with the authors on many issues but respect their experience and believe their writings to be beneficial.

Balch, Phyllis, C.N.C. and Balch, James F., M.D.;
Prescription for Cooking and Dietary Wellness (P.A.B. Publishing, Inc., Greenfield, IN, 1992)

Bragg, Paul C., N.D., Ph.D.;
The Miracle of Fasting (Health Science, Santa Barbara, CA, 1985)

Bragg, Paul C. and Patricia N.D., Ph.D.,
The Shocking Truth about Water (Health Science, Santa Barbara, CA, 1985)

de Bairacli Levy, Juliette;
The Complete Herbal Handbook for Farm and Stable (Faber and Faber, London Boston, 1984)

de Waal, M., Dr.;
Medicinal Herbs in the Bible (Samuel Weiser, Inc., York Beach, ME 1980)

Harper, Joan;
The Healthy Cat and Dog Cook Book (E.P. Dutton, a Division of El sevir - Dutton, Publishing Co., Inc., New York 1979)

Hutchens, Alma R.;
Indian Herbalogy of North America (Merco; Windsor 14, Ontario, Canada, 1983)

Jackson, Mildred, N.D. and Teague, Terri, N.D., D.C.;
The Handbook of Alternatives To Chemical Medicine (Bookpeople, Berkely, CA 1985)

Kadans, Joseph N.D., Ph.D.;
Encyclopedia of Medicinal Herbs (Arco Publishing, Inc., New York 1984)

Kirschner, W.E., M.D.;
Live Food Juices (H.E. Kirschner Publications, Monrovia, CA, 1983)

Kirschmann, John D.;
Nutrition Almanac (McGraw Hill Book Company, Revised 1979)

Mowrey, Daniel B., Ph.D.;
The Scientific Validation of Herbal Medicines (Keats Publishing, Inc.; New Canaan, CT 1986)

Royal, Penny C.;
Herbally Yours (Sound Nutrition; Provo, UT 1982)

Thatcher, Emily;
The Vinegar Book (Tresco Publishers; Canton, OH 1994)

Walker, N.W., D.Sci.;
Raw Vegetable Juices (JOVE Publications, New York, NY, 1970)

Weiss, Gaea and Shandor;
Growing and Using Healing Herbs (Rodale Press, Inc.; Emmaus, PA 1985)

Winter, Ruth;
A consumer's Dictionary of Food Additives (Crown Publishers, Inc., New York 1978)

A Letter of Gratitude to My Sponsors

It has now been more than sixteen months that I have known personally and professionally Connie Livengood, the president of Livengood International, Inc. as well as her husband, Don, and her immediate family. We met through their son and daughter-in-law who had need of my professional services.

The Livengoods have shown a trust and concern that I considered a must to make the dream of <u>Let the Mocking Bird Sing Herbal Praise (from the Old Barn)</u> a reality I desired to share.

I can declare, with full confidence, the integrity and commitment which the Livengoods have demonstrated to me in the year-and-a-half I have known them.

I wish to express my gratitude, Connie and Don; D.J. and Belinda, for being there through all the re-writes, tribulations and trials.

Livengood International, Inc. has a full line of health products and more, too numerous for me to mention; one of which I briefly discuss in a section of this book entitled, "FruitAloe May Be the Product for You." The health products offered by LII are inclusive to pets as well as humans.

If you don't already have a favorite source of health products I do encourage you to try my friends.

Again, many thanks to you Connie and Don.

FruitAloe - May Be The Product For You

1. FruitAloe is a one of its kind herbal beverage drink manufactured by Live-N-Good International, Inc.

2. Although you may find aloe vera drinks and gel less affordable, nutritionally FruitAloe offers a blend I have not yet seen that is a nutritional support as well. I dare to say seemingly therapeutic in specific cases with results to my own surprise. For example, when the nail went through my foot, fresh aloe plant, FruitAloe and honey were the only substances effective in reducing the swelling and most of the pain using external applications. Other herb combinations and liniments were used periodically. Many skin and gastrointestinal disorders have improved in patients as well.

3. FruitAloe in its four different flavors, Papaya, Pep-N-Go, Cranapple and Electrolyte Replacement, has been excellent to wash down a Super Garlic capsule, in my experience, restoring a natural surge of energy and sense of well being.

4. FruitAloe and Live-N-Good International products <u>are not the only good source of herbal and natural items</u>, but if you don't have a favorite, I urge you to try ours.

a Sample Bibliography on
Aloe Vera.

Use of Aloe Vera
Scientific Documentation

Scientific References
from the Health Sciences Library of Emory University MEDLINE

1. Antimicrobial Agents and Chemotherapy. 12-91. pp 2463-2466
2. Digestion. 1991. 49 (2). pp 65-71
3. Journal - Am-Podiatric-Med-Assoc. 1-89. pp 24-26
4. Journal - Amer Acad Dermatology. 4-88. pp 714-720
5. Hormone Research. 1986. 24 (4). pp 288-294
6. Planta-Med. 12-89. 55 (6). pp 509-512
7. Journal - Am-Podiatric-Med-Assoc. 11-89. 79 (11). pp 559-562
8. Journal - Am-Podiatric-Med-Assoc. 8-89. 79 (8). pp 395-397
9. New England Journal Medicine. 8-9-84. 311 (6). p 413
10. Journal-Pharm-Science. 1-84. 73 (1). pp 62-65
11. Japan-Journal-Pharmacology. 2-82. 32 (1). pp 139-142
12. Journal-Amer-Podiatry Assoc. 6-82. 72 (6). pp 275-284
13. Experientia. 11-15-81. 37 (11). pp 1186-1187
14. Journal-Biochem (Tokyo). 1-79. 85 (1). pp 163-171
15. Lloydia. 7&8-76. 39 (4). pp 223-224
16. Internal Journal Dermatology. 1&2-73. 12 (1). pp 68-73
17. American Surgery. 6-72. 38 (6). pp 343-345
18. Lloydia. 6-71. 34 (2) pp 204-255
19. Planta-Med. 8-70. 18 (4). pp 361-365
20. Journal-Pharm-Science. 2-69. 58 (2). pp 197-200
21. So. African Medical Journal. 10-7-67. 41 (38) p 984
22. J-Am-Podiatric-Med-Assoc. 3-92. 82 (3). pp 140-148
23. Ear-Nose-Throat Journal. 2-91. 70 (2). p 119
24. J-Am-Podiatric-Med-Assoc. 1-91. 81 (1). pp 1-9
25. International Journal Immunopharmacology. 1990. 12 (4). pp 427-434
26. Journal-Dermatology-Surg-Oncology. 5-90. 16 (5). pp 460-467
27. Journal-Am-Podiatric-Med-Assoc. 6-89. 79 (6). pp 263-276
28. Plastic-Reconstr-Surg. 6-89. 83 (6). pp 1075-1076
29. Plast-Reconstr-Surg. 1-89. 83 (1). pp 195-196
30. Arerugi. 12-87. 36 (12). pp 1094-1101
31. J-Am-Podiatric-Med-Assoc. 2-88. 78 (2). pp 60-68
32. Planta-Med. 6-85. (3). pp 273-275
33. J-Am-Podiatric Med-Assoc. 5-85. 75 (5). pp 229-237
34. J-Bergen-Cty-Dent-Soc. 5-84. 50 (8). pp 11-13
35. Am-Jour-Botany. 1947. (34). p 597
36. Journal-Amer-Phar-Sci. 1964. (53). p 1287
37. Radiology-Review-Chicago-Med-Recorder. 6-35. (37). pp 137-138
38. Internat-College-Angiology-Annual Meeting. 1984. San Antonio, Tx.
39. Nutritional Analysis. Wooden and Tennensen Laboratories.

Uses of Aloe Vera
Scientifically Documented

(numbers following examples refer to Scientific References on left hand page)

. . . Antiviral. Inactivates many viruses. 1, 36

. . . Antibacterial. 4, 17, 21, 25, 30, 32, 36

. . . Antifungal. 4, 36

. . . Effective laxative and cleanser. 2, 19

. . . Antiinflammatory. 3, 8, 22, 24, 27

. . . Improves healing of wounds, burns, radiation ulcers and bed sores. 3, 4, 7, 9, 16, 23, 26, 28, 29

. . . Lowers blood glucose levels. 5, 38

. . . Enhances antibody production. 6

. . . Improves arthritis. 11, 12, 33

. . . Inhibits edema (swelling). 10, 31

. . . Reduces bleeding time (Strong clotting activity). 14

. . . Inhibits growth of cancers (tumors). 13, 15, 18

. . . Anti diabetes activity. 3

. . . Successful treatment of Tic Douloureaux (Trigeminal Neuralgia). 34

. . . Anesthetizes tissue and relieves pain. 35

. . . Antipyretic - Reduces heat of sores and ulcers. 3, 7, 23, 26, 37

. . . Antipruretic - Stops itching. 3, 4

. . . Reduces angina attacks, reduces cholesterol and triglycerides. 38

. . . Highly nutritional, supplying a wide range of vitamins, minerals, amino acids and complex carbohydrates. 39

. . High degree of safety comparable to consuming vegetables and fruits. <u>Most listed references</u>